Race and IQ
Expanded Edition

Race and IQ
Expanded Edition

Edited by
ASHLEY MONTAGU

OXFORD
UNIVERSITY PRESS

OXFORD
UNIVERSITY PRESS

Oxford   New York

Auckland   Bangkok   Buenos Aires
Cape Town   Chennai   Dar es Salaam   Delhi   Hong Kong   Istanbul
Karachi   Kolkata   Kuala Lumpur   Madrid   Melbourne   Mexico City   Mumbai
Nairobi   São Paulo   Shanghai   Singapore   Taipei   Tokyo   Toronto

and an associated company in Berlin

First edition published by Oxford University Press, New York, 1975
Second expanded edition published by Oxford University Press, 1999
First published as an Oxford University Press paperback, 2002

198 Madison Avenue, New York, New York 10016
www.oup.com

Oxford is a registered trademark of Oxford University Press

Library of Congress Cataloging-in-Publication Data
Race and IQ / edited by Ashley Montagu. --Expanded ed.
p. cm.
Includes bibliographical references.
ISBN 978-0-19-510221-5
Contents: The debate over race / Leonard Lieberman -- What can biologists solve? /
S.E. Luria -- The magical aura of the IQ / Jerome Kagan -- An examination of Jensen's theory concerning
educability, heritability, and population differences / S. Biesheuvel -- An affluent society's excuses for inequality /
Edmund W. Gordon with Derek Green -- Natural selection and the mental capacities of mankind / Th. Dobzhansky
and Ashley Montagu -- Nature with nurture / Urie Bronfenbrenner -- Racist arguments and IQ / Stephen Jay Gould --
On creeping Jensenism / C. Loring Brace and Frank B. Livingstone -- Race and Intelligence /
Richard C. Lewontin -- Heritability analyses of IQ scores / David Layzer -- On the causes of IQ differences
between groups and implications for social policy / Peggy R. Sanday -- Race and IQ: the genetic
background / W.F. Bodmer -- Is early intervention effective? Some studies of early
education in familial and extra-familial settings / Urie Bronfenbrenner.
1. Intelligence tests.
2. Race.
3. Nature and nurture.
4. Racism in psychology.
I. Montagu, Ashley, 1905-
BF432.AIR3   1996
155.8'2--dc20   95-36397

Printed in the United States of America

To the Memory
of
Jean Finot (1856–1922)
author of the best book ever
written on the subject of "race,"
Race Prejudice, (1907)

Contents

1

INTRODUCTION

Ashley Montagu

"Race" and "IQ" are terms which seemingly possess a clear and well-defined meaning for millions of people. Their common usage implies the belief in a reality which is beyond question. When, on occasion, the suggestion is made that these terms correspond to no reality whatever, but constitute an amalgam of erroneous and stultifying ideas of the most damaging kind, the suggestion is received either with blank incredulity or open derision. Nevertheless, the truth is that these terms not only are unsound but in fact correspond to no verifiable reality, and have, indeed, been made the basis for social and political action of the most heinous kinds.

What is considered so obvious and beyond question is the apparent fact that the physical differences which allegedly mark off the "races" from one another are indissolubly linked with individual and group achievement. Some "races," it is held, are in all these respects inferior to others. Hence, all that is necessary in order to arrive at a proper estimate of an individual's potential general abilities is to identify, usually by his external appearance, his "racial" membership, and this will at once tell one what the limits of that individual's capacities are, what he is likely to be able to accomplish, and, furthermore, what his particular "race" will be able to achieve. These three phenomena, physical appearance, individual ability, and group achievement, are inseparably linked with each other by heredity. This "manifest reality" is what is generally understood by "race." It is the popular, or *social*, con-

ception of "race," and is not to be confused with the biological
concept of "race"—held in a variety of different forms—in which
no linkage is implied between physical appearance, individual abilities, and group achievement.[1]

What is wrong with the social or racist view of "race" is that,
among other things, there happens to be no genetic association
or linkage between genes for physical appearance, for individual
behavior, and for group achievement. Nevertheless, believers in
the doctrine of "race" choose to take it for granted that there
is. How else, indeed, they ask, can one account for differences
in individual abilities and group achievement of the different
"races"?

This is a legitimate question, and the answer to it is that when
the facts are considered the weight of the evidence indicates that
the differences are primarily due to the differences in the history of the experiences the individuals and their groups have
undergone. The development of civilization, for example, brought
with it enormously complex technological and other changes,
changes of a kind that simply did not occur among the isolated peoples of the world. The latter were wholly bypassed
by the civilizing influences that affected the peoples of the
culturally busier parts of the world. With rare exceptions, if,
indeed, there are any, what is required for the development of
civilization is the fructifying influence of contacts with other cultures. Such contacts must usually occur over considerable periods
of time.[2] Hence, when from the ethnocentric viewpoint of the
civilized peoples of the world unfavorable conclusions are drawn
concerning the capacities of the members of nonliterate populations, those conclusions are likely to be both unfair and unsound.
There is, in fact, no possible basis on which such comparisons can
be made, since the principal necessary condition that would make
such a comparison possible is missing, namely, *a history of similar
complex cultural experiences which lead to the development of
technological abilities and group achievement.*

Not alone is this requirement lacking in such cross-cultural comparisons, but it is also lacking in comparisons made between ethnic groups within the same nation. It is lacking, for example, in the case of Blacks and Whites, because Blacks have never enjoyed equal cultural and socioeconomic opportunities in any white society. Blacks in America have, in fact, been deprived, oppressed, discriminated against, impoverished, ghettoized, and generally excluded from the brotherhood of man.[3] Hence, it should not be surprising that there have been and continue to be significant differences in the achievements of Blacks and Whites as "measured" by tests which have been arbitrarily standardized on middle-class Whites.

For reasons which would themselves make a study of singular interest, while it has been generally agreed that IQ tests "measure" the combined effects of genetic and experiential influences on the learned ability to respond to such tests some writers have manifested an extreme biologistic bias in the evaluation of the meaning of the test scores. The tests for these writers have come to represent a measure of innate intelligence.[4] This is a view which is demonstrably unsound and is one that most authorities reject.

An intelligence test consists of a series of tasks yielding a score which is supposed to represent a rating of the standard of intelligence of that individual. The problem-solving tasks are standardized by finding the average performances of *White* individuals who by independent criteria are of known degrees of levels of test-solving ability at a particular chronological age, that is, *mental age*. The IQ score is obtained by dividing mental age by chronological age and multiplying by one hundred.

One of the many difficulties surrounding IQ tests is that no one really knows what intelligence is. What is usually said is that intelligence is what intelligence tests test. But such a "definition" of intelligence is hardly likely to advance our understanding of it. It might perhaps be agreed that such tests provide a rough estimate of certain problem-solving abilities. But abilities represent trained capacities, and therefore experience and learning enter substantially into their development. Since the tested ability to a large extent represents the trained expression of a capacity, the "measurement" of the ability can tell us nothing about the original quality of the capacity. The genetic capacity may have been considerably altered by the operation of environmental conditions, both prenatal and postnatal, long before its complex elements have been exposed to the more socially complex conditions of the cultural environment.

Alfred Binet and Theodore Simon, the original inventors of the "intelligence scale," thoroughly rejected any notion of the kind of precision that subsequent intelligence testers claimed for their test or any of its revisions. When in 1960 Simon discussed this matter with Dr. Theta Wolf he referred to the history of IQ testing as a betrayal of the purpose of the Binet-Simon test.[5]

Binet and Simon always considered their test an "intelligence scale," something that might give one an idea of the general intelligence of a child, but never a precise measure of specific abilities. The Binet-Simon Scale was published in 1905, with revisions appearing in 1908 and 1911, the latter being the year of Binet's death at the age of fifty-four. Binet's conception of what he was doing when giving his intelligence tests differed very markedly from that of those who adopted and "improved" them, especially in America. Binet's objective, in his own words, was to "measure the useful effects of adaptation, and the value of the difficulties overcome by them." This was as near as he hoped to get to intelligence, but he was never for a moment under the illusion that he had succeeded in the task of measuring intelligence in the sense that all too many American and English intelligence testers believed to have been done.

As for the term "Intelligence Quotient," embodied in the letters "IQ," which have now become as much a part of the English language as "OK," Binet never used it. The idea of a "mental" quotient—far better than "intelligence" quotient—had been suggested by the German psychologist William Stern in 1912;[6] but it was the American psychologist Lewis M. Terman who coined

"Intelligence Quotient." [7] Binet altogether refused to have anything to do with even the remotest possibility of a quotient on several grounds: first, because the tests he employed were in his view not exact enough to warrant the appearance of precision a quotient would give and, second, because "mental age" varies so greatly for each of the different items in any test that any averaging of such test results would yield a specious score; and so Binet preferred to speak of "mental level" rather than "mental age" simply because "level" was non-committal and "age" was not. With "mental level" much was left open, with "mental age" too much was taken for granted.

The excessive enthusiasm with which intelligence tests were greeted in the United States drew the criticism of Walter Lippmann, who, in a series of six articles published in the fall of 1922 in *The New Republic*, wrote what will always remain one of the most cogently critical anatomies of intelligence testing. Lippmann pointed out that the intelligence testers were claiming not only that they were measuring intelligence, but also that "intelligence is innate, hereditary, and predetermined." And, he went on to say, "Intelligence testing in the hands of men who hold this dogma could not but lead to an intellectual caste system." [8] And that is precisely what such modern writers as A. R. Jensen, R. J. Herrnstein, William Shockley, and H. J. Eysenck claim the test results should lead to.

Lippmann's articles drew a rather patronizing response from Terman,[9] the chief proponent of intelligence testing in America, which in no way met Lippmann's thoroughly sound criticisms. What Terman really believed he made quite clear in an autobiographical account of his scientific development. One of his credos was "That the major differences in the intelligence test scores of certain races, as Negroes and Whites, will never be fully accounted for on the environmental hypothesis." [10] In other words, Terman believed that genetic factors were largely responsible for the differences in the test scores between Negroes and Whites.

That IQ tests were ethnocentrically structured, and therefore, unfair when applied to members of ethnic groups other than those of the cultures upon which they had been standardized, did not bother Terman at all. Not only this, his confidence in IQ tests was such that he felt himself capable of applying them even to the dead. Thus, he and his associate Catherine Cox were able to compute the IQ of such figures as Napoleon, Lincoln, Goethe, Da Vinci, Galileo, and some three hundred others! The inference left for the reader to draw was that some people are born with low IQs and some with high IQs.

It is also evident that Terman considered intelligence to be a fairly fixed entity—an idea which would have appalled Binet who, in 1909, had already commented on some recent writers who appeared "to have given their moral support to the deplorable verdict that the intelligence of an individual is a fixed quantity. . . . We must protest and act against this brutal pessimism." [11]

William Stern had early drawn attention to the dangers of drawing incomplete and unjustifiable conclusions from intelligence quotients. "To be sure," he wrote, "there has been and still is an exaggerated faith in the power of numbers. For example, an 'intelligence quotient' may be of provisional value as *a first crude approximation* when the mental level of an individual is sought; but whoever imagines that in determining this quantity he has summed up 'the' intelligence of an individual once and for all, so that he may dispense with the more intensive qualitative study, leaves off where psychology begins" (italics added).[12]

"A first crude approximation," is exactly how Binet and Simon thought of their test, as part of the qualitative evaluation of the person as a whole—something that none of the traditional IQ tests have attempted, and which they, indeed, thoroughly disregard.

Because of the extreme bias of IQ tests favoring white urbanites as compared with other ethnic groups and socially disadvantaged classes, even if the tests were to measure intelligence—which they do not—any conclusions drawn from such tests as to the comparative quality of the intelligence and future possibilities of those subjected to them would be quite unsound.[13] Nevertheless psychologists like Arthur R. Jensen continue to commit all the errors that IQ testers have habitually committed, namely, of assuming (1) that the tests measure intelligence; (2) that the ethnic groups on whose members they carry out these tests are sufficiently comparable to permit valid inferences to be drawn as to the quality of their intelligence; and (3) that what IQ tests measure is to the largest extent intelligence determined by genes.

In a 123-page study entitled "How Much Can We Boost IQ and Scholastic Achievement?" published in the *Harvard Educational Review* in the winter of 1969, Professor Arthur R. Jensen of the University of California at Berkeley, after a detailed examination of the evidence, concluded that it is "a not unreasonable hypothesis that genetic factors are strongly implicated in the average Negro-white intelligence difference" (p. 82). According to Professor Jensen heritability measures indicate that about 80 per cent of the determinance of intelligence is due to genes and about 20 per cent to environment. By *heritability* is meant the portion of the total phenotypic or trait variance that is genetic.[14] Professor Jensen makes much of his heritability measures, but the truth is that the so-called heritability coefficient is an especially undependable measure when applied to the human species, an application which has been criticized from its very inception by mathematical geneticists such as R. A. Fisher, as well as others. Fisher, one of the founders of modern statistics and mathematical genetics, referred to the coefficient of heritability "as one of those unfortunate short-cuts which have emerged in biometry for lack of a more thorough analysis of the data."[15] Jensen's application of the heritability estimate has been dealt with by Lewontin[16] and thoroughly demolished by Layzer[17] in the contributions reprinted in this volume, and the 80/20 per cent difference claimed to have been found by Jensen is shown to belong to numerology rather than science. There have been other criticisms of this heritability estimate.[18] The truth is that the nature of the genetic contribution to intelligence as "measured" by intelligence tests is unknown both for individuals and for populations, and therefore, on this ground alone, heritability estimates constitute, as one critic has put it, "little more than a hollow quantification." [19]

Jensen tells us that his discussions with a number of geneticists concerning the question of a genetic basis for differences among races in mental abilities revealed to him a number of rather consistently agreed-upon points. These points are: "Any groups which have been geographically or socially isolated from one another for many generations are practically certain to differ in their gene pools, and consequently are likely to show differences in any phenotypic characteristics having a high heritability." Furthermore, "genetic differences are manifested in virtually every anatomical, physiological, and biochemical comparison one can make between representative samples of identifiable racial groups (Kuttner, 1967). There is no reason why the brain should be exempt from this generalization." [20]

As a generalization the first statement is quite sound. The second statement is quite unsound, and the third highly probably unsound. Jensen's reference to Kuttner as his authority for the second statement is not supported by the latter's own paper which is restricted to a review of the biochemical differences between so-called "races." [21] In any event, far from genetic differences being manifested in virtually every anatomical, physiological, and biochemical trait between "racial" groups, the likenesses in all these classes of traits are far greater than the differences. It is as absurd to exaggerate the differences as to minimize them. Differences in all these areas of structure and function exist, but to argue from the existence of such organic differences that *therefore* it is reasonable to suppose that similar differences must exist for the genetic distribution of mental functions among the "races" is simply no more than to make words do service for the work of examining the evidence. "There is no reason why the brain should be exempt from this generalization," writes Jensen, the generalization that there exist genetic differences in "virtually" every organic trait between the "races." By "brain" Jensen presumably means the neural circuitry which under the appropriate experiential conditions or organization will function as mind. Since the brain is an organic structure it can easily be slipped into Jensen's generalization and there quite erroneously equated with "mind." Certainly the brain has undergone considerable evolutionary change, but the pressures of natural selection have not acted directly on the brain but indirectly through its functions, especially capacities for its culturally acquired functions. The complexity and size of the human brain represent the end-effects of the action of selection on the functions of human behavior in human environments. What has been under selective pressure is not the brain as an organ, but *the skill in using it and its competence in responding as a culturally adaptive organ.*

Contrary to Jensen, there is every reason why the brain should be exempt from his generalization. This aspect of the manner of humanity's unique evolution was first dealt with in a joint paper by Professor Theodosius Dobzhansky and the writer as long ago as 1947.[22] In that contribution, reprinted in the present volume, it will be seen, as Professor George Gaylord Simpson later independently put it, "There are biological reasons why significant racial differences in intelligence, which have not been found, would not be expected. In a polytypic species, races adapt to differing local conditions but the species as a whole evolves adaptations advantageous to all its races, and spreading among them all under the influence of natural selection and by means of interbreeding. When human races were evolving it is certain that increase in mental ability was advantageous to *all* of them. It would, then, have tended over the generations to have spread among all of them in approximately equal degrees. For any one race to lag definitely behind another in over-all genetic adaptation, the two would have to be genetically isolated over a very large number of generations. They would, in fact, have to become distinct species; but human races are all interlocking parts of just one species." [23] And as the geneticists Professors Paul David and L. H. Snyder have written, "flexibility of behavioral adjustment to different situations is likely to have had a selective advantage over any tendency toward stereotyped reactions. For it is difficult to conceive of any human social organization in which plasticity of response, as reflected by ability to profit from experience (that is, by intelligence) and by emotional and temperamental resilience, would not be at a premium and therefore favored by natural selection. It therefore seems to us highly improbable that any significant genetic differentiation in respect to particular response patterns, populations or races has occurred in the history of human evolution." [24] "To assert the biological unity of mankind," write Professors Sherwood L. Washburn and C. S. Lancaster, "is to affirm the importance of the hunting way of life. It is to claim that however such conditions and customs may have varied locally, the main selection pressures that forged the species were the same." [25]

The foodgathering-hunting way of life was pursued by the human species the world over during the greater part of its evolutionary history. It is only during the last 15,000 years or so that some societies developed technologically more complex ways of controlling the environment.

In an editorial in *Nature* it was stated that "In circumstances in which it is plain that intelligence has been a crucial asset in survival, it is only reasonable to suppose that all of the races now extant are much of a muchness in intelligence." [26] Professor Jensen believes this to be a mistaken inference because it equates intelligence with Darwinian fitness or the ability to produce surviving progeny. But the editorial does nothing of the sort. A trait either has adaptive value—another name for Darwinian fitness—or it has not. Intelligence as a problem-solving ability is most certainly a trait possessing high adaptive value in all environments, and as such has been subject to the pressures of natural selection.

Professor Jensen thinks it not unlikely that "different environments and cultures could make differential genetically selective demands on various aspects of behavioral adaptability . . . Europeans and Africans have been evolving in widely separated areas and cultures for at least a thousand generations, under different conditions of selection which could have affected their gene pools for behavioral traits just as for physical characteristics." [27]

What Professor Jensen confuses here is the environmental pressures of widely separated geographic areas upon the *physical* evolution of the human species, and the virtually identical cultural pressures upon the *mental* development of people living a foodgathering-hunting existence. These are two totally different kettles of fish, and it does nothing but add confusion to the subject to treat the pressures of the physical environment as if they acted in the same way upon man's mental evolution. The challenges, in fact, to man's problem-solving abilities were of a very different order from those which eventually resulted in kinky or straight hair, a heavily or a lightly pigmented skin, a broad or a narrow nose, small or large ears, and so on.

While physical environments have varied considerably, the cultural environments of man during the whole of his evolutionary history, right up to the recent period, have been fundamentally alike, namely, that of foodgathering hunters.[28]

The important fact that Professor Jensen fails to understand is that while physical environments may have differed in the extreme, the conditions of selection under which man's mental evolution occurred were everywhere alike. The cultural differences between a Congo Pygmy and an Eskimo of the Far North are only superficially different. If you live in the Congo you need neither clothes nor sleds; if you live in the Far North you need both. There are great differences in detail between the foodgathering-hunting cultures, but in the responses they have made to their particular environments they are strikingly and fundamentally alike. They are alike in their material culture, in their social organization, in the absence of chieftains, political or state organization, permanent councils, belief in gods, warfare, and the like. The genetical-anthropological aspects of this subject are discussed by Professor Dobzhansky and myself in the contribution already referred to (see pp. 104–13).

"How much can we boost IQ and scholastic achievement?" There is an answer to that question which is highly encouraging, despite Professor Jensen's belief that not very much can be done that way. He pleads for a greater diversity of approaches and aims in tackling the problems of educating the young, especially the disadvantaged young. In that plea we can all join him. New approaches are, indeed, called for. In that connection the Department of Health, Education and Welfare report of 1974, *Report on Longitudinal Evaluations of Preschool Programs*,[29] has some clear and unequivocal answers to Professor Jensen's question: IQ and scholastic achievement can be boosted significantly by improving the conditions of life of the child. In volume one of the *Report* eight independent studies are presented, and Dr. Sally Ryan summarizes these by underscoring the fact that although the most frequently reported gain is a significant rise in IQ points there is also good evidence of some gains in the personal-social adjustment of children as well. Professor Urie Bronfenbrenner in volume 2 of the *Report* examines a dozen studies relating to the effects of early intervention, and concludes that whenever it is possible to improve the human environment of the child its performance on IQ tests rises significantly. By special effort mothers can be encouraged to improve the care of their children, often to such an extent that they become effective workers with other mothers and children. Where the conditions have not been favorable for maternal participation in the project a highly trained teacher was assigned to the child, in the Milwaukee project, when it was as young as three months of age.[30] The teacher was responsible for its total care and gave it a good deal of cuddling and soothing, and organized its learning and implemented the educational program by working with the child in the home from two to eight weeks—until the mother expressed enough confidence to allow the child to go to the center, where the teachers could work with the children on a very intimate one-to-one basis. At five and a half years the cared-for children had a mean IQ of 124 points while the uncared for controls had a mean IQ of 94, a difference of 30 points.[31]

Such findings not only constitute the answer to Professor Jensen's question, but the recommendations to which they lead for the improvement of the learning abilities of the child are so important that, with the kind permission of Professor Bronfenbrenner the final section of his monograph is reprinted here as our concluding chapter. It is good to be able to end this volume on so constructive and encouraging a note. Professor Bronfenbrenner's analysis of recent research strengthens our faith, as he writes, "in the capacity of parents, of whatever background, to enable their children to develop into effective and happy human beings, *once our society is willing to make conditions of life viable for all its families*" (Author's italics).

Clearly it is not so much IQ and scholastic achievement that need to be boosted as the motivation to bring about the changes in social conditions that make deprived and unfulfilled and frustrated lives possible.

The papers in this volume speak for themselves, I am indebted to the authors and publishers for permission to reprint them here. The hope is that they will provide the reader interested in this difficult subject with the means of understanding the defects not alone of Professor Jensen's claims concerning the value of IQ tests in yielding a dependable measure of innate intelligence, but also the defects of such tests when applied to the measurement of "racial" differences in intelligence.

In this introduction I have attempted to trace something of the history of the "IQ test," in order to show how the original work of Binet and Simon soon came to be abused, especially in the United States. I have stated, and I think the statement long overdue, that both the term "race" and the term "IQ" are fraudulent, because in the one case the social conception of "race" was the deliberate concoction of a slave-owning caste attempting to justify its conduct, and in the other case because "IQ" tests do not measure what they have generally been claimed to measure, namely, innate intelligence. It is most unfortunate that vested interests (including an unregulated multimillion dollar industry based on them) have made a cult of the "IQ" and, in the face of the contrary evidence, persist in perpetuating claims for such tests that are quite untenable.

Intelligence is a complex function of highly complex variables, so complex, indeed, that we can hardly be said to have made a beginning in understanding any of them. No one can really define intelligence. The best we can do is to make rather general statements about this complex function, but no serious student of the subject pretends that such statements represent anything more than the crudest kinds of remote approximations.

As for the genetics of intelligence, our knowledge is virtually non-existent. Intelligence is clearly a function of many genes in interaction with the environment. The fact that we have no idea how many genes may be involved would not in itself constitute a sufficient impediment to the study of the genetics of intelligence *were we able to separate out the contribution made by the environment toward influencing the expression of intelligence.* But we are unable to do that, and the best authorities agree that it does not seem likely that we shall ever—even though "ever" is a long time—be able to make such a separation. For this reason, especially when making comparisons between different groups, it is false to claim that there has been any success in distinguishing the genetic from the environmental contributions to the development of intelligence.

There can, of course, be not the slightest doubt that in many cases genetic influences enter into the production of some of the differences in intelligence observed between different individuals within any group. It is, however, impossible at the present time to discover to what extent genes have contributed to those differences. To repeat once again the point that cannot be too often repeated, since genes never function in isolation, but always in interaction with the environment, it does not appear likely that we shall ever be able to say to what extent differences in intelligence are on the one hand due to genes and on the other to environment.

In addition, it is quite clear that there are many unknowns involved in the development of intelligence, as for example, aspects of physiological, biochemical, neurological, neurohumoral, molecular, and social conditions, conditions which it is quite impossible to take into account because they are unknown. All of which leads to the conclusion that those who tell us that "IQ" tests measure innate intelligence by that very statement make it clear that they simply do not understand the complexity of the problem, and in claiming to have solved it and making their specious recommendations, deceive both themselves and the public. They perceive cause and effect relations between variables, such as test scores and assumed genetic determinants, where in fact no such cause and effect relations exist. The statistical treatment of the data in any investigation may be quite unexceptionable, but when unexceptionable statistical methods are applied to the analysis of unsound data to begin with, based on assumptions that are equally unsound, one can only end up with conclusions that are equally unsound. Such are the erroneous constructs of "race" and "IQ." This book deals with some of the principal unsound assumptions of Professor Jensen's writings in the hope, among other things, that the demonstration of the errors into which he has fallen may serve to set the record straight.

NOTES

1. Ashley Montagu (editor), *The Concept of Race*. New York, The Free Press, 1964.
2. Stuart Piggott, *The Dawn of Civilization*. New York, McGraw-Hill, 1961; Michael Grant (editor), *The Birth of Western Civilization*. New York, McGraw-Hill, 1964; Grahame Clark, *From Savagery to Civilization*. London, Cobbett Press, 1946; V. Gordon Childe, *Man Makes Himself*. New York, New American Library, 1960.
3. John S. Haller, Jr., *Outcasts from Evolution*. Urbana, University of Illinois Press, 1971; Winthrop D. Jordan, *White Over Black*. Chapel Hill, N.C., University of North Carolina Press, 1968; George M. Fredrickson, *The Black Image in the White Mind*. New York, Harper & Row, 1971; Thomas P. Gossett, *Race: The History of an Idea*. Dallas, Southern Methodist University Press, 1963.
4. R. J. Herrnstein, "I. Q.," *The Atlantic Monthly*, September 1971, pp. 43–64; R. J. Herrnstein, *I.Q. in the Meritocracy*. Boston, Little, Brown, 1973; H. J. Eysenck, *Race, Intelligence and Education*. London, Temple Smith, 1971; H. J. Eysenck, *The IQ Argument*. New York, The Library Press, 1971.
5. Theta H. Wolf, *Alfred Binet*. Chicago, University of Chicago Press, 1973, p. 203.
6. Wilhelm Stern, *Die Intelligenz der Kindes und Jugendliche und die Methoden ihrer Untersuchung*. Leipzig, 1912.
7. Lewis M. Terman. *The Measurement of Intelligence*. Boston, Houghton, Mifflin, 1916.
8. Walter Lippmann, "The Mental Age of Americans," *The New Republic*, 25 October 1922, pp. 213–15; "The Mystery of the 'A' Men." 1 November 1922; "The Reliability of Intelligence Tests." 8 November 1922; "The Abuse of the Tests." 15 November 1922; "Tests of Hereditary Intelligence." 22 November 1922; "The Future of the Tests." 29 November 1922.
9. Lewis M. Terman, "The Great Conspiracy or The Impulse Imperious of Intelligence Testers, Psychoanalyzed and Exposed by Mr. Lippmann." *The New Republic*, 27 December 1922, pp. 116–20. See also Walter Lippmann, "The Great Confusion: A Reply to Mr. Terman." *The New Republic*, 3 January 1923, pp. 145–46.
10. Lewis M. Terman, in Carl Murchison (editor), *A History of Psychology in Autobiography*, vol. 2, Worcester, Mass. Clark University Press, 1932, p. 329.
11. Alfred Binet, *Les Idées modernes sur les enfants*. Paris, Flammarion, 1909.

12. William Stern, *General Psychology*. New York, Macmillan, 1938, p. 60.
13. Ken Richardson, David Spears, and Martin Richards (editors), *Race, Culture, and Intelligence*. Baltimore, Penguin Books, 1972; Evelyn Sharp, *The IQ Cult*. New York, Coward, McCann & Geoghegan, 1972; Carl Senna (editor), *The Fallacy of the I.Q.* New York, The Third Press, 1973; John Garcia, "IQ: The Conspiracy," *Psychology Today*, September 1972, pp. 40–43, 92–94; Peter Watson, *Psychology and Race*. New York, Basic Books, 1974; Robert L. Williams, "Scientific Racism and IQ: The Silent Mugging of the Black Community," *Psychology Today*, May 1974, pp. 32–41, 101.
14. *Heritability* is the proportion of the genetic to the total phenotypic variance. It is a group or population measure, and cannot be determined on an individual. For any particular trait in a specified population H (Heritability) is obtained by genetic variance divided by phenotypic variance, that is, in the present instance the observable trait yielded as the IQ score and called "intelligence," as $H = V_G/V_P$ or $V_G + V_E$ (V_G = genetic variance; V_P = phenotypic variance; V_E = environmental variance). Genetic variance denotes that portion of the phenotypic variance which is caused by variation in the genetic constitution of the individuals in a population.
15. R. A. Fisher, "Limits to Intensive Production in Animals," *British Agricultural Bulletin*, vol. 4, 1951, pp. 317–18.
16. See pp. 174–191 of the present volume.
17. See pp. 192–219 of the present volume.
18. Jerry Hirsch, "Behavior-Genetic Analysis and Its Biosocial Consequences," In Robert Cancro (editor), *Intelligence: Genetic and Environmental Influences*. New York: Grune & Stratton, 1971, pp. 88–106; Vernon W. Stone, "The Interaction Component Is Critical," *Harvard Educational Review*, vol. 39, 1969, pp. 628–30; R. M. C. Huntley, "Heritability of Intelligence," in J. E. Meade and A. S. Parkes (editors), *Genetic and Environmental Factors in Human Ability*. New York, Plenum Press, 1966, pp. 201–18; Theodosius Dobzhansky, "Genetics and the Social Sciences," in David C. Glass (editor), *Genetics*. New York, The Rockfeller University Press, 1968, pp. 129–42.
19. Vernon W. Stone, "The Interaction Component Is Critical," *Harvard Educational Review*, vol. 39, 1969, pp. 628–39, p. 629.
20. Arthur R. Jensen, "How Much Can We Boost IQ and Scholastic Achievement?" *Harvard Educational Review*, vol. 39, 1969, p. 80.
21. Robert E. Kuttner, "Biochemical Anthropology," in Robert E. Kuttner (editor), *Race and Modern Science*. New York, Social Science Press, 1967, pp. 197–222.
22. Theodosius Dobzhansky and Ashley Montagu, "Natural Selection and the Mental Capacities of Mankind," *Science*, vol. 105, 1947, pp. 587–90.
23. George Gaylord Simpson, *Biology and Man*. New York, Harcourt, Brace and World, 1969, p. 104.
24. Paul David and Laurence H. Snyder, "Genetic Variability and Human Behavior," in John H. Rohrer and Muzafer Sherif (editors), *Social Psychology at the Crossroads*. New York, Harper & Bros., 1951, p. 71.
25. Sherwood L. Washburn and C. S. Lancaster, "The Evolution of Hunt-

ing," in Richard B. Lee and Irven De Vore (editors), *Man the Hunter*. Chicago, Aldine Publishing Co., 1968, p. 303.

26. Editorial, "Fear of Enlightenment," *Nature*, vol. 228, 1970, pp. 1013–14.

27. Arthur R. Jensen, *Educability and Group Differences*. New York, Harper & Row, 1973, p. 24.

28. Richard B. Lee and Irven De Vore (editors), *Man the Hunter*. Chicago, Aldine Publishing Co., 1968; Elman R. Service, *The Hunters*. Englewood Cliffs, N.J., Prentice-Hall, 1966; Carleton S. Coon, *The Hunting Peoples*. Boston, Little, Brown, 1971.

29. *A Report on Longitudinal Evaluations of Preschool Programs*. Vol. 1, Sally Ryan, *Longitudinal Evaluations*, vol. 2, Urie Bronfenbrenner, *Is Early Intervention Effective?* Washington, D.C., DHEW Publication Nos. (OHD) 72–75, 1974.

30. R. Heber, H. Garber, S. Harrington, and C. Hoffman, *Rehabilitation of Families at Risk for Mental Retardation*. Madison, Wisconsin, Rehabilitation and Research Center in Mental Retardation, University of Wisconsin, 1972.

31. For a good discussion of this subject, see A. Whimbey with L. S. Whimbey, *Intelligence Can Be Taught*. New York, Dutton, 1975.

2

NATURAL SELECTION AND THE
MENTAL CAPACITIES OF MANKIND

Th. Dobzhansky and Ashley Montagu

The fundamental mechanisms of the transmission of heredity from parents to offspring are surprisingly uniform in most diverse organisms. Their uniformity is perhaps the most remarkable fact disclosed by genetics. The laws discovered by Mendel apply to human genes just as much as to those of the maize plant, and the processes of cellular division and germ cell maturation in man are not very different from those in a grasshopper. The similarity of the mechanisms of heredity on the individual level is reflected on the population level in a similarity of the basic causative factors of organic evolution throughout the living world. Mutation, selection, and genetic drift are important in the evolution of man as well as in amoebae and in bacteria. Wherever sexuality and cross-fertilization are established as exclusive or predominant methods of reproduction, the field of hereditary variability increases enormously as compared with asexual or self-fertilizing organisms. Isolating mechanisms which prevent interbreeding and fusion of species of mammals are operative also among insects.

Nevertheless, the universality of basic genetic mechanisms and of evolutionary agents permits a variety of evolutionary patterns to exist not only in different lines of descent but even at different

From *Science*, Vol. 105, 1947, pp. 587–90. Reprinted by permission.

times in the same line of descent. It is evident that the evolutionary pattern in the dog species under domestication is not the same
as in the wild ancestors of the domestic dogs or in the now living wild relatives. Widespread occurrence of reduplication of
chromosome complements (polyploidy) in the evolution of plants
introduces complexities which are not found in the animal kingdom, where polyploidy is infrequent. Evolutionary situations
among parasites and among cave inhabitants are clearly different
from those in free-living forms. Detection and analysis of differences in the evolutionary patterns in different organisms is one
of the important tasks of modern evolutionists.

It can scarcely be doubted that man's biological heredity is
transmitted by mechanisms similar to those encountered in other
animals and in plants. Likewise, there is no reason to believe that
the evolutionary development of man has involved causative factors other than those operative in the evolution of other organisms. The evolutionary changes that occurred before the prehu-
man could become human, as well as those which supervened
since the attainment of the human estate, can be described causally
only in terms of mutation, selection, genetic drift, and hybridization—familiar processes throughout the living world. This reasoning, indisputable in the purely biological context, becomes a fallacy, however, when used, as it often has been, to justify narrow
biologism in dealing with human material.

The specific human features of the evolutionary pattern of man
cannot be ignored. Man is a unique product of evolution in that
he, far more than any other creature, has escaped from the bond-
age of the physical and the biological into the multiform social
environment. This remarkable development introduces a third dimension in addition to those of the external and internal environments—a dimension which many biologists, in considering the
evolution of man, tend to neglect. The most important setting of
human evolution is the human social environment. As stated
above, this can influence evolutionary changes only through the

media of mutation, selection, genetic drift, and hybridization. Nevertheless, there can be no genuine clarity in our understanding of man's biological nature until the role of the social factor in the development of the human species is understood. A biologist approaching the problems of human evolution must never lose sight of the truth stated more than 2,000 years ago by Aristotle: "Man is by nature a political animal."

In the words of Fisher, "For rational systems of evolution, that is, for theories which make at least the most familiar facts intelligible to the reason, we must turn to those that make progressive adaptation the driving force of the process." It is evident that man by means of his reasoning abilities, by becoming a "political animal," has achieved a mastery of the world's varying environments quite unprecedented in the history of organic evolution. The system of genes which has permitted the development of the specifically human mental capacities has thus become the foundation and the paramount influence in all subsequent evolution of the human stock. An animal becomes adapted to its environment by evolving certain genetically determined physical and behavioral traits; the adaptation of man consists chiefly in developing his inventiveness, a quality to which his physical heredity predisposes him and which his social heredity provides him with the means of realizing. To the degree to which this is so, man is unique. As far as his physical responses to the world are concerned, he is almost wholly emancipated from dependence upon inherited biological dispositions, uniquely improving upon the latter by the process of learning that which his social heredity (culture) makes available to him. Man possesses much more efficient means of achieving immediate or long-term adaptation than any other biological species: namely, through learned responses or novel inventions and improvisations.

In general, two types of biological adaptation in evolution can be distinguished. One is genetic specialization and genetically controlled fixity of traits. The second consists in the ability to re-

spond to a given range of environmental situations by evolving
traits favorable in these particular situations; this presupposes
genetically controlled plasticity of traits. It is known, for example,
that the composition of the blood which is most favorable for life
at high altitudes is somewhat different from that which suffices
at sea level. A species which ranges from sea level to high altitudes on a mountain range may become differentiated into several altitudinal races, each having a fixed blood composition favored by natural selection at the particular altitude at which it
lives; or a genotype may be selected which permits an individual
to respond to changes in the atmospheric pressure by definite alterations in the composition of the blood. It is well known that
heredity determines in its possessor not the presence or absence
of certain traits but, rather, the responses of the organisms to its
environments. The responses may be more or less rigidly fixed, so
that approximately the same traits develop in all environments in
which life is possible. On the other hand, the responses may differ
in different environments. Fixity or plasticity of a trait is, therefore, genetically controlled.

Whether the evolutionary adaptation in a given phyletic line
will occur chiefly by way of genetic fixity or by way of genetically controlled plasticity of traits will depend on circumstances.
In the first place, evolutionary changes are compounded of muta-
tional steps, and consequently the kind of change that takes place
is always determined by the composition of the store of muta-
tional variability which happens to be available in the species
populations. Secondly, fixity or plasticity of traits is controlled
by natural selection. Having a trait fixed by heredity and hence
appearing in the development of an individual regardless of environmental variations is, in general, of benefit to organisms whose
milieu remains uniform and static except for rare and freakish
deviations. Conversely, organisms which inhabit changeable environments are benefited by having their traits plastic and modified by each recurrent configuration of environmental agents in

a way most favorable for the survival of the carrier of the trait in question.

Comparative anatomy and embryology show that a fairly general trend in organic evolution seems to be from environmental dependence toward fixation of the basic features of the bodily structure and function. The appearance of these structural features in the embryonic development of higher organisms is, in general, more nearly autonomous and independent of the environment than in lower forms. The development becomes "buffered" against environmental and genetic shocks. If, however, the mode of life of a species happens to be such that it is, of necessity, exposed to a wide range of environments, it becomes desirable to vary some structures and functions in accordance with the circumstances that confront an individual or a strain at a given time and place. Genetic structures which permit adaptive plasticity of traits become, then, obviously advantageous for survival and so are fostered by natural selection.

The social environments that human beings have created everywhere are notable not only for their extreme complexity but also for the rapid changes to which immediate adjustment is demanded. Adjustment occurs chiefly in the psychical realm and has little or nothing to do with physical traits. In view of the fact that from the very beginning of human evolution the changes in the human environment have been not only rapid but diverse and manifold, genetic fixation of behavioral traits in man would have been decidedly unfavorable for survival of individuals as well as of the species as a whole. Success of the individual in most human societies has depended and continues to depend upon his ability rapidly to evolve behavior patterns which fit him to the kaleidoscope of the conditions he encounters. He is best off if he submits to some, compromises with some, rebels against others, and escapes from still other situations. Individuals who display a relatively greater fixity of response than their fellows suffer under most forms of human society and tend to fall by the way. Suppleness, plasticity, and, most important of all, ability to profit by experience and education are required. No other species is comparable to man in its capacity to acquire new behavior patterns and discard old ones in consequence of training. Considered socially as well as biologically, man's outstanding capacity is his educability. The survival value of this capacity is manifest, and therefore the possibility of its development through natural selection is evident.

It should be made clear at this point that the replacement of fixity of behavior by genetically controlled plasticity is not a necessary consequence of all forms of social organization. The quaint attempts to glorify insect societies as examples deserving emulation on the part of man ignore the fact that the behavior of an individual among social insects is remarkable precisely because of the rigidity of its genetic fixation. The perfection of the organized societies of ants, termites, bees, and other insects is indeed wonderful, and the activities of their members may strike an observer very forcibly by their objective purposefulness. This purposefulness is retained, however, only in environments in which the species normally lives. The ability of an ant to adjust its activities to situations not encountered in the normal habitats of its species is very limited. On the other hand, social organizations on the human level are built on the principle that an individual is able to alter his behavior to fit any situation, whether previously experienced or new.

This difference between human and insect societies is, of course, not surprising. Adaptive plasticity of behavior can develop only on the basis of a vastly more complex nervous system than is sufficient for adaptive fixity. The genetic differences between human and insect societies furnish a striking illustration of the two types of evolutionary adaptations—those achieved through genetically controlled plasticity of behavioral traits and those attained through genetic specialization and fixation of behavior.

The genetically controlled plasticity of mental traits is, biologically speaking, the most typical and uniquely human characteristic. It is very probable that the survival value of this characteristic in human evolution has been considerable for a long time, as measured in terms of human historical scales. Just when this characteristic first appeared is, of course, conjectural. Here it is of interest to note that the most marked phylogenetic trend in the evolution of man has been the special development of the brain, and that the characteristic human plasticity of mental traits seems to be associated with the exceptionally large brain size. The brain of, for example, the Lower or Middle Pleistocene fossil forms of man was, grossly at least, scarcely distinguishable from that of modern man. The average Neanderthaloid brain was somewhat larger than that of modern man, though slightly different in shape. More important than the evidence derived from brain size is the testimony of cultural development. The Middle Acheulean handiwork of Swanscombe man of several hundred thousand years ago and the beautiful Mousterian cultural artifacts associated with Neanderthal man indicate the existence of minds of a high order of development.

The cultural evidence thus suggests that the essentially human organization of the mental capacities emerged quite early in the evolution of man. However that may be, the possession of the gene system, which conditions educability rather than behavioral fixity, is a common property of all living mankind. In other words, educability is truly a species character of man, *Homo sapiens*. This does not mean, of course, that the evolutionary process has run its course and that natural selection has introduced no changes in the genetic structure of the human species since the attainment of the human status. Nor do we wish to imply that no genetic variations in mental equipment exist at our time level. On the contrary, it seems likely that with the attainment of human status that part of man's genetic system which is related to mental potentialities did not cease to be labile and subject to change.

This brings us face to face with the old problem of the likelihood that significant genetic differences in the mental capacities of the various ethnic groups of mankind exist. The physical and, even more, the social environments of men who live in different countries are quite diversified. Therefore, it has often been argued, natural selection would be expected to differentiate the human species into local races differing in psychic traits. Populations of different countries may differ in skin color, head shape, and other somatic characters. Why, then, should they be alike in mental traits?

It will be through investigation rather than speculation that the problem of the possible existence of average differences in the mental make-up of human populations of different geographical origins will eventually be settled. Arguments based on analogies are precarious, especially where evolutionary patterns are concerned. If human races differ in structural traits, it does not necessarily follow that they must also differ in mental ones. Race differences arise chiefly because of the differential action of natural selection on geographically separated populations. In the case of man, however, the structural and mental traits are quite likely to be influenced by selection in different ways.

The very complex problem of the origin of racial differentiations in structural traits does not directly concern us here. Suffice it to say that racial differences in traits such as the blood groups may conceivably have been brought about by genetic drift in populations of limited effective size. Other racial traits are genetically too complex and too consistently present in populations of some large territories and absent in other territories to be accounted for by genetic drift alone. Differences in skin color, hair form, nose shape, etc. are almost certainly products of natural selection. The lack of reliable knowledge of the adaptive significance of these traits is perhaps the greatest gap in our understanding of the evolutionary biology of man. Nevertheless, it is at least a plausible working hypothesis that these and similar traits have, or at any rate had in the past, differential survival values in the environments of different parts of the world.

By contrast, the survival value of a higher development of mental capacities in man is obvious. Furthermore, natural selection seemingly favors such a development everywhere. In the ordinary course of events in almost all societies those persons are likely to be favored who show wisdom, maturity of judgment, and ability to get along with people—qualities which may assume different forms in different cultures. Those are the qualities of the plastic personality, not a single trait but a general condition, and this is the condition which appears to have been at a premium in practically all human societies.

In human societies conditions have been neither rigid nor stable enough to permit the selective breeding of genetic types adapted to different statuses or forms of social organization. Such rigidity and stability do not obtain in any society. On the other hand, the outstanding fact about human societies is that they do change and do so more or less rapidly. The rate of change was possibly comparatively slow in earlier societies, as the rate of change in present-day nonliterate societies may be, when compared to the rate characterizing occidental societies. In any event, rapid changes in behavior are demanded of the person at all levels of social organization even when the society is at its most stable. Life at any level of social development in human societies is a pretty complex business, and it is met and handled most efficiently by those who exhibit the greatest capacity for adaptability, plasticity.

It is this very plasticity of his mental traits which confers upon man the unique position which he occupies in the animal kingdom. Its acquisition freed him from the constraint of a limited range of biologically predetermined responses. He became capable of acting in a more or less regulative manner upon his physical environment instead of being largely regulated by it. The process of natural selection in all climes and at all times have favored genotypes which permit greater and greater educability and plasticity of mental traits under the influence of the uniquely social environments to which man has been continuously exposed.

The effect of natural selection in man has probably been to render genotypic differences in personality traits, as between individuals and particularly as between races, relatively unimportant compared to their phenotypic plasticity. Instead of having his responses genetically fixed as in other animal species, man is a species that invents its own responses, and it is out of this unique ability to invent, to improvise, his responses that his cultures are born.

3

THE IQ MYTHOLOGY

Ashley Montagu

"Race" and "IQ" are terms which seemingly possess a clear and well-defined meaning for millions of people. Their common usage implies for them the belief in a reality which is beyond question. When, on occasion, the suggestion is made that these terms correspond to no reality whatever, but constitute an amalgam of erroneous and stultifying ideas of the most damaging kind, the suggestion is received either with blank incredulity or open derision. Nevertheless, the truth is that these terms not only are unsound but in fact correspond to no verifiable reality, and have, indeed, been made the basis for social and political action of the most heinous kinds.

What is considered so obvious and beyond question is the apparent fact that the physical differences which allegedly mark off the "races" from one another are indissolubly linked with individual and group achievement. Some "races," it is held, are in all these respects inferior to others. Hence, all that is necessary in order to arrive at a proper estimate of an individual's potential general abilities is to identify, usually by his external appearance, his "racial" membership, and this will at once tell one what the limits of that individual's capacities are, what he is likely to be able to accomplish, and, furthermore, what his particular "race" will be able to achieve. These three phenomena, it is commonly believed, physical appearance, individual ability, and group achievement, are taken to be inseparably linked with each other by heredity. This "manifest reality," though it is rarely so articulated, represents what is generally understood by "race." It is the popular, or *social*, conception of "race," and is not to be confused with the biological concept of "race"—held in a variety of different forms—in which no linkage is implied between physical appearance, individual abilities, and group achievement.[1]

What is wrong with the social or racist view of "race" is that, among other things, there happens to be no genetic association or linkage between genes for physical appearance, for individual behavior, or for group achievement. Nevertheless, believers in the doctrine of "race" choose to take it for granted that there is. How else, indeed, they ask, can one account for differences in individual abilities and group achievement of the different "races"?

This is a legitimate question, and the answer to it is that when the facts are considered the weight of the evidence indicates that the differences are primarily due to the differences in the history of the experiences the individuals and their groups have undergone. The development of civilization, for example, brought with it enormously complex technological and other changes, changes of a kind that simply did not occur among the indigenous peoples of the world. The latter were wholly bypassed by the civilizing influences that affected the peoples of the culturally busier parts of the world. With rare exceptions, if, indeed, there are any, what is required for the development of civilization is the fructifying influence of contacts with other cultures. Such contacts must usually occur over appreciable periods of time.[2] Hence, when from the ethnocentric viewpoint of the civilized peoples of the world unfavorable conclusions are drawn concerning the capacities of the members of indigenous populations, those conclusions are likely to be both unfair and unsound. There is, in fact, no possible basis on which such comparisons can be made, since the principal necessary condition that would make such a comparison possible is missing, namely, *a history of novel complex cultural experiences which lead to the development of technological abilities and group achievement.*

Not alone is this requirement generally lacking in such cross-cultural comparisons, but it is also lacking in comparisons made between ethnic groups within the same nation. It is lacking, for example, in the case of blacks and whites, because blacks have never enjoyed equal cultural and socioeconomic opportunities in any white society. Blacks in America have, in fact, been deprived, oppressed, discriminated against, impoverished, ghettoized, and generally excluded from the brotherhood of man.[3] Hence, it should not be surprising that there have been and continue to be significant differences in the achievements of blacks and whites as "measured" by tests which have been arbitrarily standardized on middle-class whites.

For reasons which would themselves make a study of singular interest, while it is thought that IQ tests "measure" the *combined effects* of genetic and experiential influences on the learned ability to respond to such tests, some writers have manifested an extreme biologistic bias in the evaluation of the meaning of the test scores. The tests for these writers have come to represent a measure of innate intelligence.[4] This is usually a biased view which is demonstrably unsound and is one that most authorities reject.

An intelligence test consists of a series of tasks yielding a score which is supposed to represent a rating of the standard of intelligence of that individual. The problem-solving tasks are standardized by finding the average performances of *white* individuals who by independent criteria are of known degrees of levels of test-solving ability at a particular chronological age, that is, *mental age*. The IQ score is obtained by dividing mental age by chronological age and multiplying by one hundred.

One of the many difficulties surrounding IQ tests is that no one really knows what the structure of intelligence is. What is usually said is that intelligence is what intelligence tests test. But such a "definition" of intelligence is hardly likely to advance our understanding of it. It might perhaps be agreed that such tests provide a rough estimate of certain problem-solving abilities. But abilities rep-

resent trained capacities, and therefore experience and learning enter substantially into their development. Since the tested ability to
a large extent represents the trained expression of a capacity, the
"measurement" of the ability can tell us nothing about the original
quality of the capacity. The genetic capacity may have been considerably altered by the operation of environmental conditions, both
prenatal and postnatal, long before its complex elements have been
exposed to the more socially complex conditions of the cultural environment.

Alfred Binet and Theodore Simon, the original inventors of the
"intelligence scale," thoroughly rejected any notion of the kind of
precision that subsequent intelligence testers claimed for their test
or any of its revisions. When in 1960 Simon discussed this matter
with Dr. Theta Wolf he referred to the history of IQ testing as a
betrayal of the purpose of the Binet-Simon test.[5]

Binet and Simon always considered their test an "intelligence
scale," something that might give one an idea of the general intelligence of a child, but never a precise measure of specific abilities.
The Binet-Simon Scale was published in 1905, with revisions appearing in 1908 and 1911, the latter being the year of Binet's death
at the age of fifty-four. Binet's conception of what he was doing
when giving his intelligence tests differed very markedly from that
of those who adopted and "improved" them, especially in America.
Binet's objective, in his own words, was to "measure the useful effects of adaptation, and the value of the difficulties overcome by
them." This was as near as he hoped to get to intelligence, but he
was never for a moment under the illusion that he had succeeded
in the task of measuring intelligence in the sense that all too many
American and English intelligence testers believed they had done.

As for the term "Intelligence Quotient," embodied in the letters
"IQ," which have now become as much a part of the English language as "OK," Binet never used it. The idea of a "mental" quotient—far better than "intelligence" quotient—had been suggested
by the German psychologist William Stern in 1912.[6] It was the

American psychologist Lewis M. Terman who coined the term "Intelligence Quotient."[7] Binet altogether refused to have anything to do with even the remotest possibility of a quotient on several grounds: first, because the tests he employed were in his view not exact enough to warrant the appearance of precision a quotient implied and, second, because "mental age" varies so greatly for each of the different items in any test that any averaging of such test results would yield a specious score; and so Binet preferred to speak of "mental level" rather than "mental age" simply because "level" was non-committal and "age" was not. With "mental level" much was left open, with "mental age" too much was closed off.

The excessive enthusiasm with which intelligence tests were greeted in the United States drew the fire of Walter Lippmann, America's most distinguished journalist, who, in a series of six articles published in the fall of 1922 in *The New Republic*, wrote what will always remain one of the most cogently critical anatomies of intelligence testing. Lippmann pointed out that the intelligence testers were claiming not only that they were measuring intelligence, but also that "intelligence is innate, hereditary, and predetermined." And, he went on to say, "Intelligence testing in the hands of men who hold this dogma could not but lead to an intellectual caste system."[8] And that is precisely what such modern writers as A. R. Jensen, R. J. Hernstein, C. Murray, William Shockley, and H. J. Eysenck claim the test results should lead to.

Lippmann's articles drew a rather patronizing response from Terman,[9] the chief proponent of intelligence testing in America, which in no way met Lippmann's thoroughly sound criticisms. What Terman really believed he made quite clear in an autobiographical account of his scientific development. One of his credos was "That the major differences in the intelligence test scores of certain races, as negroes and whites, will never be fully accounted for on the environmental hypothesis."[10] In other words, Terman believed that genetic factors were largely responsible for the differences in the test scores between blacks and whites.

That IQ tests were ethnocentrically structured, and therefore unfair when applied to members of ethnic groups other than those of
the cultures upon which they had been standardized, did not bother
Terman at all. Not only this, his confidence in IQ tests was such
that he felt himself capable of applying them even to the dead. Thus,
he and his associate Catherine Cox were able to compute the IQ of
such figures as Napoleon, Lincoln, Goethe, Da Vinci, Galileo, and
some three hundred others! The inference left for the reader to
draw was that some people are born with low IQs and some with
high IQs.

It is also evident that Terman considered intelligence to be a fairly
fixed entity—an idea which would have appalled Binet who, in 1909,
had already commented on some recent writers who appeared "to
have given their moral support to the deplorable verdict that the
intelligence of an individual is a fixed quantity. . . . We must protest
and act against this brutal pessimism."[11]

William Stern had early pointed to the dangers of drawing incomplete and unjustifiable conclusions from intelligence quotients.
"To be sure," he wrote, "there has been and still is an exaggerated
faith in the power of numbers. For example, an 'intelligence quotient' may be of provisional value as *a first crude approximation* when
the mental level of an individual is sought; but whoever imagines
that in determining this quantity he has summed up 'the' intelligence of an individual once and for all, so that he may dispense with
the more intensive qualitative study, leaves off where psychology
begins" (italics added).[12]

"A first crude approximation," is exactly how Binet and Simon
thought of their test, as part of the qualitative evaluation of the
person as a whole—something that none of the traditional IQ tests
have attempted, and which they, indeed, thoroughly disregarded.

Because of the extreme bias of IQ tests favoring white urbanites
as compared with other ethnic groups and socially disadvantaged
classes, even if the tests were to measure intelligence—which
they do not—any conclusions drawn from such tests as to the

comparative quality of the intelligence and future possibilities of those subjected to them would be quite unsound.[13] Nevertheless psychologists like Arthur R. Jensen continue to commit all the errors that IQ testers have habitually committed, namely, of assuming (1) that the tests measure intelligence; (2) that the ethnic groups on whose members they carry out these tests are sufficiently comparable to permit valid inferences to be drawn as to the quality of their intelligence; and (3) that what IQ tests measure is to the largest extent intelligence determined by genes.

In a 123-page study entitled "How Much Can We Boost IQ and Scholastic Achievement?" published in the *Harvard Educational Review* in the winter of 1969, Professor Arthur R. Jensen of the University of California at Berkeley, after a detailed examination of the evidence, concluded that it is "a not unreasonable hypothesis that genetic factors are strongly implicated in the average Negro-white intelligence difference" (p. 82). According to Professor Jensen heritability measures indicate that about 80 percent of the determinance of intelligence is due to genes and about 20 percent to environment. *Heritability* is alleged to mean the portion of the total phenotypic or trait variance that is genetic.[14] Professor Jensen makes much of his heritability measures, but the truth is that the so-called heritability coefficient is an especially undependable measure when applied to the human species, an application which has been criticized from its very inception by mathematical geneticists such as R. A. Fisher, as well as others. Fisher, one of the founders of modern statistics and mathematical genetics, referred to the coefficient of heritability "as one of those unfortunate short-cuts which have emerged in biometry for lack of a more thorough analysis of the data."[15] The great appeal of heritability to racialist writers like Murray and Hernstein is their erroneous belief that it means unchangeability. Jensen's application of the heritability estimate has been dealt with by Lewontin[16] and independently thoroughly demolished by Layzer as well as by Block[17] in the contributions reprinted in this volume, and the 80/20 percent difference claimed to have been found by Jensen is shown to belong to numerology rather than science. There have been other criticisms of this heritability estimate.[18] The truth is that the nature of the genetic contribution to intelligence as "measured" by intelligence tests is unknown both for individuals and for populations, and therefore, on this ground alone, heritability estimates constitute, as one critic has put it, "little more than a hollow quantification."[19]

Jensen tells us that his discussions with a number of geneticists, whose names he does not reveal, concerning the question of a genetic basis for differences among races in mental abilities revealed to him a number of rather consistently agreed-upon points. These points are: "Any groups which have been geographically or socially isolated from one another for many generations are practically certain to differ in their gene pools, and consequently are likely to show differences in any phenotypic characteristics having a high heritability." Furthermore, "genetic differences are manifested in virtually every anatomical, physiological, and biochemical comparison one can make between representative samples of identifiable racial groups (Kuttner, 1967). There is no reason why the brain should be exempt from this generalization."[20]

As generalizations, the first statement is quite sound. The second statement is quite unsound, and the third probably highly unsound. Jensen's reference to Kuttner as his authority for the second statement is not supported by the latter's own paper, which is restricted to a review of the biochemical differences between so-called "races."[21] In any event, far from genetic differences being manifested in virtually every anatomical, physiological, and biochemical trait between "racial" groups, the likenesses in all these classes of traits are consistently far greater than the differences. It is as absurd to exaggerate the differences as to minimize them. Differences in all these areas of structure and function exist, but to argue from the existence of such physical differences that *therefore* it is reasonable to suppose that similar differences must exist for the genetic distribution of mental functions among the "races" is simply no more than to make words do service for the work of examining the evidence. "There is no reason why the brain should be exempt from this generalization," writes Jensen, the generalization that there exist genetic differences in "virtually" every physical trait between the "races." By "brain" Jensen presumably means the neural circuitry which under the appropriate experiential conditions or organization will function as mind. Since the brain is an organic structure it can easily be slipped into Jensen's generalization and there quite erroneously equated with "mind." Certainly the brain has undergone considerable evolutionary change, but the pressures of natural selection have not acted directly on the brain but indirectly through its functions, especially capacities for its culturally acquired functions. The complexity and size of the human brain represent the end-effects of the action of selection on the functions of human behavior in human environments. What has been under selective pressure is not the brain as an organ, but *the skill in using it and its competence in responding to the challenges of the environment as a culturally adaptive organ.*

Contrary to Jensen, there is every reason why the brain should be exempt from his generalization. This aspect of the manner of humanity's unique evolution was first dealt with in a joint paper by Professor Theodosius Dobzhansky and the writer as long ago as 1947.[22] In that contribution, reprinted in the present volume (p. _____), it will be seen, as Professor George Gaylord Simpson later independently put it, "There are biological reasons why significant racial differences in intelligence, which have not been found, would not be expected. In a polytypic species, races adapt to differing local conditions but the species as a whole evolves adaptations advantageous to all its races, and spreading among them all under the influence of natural selection and by means of interbreeding. When human races were evolving it is certain that increase in mental ability was advantageous to *all* of them. It would, then, have tended over the generations to have spread among all of them in approximately equal degrees. For any one race to lag definitely behind another in over-all genetic adaptation, the two would have to be genetically isolated over a very large number of generations. They would, in fact, have to become distinct species; but human races are all interlocking parts of just one species."[23] And as the geneticists Professors Paul David and L. H. Snyder have written, "flexibility of behavioral adjustment to different situations is likely to have had a selective advantage over any tendency toward stereotyped reactions. For it is difficult to conceive of any human social organization in which plasticity of response, as reflected by ability to profit from experience (that is, by intelligence) and by emotional and temperamental resilience, would not be at a premium and therefore favored by natural selection. It therefore seems to us highly improbable that any significant genetic differentiation in respect to particular response patterns, in populations, or races has occurred in the history of human evolution."[24] "To assert the biological unity of mankind," write Professors Sherwood L. Washburn and C. S. Lancaster, "is to affirm the importance of the hunting way of life. It is to claim that however such conditions and customs may have varied locally, the main selection pressures that forged the species were the same."[25]

The foodgathering-hunting way of life was pursued by the human species the world over during the greater part of its evolutionary history. It is only during the last 15,000 years or so that some societies developed technologically more complex ways of controlling the environment, but even here the challenges required much the same responses, however complex.

In an editorial in *Nature* it was stated that "In circumstances in which it is plain that intelligence has been a crucial asset in survival, it is only reasonable to suppose that all of the races now extant are much of a muchness in intelligence."[26] Professor Jensen believes this to be a mistaken inference because it equates intelligence with Darwinian fitness or the ability to produce surviving progeny. But the editorial does nothing of the sort. A trait either has adaptive value— another name for Darwinian fitness—or it has not. Intelligence as a problem-solving ability is most certainly a trait possessing high adaptive value in all environments, and as such has been subject to the pressures of natural selection.

Professor Jensen thinks it not unlikely that "different environments and cultures could make differential genetically selective demands on various aspects of behavioral adaptability . . . Europeans and Africans have been evolving in widely separated areas and cultures for at least a thousand generations, under different conditions of selection which could have affected their gene pools for behavioral traits just as for physical characteristics."[27]

What Professor Jensen confuses here is the environmental pressures of widely separated geographic areas upon the *physical* evolution of the human species, and the virtually identical cultural pressures upon the *mental* development of people living a foodgathering-hunting existence. These are two totally different kettles of fish, and it does nothing but add confusion to the subject to treat the pressures of the physical environment as if they acted in the same way upon humankind's mental evolution. The challenges, in fact, to humankind's problem-solving abilities were of a very different order from those which eventually resulted in kinky or straight hair, a heavily or a lightly pigmented skin, a broad or a narrow nose, small or large ears, and so on.

While physical environments have varied considerably, the cultural environments of humankind's existence during the whole of its evolutionary history, right up to the recent period, have been fundamentally alike, namely, that of foodgathering-hunters.[28]

The important fact that Professor Jensen fails to understand is that while physical environments may have differed in the extreme, the conditions of selection under which humankind's mental evolution occurred were everywhere alike. The cultural differences between a Congo Pygmy and an Eskimo of the Far North are only superficially different. If you live in the Congo you need neither clothes nor sleds; if you live in the Far North you need both. There are great differences in detail between the foodgathering-hunting cultures, but the problem-solving responses they were required to make to the challenges of the particular environments, however different they were, are strikingly and fundamentally alike. They are generally alike in their material culture, in their social organization, permanent councils, belief in gods, warfare, and the like. The genetical-anthropological aspects of this subject are discussed by Professor Dobzhansky and myself in the contribution already referred to (see pp. _____-_____).

"How much can we boost IQ and scholastic achievement?" There is an answer to that question too which is highly encouraging, despite Professor Jensen's belief that not very much can be done that way. He pleads for a greater diversity of approaches and aims in tackling the problems of educating the young, especially the disadvantaged young. In that plea we can all join him. New approaches are, indeed, called for. In that connection the Department of Health, Education and Welfare report of 1974, *Report on Longitudinal Evaluations of Preschool Programs,* [29] is typical in its clear and unequivocal answers to Professor Jensen's question: IQ and scholastic achievement can be boosted significantly by improving the conditions of life of the child. In volume one of the *Report* eight independent studies are presented, and Dr. Sally Ryan summarizes these by underscoring the fact that although the most frequently reported gain is a significant rise in IQ points there is also good evidence of some gains in the personal-social adjustment of children as well. Professor Urie Bronfenbrenner in volume two of the *Report* examines a dozen studies relating to the effects of early intervention, and concludes that whenever it is possible to improve the human environment of the child its performance on IQ tests rises significantly. By special effort mothers can be encouraged to improve the care of their children, often to such an extent that they become effective workers with other mothers and children. Where the conditions have not been favorable for maternal participation in the project a highly trained teacher was assigned to the child, in the Milwaukee project, when it was as young as three months of age. [30]

The teacher was responsible for the child's total care and gave it a good deal of cuddling and soothing, and organized its learning and implemented the educational program by working with the child in the home from two to eight weeks—until the mother expressed enough confidence to allow the child to go to the center, where the teachers would work with the children on a very intimate one-on-one basis. At five and a half years the cared-for children had a mean IQ of 124 points while the uncared for controls had a mean IQ of 94, a difference of 30 points.[31]

Such findings not only constitute the answer to Professor Jensen's question, but the recommendations to which they lead for the improvement of the learning abilities of the child are so important that, with the kind permission of Professor Bronfenbrenner the final section of his monograph is reprinted here as our concluding chapter. It is good to be able to complete this volume on so constructive and encouraging a note. Professor Bronfenbrenner's analysis of recent research strengthens our faith, as he writes, "in the capacity of parents, of whatever background, to enable their children to develop into effective and happy human beings, *once our society is willing to make conditions of life viable for all its families*" (Author's italics).

Clearly it is not so much IQ and scholastic achievement that need to be boosted as the motivation to bring about the changes in social conditions that make deprived and unfulfilled and frustrated lives possible.

The papers in this volume speak for themselves; I am indebted to the authors and publishers for permission to reprint them here. The hope is that they will provide the reader interested in this difficult subject with the means of understanding the defects not alone of Professor Jensen's claims concerning the value of IQ tests in yielding a dependable measure of innate intelligence, but also the defects of such tests when applied to the measurement of "racial" differences in intelligence.

In this essay I have attempted to trace something of the history of the "IQ test," in order to show how the original work of Binet and Simon soon came to be abused, especially in the United States. I have stated, and I think the statement long overdue, that both the term "race" and the term "IQ" are delusive because in the one case the social conception of "race" was the deliberate invention of a slave-owning caste attempting to justify its conduct, and in the other case because "IQ" tests do not measure what they have generally been claimed to measure, namely, innate intelligence. It is most unfortunate that vested interests (including an unregulated multi-million dollar industry based on them) have made a cult of the "IQ" and, in the face of the contrary evidence, persist in perpetuating claims for such tests that are quite untenable.

Intelligence is a complex function of highly complex variables, so complex, indeed, that we can hardly be said to have made a beginning in understanding any of them. No one can really define intelligence. The best we can do is to make rather general statements about this complex function, but no serious student of the subject pretends that such statements represent anything more than the crudest kinds of remote approximations.

As for the genetics of intelligence, our knowledge is virtually non-existent. Intelligence is clearly a function of many genes in inter-action with the environment. The fact that we have no idea how many genes may be involved would not in itself constitute a suffi-cient impediment to the study of the genetics of intelligence *were we able to separate out the contribution made by environmental factors toward influencing the expression of intelligence.* But we are unable to do that, and the best authorities agree that it will be a long time, if ever, before we shall be able to make such a separation. For this reason, especially when making comparisons between different groups, it is false to claim that there has been any success in distin-guishing the genetic from the environmental contributions to the development of intelligence.

There can, of course, be little doubt that in many cases genetic influences enter into the production of some of the differences in intelligence observed between different individuals within any group. It is, however, impossible at the present time to discover to what extent genes have contributed to those differences. To repeat once again the point that cannot be too often repeated: since genes never function in isolation, but always in interaction with the environment, it does not appear likely that we shall ever be able to say to what extent differences in intelligence are on the one hand due to genes and on the other to environment.

In addition, it is quite clear that there are many unknowns involved in the development of intelligence, as, for example, aspects of physiological, biochemical, neurological, neurohumoral, molecular, personal, and social conditions, conditions which it is quite impossible to take into account because they are unknown. All of which leads to the conclusion that those who tell us that "IQ" tests measure innate intelligence by that very statement make it clear that they simply do not understand the complexity of the problem, and in claiming to have solved it and making their specious recommendations, deceive both themselves and the public. They perceive cause and effect relations between variables, such as test scores and assumed genetic determinants, where in fact no such cause and effect relations exist. The statistical treatment of the data in any investigation may be quite unexceptionable, but when unexceptionable statistical methods are applied to the analysis of unsound data to begin with, based on assumptions that are equally unsound, one can only end up with conclusions that are equally unsound. Such are the erroneous constructs of "race" and "IQ." This book deals with some of the principal unsound assumptions of racialist writers in the hope, among other things, that the demonstration of the errors into which they have fallen may serve to set the record straight.

NOTES

1. Ashley Montagu (editor), *The Concept of Race*. New York, The Free Press, 1964.
2. Stuart Piggott, *The Dawn of Civilization*. New York, McGraw-Hill, 1961; Michael Grant (editor), *The Birth of Western Civilization*. New York, McGraw-Hill, 1964;

Grahame Clar, *From Savagery to Civilization*. London, Cobbett Press, 1946; V. Gordon Childe, *Man Makes Himself*. New York, New American Library, 1960; Albert Jacguard, *In Praise of Difference*. New York, Columbia University Press, 1984.

3. John S. Haller, Jr., *Outcasts from Evolution*. Urbana, University of Illinois Press, 1971; Winthrop D. Jordan, *White Over Black*. Chapel Hill, N.C., University of North Carolina Press, 1968; George M. Fredrickson, *The Black Image in the White Mind*. New York, Harper & Row, 1971; Thomas P. Gossett, *Race: The History of an Idea*. Dallas, Southern Methodist University Press, 1963; Joel Williamson, *The Crucible of Race*. New York: Oxford University Press, 1984; Paul M. Sniderman & Thomas Piazza, *The Scar of Race*. Cambridge, Harvard University Press, 1993; Ronald Takski, *A Different Mirror*. Boston, Little, Brown, 1993.

4. R. J. Hernstein, "I. Q." *The Atlantic Monthly*, September 1971, pp. 43–64; R. J. Hernstein, *I.Q. in the Meritocracy*. Boston, Little, Brown, 1973; H. J. Eysenck, *Race, Intelligence and Education*. London, Temple Smith, 1971; H. J. Eysenck, *The IQ Argument*. New York, The Library Press, 1971; C. Murray & R. J. Hernstein, *The Bell Curve*. New York, The Free Press, 1994.

5. Theta H. Wolf, *Alfred Binet*. Chicago, University of Chicago Press, 1973, p. 203.

6. Wilhelm Stern, *Die Intelligenz der Kindes und Jugendliche und die Methoden ihrer Untersuchung*. Leipzig, 1912.

7. Lewis M. Terman, *The Measurement of Intelligence*. Boston, Houghton, Mifflin, 1916.

8. Walter Lippmann, "The Mental Age of Americans," *The New Republic*, 25 October 1922, pp. 213–15; "The Mystery of the 'A' Men." 1 November 1922; "The Reliability of Intelligence Tests." 8 November 1922; "The Abuse of the Tests." 15 November 1922; "Tests of Hereditary Intelligence." 22 November 1922; "The Future of the Tests." 29 November 1922.

9. Lewis M. Terman, "The Great Conspiracy or The Impulse Imperious of Intelligence Testers, Psychoanalyzed and Exposed by Mr. Lippmann." *The New Republic*, 27 December 1922, pp. 116–20. See also Walter Lippmann, "The Great Confusion: A Reply to Mr. Terman." *The New Republic*, 3 January 1923, pp. 145–46.

10. Lewis M. Terman, in Carl Murchison (editor), *A History of Psychology in Autobiography*, vol. 2. Worcester, Mass., Clark University Press, 1932, p. 329.

11. Alfred Binet, *Les Idées modernes sur les enfants*. Paris, Flammarion, 1909.

12. William Stern, *General Psychology*. New York, Macmillan, 1938, p. 60.

13. Ken Richardson, David Spears, and Martin Richards (editors), *Race, Culture, and Intelligence*. Baltimore, Penguin Books, 1972; Evelyn Sharp, *The IQ Cult*. New York, Coward, McCann & Geoghegan, 1972; Carl Senna (editor), *The Fallacy of the I.Q.* New York, The Third Press, 1973; John Garcia, "IQ: The Conspiracy." *Psychology Today*, September 1972, pp. 40–43, 92–94; Peter Watson, *Psychology and Race*. New York, Basic Books, 1974; Robert L. Williams, "Scientific Racism and IQ: The Silent Mugging of the Black Community." *Psychology Today*, May 1974, pp. 32–41, 101.

14. *Heritability* is the proportion of the genetic to the total phenotypic variance. It is an unsound group or population measure, and cannot be determined on an individual. For any particular trait in a specified population H (Heritability) is obtained by genetic variance divided by phenotypic variance, that is, in the present instance the observable trait yielded as the IQ score and called "intelligence," as $H = V_G/V_P$ or $V_G + V_E$ (V_G = genetic variance; V_P = phenotypic variance;

V_E environmental variance). Genetic variance denotes that portion of the phenotypic variance which is caused by variation in the genetic constitution of the individuals in a population. For a critical examination of H, see Black in this volume, pp _____-_____).

15. R. A. Fisher, "Limits to Intensive Production in Animals," *British Agricultural Bulletin*, vol. 4, 1951, pp. 317–18.
16. See pp. _____-_____ of the present volume.
17. See pp. _____-_____ of the present volume.
18. Jerry Hirsch, "Behavior-Genetic Analysis and Its Biosocial Consequences," in Robert Cancro (editor), *Intelligence: Genetic and Environmental Influences*. New York: Grune & Stratton, 1971, pp. 99–106; Vernon W. Stone, "The Interaction Component Is Critical," *Harvard Educational Review*, vol. 19, 1969, pp. 628–30; R. M. C. Huntley, "Heritability of Intelligence," in J. E. Meade and A. S. Parkes (editors), *Genetic and Environmental Factors in Human Ability*. New York, Plenum Press, 1966, pp. 201–18; Theodosius Dobzhansky, "Genetics and the Social Sciences," in David C. Glass (editor), *Genetics*. New York, The Rockefeller University Press, 1968, pp. 129–42.
19. Vernon W. Stone, "The Interaction Component Is Critical." *Harvard Educational Review*, vol. 39, 1969, pp. 628–39, p. 629.
20. Arthur R. Jensen, "How Much Can We Boost IQ and Scholastic Achievement?" *Harvard Educational Review*, vol. 39, 1969, p. 80.
21. Robert E. Kuttner, "Biochemical Anthropology," in Robert E. Kuttner (editor), *Race and Modern Science*. New York, Social Science Press, 1967, pp. 197–222.
22. Theodosius Dobzhansky and Ashley Montagu, "Natural Selection and the Mental Capacities of Mankind." *Science*, vol. 105, 1947, pp. 587–90.
23. George Gaylord Simpson, *Biology and Man*. New York, Harcourt, Brace and World, 1969, p. 104.
24. Paul David and Laurence H. Snyder, "Genetic Variability and Human Behavior," in John H. Rohrer and Muzafer Sherif (editors), *Social Psychology at the Crossroads*. New York, Harper & Bros., 1951, p. 71.
25. Sherwood L. Washburn and C. S. Lancaster, "The Evolution of Hunting," in Richard B. Lee and Irven De Vore (editors), *Man the Hunter*. Chicago, Aldine Publishing Co., 1968, p. 303.
26. Editorial, "Fear of Enlightenment," *Nature*, vol. 228, 1970, pp. 1013–14.
27. Arthur R. Jensen, *Educability and Group Differences*. New York, Harper & Row, 1973, p. 24.
28. Richard B. Lee and Irven De Vore (editors), *Man the Hunter*. Chicago, Aldine Publishing Co., 1968; Elman R. Service, *The Hunters*. Englewood Cliffs, N.J., Prentice-Hall, 1966; Carleton S. Coon, *The Hunting Peoples*. Boston, Little, Brown, 1971; Tim Ingold, David Riches, and James Woodburn (editors), *Hunters and Gatherers*. 2 vols. Berg Publishers, 1988.
29. *A Report on Longitudinal Evaluations of Preschool Programs*. Vol. I. Sally Ryan, *Longitudinal Evaluations*, vol. 2. Urie Bronfenbrenner, *Is early Intervention Effective?* Washington, D.C., DHEW Publication Nos. (OHD) 72–75, 1974.
30. R. Heber, H. Garber, S. Harrington, and C. Hoffman. *Rehabilitation of Families at Risk for Mental Retardation*. Madison, Wisconsin, Rehabilitation and Research Center in Mental Retardation, University of Wisconsin, 1972.
31. For a good discussion of this subject, see A. Whimbey and L. S. Whimbey, *Intelligence Can Be Taught*. New York, Dutton, 1975.

4

THE DEBATE OVER RACE: THIRTY YEARS AND TWO CENTURIES LATER

Leonard Lieberman, with Alice Littlefield and Larry T. Reynolds

. . . the new immigration, while it included many strong elements from the north of Europe, contained a large and increasing number of the weak, the broken and the mentally crippled of all races drawn from the lowest stratum of the Mediterranean basin and the Balkans together with hordes of the wretched, submerged populations of the Polish ghettoes. Our jails, insane asylums and almshouses are filled with the human flotsam and the whole tone of American life, social, moral and political has been lowered and vulgarized by them. . . . Nature had granted to the Americans of a century ago the greatest opportunity in recorded history to produce . . . a powerful and racially homogeneous people and had provided for the experiment a pure race of one of the most gifted and vigorous stocks on earth. . . . Our grandfathers threw away this opportunity.

(Madison Grant, *The Passing of the Great Race*, 1924)

The following paper consists of two parts. First, there is an analysis of the way the race concept has been shaped by social influences. Emphasis is placed on the debate of the 1960s concerning the validity of the idea of race. This part of the paper was originally published in 1968 and has been partly revised here. The second part of the paper reports on the passing of the great consensus on the reality of race, and the factors that brought that about.

The year of Madison Grant's fourth edition, quoted above, was 1924. The book was powerfully influential in bringing about passage by the United States Congress of legislation sharply restricting immigration of "races" from southern and eastern Europe. Also influential in bringing this about were the IQ tests administered at Ellis Island reporting eighty percent of immigrant Jews, Poles, Hungarians, and Russians were morons. The IQ tests had also been administered to 1.7 million army recruits in World War I. Within twenty years of the passage of the immigration legislation millions of people in those regions would be dead in the cause of Nazi racial purification. Many of these would otherwise have left Europe and today their children and grandchildren would be citizens of the United States. The widely publicized results of the army tests were also said to prove that blacks were inferior due to heredity. That conclusion was used to justify the system of rigid Jim Crow segregation that kept blacks in poverty and made them victims of every injustice. Two of the powerful conceptual weapons used in bringing about these events were "race" and "IQ." Other papers in this collection examine "IQ"; here I explain the social origins of the concept of race, and why it no longer enjoys consensus among anthropologists.

PART ONE: THE DEBATE OF THE 1960s
Leonard Lieberman

The sociology of knowledge invites us to discover how reason is shaped by social factors (Coser and Rosenberg 1964, 661–684), while the sociological imagination suggests that the social function of reason is "to formulate choices, to enlarge the scope of human decision in the making of history" (Mills 1959, 174). The concept of race provides a case study in the growth of distorted reason and the formulation of choices within changing social structures.

In the seventeenth century, following the era of worldwide exploration, Europeans awoke to renewed awareness of the fact that there were many other peoples different in their appearance and customs. In the eighteenth century, the concept of race emerged in the effort to assimilate this new information into scientific taxonomies. In scientific circles it was first debated whether the races had separate origins. Scientific and popular ideas influenced each other, and both served the cause of ideologically justifying European colonialism, slavery, nationalism, and imperialism.

In the first decade of the twentieth century, anthropologists, sociologists, and psychologists took up the issue of inequality, debated it, and with the aid of a changing social structure succeeded in shifting the majority opinion of scientists and educated persons from racism to egalitarianism. Having helped persuade many that races are not unequal, some anthropologists then began to argue that races do not exist. They argued that race is a fiction or a myth which must be exorcised like ghosts, the humors, instincts, and phlogiston.

The ultimate phase in the debate has been underway among physical anthropologists for three decades beginning in the 1940s. The affirmative position states that races exist, the negative that race is a myth. Their discourse was the most recent in a tournament lasting over two centuries. I shall analyze the debate from the perspective of the sociology of knowledge, which leads to the question of how ideas have been shaped by existing ideology, social structure, social problems, scientific ideas and data, and the debating process itself.

THE DEBATE: SPLITTERS VS. LUMPERS

In the context of this debate among anthropologists, splitters classify the human species into biological units called races, while lumpers do not believe there is evidence to support such divisions, and they assert that there is in fact contrary evidence. The splitters, adherents of the position that races exist, include Dobzhansky, Garn, Laughlin, Mayr, Newman, and others. The lumpers, who argue that races do not exist, include Livingstone, Montagu, Brace, Hiernaux, Hogben, and Fried.

The splitters claim that:

1. Races are the taxonomic unit below the species level, and if such units are not called race, "it still has exactly the same taxonomic meaning" (Garn 1964, 316).
2. Races vary from populations "differing only in the frequencies of a few genes to those groupings that have been totally isolated for tens of thousands of years and are at least incipient species" (Garn 1964, 314).
3. Clines (gradations) exist but it is necessary to distinguish clines between subspecific populations and clines within subspecific populations. Interracial clines are found in intermediate populations between subspecific populations or races (Coon 1962, 314).

The position of lumpers holds that:

1. Biological variability exists, but "this variability does not conform to the discrete packages labelled races" (Livingstone 1962, 279).
2. So-called racial characteristics are not transmitted as complexes (Montagu 1942, 33).
3. Human differentiation is the result of natural selection forces which operate in ecological zones, and such forces and their zones do not coincide with population boundaries. Furthermore, different selective forces may operate in overlapping ecological zones (Brace 1964a, 320). Thus, geographic distributions of more than one trait have no necessary correlation (Brace 1964a, 313).
4. Races do not exist, because isolation of groups has been infrequent; populations have always interbred (Fried 1965, 22).
5. "Boundaries between what have been called 'races' are com-

pletely arbitrary, depending primarily upon the wishes of the classifier" (Brace 1964a, 313).

The debate over an issue may help clarify it by generating finer distinctions. Thus, among the lumpers and splitters it is possible to distinguish polar positions and moderate views about the number of races and their existence:

1. No races exist now or ever did (Fried 1965).
2. Very few races have existed (Hiernaux 1964, 42–43).
3. In its anthropological sense, the word *race* should be reserved for groups of mankind possessing well-developed and primarily inheritable physical differences from other groups. Many populations can be so classified but, because of the complexity of human history, there are also many populations which cannot easily be fitted into a racial classification (*Physical Anthropologists and Geneticists* 1961, 304–306).
4. The number of races varies with the size of unit studied and/ or the scope of the definition (Garn and Coon 1960, 9).
5. A race is a breeding population; hence, there are thousands of races (Garn and Coon 1960, 13–14).

The first thought that might occur to an observer of this debate has to do with the arbitrary nature of definitions. Similar problems have been discussed by distinguishing realism and nominalism, absolutism and arbitrariness, reality and ideal types. But in this debate many on both sides accept essentially the same definition. It is a view of race as it was formulated in the 1950s as an expression of the synthetic theory with its more precise reference to gene frequencies. The immunologist William Boyd expressed it this way: "We may define a human race as a population which differs significantly from other human populations in regard to the frequency of one or more of the genes it possesses. It is an arbitrary matter which, and how many, gene loci we choose to consider as a significant constellation . . ." (Boyd 1950, 207).

The common meaning of the above definition of race is a population which can be distinguished from other populations on the basis of inherent physical characteristics. Given the ecological and geographic basis of evolutionary and population biology, there must be some identifiable boundary where one population ends and another begins. The general acceptance of boundary lines in fact or as an arbitrary necessity leave the two sides contending over the issue of whether or not one can locate boundaries and thereby prove that races exist, or settle for population means which reinforce the obsolete notion of types or essences.

The reader of this book may be impatient that I have not yet discussed my preferred definition of race, the central concept under discussion. In fact, I have no preferred definition, nor has the centuries-long debate generated any consensus on a precise or useful definition. Molnar's 1992 book, *Human Variation, Races, Types and Ethnic Groups, the Problem of Human Variation,* is the most recent extended analysis of the concept of race by a physical anthropologist. He lists eight *different* definitions by prominent biologists and physical anthropologists and identifies two features that are emphasized: (a) the role of geographic distribution in race formation, and (b) the importance of breeding populations. He also reports "that at least fourteen different race typologies have been described in this century." Molnar states that "the more we learn about the variability of [groups], the more difficult it becomes to fix boundaries between them" (23–24). Race has been defined, and races have been counted, not by reference to a precise definition, or set of rules, but in whatever way seems useful to each researcher, as indicated in the second sentence of Boyd's definition. If taxonomists did the same, there would be no agreement about species or higher taxa and there would be no science in taxonomy.

The debate sketched above is not an argument in which a minority is opposed to a majority or in which experts oppose nonexperts. Both debate "teams" include widely recognized specialists in

physical anthropology. Briefly, the argument hinges on the significance of the geographically distributed gradation of genetically
based physical characteristics. The no-race supporters argue that
these genetic gradations are not intergradations but are overlapping
gradients, or clines, which are not confined to the boundaries of
particular populations. Furthermore, the no-race position emphasizes that each hereditary trait must first be analyzed separately and
its gradient mapped. When several such gradients or clines are
viewed in an overlay map it becomes evident that they do not agree
in their spatial distribution; they are usually discordant to some degree. For example, the allele for B-type blood in Europe is generally
distributed in an increasing frequency from West to East, but the
gradient for skin pigmentation decreases northward from the equa-
tor, while hemoglobin S (sickling) varies on at least two dimensions
in Africa and around the Mediterranean. The discordant distribution of clines indicates that boundary lines between races are arbitrary.

Although the early physical anthropologists were aware of the
conflict between their taxonomy and the existence of gradations, the
issue lay dormant until the 1950s. The eruption of the debate was
stimulated by the availability of clinal data. The dispute was concentrated in the pages of *Current Anthropology*, where, in three issues
in 1962–64, some twenty-four 8 × 11 triple-column pages in small
print were given over to the topic. While the new data were better
and more abundant, they seemed initially to intensify the debate
rather than resolve it.

Race as a concept appeared before there were techniques for measuring physical attributes. For some time the major sources of information on race characteristics depended upon whatever struck
the fancy of explorers and travelers, and often this was skin color
and hair texture. In 1940 Boas had recognized the arbitrary nature
of the selection of genes or traits said to represent a race:

> Actually the type of a population is always an abstraction of the strik-
> ing peculiarities of the mass of individuals which are assumed to be

represented combined in a single individual. *What the striking peculi-arities are depends largely upon the previous experiences of the observer*, not upon the morphological value of the observed traits. This explains the diversities of opinion in taxonomic classification (Boas 1940, 173, emphasis added).

Several biometric techniques were developed before Darwin's publication of *The Origin of Species* in 1859; the selection of traits to measure was one based on experience or convenience. Camper (1722–1789) developed the facial angle, "the interior angle the face makes with the horizontal" (Stanton 1960:25). In 1842 Retzius introduced the cephalic index, the ratio of head length to width. By 1900 A. von Torok had enough techniques available to take 5,000 measurements on a single skull (Barzun 1965, 117).

The old data were external phenotypical traits; the new data are genetic in character. Examples of genes which have been identified and used in studying taxonomy and variations in humans include: the Rh series of alleles, the ABO system, the sickle-cell trait, the gene for M blood type in the MNS series, and the frequency of tasting phenylthiocarbamide (Edmondson 1965).

Examples of the uses of this kind of data will indicate how they can be used to support either position. Glass and Li compared blood types of blacks in the United States with those of African blacks and concluded that North American blacks have about thirty percent genes from white populations. The authors estimated that at the same rate of gene-flow black North Americans will be indistinguishable from white Americans in about a thousand years (Glass and Li 1953). In this way the authors use the new genetic viewpoint to investigate change but do so with the old taxonomy of races.

An ambitious taxonomic undertaking by Edmondson (1965) used 124 populations from all over the world and classified twenty-four genetic traits to construct a measure of population distance. Splitters might say that the distances identify races. The lumpers might argue that distance measures ignore clines, that the twenty-four genes are not a random representation of the much larger number of genes, and that it is not clear which of these traits are environmentally adaptive.

Another study in Africa, by Hiernaux, questions the general validity of race taxonomies. Hiernaux asks whether "human populations . . . form clusters within which the distances are less than the inter-cluster distances." Hiernaux answers the question with research on fifteen populations in central Africa. He finds "one cluster of two closely related populations (the Tutsi of Rwanda and those of Burandi) is clearly apart, but the remaining thirteen populations allow no further clustering." Hiernaux believes a similar situation would apply to published data on Asia or America (Hiernaux 1964, 36–37). The splitters might argue that Hiernaux has identified at least two races, perhaps three, and thus races not only do exist but better techniques might reveal the existence of still more.

The studies relating to the no-race position include the classic study on sickle-cell anemia in which one sickling gene provides resistance to malaria, and inheritance of two sickling genes causes anemia and early death. The populations studied revealed a series of clines ranging from West Africa where twenty-nine percent of the genes for hemoglobin are of the sickling type to populations in the circum-Mediterranean area and South Asia with few sickling genes (Livingstone 1958). Livingstone interprets these clines as indicating that boundaries between races are nonexistent; hence, the species can not be divided into races.

The response of the splitters and lumpers to the improvement in data is not unlike that of debaters. The splitters are on the defensive and argue that more data and methods are needed to identify races properly. "There are valid races but biology is only beginning to properly discern and define them" (Newman 1963, 189). New mathematical models are needed better "fitting the human condition" (Garn 1963, 197).

The lumpers, on the offensive, find that present data provide sufficient ammunition to argue that humankind cannot be split into races. "The theoretical analysis of clines has barely begun but there seems to be no need for the concept of race in this analysis" (Livingstone 1962, 279). From their strategically superior position the lumpers generally do not concede that further data are needed to clarify the taxonomic question of the existence of races. Instead, they view further data as necessary to study current processes of evolution. On this point the lumpers seem to have the splitters on the defensive since more data tend to show more overlapping clines, to which the splitters can only reply that new methods and data are needed.

If science were a totally self-correcting inquiry, then checking the concept against better data in time should be all that is necessary to clarify the question of race. But science is not free of social influences; and while a theory may be pulled towards validity by data, it may be pulled either way by ideology, social structure, and social problems. Even the best of data must be interpreted, and the interpretation itself must be analyzed by inquiring into the social process in which ideas are formulated.

CHANGES IN SOCIAL STRUCTURE, CONCEPT, AND IDEOLOGY: THE EMERGENCE OF "RACE"

The idea of inherited differences is ancient, but human populations have not always been classified into races. "No such word exists in classical Latin or Greek, nor in any of the earlier Indo-European tongues. Nor is it Semitic" (Hierschfeld 1938, 51). Whatever they may be called, Europeans had, at least since classical times, conceptualized the existence of other peoples who were humanlike, yet biologically monstrous (Mason 1990, 7–8). The persistence of these ideas is found in Linnaeus's (1758) listing, alongside *Homo sapiens*, another nonsapiens species containing six varieties of people who were small, or large, or infertile, or conical-headed, or flat-headed, or beardless. These monstrous varieties suggest that Europeans were ready to think in terms of race, or some such biological concept.

The notion of race is a comparatively recent development (Snyder 1962, 25). The emergence of the scientific concept of race began in the seventeenth century following upon the explorations of the preceding two centuries, in which Europeans ranged the globe, established themselves as conquerors and colonizers, and brought back reports of aborigines and sometimes the aborigines themselves. The effect was to create vivid awareness of differences among humans.

The first known use of the word *race* was in 1606 by Tant in *Thrésor de la Langue Française*. The seventeenth century was a period in which race was not yet a concept in wide use. During the whole of the seventeenth century only five discussions relating to the varieties of mankind have been identified (Montagu 1965, 9–10). In 1749 Buffon introduced into the scientific literature a classification of six human varieties (Herschfeld 1938, 52). Later in the eighteenth century the idea of four varieties of the human species was introduced by Linnaeus into a revised version of his *Systema Naturae* (1758). He saw the human species as a fixed and unchanging entity made up of four varieties identified by color, clothing, and customs. Although he was aware that some characteristics depended on the situation, his descriptions mixed biology and cultural behavior in a way that linked them together and formed a hierarchy from lower varieties to the highest, with Europeans occupying the superior position. In 1770 Blumenbach proposed four varieties, in 1781 he thought there were five, and in 1790 Cuvier would identify three (Molnar 1975, 7).

The classification of *Homo sapiens* into varieties was the way in which the idea of race began its development in the emerging science of natural history. At the same time there was an increase in the use of race or its equivalent in West European languages (Banton 1987, 45). According to Banton, "viewing the classifications of Linnaeus, Buffon, Kant, and Blumenbach as *racial* classifications is to see them from the perspective of a later generation." They were not seeking to develop scientific ideas, but to "know God through nature" in an era in which the world was seen in a religious perspective (Banton 1987, 47). Nonetheless, I believe that this did not preclude the development of racial classification, and may have encouraged it. Buffon and Blumenbach would later be recognized as founding fathers of biology, giving respectable lineages to the idea of race.

The earliest contacts by Europeans with peoples of the Americas involved the question of whether these people had souls and were fully human. In the eighteenth and nineteenth centuries, after this question had been generally answered in the affirmative, the race concept held by scientists went through a polygenic vs. monogenic debate which helped influence the growth of the ideology of racism and was in turn influenced by it. The polygenic view held that races had separate origins and were possibly separate species. The monogenic view held that the races had a common origin. Having looked at the world through taxonomic glasses, the debaters explained taxonomy in terms of existing cosmology, and so in the eighteenth century they asked if God had created these races all at once or had created them separately.

The monogenic view had been held earlier by Linnaeus and came to be the position of the leading naturalists and intellectuals of the eighteenth century and the early nineteenth century, including Buffon, Blumenbach, Kant, Cuvier, Camper, and Herder. They were in agreement that there was one common source for the races, and most of them held that race differences intergraded (Greene 1959, 222–224). Blumenbach described the intergradation in 1793: "No variety of mankind exists, whether of colour, countenance, or stature, etc., so singular as not to be connected with others of the same kind by such an imperceptible transition, that it is very clear they are all related, or only differ from each other in degree" (Blumenbach, cited in Montagu 1942, 15).

Today Blumenbach would be classified as a splitter, but in his time he was a lumper. The splitters of that day held the polygenic view. Many were nonscientists, such as Voltaire, or lesser writers, such as Nott, Gliddon, Morton, and others (Greene 1954, 22), who held that the different races were products of creation and that changes occurred by hybridization (Stanton 1960:195). In the first half of the nineteenth century Gliddon, Morton, and Nott expressed the polygenic position dominant in the United States among scientists and laymen. It fitted their reading of the Book of Genesis and helped justify their view of themselves as children of God among the barbaric Canaanites—the Canaanites being any Indians occupying desirable land. But many Southerners found the polygenic view too much at odds with their fundamentalist interpretation of Genesis, and so they took the monogenic stance. Their virtue was rewarded by the idea that one of Noah's sons had seen his father's nude body and been cursed for it; as a consequence, his descendants had turned black and had become the servants of the white man.

Polygenism had its beginnings in the eighteenth century, but became "much more widespread by the middle of the nineteenth century" and was "probably the dominant current among those who in retrospect might be called 'physical anthropologists' " (Stocking 1968, 39). By the 1850s in England, the polygenists had won considerable support for three ideas: races occupied a hierarchical scale, there were innate differences in the brain of different races, and races were fixed and not subject to environmental influences (Stepan, 1982, 86). The views of the polygenists were strongly influenced by the concept of *type*, which was an expression of underlying essential nature, an idea stemming from Plato and imbedded in Western thought. If the observations did not coincide with the essential type then they were deviations from it (Odom 1967, 6). Scientists of the time were so committed to the idea of racial types, and their fixed and unequal nature, that the Darwinian theory of biological change was ignored (Stepan, 110).

The debate over the equality of man followed the monogenic-polygenic debate. During the later portion of the nineteenth century it was hardly a debate at all, since the polygenic inequality of races was the predominant view of scientists and intellectuals. According to Gosset, American thought from 1880 to 1920 "generally lacks any perception of the Negro as a human being with potentialities for improvement. Most of the people who wrote about Negroes were firmly in the grip of the idea that intelligence and temperament are racially determined and unalterable" (Gossett 1964, 286).

EUROPEAN DEVELOPMENT AND THE GROWTH OF RACISM

From its beginnings, the concept of race incorporated a hierarchical concept which we would today call racism. I believe that racist beliefs were at the passionate core of the idea of race, and that racism had to be reduced before the validity of the race concept could be challenged. These two concepts were constructed along with Europe's worldwide colonization in the two centuries from 1700 to 1900, but especially in the nineteenth century. By the year 1900 European nations and the offshoots of Western civilization controlled eighty-five percent of the earth's land surface. During this period of time the awareness of constitutional differences was converted into an ideology of racism and a scientific conception of the biological divisions in the human species. Some authors emphasize that the idea of race typologies received its major stimulus from the slave trade and the ensuing controversy (Dobzhansky 1962). Banton stresses origins of that kind of thinking not in relations between black and white peoples, but rather in the revolutionary events in Europe in 1848. National origins were traced to myths of Saxon, Frankish, or Aryan roots (Banton 1977). Populations could be urged to unite behind the national fatherland against its alien enemies, both within and without. The origins of racism, which constituted the essence of racial typologies, had yet another historical source in the conquest and forced migration, and concentration on reservations, of native populations in the New World (Horsman 1981, Cooper and David 1986, 99).

The word "racism" first appears in the English language in the

1930s (Herschfeld 1938). *Racism* is defined here as an ideological conviction and set of practices. As an ideology it involves the belief that the world is divided into distinct biological races, that biological race and cultural attributes are linked in heredity, that races have a hierarchical order ranging from superior to inferior (Miles 1982, 285), and that races are unchanging or slow to change. An *ideology* is defined as a cluster of ideas that is widely shared and emotionally defended by the members of a society as a justification for their activities. The ideology of racism is used to justify institutionalized behavior patterns and processes that maintain domination of one group over others (Blauner 1972, 9–10; Miles 1989, 51).

According to Stepan (1982), prior to the age of black slavery black Africans were depicted by European artists in a wide range of representations, "never uniform and rarely negative" (Stepan 1982, 190). This view is contradicted by Walvin's (1973) analysis of exaggerated stereotypical cartoons and literature of the eighteenth century, with their roots in precolonial times. Scientific ideas of race did not replace ideas of "the other" in savagery or barbarism, but intertwined with them (Miles 1989). Miles, referring to a more abstract aspect, believes that "up to the end of the eighteenth century, the predominant European (view) . . . conceded that biological differences . . . were not inherent in the sense of fixed and inevitable." Further, the predominant view was that although the Africans were "part of God's creation," their "characteristics are subject to environmental influence," and that they were humans but inferior ones (1989, 30). Miles believes that the *beginnings* of the enslavement of Africans were "not widely legitimated by an argument which alleged that the African was biologically suited to slavery" (30); rather, "racism was the consequence of slavery" (Williams 1944, 7, quoted by Banton 1987, 49).

Smedley (1993) describes how the elite of the thirteen colonies developed a constitution embodying the world's greatest guarantees of individual rights and the most absolute denial of human rights in the history of slavery, reducing Africans to mere property. Fredrickson (1988) traces how efforts developed over time to assure that the status of the highest black was lower than that of the lowest white, and that there existed a kind of "pseudo-equality" among whites poor and prosperous. Racist practices came under intense challenge from the northern abolitionists in the 1830s, and in response pro-slavery Southerners developed a racist theory. "Racist thought did not reach a crescendo until the end of the nineteenth century, when it latched on to Darwinism," and scientists provided it with the appearance of justification (Fredrickson 1988, 202–205; Miles 1989, 31).

The ideology of racism became particularly intense in the second half of the nineteenth century. A major phenomenon which intensified the existing racism, in addition to the emancipation movement, was the spread of nationalism. These forces were intensified later in the century by Europe's and the United States's adventures in imperialism, and, in the United States from 1890 to 1920, by massive immigration from South and East Europe and the resistance to it in the pattern of events known as nativism, as well as the eugenic movement. In 1928 an eminent sociologist wrote that "perfect agreement of all these tests: the historic-cultural, the mental, the absence of geniuses . . . seems to indicate strongly . . . that the cause of such a difference in the Negro is due not only, and possibly not so much to environment, as to heredity" (Sorokin 1928, 297–298).

Scientific racism extended also to psychologists. G. Stanley Hall, a pioneer psychologist, held that primitive races were at earlier evolutionary stages (Gosset 1964, 154). By 1916 the Binet intelligence test was regarded as perfected, and "a powerful school of psychologists appeared which took up the old argument that intelligence is largely hereditary and little affected by environment." Racists found support in the idea that some persons could not benefit from education as much as others (Gossett 1964, 363, 368).

In literary circles the list of those believing in the inequality of races included James Fenimore Cooper, Henry Adams, Frank Norris, Jack London, Owen Wister, and Henry James (Gossett 1964, 198). In Europe a comparable group of writers included Kipling and Sir Walter Scott, whose *Ivanhoe* converted a feudal class struggle into an affair of "self-conscious racial conflict" between Saxon and Norman (MacRae 1960, 80).

That the majority of intellectuals and scientists had hierarchical ideas helped to keep race and racism from being questioned. There were, however, some intellectuals and scientists who were not racists. Most of the opponents of racism were humanitarians and intellectuals, such as George Washington Cable, Winslow Homer, Mark Twain, Stephen Crane, and J. S. Mill. Among scientists the list includes Adolf Bastian, Rudolph Virchow, William Ripley, Theodore Waitz, Friedrich Ratzel, Henry Rowe Schoolcraft, Lewis Henry Morgan, and John Wesley Powell (Gossett 1964, 245). But they were not active anti-racists. They were forerunners of a reformed view of race who generally held races differed only in minor respects.

The debate over the inequality of races was largely one-sided until the 1920s. The historian Gosset (1964, 429–430) writes that the stemming of the tide was the work of "one man, Franz Boas, who was an authority on several fields which had been the strongest sources of racism." He asked for proof that race determines mentality and temperament. From then on "it would be the racists who were increasingly on the defensive . . . it was clearly Boas who led the attack." In 1912 he published work in physical anthropology demonstrating changes in head shape in children of immigrants. It weakened the older concept of the fixity of race and the implication that mentality was also racially determined.

But Boas's influence on racism was even more significant through his leadership in cultural anthropology. According to Gosset (1964, 416), the ethnographic work his students began "had the utmost importance for race theory because the close and detailed knowledge of . . . primitive peoples showed how directly ideas and customs are interrelated and how fallacious is the idea that any society can be meaningfully interpreted in terms of its racial inheritance." Gosset holds that what was needed to break through the dominant misconception was a way to explain character as an outcome of institutions, history, and environment. Boas and his students did that by building the culture concept on the foundation left by Tylor, by their development of the relativistic approach to cultural differences, and by their insistence on masses of evidence. Gosset (1964, 418) believes "it is possible that Boas did more to combat race prejudice than any other person in history."

A broader explanation is needed in terms of how Boas's ideas came to be part of anti-racist theory in the social sciences and then how they gained wide popular acceptance. Elazar Barkan (1987, 4–5) describes three stages in the development of anti-racism. First was the growth in the 1920s of an alternative program, seen especially in the development of the idea of culture and society as distinct from biological race. The second stage was the rejection of racial typologies. In the third phase scientists were pushed and dragged by Franz Boas and his allies into making public anti-racist commitments as part of an effort to influence public thought (Kuznick 1987).

Boas's influence on his students helps explain the spread of his views into anthropology. One of Boas's most prominent students was Kroeber, whose 1917 article, "The Superorganic," was one of the influential statements calling for a social rather than an organic interpretation of human behavior. Social psychologists began to shift their position. Otto Klineberg (1935) was one psychologist who had contact with Boas and his students. He later gathered empirical support for the culture concept through his work on the changing IQ of black children as they moved from South to North. In sociology the same trend occurred but under differing influences:

Racial explanation disappears from serious sociology with the great generation of the early twentieth century: Pareto, Durkheim, Hob-

house and Max Weber made the issue of race irrelevant by the introduction of new canons of analysis and by their attempt to explain the
social by the social (MacRae, 1960, 445).

What numerous social scientists had done was to respond to racism with a scientific rebuttal. Scientific anti-racism came to be the
accepted position in the social sciences and among intellectuals. The
idea was soon to spread and become a new popular ideology partly
replacing racism and engaged in competing with it. But a set of ideas
does not become an accepted ideology simply because it is scientific.
It spreads when cultural conditions are appropriate. The earlier
ideas ran against the tide of conditions causing racism. But in the
1940s a social base for anti-racism was emerging.

Gossett (1964, 445) lists several of these conditions and comments
that "We owe something to impersonal forces in the decline of
racism, but the trouble with impersonal forces is that they can as
easily work one way as another. We owe far more to the people and
the organizations motivated by a concern for equality of all." Gosset's position seems to be that of the historian and humanist: men
and ideas make history. The view that must be added concerns the
influence of social and cultural conditions through people and organizations. Boas's ideas could only spread when the social structure
was ready. Humans may make history, but they do not do so uni-
laterally.

In the early decades of the century the forces for egalitarian beliefs began to develop in the United States through the emergence
of the social sciences as organized disciplines and through the advanced growth of urbanism and industrialism. To these must be
added the transcendent influence of World War II. The propaganda
developed during the War was based on the fact that Nazi Germany
was totalitarian and racist. Since the enemy was racist, America had
to become anti-racist. The massive anti-racist propaganda and the
racist enemy undermined the strength of racist groups in the Untied
States that had been so vocal in the 1930s.

Scientists in the United States and in Britain (Stepan 1982, 160) began to see the need to combat racism in science. The decline of racism among policymakers was clearly evident in the 1954 United States Supreme Court rejection of the established rationale of "separate but equal," and the Court's mandating of desegregated schools. More than that, what the court did was to accept the statements of social scientists concerning the belief that a number of alleged "racial" behaviors were not in fact hereditary, but were in fact a product of environment and learning (Barkan 1987, 3).

Racism began to recede on the surface and to be replaced by an appearance of genteel tolerance as a public policy, a trend aided by the shift in the American social classes in which the middle class increased in size, education, and level of living. The changes among scientists were not unidirectional or consistent. Elazar Barkan (1987) traces the complex and fascinating developments in which racist and anti-racist scientists maintained continuing associations with each other, in which Boas would recruit racist scientists to support anti-racist statements, how strands of racism and reformed views of race were expressed by the same scientists at the same time, how the views of a number of them changed over time, and how the public statements opposing racism by some scientists were totally contradicted in their personal correspondence. The change developing among scientists had its beginning prior to the Second World War in the reaction against social Darwinism, and in the debate over nature vs. nurture occurring among scientists in several disciplines.

THE CURRENT DEBATE AND ITS RELATIONSHIP TO PAST AND PRESENT IDEOLOGY

The major debates of the past two centuries were over the issues of separate or common origins for races, and the equality or inequality of races. The third debate, that of the 1960s, concerned the validity and utility of the concept of race. The three debates all pivot on one common problem: equality. Each emphasized a different aspect of equality: equality of origins, equality of intelligence, and taxonomic equality; but in each debate the same issue of equality of rights has been implicitly present.

The influence of ideology in the third debate can be discovered in the statements of two men who take opposite positions as lumpers and splitters. Consider the position of Montagu, who for decades has held that race is a myth:

> How many times will it have to be reiterated that human beings are not "races" or for the simple principle that all men, by virtue of their humanity, have a right . . . to fulfill themselves. None of the findings of physical or cultural anthropology . . . can in any way affect this principle, which is an ethical one—an ethical principle which happens in every way to be supported by the findings of science (Montagu 1963, 144–145).

Carleton Coon, an ardent splitter, takes a position opposite to Montagu's. Coon's thesis (1962) is that 500,000 years ago man was one species, *Homo erectus*, which perhaps already was divided into five geographic races or subspecies. *Homo erectus* then evolved into *Homo sapiens* five times as each subspecies or race living in different territories passed a threshold from erectus to sapiens state. In this parallel evolution the races passed over the threshold from erectus to sapiens species at different times: Caucasoid was first at 250,000 years ago; then Mongoloid, 150,000 years ago; Australoid, 40,000 years ago; Congoloid (Negroes and Pygmies), 40,000 years ago; and then the Capoid (Bushmen, Hottentots).

Coon's values may be inferred from several scattered statements in *The Origin of Races* (1962):

> . . . it is a fair inference that fossil men now extinct were less gifted than their descendants who have larger brains, that the subspecies that crossed the evolutionary threshold into the category of *Homo sapiens* the earliest have evolved the most, and that the obvious correlation between the length of time a subspecies has been in the *sapiens* state

and the levels of civilization attained by some of its populations may be related phenomena (IX–X).

... the Australian aborigines come closest to any living peoples, to the *erectus-sapiens* threshold (427).

[If Africa was the cradle of mankind] it was only an indifferent kindergarten. Europe and Asia were our principal schools (656).

As far as we know now, the Congoloid line started on the same evolutionary level as the Eurasiatic ones in the Early Middle Pleistocene and then stood still for half a million years, after which Negroes and Pygmies appeared as if out of nowhere (658).

Genes in a population are in equilibrium if the population is living a healthy life as a corporate entity. Racial intermixture can upset the genetic as well as the social equilibrium of a group, and so newly introduced genes tend to disappear or to be reduced to a minimum percentage unless they possess a selective advantage over their local counterparts (661).

It is a common observation among anthropologists who have worked in many parts of the world in intimate contact with people of different races that racial differences in temperament also exist and can be predicted (116).

The polar positions of Montagu and Coon on the question of the *existence* of races also involve opposite positions on the *equality* of populations or races. But most anthropologists who take a position on this matter are egalitarians. A racist can only be a splitter, a lumper can only be an egalitarian, but an egalitarian has the choice of being a lumper or a splitter. Since lumpers can logically be only egalitarian, it is worth noting that the debate over the existence of races can be kept active only by the lumpers. There would be no issue if the lumpers, as challengers of the status quo, did not contend that races do not exist. These lumpers draw on the evidence of genetics and clines, and express the values of egalitarianism.

CONCLUSION

The division of anthropologists into lumpers and splitters when most of them are egalitarian requires further explanation. The general liberal orientation of most anthropologists may relate to their selection of anthropology as a career. It is also supported by group definition and pressure in the social organization of the profession. It is no longer necessary to minimize race by arguing there are only three or only a few very similar races; and then, too, the argument that there are many races is a way of quietly saying that race is not important. Thus egalitarians can comfortably be either lumpers or splitters. Their egalitarian values are manifest in their opposition to racism. Lumpers generally oppose splitting as invalid and playing into the hands of bigotry, and splitters generally oppose lumping as unrealistic and playing into those same hands. Dobzhansky takes this latter view:

> Nowadays, a scientist cannot ignore the uses and misuses of his findings by politicians and special pleaders. He certainly cannot and should not refrain from recording the facts which he discovers, but he had better see to it that the language he uses to describe the facts does not invite misrepresentation. To say that we have discovered that races of man do not exist is such an invitation. It is far better to find out, and to explain to others, the real nature of the observable phenomena which is, and will continue to be, called "race" (1963, 197).

Can racism be fought by persuasion, semantics, and data? Fried, Montagu, and others think so. Race is an erroneous and dangerous concept, says Montagu (1962), and therefore should be fought. It is too ambiguous to be redefined, and so he proposes to substitute the concept of "ethnic group." He claims that "ethnic group," being noncommittal and of uncertain meaning, would raise questions and clarify thinking.[1] The term "ethnic group" is given cultural meaning by anthropologists and sociologists to clarify the idea that groups are identified by cultural *beliefs*, not by biological differences. I argue that a cultural concept such as ethnic group is needed to encourage thinking in social and cultural terms, rather than a concept that supports the belief that biological differences subdivide the species into racial units. There is also a need for a biological alternative to race. The concept of gradation, or clines, is useful for conceptualizing and measuring human hereditary variation one trait at a time, and without resorting to the concept of race. Studies of particular populations which sample their genetic and morphological characteristics are just that, studies of *populations*, for which the term race, with its lack of clarity and its hierarchical baggage, is unnecessary and unjustified.

Several propositions are suggested by the above view of the debate over races:

1. The race concept developed in a dialectic that has been controlled largely by the same structural forces that generated the growth of racist ideology.
2. The specific issue debated has shifted with changing social structure.
3. Whatever the specific issue under discussion, the underlying theme has been the equality or inequality of different populations.
4. With one exception, it is possible to take any side of the issue and debate for or against the equality of these populations. The exception is that of the nonexistence of races, which views all human populations as equal in their potential.
5. Although the data push towards greater similarity of groups, it is argued here that the fate of race as a concept and racism as an ideology will depend upon the range of possibilities created by changes in social structures.

The role of scientific data in past disputes over race, and the present dispute over the existence of races, has been largely controlled or made possible by changes in social structure. The role of science in this view is that of a catalytic agent which can speed and channel the change by developing one or another of the possible alternative formulations for conceptualizing biological differences. We have already seen this occur in the case of the race concept. It is the hope of action-oriented scientists and intellectuals that adopting one formulation rather than another will lead to changes which transcend the limits of the social structure that made the formulation possible.

In the conclusion to the 1968 version of "The Debate Over Race," I wrote that "Improvement in data has not helped bring consensus about the nature of race because the concept is polarized between two groups influenced by the ideology of equality. Splitters believe that equality . . . is a matter of values and that the idea of the existence of many overlapping races will erode racism faster than the idea of the non-existence of races. The lumpers accept the unity of the human species and argue against race as our "most dangerous myth" (141). Each side believed the data supported its point of view. In 1968 when a version of this paper was first published, splitting was the dominant mode of thought. It appeared as if lumping would remain a lesser viewpoint or even fade and be forgotten. In the decades that have followed lumping has in fact flourished and support for the race concept has declined. In the next section I discuss the change that has occurred in beliefs about the existence of race among anthropologists since the debate described above. In what follows I shall hold that clinal data provided a catalytic influence along with several social influences.

PART TWO: THIRTY YEARS AFTER THE DEBATE OVER RACE: THE PASSING OF THE GREAT CONSENSUS
With Alice Littlefield and Larry T. Reynolds

Finally, the concept of race itself was shown to be devoid of biological justification. . . . Consequently, the whole enterprise of racial classification once at the core of professional physical anthropology, was deprived of its scientific credibility and basically ceased to exist. The social scientist, cognizant of the inequities and injustices perpetuated in the name of "race," could well cry "good riddance" (Brace and Hunt 1990. 342).

The "Passing of the Great Race," so lamented by Madison Grant and those who favored eugenic and anti-immigration policies in the 1920s in order to keep out those of low IQ, was the great red herring produced by believers in race purity and racial explanations of history. The acceptance of those beliefs and explanations has diminished in popular culture since the mid-twentieth century and was rejected even earlier in anthropology. More recently, in anthropology the grand consensus on the reality of human races has been shattered. Race, culture, and evolution had long been recognized as the central concepts of anthropology (Stocking 1968; Cravens 1978). In the latter decades of the twentieth century, human variation, culture, and evolution promise to remain essential foci for the future of anthropology. In support of this, I will present data indicating that a majority of anthropologists no longer agree among themselves that there are biological races in the species *Homo sapiens*. The debate over race that occurred in the 1960s challenged a concept that had its popular roots in the era of eighteenth and nineteenth century colonialism, and its scientific roots in the biological science that developed during that era. In 1904 Franz Boas (1974, 262) stated that:

> The biological side of anthropology . . . owes its origins to the great zoologists of the 18th century. . . . [Their] many efforts were directed towards a classification of the races of man and to the discovery of valid characteristics by means of which the races would be described. . . . The attempts at classifications were numerous, but no new point of view was developed.

In the 1960s it was possible to say that what Boas identified in the eighteenth and nineteenth centuries was still true in the twentieth.

No new knowledge had resulted from the use of the race concept that could not have been arrived at by using other means. Yet in 1968 while it was possible to observe that prominent anthropologists disagreed on the utility and validity of race, the viewpoint of the rank and file was unknown. Therefore it could be assumed that the great consensus on this most colonial of concepts still prevailed. We believe that the concept of race was assumed by most anthropologists to be central to the discipline, especially to physical anthropologists, until the debate of the 1960s. We present evidence that in the years following that debate the race concept lost the supporting consensus that is expected of a concept which occupies a central role in a discipline.

CONSENSUS LOST: RACE IN THE LAST QUARTER OF THE TWENTIETH CENTURY

The word is out, the earth is no longer the center of this universe. The word is spreading, the human species is not divided into discrete races. A revolution is occurring in scientific thinking. I will present five kinds of evidence to show the change that is underway: a survey of anthropologists, content analysis of textbooks, monographs on human variation, research on human variation, and articles in newspapers and magazines.

The Survey

In the mid-1980s my colleagues and I inquired into the acceptance of the race concept (Lieberman, in press; Lieberman, Stevenson and Reynolds 1989). We refer to this as the 1985 study. We asked the respondents whether they agreed that "There are biological races within the species *Homo sapiens.*" Acceptance of the concept among physical anthropologists ran fifty percent among responding faculty at Ph.D.-granting departments, fifty-four percent among B.A./M.A. faculty, and forty-four percent from community-college faculty.

Rates of rejection of the concept were, respectively, forty-two per-cent, thirty-eight percent, and forty-one percent ($X^2 = p < .00$). Clearly, the overwhelming acceptance of the race concept that pre-vailed in physical anthropology for two centuries had been aban-doned by 1985.

We concluded that the 1985 data indicate that only about half of physical anthropologists at Ph.D. institutions support the concept. Considering the role of Ph.D. institutions in conserving and devel-oping the discipline's basic concepts, we conclude that the race con-cept no longer enjoys consensus among physical anthropologists. Furthermore, among *cultural* anthropologists at each of the three institutional types, about one-third of respondents accept the con-cept and a majority reject it: fifty-two percent at Ph.D.-granting institutions, fifty-four percent at B.A./M.A. institutions, and fifty-three percent at two-year colleges. Response rates were sixty-nine percent, seventy percent, and twenty-two percent, respectively. Since cultural anthropologists are more numerous than physical an-thropologists, it can also be concluded that the race concept is re-jected by a majority of members of the discipline of anthropology in the United States. It might be contended that this is a question of whether the glass is half-full or half-empty since half of physical anthropologists accept the race concept, and just over half of cul-tural anthropologists reject it. Whether half-full or half-empty, the more important point is that the idea of race, supported by almost all anthropologists until the 1950s, no longer enjoys the consensus expected of a core concept.

Monographs on Race

The decade of the 1960s saw the race debate reach a peak of intensity, with the discipline moving away from the concept in the 1970s. The decade of the 1960s opened with Stanley Garn's *Human Races* (1961). The book presented a scholarly classification system consisting of geographical, local, and micro-races, and several chapters on the biology, physiology, and origins of racial variation. It concludes with a taxonomy of nine geographic races and thirty-two local races.

Carleton Coons's *The Origin of Races* was published in 1962 and reviewed with enthusiasm by biologists, but almost all anthropologists rejected it (Marks 1991) for its racialist interpretation of the fossil record and racial origins. The response indicated that alertness to signs of racism had become an established tradition among anthropologists, and that they were ready to debate the race concept. In the 1960s they did just that (see Chapter 2) through the papers published primarily in *Current Anthropology*.

Ashley Montagu summarized his views in his 1965 book on *The Idea of Race* and included a summary of the ideas generated in the debate over race published in papers in *Current Anthropology* in the early 1960s. In 1964 he made these and other papers more broadly available in his reader *The Concept of Race*. Monographs published since 1970, in which biological race or human variation is the central subject matter, provide an additional view on the changes that have occurred. Few books by biologists on human races have appeared since the 1970s, suggesting that the topic is being left to anthropologists.

Among anthropologists, a series of books appeared that reflected the shift occurring in the discipline. *The Kinds of Mankind: An Introduction to Race and Racism* (1971), by Morton Klass and Hal Hellman, represented the new approach to race that emerged following the debate over race. It emphasized human differences, their origins, the difference between biological and social explanations, and the nature of racism, and definitely avoided a typological approach in favor of the cline concept. Stephen Molnar's 1975 *Races, Types and Ethnic Groups: The Problem of Human Variation* emphasizes the confusion in the definitions of race, proposes a combination of population and cline as the alternative, and advocates viewing human diversity as the result of response to the "stress of natural selection as modified by man's behavior or culture" (1975, 187, see also

Molnar 1992, 27). Kenneth A. R. Kennedy's *Human Variation in Space and Time* (1976) presents the origins of the race concept, summarizes the sources of human variation, and explains that the rejection of subspecific taxonomic units began as biologists "came to recognize that discordant variation is the rule for all species, and the assumption of coordinated variation was insupportable" (78). Two books by Jane H. Underwood, *Biocultural Interactions and Human Variation* (1975) and *Human Variation and Human Microevolution* (1979), emphasized the processes of change in gene frequencies, and neither book mentioned race. Alice M. Brues's *People and Races*, first published in 1977, was reissued in 1990. It presented a summary of the genetics, biology, and physiology of human variation, sandwiched between a brief introduction to "Races Large and Small" (19) and a penultimate chapter on "The Geography of Human Races." Aside from Brues's chapters on human races, the trend in scholarly books and monographs on race is clearly away from the use of the concept in anthropology. No major work in biology or anthropology published since 1975 has taken a traditional approach to biological race among humans, except the 1982 *Racial Adaptations* by Carleton Coon.

Research

A similar pattern is apparent in research papers. Abstracts in the proceedings of the annual conference of the American Association of Physical Anthropologists seldom explicitly utilize the race concept. The more usual approach is to present analysis of genetic variation in terms of populations, genetic distance, and dendrograms. Few of those using dendrograms interpret them in racial terms.

Two areas of research utilizing the race concept exist. The first concerns the various models for the origin of modern *Homo sapiens*. Most prominent among them are the multiregional and the mitochondrial approach. The latter asserts that moderns originated about 200,000 years ago in Africa, migrated into Asia and Europe displacing the earlier *Homo erectus* and evolving into the different races. This model implies races are of very recent origin, but leaves open the possibility of widespread genocide as the *sapiens* displace the *eructus* population (Cann 1987). The multiregional model assumes *Homo erectus* left Africa about one million years ago, migrated to Asia and Europe and evolved into modern races and *Homo sapiens* in each area, with gene flow between the regions maintaining a unified species (Wolpoff 1989). In this case races have a longer period in which greater variation can develop. Utilization of either of these models encourages continued use of the race concept (Lieberman and Jackson 1995). It should be noted that the concept is used only as a familiar label. At this time the future of the race concept depends in part on encouragement from these models. Yet, neither model gains explanatory power by use of the idea. Simple designators such as "population" or geographic identifiers would do as well.

The second area of research is that of forensic anthropology. Forensic specialists identify the age, sex, height, and "race" of skeletal material for use in the criminal justice system. Almost all forensic specialists utilize the race label to report their findings to police investigators, and in their published research. Yet most of them qualify their books and manuals by referring to the difficulty of identifying individuals whose ancestors originated in two or more regions of the world. One forensic anthropologist who rejects the race concept suggests that geographic designators would be more precise (Sauer 1988).

The claim has been made that the rejection of the race concept leads physical anthropologists and other scientists to neglect research on the differences between human beings (see Shipman 1994). Beginning in 1964 C. Loring Brace was one who advocated abandonment of the race concept, but also urged research on clinal variations, that is thinking in terms of gradations rather than discrete races. It was then and remains now an idea disconcerting to those who prefer the romance of race. He has also conducted research that proves you can study human variation without "race."

He has recently completed a study consuming years of time and requiring worldwide travel to measure craniofacial variation in museum collections around the world. The study required multiple measurements of nonadaptive craniofacial variations and made it possible to establish that these traits clustered together within a geographic area. These similarities also resembled populations in adjacent areas more than those in more distant regions. Since the traits had no apparent adaptive value, they were not racial and it was likely that they were the result of genetic drift into an area, followed by population expansion. Brace refers to the resulting population with its cluster of traits as bearing a *family* level resemblance writ large. In this way he provides a way of understanding human similarities in a region without the use of the idea of race. Another work that demonstrates this possibility is *The History and Geography of Human Genes*, containing hundreds of pages of clinal maps encompassing the entire globe by L. L. Cavalli-Sforza, Paola Menozzi, and Albert Piazza (1994). In this group of pioneers who have demonstrated the fruitfulness of clinal analyses of human variation are Frank Livingstone (1958) for his analysis of sickle-cell, and Joseph B. Birdsell (1993) for his research in Australia.

The Historical Record of the Textbooks: The Decline of Race, the Rise of Cline

The transformation that has occurred in physical anthropology can also be documented by examining the introductory textbooks used in colleges and universities. These textbooks are written by professors in an effort to represent the theory, concepts, and data of that discipline. Physical anthropology is that subfield of the discipline of anthropology within universities and colleges in the United States which concerns itself with the evolution of human and nonhuman primates, including human heredity variation and the evolutionary processes involved in biological adaptation to a habitat. Therefore, human hereditary variation and the critique of the concept of human races are the domain of physical anthropology.

The authors of textbooks wish to present a thorough, credible, and up-to-date text because of the necessity of seeking adoption of the text by other professors, and for the sake of their own standing in the field. When *dissensus* exists on a concept, such as was reflected in the debate over race in the late 1960s, we can expect different authors of textbooks to take diverse points of view. Analysis of textbooks can provide a record of conceptual changes in a discipline. It is already documented that the decline in the acceptance of the race concept was reflected in the textbooks beginning after 1974, just long enough for the debate over race to play its role. We have also documented the use of the cline concept in most of the textbooks rejecting the race concept, and argued that this concept and its reference to gene frequencies provided the hard data necessary to reject the race concept (Littlefield, Lieberman, and Reynolds 1982).

We have analyzed all introductory textbooks that could be identified, from the earliest, *Up From the Ape* by Earnest Hooton in 1932, to the most recent as of 1984. A panel of students classified each textbook's approach to race and cline in order to identify the interpretation of the material by its intended audience. We examined textbooks because they represent their author's views of the state of knowledge in their field, because texts reach a large number of students and teachers and may influence world views, and because changes originating outside the universities and colleges have an impact on the acceptance of scientific ideas, and textbook authors competing for markets are likely to be responsive to these influences.

Of the thirty-six texts published in the United States from 1932 to 1974 some twenty expressed the view that races exist, while seven rejected the concept. The "reality of race" was the reigning outlook. A conceptual revolution appears in the 1975–84 period: in thirty-three texts, only seven clearly supported the concept of race, thirteen rejected it, and the remaining thirteen were intermediate (p = <.02). It should also be noted that the proportion of textbooks that were intermediate (did not mention race or where the panel did not agree on classification) increased over the three periods reported, indicating that more change could be expected. I have further explored this proposition by examining textbooks published from 1984 to 1994, and found thirteen rejected the "race" concept and only one accepted it. We conclude that the concept of race has fallen to a very low acceptance level and may have lost more than consensus; that is, it may be on the way to losing legitimacy.

The textbook study, summarized above, has been criticized by Arthur Jensen:

> If central concepts in physical anthropology can be pushed around by such nonscientific considerations as those described by Littlefield et al., it would seem to be high time for those in the field to take stock of its status as objective science. I would say the same thing for my own field (psychology) and, indeed, for all of the behavioral and human sciences.
>
> Concepts in science, even if we would wish it, cannot be importantly changed or permanently killed off by ideological edicts or by religious, political, or social attitudes. Scientific concepts change only through replacement by new ones which more clearly comprehend the objectively observable phenomena that gave rise to them, as oxidation replaced phlogiston in understanding the phenomena of combustion (Jensen 1982, 649–650).

The statement by Jensen ignores the scientific reasons for abandoning race which were presented in the paper in question. These included the development of new concepts of cline and ethnicity. In part, we agree with the statement that concepts change through "replacement by new ones which more clearly comprehend the objectively observable phenomena." But are Littlefield, Lieberman, and Reynolds, *or* Jensen, exempt from the social forces that affected Darwin and Wallace? It should be noted, from a sociology of science perspective, that authors who use the race concept, and those who reject it, may have vested interests to defend and may be responsive to ideology, but the concept of cline is a far more precise way of comprehending "observable phenomena" than is the race idea.

Reaching Popular Culture: Magazines and Newspapers

Do the above developments diffuse into everyday American culture beliefs? What is taught in college classroom must diffuse to some degree. Beyond the school, an agency of broader diffusion is the popular media. In the mid-1990s the major weekly newsmagazines, newspapers, and one monthly published articles quoting anthropologists who question the race concept.

Discover magazine for November 1994 carried this cover title "Race, what is it good for? Science Looks at Flesh and Bones, Genes and Behavior." The entire issue is devoted to quotations and articles in which scientists question the utility and accuracy of the race concept (Gould 1994, Diamond 1994, Shreve 1994, William 1994). *Time*, in an issue following its article supporting *The Bell Curve*, carried an article about the publication of *The History and Geography of Human Genes* (Cavalli-Sforza et al. 1994). The article was titled "The Story in Our Genes: A Landmark Global Study Flattens *The Bell Curve* Proving that Racial Differences are only Skin Deep" (*Time* Jan. 16, 1995). On February 13, 1995 *Newsweek* carried a cover story entitled "What Color is Black: Science, Politics and Racial Identity." The article contains this comment: "Partly because of immigration—and partly because diversity is suddenly hip—America is beginning to revise its two-way definition of race. Though this process will surely take years, it is already blurring our sense that racial identity is fixed. . . . [T]he idea of race itself is now coming under attack by science" (63–64). In that same issue a second article is titled "Three is not Enough, Surprising New Lessons from the Controversial Science of Race," and explains that a majority of anthropologists reject race as a biological category" (67).

Foremost among newspapers with national reputations and wide circulations is *The New York Times*. In 1994 it carried an article in which it stated that "in recent years there is a surprising lack of agreement among scientists over the popular notions of what constitutes a racial group" (1994, 5). *The Los Angeles Times* carried a syndicated article that appeared in a number of newspapers across the country. The *Flint Journal* printed a version of it under the title "Concept of Race Shouldn't Exist, Scientists Should Abandon it— experts" (Feb. 20, 1995). Other newspapers carrying this and similar themes include the *Houston Chronicle* (1991), the *Tampa Tribune* (1992), the *Detroit Free Press* (1988, 1993, 1994), the *Columbus Dispatch* (1995), and the *Detroit News* (1995).

The *Times Picayune* of New Orleans ran an extraordinary series of eight multipage sections on Sundays from May 1993 to December 1993. The series was captioned "Together Apart: The Myth of Race." One segment was headed "What is Race?" (August 15:53–72). And for administrators, and some academics, the *Chronicle of Higher Education* (Feb. 17, 1995) carried on its first page this statement: "After several hundred years in which people have been trying to deal with race, there has never been a workable definition." The article itself, covering several pages, is titled: "A Growing Number of Scientists Reject the Concept of Race: Many Say Racial Classifications are Meaningless and Unscientific" (A8–9).

Of course readers may ignore or selectively perceive media information, but it does represent communication to the reading public that there are serious scientific reasons for questioning the concept of race. What Montagu had begun in 1942 had reached the public's attention first through his book *Man's Most Dangerous Myth* and again over fifty years later in the 1990s through newspapers and magazines.

CONCLUSION

Reasons for the Decline of Race

Concepts central to a discipline are not easily relinquished. The loss of consensus on "race" was the result of a complex of factors. As stated above, in order to understand the change it is necessary to examine the history of social and cultural conditions and their expression and interaction with people and organizations. The efforts of Franz Boas to combat racism and to challenge the notion of races as fixed biological entities was portrayed in part one of this paper. Boas and his students constituted the first generation of twentieth-century American anthropologists. They differed from those who had passed before by challenging racism and building the culture concept (Benedict 1934, Kroeber 1917, Lowie 1920, Mead 1928). With culture as an explanatory concept, it was possible to avoid using biological race and a Lamarckian explanation for human behavior. In the battle between nurture and nature that occupied the first half of the century, the culture concept at last provided powerful focus around which evidence could be organized.

Boas and his students did not challenge the idea that races are a reality. But they vigorously confronted racism and the idea that races do not change. Contesting racism and race fixity were necessary preludes to viewing race as a concept without validity. Racism was the passionate core of the idea of race—remove that romantic core and the concept no longer excites the loyalty of many of its adherents. As we have seen the first person in the United States to declare race was an invalid concept was Ashley Montagu. Most anthropologists were not ready for this iconoclastic view. In the two decades that followed Montagu's paper and book, published works by others did not reflect these new views. Then came the debate over the existence of race described in the previous section. That debate was crucial to developing support for the view that races did not exist. The heat of the debate in fact cast much light. Anthropologists became informed, examined the new ideas and the new data, and the number of those who rejected or were more critical of race increased.

Other events internal to science were predecessors of the shift. Two relatively new concepts and new data were promoted by the debate. The concept of ethnic group provided a cultural way of explaining differences between the groups by referring to common origins or identity based on nationality, religion, or ancestry. The concept of cline, originally proposed by Julian Huxley (1938), referred to geographic gradations of a gene frequency or a phenotypic characteristic. As explained in the first part of this paper, this directed analysis to one trait at a time, as C. L. Brace had advocated (1964b) indicating gradations rather than sharp lines between populations. Analyses of several traits simultaneously revealed that the clines were distributed in patterns that traveled in different directions creating a picture in which racial boundary lines could not be identified.

The concepts and the data were there, the debate drew attention to the data. New recruits into anthropology were from families of immigrant, African-American, or Third-World origin, and more likely to take the new data seriously. Also sensitizing them to reexamine old concepts in the light of the new were the social movements of the 1960s and the memory of the Nazi extermination of Jews, Gypsies, and Poles in order to achieve race purification.

It has been over two hundred years since race became a concept used by scientists. In that time no cumulative body of knowledge has developed. The concept remains loosely defined and unproductive in research. There is no agreement on the number of races or how to identify their boundary lines. A majority of anthropologists believe that there are no biological races in the species *Homo sapiens*. Human biological variation exists and is studied, but each characteristic is distributed in a geographic gradation that defies establishing any clear boundary line between so-called races. Races are not the product of precise observation, but are derived from selective perception in which stereotypes were constructed in the cultural period when Europeans had become aware of people from far-away places, but generally unaware of the gradations connecting them, let alone of the discordant nature of these gradations (Brace 1964b). "Races" are not homogenous populations. There is more variation within a "race" than between races (Lewontin 1973). Geographical races in numerous other species differ by about 20.5 percent of gene frequency (Graves and Place 1995, 40–41). The amount of genetic differences between the three "racial" groups is no greater than 7.8 percent (Nei and Livshits 1989), another study found 5.0 percent (Cann et al. 1987), and a third 4.5 percent (Brown 1980).

Add to this the extensive interbreeding that has occurred as populations migrated. "Genetically, human populations are all mongrels, because people always breed outside their local group at every opportunity. This is [part of] why anthropologists have largely abandoned the idea of race as a scientific biological concept" (Lieber 1994, Sect. 4, 3). Studies of African-Americans suggest that from twenty to thirty percent of their genes are from European populations (Glass and Li 1953).

Those who study IQ scores of different groups do so with the assumption that there are homogenous races, when in fact that is not the case. Populations being very similar to each other to begin with, and being interbred with each other—and humans have interbred throughout their evolution—makes it impossible to explain differences in IQ scores largely on the basis of heredity.

Just as there is no cumulative scientific literature on the nature of races, so also is the fact that after a century of IQ research there is no accumulated "body of knowledge about the role of heredity in human intellectual variation . . ." (Evans and Waites 1981, 177–178). While individuals vary in their inherited intelligence, the claim that large subdivisions of the human species also vary in that regard has been demonstrated by a century of debate over race and IQ to be no more than a product of pseudoscientific imagination.

REFERENCES

Banton, Michael.
1977. *The Idea of Race*. London: Tavistock.
1987. *Racial Theories*. Cambridge: Cambridge University Press.
Barkan, Elazar.
1987. *From Race to Ethnicity: Changing Concepts of Race in England and the United States Between the Two World Wars*. Waltham, Ma.: Brandeis University. PhD dissertation.
Barzun, Jacques.
1965. *Race: A Study in Modern Superstition*. N.Y.: Harper and Row (1937).
Beck, Joan.
1991. Ending Concept of Race a Good Idea. *Houston Chronicle* March 16:32A.
Benedict, Ruth.
1934. *Patterns of Culture*. Boston: Houghton Mifflin Co.
Begley, Sharon.
1995. Three is not enough: Surprising new lessons from the controversial science of race. *Newsweek* Feb. 13:67–69.
Birdsell, Joseph B.
1993. *Microevolutionary Patterns in Aboriginal Australia*. N.Y.: Oxford University Press.
Blauner, Bob.
1972. *Racial Oppression in America*. N.Y.: Harper and Row.
Blumenbach, Johann Friedrich.
1770. *On the Natural Varieties of Mankind*. Trans. Thomas Benyshe. N.Y.: Bergman. In *The Anthropological Treatises of Joann Friedrick Blumenbach*. London: Longman, Green (1865).
Boas, Franz.
1940. The relations between physical and social anthropology. In *Race, Language and Culture*, 172–175. N.Y.: The Free Press.
1974. History of anthropology (1904). In *Readings in the History of Anthropology*, Regna Darnell, ed., 260–273. N.Y.: Harper and Row.
Boyd, William C.
1950. *Genetics and the Races of Man*. Boston: Little, Brown and Company.
Brace, C. Loring.
1964a. On the race concept. *Current Anthropology* 5:313–320.
1964b. A nonracial approach toward the understanding of human diversity. In *The Concept of Race*, Ashley Montagu, ed., 103–152. N.Y.: Free Press.
Brace, C. Loring and Kevin D. Hunt.
1990. A nonracial craniofacial perspective on human variation: (A)ustralia to Z(uni). *American Journal of Physical Anthropology* 82:341–360.
Brown, W. M.
1980. Polymorphism in Mitochondrial DNA of Humans as Revealed by Restrictive Endonuclease Analysis. *Proceeds of National Academy of Science, USA* 77:3605–3609.
Brues, Alice M.
1977. *People and Races*. New York: Macmillan. Reprinted 1990.
Buffon, George L. L.
1749. *Histoire Naturelle, Générale et Particuliére*. Sanson and cie.
Camper, Petrus.

1792. *Dissertation sur les variétés naturelles qui caractérisent la physiononie des hommes des divers climates et différens ages*. Paris: H. J. Jansen.

Cann, Rebecca L., M. Stoneking and Alan C. Wilson.

1987. Mitochondrial DNA and Human Evolution. *Nature* 325:31–36.

Cavalli-Zforza, L. Luca, Paolo Menozzi, and Alberto Piazza.

1994. *The History and Geography of Human Genes*. Princeton: Princeton University Press.

Coon, Carleton S.

1962. *The Origin of Races*. New York: Knopf.

1982. *Racial Adaptations*. Chicago: Nelson-Hall.

Cooper, Richard and Richard David.

1986. The biological concept of race and its application to public health and epidemiology. *Journal of Health Politics, Policy and Law* 11:97–116.

Coser, Lewis A. and Bernard Rosenberg.

1964. The Sociology of Knowledge. In *Sociological Theories*, L. Coser and B. Rosenberg, eds., 661–684. N.Y.: Macmillan.

Cravens, Hamilton.

1978. *The Triumph of Evolution: American Scientists and the Heredity-Environment Controversy 1900–1941*. Phila.: University of Pennsylvania Press.

Cuvier, Georges.

1829. *Le Régne Animel*. Paris: Déterville.

Darwin, Charles.

1859. *The Origin of Species*. London: J. Murray.

Diamond, Jared.

1994. Race without color. *Discovery* 15:82–89.

Dobzhansky, Theodosius.

1962. Comment on Livingstone. *Current Anthropology* 3:279–280.

1963. Comment. *Current Anthropology* 4:197.

Edmondson, Munro S.

1965. A Measurement of Relative Racial Differences. *Current Anthropology* 6:167–198.

Evans, Brian and Bernard Waites.

1981. *IQ and Mental Testing: An Unnatural Science and its Social History*. Atlantic Highlands, N.J.: Humanities Press.

Flint Journal

1995. Concept of Race "Shouldn't Exist." Feb. 20.

Fredrickson, George M.

1988. *The Arrogance of Race: Historical Perspectives on Slavery, Racism, and Social Inequality*. Middletown, Ct.: Wesleyan University Press.

Fried, Morton.

1965. A four letter word that hurts. *Saturday Review* 68 (Oct. 2):22.

Garn, Stanley M.

1961. *Human Races*. Springfield, Il.: C. C. Thomas. 3rd revised edition, 1971.

1963. Comment. *Current Anthropology* 4:197.

1964. *Culture and the Direction of Human Evolution*. Detroit: Wayne State University Press.

Garn, Stanley and Carleton Coon.

1960. On the Number of Races of Mankind. In *Readings on Race*, Stanley Garn, ed. Springfield, Illinois.

Glass, Beutley and C. C. Li.
1953. The Dynamics of Racial Intermixture—An Analysis Based on the American Negro. *American Journal of Human Genetics* 5:1–20.
Goodman, Alan H. and George J. Armelagos.
In Press. The Resurrection of Race: The Concept of Race in Physical Anthropology in the 1990s. In *Race and Other Misadventures: Essays in Honor of Ashley Montagu.* Dix Hills, N.J.: General Hall Press.
Gossett, Thomas F.
1964. *Race: The History of an Idea in America.* Dallas: The University of Texas Press.
Gould, Stephen Jay.
1994. The Geometer of Race. *Discover* 15:64–69.
Grant, Madison.
1924. *The Passing of the Great Race.* New York: Charles Scribner's Sons. 4th revised ed.
Graves, Joseph L. Jr. and Terri Place.
1995. Race and IQ Revisited: figures never lie but often liars figure. Department of Life Sciences: Arizona State University.
Greene, John C.
1959. *The Death of Adam, Evolution, and Its Impact on Western Thought.* Ames: Iowa State University Press.
Hiernaux, Jean.
1964. The concept of race and the taxonomy of mankind. In *The Concept of Race,* Ashley Montagu, ed., 29–45. New York: Collier-Macmillan.
Hirschfeld, Magnus.
1938. *Racism.* Trans. and ed. Eden and Cedar Paul. London: Victor Gollancz.
Holmes, Steven A.
1994. You're Smart if you know what race you are. *New York Times* Oct. 23:5.
Holz, Robert Lee.
1994. *Los Angeles Times/New York Times*
Hooton, Earnest.
1932. *Up From the Ape.* N.Y.: Macmillan. Revised 1946.
Horsman, Reginald.
1981. *Race and Manifest Destiny: The Origins of American Racial Anglo-Saxonism.* Cambridge: Harvard University Press.
Hotz, Robert Lee.
1995. Scientists push classification not based on race. *Detroit News* April 16: 4A.
Huxley, Julian S.
1938. Clines: An auxiliary taxonomic principle. *Nature* 142:47.
Jensen, Arthur.
1982. Comment. *Current Anthropology* 22:649–650.
Kennedy, Kenneth A. R.
1976. *Human Variation in Space and Time.* Dubuque, Io.: W. C. Brown.
Klass, Morton and Hal Hellman.
1971. *The Kinds of Mankind: An Introduction to Race and Racism.* Phila.: Lippincott.
Klineberg, Otto.
1935. *Race Differences.* N.Y.: Harper.
Kong, Delores.
1988. The fallacy of focusing on skin color. *Detroit Free Press.*
Kroeber, Alfred Louis.

1917. The superorganic. *American Anthropologist* 19:163-213.
Kuznick, Peter J.
1987. *Beyond the Laboratory: Scientists as Political Activists in 1930's America*. Chicago: University of Chicago Press.
Laitner, Bill.
1993. Research on Athletics: Race is Inconclusive. *Detroit Free Press* July 27.
Lewontin, Richard.
1973. The Apportionment of Human Diversity. *Evolutionary Biology* 6:381-397.
Lieber, Michael.
1994. An Anthropological Look at Race and Intelligence. *Chicago Tribune* Section 4, 3.
Lieberman, Leonard.
1968. The debate over race: A study in the sociology of knowledge. *Phylon* 39:127-141.
In Press. *Outrageous Concepts: Race, Genes and IQ*. Dix Hills, Ny: General Hall.
Lieberman, Leonard, Blaine Stevenson and Larry T. Reynolds.
1989. Race and anthropology: A core concept without consensus. *Anthropology and Education Quarterly* 20(2) June:7-73.
Lieberman, Leonard and Fatimah Jackson.
1995. Race and Three Models of Human Evolution. *American Anthropologist* 97:--.
Linnaeus, Carolus.
1758. *Systema Naturae*. Stockholm: G. Keisewetter. 10th edition.
Littlefield, Alice, Leonard Lieberman and Larry T. Reynolds.
1982. Redefining Race: The potential demise of a concept. *Current Anthropology* 23: 641-647.
Livingstone, Frank B.
1962. On the Non-Existence of Human Races. *Current Anthropology* 3:279-281, 470.
1958. Anthropological implications of sickle cell gene distributions in West Africa. *American Anthropologist* 30:533-562.
1962. On the non-existence of human races. *Current Anthropology* 3:279-281, 470.
Lore, David.
1995. Science Debates Racial Identities. *Columbus Dispatch* Sunday, Feb. 26: 7E.
Lowie, Robert.
1920. *Primitive Society*. N.Y.: Boni and Liveright.
MacRae, Donald G.
1960. Race and sociology in history and theory. In *Man, Race and Darwin*, Phillip Mason, ed., 76-86. London: Oxford University Press.
Marks, Jonathan.
1991. Personal Communication.
Mason, Peter.
1990. *Deconstructing America, Representatives of the Other*. London and N.Y.: Routledge.
Mead, Margaret.
1928. *Coming of Age in Samoa*. New York: William Morrow.
Miles, Robert.
1982. Racism and nationalism in Britain. In *Britain: Continuity and Change*, Charles H. Hubbard, ed., 279-300. London: Hutchins.
1989. *Racism*. London and N.Y.: Routledge.
Mills, C. Wright.

1959. *The Sociological Imagination*. N.Y.: Grove Press.
Molnar, Stephen.
1975. *Races, Types, and Ethnic Groups: The Problem of Human Variation*. Englewood Cliffs, N.J.: Prentice-Hall.
1992. *Human Variation: Races, Types and Ethnic Groups*, 3rd edition. Englewood Cliffs, N.J.: Prentice-Hall.
Montagu, Ashley.
1941. The Concept of Race in the Human Species in the Light of Genetics. *Journal of Heredity* 23:243–247.
1942. *Man's Most Dangerous Myth: The Fallacy of Race*. N.Y.: Columbia University Press.
1962. The concept of race. *American Anthropologist* 64:919–928.
1963. *Race, Science, and Humanity*. Princeton: Van Nostrand.
1964. *The Concept of Race*. N.Y.: Free Press of Glencoe.
1965. *The Idea of Race*. Lincoln: University of Nebraska Press.
Nei, Masatoski and G. Livshits.
1989. The Genetic Relationship of Europeans, Asians, and Africans and the Origin of Modern Homo sapiens. *Human Heredity* 39:276–281.
Newman, Marshall T.
1963. Geographic and microgeographic races. *Current Anthropology* 4 (April):189.
Morganthau, Tom.
1995. What Color is Black? *Newsweek* Feb. 13:63–65.
Odom, Herbert H.
1967. Generalizations on race in nineteenth-century physical anthropology. *Isis* 58: 5–18.
Physical Anthropologists and Geneticists.
1961. On the Nature of Race and Race Differences by Physical Anthropologists and Geneticists. In *Current Anthropology* 2:304–306.
Retzius, Anders.
1859. Present state of Ethnology in Relation to the Form of the Human Skull. In *Smithsonian Institution Annual Report* 1860. Washington, D.C.
Sauer, Norman J.
1992. If Races Don't Exist, How Come Forensic Anthropologists are so Good at Identifying Them? *Social Science and Medicine* 34:107.
Shipman, Pat.
1994. The Evolution of Racism. N.Y.: Simon and Schuster.
Shreve, James.
1994. Terms of Estrangement. *Discover* 15:56–63.
Smedley, Audrey.
1993. *Race in North America: Origin and Evolution of a Worldview*. Boulder: Westview Press.
Snyder, Louis.
1962. *The Idea of Racialism*. N.Y.: Van Nostrand and Rheinhold.
Sorokin, Pitrim A.
1928. *Contemporary Sociological Theories*. N.Y.: Harper and Row.
Stanton, William.
1960. *The Leopard's Spots: Scientific Attitudes Toward Race in America 1815–59*. Chicago: University of Chicago Press.
Stepan, Nancy.

1982. *The Idea of Race in Science: Great Britain 1800–1960.* Hampton, Ct.: Shoestring Press.

Stocking, George W. Jr.

1968. *Race, Culture and Evolution: Essays in the History of Anthropology.* N.Y.: The Free Press.

Siegel, Suzie.

1992. The Human Family. *Tampa Tribune* Feb. 25:1–2.

Subramanian, Sribala.

1995. The Story in Our Genes. *Time* Jan. 16:54–55.

The Times-Picayune

1993. Together Apart: The Myth of Race. May 9:1–12.

1993. Chained to History. June 13:13–36.

1993. What is Race? Aug. 15:53–72.

1993. Early Lesson Last a Lifetime. Sept. 12:73–88.

1993. Black Culture White Culture. Oct. 17:109–122.

1993. Our Separate Ways. Nov. 14:123–146.

1993. Speak Up Part III. Aug.–Dec.: 147–166.

Underwood, Jane H.

1975. *Biocultural Interactions and Human Variation.* Dubuque, Io.: W. C. Brown.

1979. *Human Variation and Human Microevolution.* Englewood Cliffs, N.J.: Prentice-Hall.

1995. Speak Up Part II. June–Aug.:89–108.

Unesco *Statement on Race,* 1950.

Walvin, James.

1973. Black caricature: The roots of racialism. In *Black and White: The Negro and English Society 1555–1945,* Charles Husband, ed., 159–66. London: Allen Lane, Penguin Press.

West. Erika McPhail and Sharon McPhail.

1994. It's Not Black and White. *Detroit Free Press Magazine* Oct. 9:6–8, 10–12, 16–17.

Wheeler, David L.

1995. A Growing Number of Scientists Reject the Concept of Race: Many Say Racial Classifications are Meaningless and Unscientific. *The Chronicle of Higher Education* Feb. 17: A8–A9, A15.

William, Juan.

1994. Violence, Genes and Prejudice. *Discover* 15:92–102.

Wolpoff, Milford H.

1989. Multiregional Evolution: The Fossil Alternative to Eden. In *The Human Revolution,* P. Mellars and C. Stringer, eds. Princeton: Princeton University Press.

5

WHAT CAN BIOLOGISTS SOLVE?

S. E. Luria

What is the relation of biology to social concerns, aside from work that is primarily medical? We hear from all sides that biology, and in fact all pure science, has become irrelevant, neglecting its obligation to pursue goals of physical betterment of man. We all know the fallacy of this viewpoint. We know that all science can find applications in appropriate times and circumstances. Even the most esoteric studies on bacterial gene action and on DNA and RNA synthesis have suddenly become central to the cancer problem. For example, viruses cause cancers, and scientists are searching within human cells for genetic material that may resemble cancer-producing viruses.

One could give many similar examples in defense of pure research; but that is not the point I wish to make. I do not disagree with the demand that scientists concern themselves with the consequences of their work. On the contrary, I firmly believe that such concern is very important. But I also believe that an intense guilt feeling about the "irrelevance" of one's work is counterproductive both to good research and to relevant research.

From *The New York Review of Books*, 7 February 1974, pp. 27–28. Copyright © 1974 Nyrev, Inc. Reprinted by permission.

There is another, more insidious aspect to the relevance question: the attempt to saddle science with the burden of tasks that have little or nothing to do with science. Specifically, I believe that today biologists are being pressed to take on, as their professional responsibility, the study of certain problems that are not, or at least not primarily, biological problems, but social problems. In my opinion this is not an accident: it is part of a technocratic tendency to see only the technical aspects of human problems— and, when these aspects do not exist, to invent them. Let me give you several examples of what I have in mind.

The first example concerns the so-called ecological crisis and the pollution of the environment. Well-known biologists as well as other earnest persons have joined in alerting the public to the worrisome state of our air, our waters, our soil. That is fine. But, in the face of the crisis, if a crisis does in fact exist, biologists and other scientists have now been called upon not only to help correct the immediate consequences of pollution and to advise on future policies, but to assume responsibility for new approaches to the management of our environment. Universities have established courses and programs in ecological science, environmental biology, and other new specialties—often without any specialists to man these programs.

I do not question that applied biology can help to correct some ecological troubles. But it seems clear to me that the central problems are not biological. Neither are they scientific or even technological. They are social, and their solution depends on radical changes in social priorities and on improved machinery to enforce those priorities.

If the ecological crisis exists it is a social and political crisis, brought about in part by population increase and urbanization, and in great part, at least in this country, by unfettered and selfish exploitation of natural resources by industry—aided and abetted by the government. To call on scientists to solve the ecological crisis is but an exercise in buck-passing, as it would be for the board of directors of the Pennsylvania Railroad to ask their train conductors to rescue the railroad from bankruptcy. If scientists are lured into claiming that they have the know-how to solve what are really social crises, they will share the responsibility for the fact that these crises remain unsolved. They actually aid and abet those who are responsible for generating and maintaining the crises. Physicians are well aware of comparable attempts to use medicine as a cover, in order *not* to attack the real roots of a variety of social problems, from drug addiction to malnutrition.

My second example is a somewhat subtler one. It has to do with violence. We are told by ethologists and by politicians that crime and violence, from murder in the city streets to the automated battlefield, are the expression of aggressions that man has inherited from his brute ancestors, only made worse by man's intellectual capacities. They are claimed to be the behavior of the "naked ape." According to ethologists, including the most famous ones, aggression is part of the biological nature of man as of cyclid fish; violence is the natural function of the limbic system of our brain; crime and drug addiction are manifestions of certain genes or groups of genes; kind-hearted social measures have "failed" to correct these evils; and it is now time for biologists to face their responsibility, their manifest destiny to save and redirect the future of the human race by improving experimentally the heredity of mankind—presumably by selecting the meek or eliminating the violent.

Such calls for biologists to take over from soft-headed sociologists and criminologists the burden of research responsibility come not only from some ethologists (and, of course, from right-wing politicians) but also from some respected experimental scientists who in their own work would never be caught misreasoning as they do in social matters. One very distinguished scientist, in advocating a biological approach, argues that crim-

inality can be an expression of the beast in man. Then he be-
moans the frightful increases in crime in the last decades, as if
here were not evidence for the social nature of the crime problem!
    It is easy to see that such biologizing of crime and aggression
serves to make people close their eyes to what crime really is:
a social illness, fed by poverty and by profit. On the one hand,
the major increases in crime have coincided with the industrializa-
tion of crime—in the prohibition period, in the Mafia, in the drug-
importing and marketing industry—in parallel with the indus-
trialization of most other activities in our society. On the other
hand, crime is a product of poverty and exploitation, as it has
always been. It is not the expression of a few genes or chromo-
somes. We biologists and medical scientists should be alert not
to let our sciences be dragged into these kinds of sterile pursuits.

    One more example: the current but not novel controversy
about race and IQ. Intelligence tests, standardized to predict success in school under present curricula, have shown an average
15-point difference between white and black Americans. A few
psychologists and educationists, on the basis of shaky and probably
meaningless evidence, have asserted that most of the difference is
attributable to heredity. Too many people have already pointed
out the pitfalls and fallacies in the methods used in these studies
for me to do the same here. One important argument, however, is
worth mentioning: according to an elegant analysis by Bowles
and Gintis, the IQ, no matter how predictive of success in school,
turns out to be almost irrelevant to economic success in life. The
son of an industrialist with an IQ of 90 has an enormously better
chance to succeed than a black boy with 120.
    There is an even more cogent argument. Even if IQ were in-
heritable and its differences between races statistically significant,
there is nothing sensible one can do about it, except possibly
abolish the IQ tests (which may not be a bad idea) or improve
school curricula (if one knew how)—unless, of course, what the

IQ enthusiasts want is to segregate the races: in schools, perhaps, or in concentration camps.

Whenever self-appointed experts state that the problem of impoverishment of IQ is a major problem facing our nation, I see racist eugenics raising once again its ugly head. Behind the urgent scientific necessity to know the truth about those miserable 15 IQ points, on which the whole future of the schools, the nation, and the species is claimed to depend, there is a movement to drop the current efforts toward integrated schools and equalized opportunities for black and white children. If biologists let themselves be enticed into the quicksands of the genetics of IQ, they will end up as the stooges of the forces of racial bigotry. How to get the most out of each person according to his or her ability is not a biological problem. It is a problem of social organization and social responsibility—as are the problems of pollution and crime.

Thus the three problems I have mentioned, although claimed to present socially relevant tasks for life scientists, turn out to be socio-political traps beyond the scope of science.

As biologists we must resist the lure of research on nonbiological social problems. For better or for worse, we must continue to develop our science along the lines we are currently pursuing, with a success comparable only to the successes of physics in the first quarter of this century. Just now the most esoteric aspects of these advances, such as synthesis of RNA and DNA or membrane chemistry, have begun to find direct applications to cancer and other diseases.

But as we pursue our own exciting business as biologists, it will not hurt us to have some grander vision. It is good even at my age to dream about greener pastures, if not for oneself at least for one's science as a collective enterprise.

I was thinking along these lines this past summer as I walked through the British Museum, going from the Elgin Marbles to my favorite set of sculptures, the Assyrian bas-reliefs of Assur-banipal. A few yards away are the beautiful hand-painted scrolls of all religions of man. Next to them, manuscript letters of the greatest minds of our culture—Shakespeare, Descártes, Newton, Voltaire, Shelley, and many others. Most touching of all, the diary written by Captain Scott, freezing to death at the South Pole in pursuit of knowledge and duty. I found myself thinking: what kind of instrument is the human mind, which plans and dares and fails and hopes? Will biology ever be able to unravel this greatest of wonders? Will man be able to understand in molecular terms how he himself thinks and feels and learns, remembers and forgets?

Such a biology of the human spirit, if I may call it that, must start, of course, from the biology of the mammalian brain: how it is constructed, how its various parts are connected, how signals originate and are processed. But ultimately it must be more than that: it must explain not only the mechanical aspects of neuro-physiology but also the remarkable superstructure that we call the mind. It must interpret in biological terms—not in terms of biological determinism—the choices that the human mind makes among different possibilities. It must explain the apparent freedom of these choices, that is, the freedom of the will. And it must come to grips with the most intriguing feature—the creativity of the human spirit. Some may believe that a biology of the mind is impossible, either on theological or on philosophical grounds. I take here a different view, that a biology of the mind is feasible and is one of the great goals of science, possibly the greatest.

The mind, whatever it may be, operates within the network of neural connections in the brain. Applied mathematics and computer science can contribute analogs of the brain network that help clarify what any model of the human brain must be able to account for. But the brain is not a computer. On the one hand, it grows: it is made anew in each individual, starting from the instructions of the genes, which provide a specific chemical program for the brain as they do for any other organ. On the other hand, the brain's creativity is beyond the combinational possibilities of any computer, if nothing else because of the thousand billions of nerve cells in a human brain.

The brain, of course, is an old invention. The vertebrate brain itself predated man by a half billion years. The synapses or connections between nerve cells that underlie the brain network are roughly similar in invertebrates as in man. The directing processes that during the development of the organism and specifically of the brain generate that network are an immediate challenge: one needs to understand the "individuality" of nerve cells that causes a given nerve fiber from the eye, for example, to make precise connection with a given cell or group of cells in the lower brain, which in turn send their fibers precisely to certain columns of cells in the brain cortex.

Dr. Stephen Roth of Johns Hopkins University has reported that in the early chick embryo the nerve cells isolated from any given part of the retina have already a tendency to stick preferentially to fragments of those parts of the chick brain to which they would later send their fibers. This is true even before the retinal cells have started to make their fibers. It seems, therefore, that the program for specific recognition is expressed independently in the retina and in the brain on the surface of the cells that have to become connected. Just as a manufacturer color codes the terminals of electric wires so that the electrician knows how to assemble an appliance, so does the genetic program mark the surface of nerve cells with specific chemical markings.

Nothing that we now know about the chemistry of cell surfaces can explain the precise specificity required to account for such precise recognition between one cell and another. Yet we are confident that phenomena of this kind will yield to ever more refined biochemical and physiochemical analyses. The brain network is hundreds of million years old and its basic features should yield to animal experimentation. But matters change when we come face to face with something uniquely human.

Human language has evolved in the last million years or so, that is, in a relatively tiny time span on the scale of evolution. It was a new invention, which not only changed the destiny of the line of descent in which it appeared but affected all living species and the fate of the earth itself. Human language permitted communication between individuals and between distant generations of men. By making conceptual thinking possible it created culture and thereby the intellectual enterprise. In turn, culture probably relegated whatever instinctual drives man had inherited from his ancestors to a secondary role—ethologists notwithstanding.

Language, of course, was not a miracle: it was a biological invention, like the wing of the bird and the fin of the fish. The study of human language, of its underlying neural mechanisms, of how these operate in the uses of language for logical and creative thinking, seems to me to be the supreme and yet attainable goal for a human biology—I would almost say a "humanistic" biology.

Is there a justification, one may ask, for attempting to biologize language while at the same time refusing to biologize aggression, or IQ, or the ecological crisis? Would it not suffice to assume that language is a socially determined set of human activities superimposed upon the enormous but unspecific complexity of a primate brain?

The justification for treating human language as a biological phenomenon comes from modern linguistics. According to Chomsky and his followers, human language, irrespective of race and culture, is based on innate grammatical and syntactic structures common to all normal human beings. To a biologist, this can mean only that somehow the inner structure of language is genetically determined. That is, language and its intellectual correlates are the functional manifestation of a specific, genetically determined system of nervous connections in the cerebral cortex. The enormous growth of the human brain cortex in the astonishingly short time of a few hundred thousand years may have been a correlate of the development of language, just as the expansion of a lobe in the brain of electric fishes was bound to the dependence of these animals on the detection of electric fields.

Note that a biology of language as I envision it here will include a biology of thinking processes such as logical structures, *a priori* ideas, artistic creation, and even ethical principles. To a very large extent the actual contents of these areas must, of course, be of environmental origin, just as the actual language you and I, or a Chinese or a Bantu, speak is dictated not by genes but by upbringing. At the same time, a biology of language could be a truly humane science since it would address itself to qualities common to all men, not to differences between men. It may generate an applied science too, by discovering better ways to teach, to learn, and to make use of what we learn.

How to approach the biology of human language and thereby also the biology of the human mind is not yet easy to see. Behavior geneticists have barely started to analyze biologically the behavior of *Escherichia coli* or of the fruitfly. And in man we cannot isolate mutants or perform controlled crosses. At any rate, the genetic basis of human language is likely to involve not one or a few genes but thousands.

A start on the biology of language can be made by observing the derangements produced by accidents or disease or genetic mutation or chemical poisoning onto linguistic functions on the one hand and on the brain network on the other hand. Some work of this kind is being done by Alexander Luria in the Soviet Union and by Norman Geschwind and others in the United States. But new techniques and ideas will probably be needed.

It may seem unwise or grandiose to put forward as a legitimate goal for biologists a study with so little immediate prospect for rapid advance. My reason for doing so is that I believe the real relevance of science is to cultivate, as immediate or ultimate goals, a vision of the resolution of the great mysteries of nature. As we toil at our individual tasks, investigating the function of a gene or the structure of a membrane or the specificity of a synapse, we gain if we connect our work with some further and grander goal.

Several years ago Peter Medawar epitomized the pursuit of science as "The Art of the Soluble." Truly and correctly, this excludes from the purview of science the pursuit of mirages generated by wishful thinking. Yet when all self-delusion is excluded, there remain true problems, still insoluble but already visible as challenges to the scientists—like the Himalayas to a mountain climber. By facing them with courage and imagination, and with proper restraint, we remain faithful to the ideals of science.

6

THE MAGICAL AURA
OF THE IQ

Jerome Kagan

Every society, or large cohesive group within a society, recognizes that in order to maintain stability a small group must possess some power over the much larger citizenry. The power is sometimes inherited, sometimes awarded, sometimes attained, and sometimes seized. In actual practice, this lean and rather raw description is usually disguised by a clever strategy—much like a magician's wrist movement—that makes select psychological traits symbolic of highly valued, status-conferring attributes—hence, they become the vessels from which power is inevitably drawn.

Tenth-century Europe awarded power to those who were assumed to be more religious than their brothers. The presumption of a capacity for more intense religiosity provided a rationale that allowed the larger society to accept the fact that a privileged few were permitted entry into marble halls. Pericles' Athens and Lee's Virginia both rationalized the subjugation of their slaves on various psychological grounds. At other times and in other

From *The Saturday Review*, 4 September 1971, pp. 92–93. Reprinted by permission of Jerome Kagan and The Saturday Review.

places sexual abstinence, sexual potency, hunting skill, a capacity for silent meditation, good soldiering, or efficient farming have been dimensions along which men were ordered and, as a consequence of that ranking, divided into unequal groups.

Contemporary American society uses intelligence as one of the bases for ranking its members, and it makes the same arguments that educated Athenians uttered 2,500 years ago. Major loci of power in the United States reside in state and federal governments, major businesses, and the universities. All three of those institutions require their members to be regarded by the citizenry as intelligent, and many meet this requirement, in part, by completing a minimal amount of formal education. Education is one of the best reflections of intelligence, the argument goes, for one could not master the school's task without intelligence.

Thus far the ritual and ideology are not very different from the Islamic Moroccan who celebrates the warrior-saint and invents ways to select him. It is more threatening, however, to note that the analogy with the Islamic Moroccan extends to our explanations of the unequal distribution of intelligence in our society. The majority of Americans believe that children are born with a differential intellectual capacity and that, as a result, some children are destined to assume positions of status and responsibility. "Nature intended it that way." A much smaller group believes that this psychological capacity has to be attained through early experience and will.

These opposing hypotheses are identical in substance to the two interpretations of differential "capacity for religiosity" held by Islamites in Morocco and Indonesia. The Moroccans believe that some are born with a greater capacity for strong and intense religious experience. The Javanese believe the greater capacity is attained following long periods of meditation. And they, like us, discover the small proportion of their population that fits the description of the pure, and allows them ascent. The Moroccans explain this phenomenon by arguing that those who possess power do so because they inherited some special capacity that, in our society, is intelligence.

I do not contest the obvious fact that there are real differences among individuals' psychological traits—such as intelligence—that our society values. But I do suggest that, given the insufficient and controversial quality of the information relevant to the causes of these differences, it is likely that deep personal attitudes rather than logic or sound empirical data dictate one's interpretations of the documented variability in IQ.

Let me try to support this rather strong statement with a fragmentary analysis of what an intelligence test is made of. For the widely publicized announcement that 80 per cent of intelligence is inherited and 20 per cent environmentally determined is based on information from two similarly constructed standardized IQ tests invented by Caucasian middle-class Western men to rank-order everyone.

The most important set of test questions (important because scores on this set have the highest correlation with the total IQ) asks the person being tested to define words of increasing rarity. Rarity is a relative quality, depending always on the language community one selects as referent. "Shilling" is a rare word in the language space of the American child, but so is "fuzz." The test constructors decided that rarity would be defined with respect to the middle-class Caucasian experience. And a child reared in a middle-class home is more likely to learn the meaning of shilling than the meaning of fuzz. If contemporary black psychologists had accepted the assignment of constructing the first intelligence test, they probably would have made a different choice.

A second set of IQ test questions poses the child some everyday problem and asks him to state what he would do in that situation. For example, one question asks a seven-year-old, "What should you do if you were sent to buy a loaf of bread and the grocer said he didn't have any more?" Clearly, this question assumes a middle-class urban or suburban environment with more than one grocery store within safe walking distance of the home. For the only answer for which maximal credit is given is, "I would go to another store." It is not surprising that rural and ghetto children are less likely to offer that answer. Recently I examined a set of protocols gathered on poor black children living in a large Eastern city and found that many of them answered the question by saying they would "go home"—a perfectly reasonable, even intelligent, answer for which they were not given credit.

A third class of IQ test questions, called analogies, has the same dubious validity that the vocabulary test does, for the concepts the child must reason about are of differential familiarity to various ethnic groups. The child is asked how a piano and a violin are alike, not how tortilla and frijole are similar.

The fourth class of questions asks the child to solve some arithmetic problems. Of course, if the child has not learned how to add, subtract, or multiply, he will not be able to solve them. If intelligence is presumed to be 80 per cent inherited, it seems inappropriate that this quality should be measured, in part, by whether one has learned to add.

Another class of IQ test items includes a line drawing of an object that has an element missing and requires the child to discover the missing feature. As one might suspect, the pictures are selected to favor middle-class children, for they depict a thermometer without mercury in the bulb and a hand without fingernail polish, rather than a door without a double lock.

One task that does not favor middle-class white children asks the testee to remember a list of four or five numbers read at the rate of one per second. It is relevant to add that this test usually yields minimal differences between class and ethnic groups in the United States.

Biases in the selection of questions comprise only part of the IQ test problem. There is also a serious source of error in the administration of the test. White middle-class examiners usually administer the tests to children of different linguistic backgrounds. The test protocols of the black children mentioned above, gathered by well-intentioned, well-trained examiners, indicated that the children often misunderstood the examiner's pronunciation. When asked to define the word "fur" some said, "That's what happens when you light a match." Clearly, the children who gave this reply had misinterpreted the word to be *fire* and received no credit. Similarly, when requested to define "hat," some children said, "When you get burned," indicating they perceived the word as *hot,* and again received no credit.

These few examples, which comprise only a small proportion of all the sources of error that could be documented, are persuasive of the view that the IQ test is a seriously biased instrument that almost guarantees middle-class white children higher IQ scores than any other group of children.

However, most citizens are unaware either of the fundamental faults with the IQ test or of the multiple bases for differences in tested intelligence. And, like the Greeks, Islamic Moroccans, and medieval Christians, we, too, need a trait whose content can form a rational basis for the awarding of power and prizes. Intelligence is an excellent candidate, for it implies alertness, language sophistication, and ease of learning new skills and ideas. Moreover, it it is a characteristic of a single individual and, like his fingerprints, is not, in theory, linked with his religion, region, or eating habits. It is our modern interpretation of saintliness, religiosity, courage, or moral intensity, and, of course, it works. It works so well that when we construct an intervention project, be it a major effort like Headstart or a small study run by a university scientist, we usually evaluate the effects of the intervention by administering a standard intelligence test or one very similar to it.

Our practice reflects the unconscious bias that a child's IQ must be the essential dimension we wish to change. If an intervention does not alter this quintessential quality, the effort is probably not worthwhile. Hence, we create conditions in which poor four-year-olds leave their homes for a few hours a day to play with other children of their own and other ethnic groups and to interact with new adults. Then we evaluate the growth-enhancing quality of this experience by administering an IQ test, rather than by determining if the child has become friendlier or less suspicious of children and adults who don't come from his family or neighborhood.

What implications are to be drawn from this acerbic analysis of the IQ? The first may seem paradoxical, considering my apparently hostile critique of the IQ test. Despite the injustice inherent in awarding privilege, status, and self-esteem to those who possess more of some attribute the society happens to value, this dynamic seems to be universal, perhaps because it is necessary. Power—and I mean here benevolent power—probably has to be held unequally. Therefore the community must invent a complex yet reasonable rationale that will both permit and explain the limited distribution of this prized resource.

Knowledge of Western language, history, and customs is not altogether unreasonable as one of the bases on which to found the award. But let us be honest about the footing of this arbitrary decision and rid ourselves of the delusion that those who temporarily possess power are biologically more fit for this role because their brains are better organized. Sir Robert Filmer made this argument in 1680 to rationalize the right of kings to govern, and John Locke's political philosophy was shaped on a brilliant critique of Filmer's thesis. Moreover, the conclusion that those in power are biologically more intelligent does not fit either the mood of objectivity hammered out during the last 300 years of modern scientific work or the historical fact that the use of power for benevolent or malevolent ends has usually been independent of size of vocabulary, arithmetic skill, or analogical reasoning.

I do not deny the existence of biological differences, many of which are inherited between and within ethnic and racial groups. But we do not regard inherited characteristics such as eye color or tendency to perspire as entitling anyone to special favor. Similarly, we should reflect on the wisdom of using fifteen-point differences on a culturally biased test—regardless of the magnitude of the genetic contribution to the IQ—as a weapon to sort some children into stereotyped categories that impair their ability to become mayors, teachers, or lawyers.

It is possible to defend the heretical suggestion that for many contemporary occupations (note that I did not say all) IQ should not be the primary attribute upon which a candidate is screened. Of course, biological factors determine a person's muscle mass, brain size, and adrenaline secretion in response to stress. But let us not unfairly exploit these hard-won facts to rationalize the distribution of secular power, which is a political and sociological dimension. To do that would be to use fair science for dark deeds.

7

AN EXAMINATION OF JENSEN'S THEORY CONCERNING EDUCABILITY, HERITABILITY AND POPULATION DIFFERENCES

S. Biesheuvel

It is difficult, within the confines of a symposium, to deal effectively with Prof. Jensen's view that the difference in performance of white and black Americans at school and in intelligence tests must be ascribed more to genetic than to environmental factors. There is obviously no time to evaluate the vast amount of research material he has reviewed in support of his hypothesis. (Symposiasts were supplied with a 385 page manuscript and a summary of its contents).[1] The best one can do is to comment on the principal arguments put forward in the summary. Here

From *Psychologia Africana*, Volume 14, No. 2, 1972, pp. 87–94. Reprinted by permission. Originally, this was a paper contributed by invitation to a symposium on "Genetic and Cultural Differences in Abilities: Educational and Occupational Implications," at the 17th International Congress of Applied Psychology, held at Liège in July 1971. The symposium was convened and chaired by Prof. P. E. Vernon, Emeritus professor of psychology at the University of London, and now professor of Educational Psychology at the University of Calgary, Alberta. Prof. A. R. Jensen, Institute of Human Learning, University of California, Berkeley, U.S.A., was the principal speaker.

too there are snags, for Jensen's position is based on a process of reasoning from unacceptable premises. To challenge the argument at a particular point compels one first to deal with prior arguments and assumptions lest one should fall into the trap of having implicitly conceded them. The following quote from the summary illustrates this point:

> To be more specific, all major facts are comprehended quite well by the hypothesis that somewhere between one-half and three-fourths of the average I.Q. difference between American Negroes and whites is attributable to genetic factors and the remainder to environmental factors and their interactions with the genetic differences. This hypothesis, if it is wrong, is sufficiently precise to be disproved by empirical evidence.

One might be tempted to take up this challenge and to seek the relevant experimental evidence, in terms of the concepts inherent in the statement of the hypothesis. On further consideration, however, a number of questions pose themselves which cast doubt on whether the hypothesis is meaningful and capable of scientific verification. Before I proceed to demonstrate this, let me first clarify my position in so far as the ideological position underlying the current controversies is concerned.

I hold that it is legitimate to pose a hypothesis concerning the involvement of genetic factors in the observed differences between whites and blacks in various test performances and in adaptations to the educational and occupational requirements of Western Societies. On evolutionary grounds, I can see no good reason why in the process of adapting, races should only have differentiated in the physical and not in the mental domain. The examination of this proposition is, however, beset by such immense experimental difficulties that so far it has not yet been possible to perform the critical experiments, (a) because we can only deal with behaviour which is the outcome of interaction between genetic endowment and the environmental factors influencing its deployment; (b) because it is impossible to control all the relevant environmental variables in representative samples; (c) because the measuring devices are themselves culture bound; (d) because of the incompleteness of our knowledge about the genetic basis of behaviour and the determinants of individual development. We have much information bearing on the question. However, on strict scientific evidence, of the kind that would be accepted in sciences less affected by ideological positions than psychology, one can only say: "We do not know. Whether there are genetic differences in intellectual endowment between races still remains an open question."

To return now to a critique of Jensen's hypothesis.

1. He uses I.Q. as if it were a behavioural entity, whereas in fact it is nothing more than a statistical index relating to tests which may measure quite different functions of behaviour. It has frequently been shown that the same test may have different factor structures in different populations. I.Q.'s from different tests applied to the same population are also factorially diverse. Jensen's methodology does not reveal which component or components of any test performance or I.Q. are hereditarily determined. Lest it be argued that the precise behavioural nature of the I.Q. is immaterial, let me refer to an old investigation of mine. (Biesheuvel, 1949.)

The Porteus Maze Test, one of the most effective indices of adaptability ever designed, showed no difference between two samples of black (Bantu) and white (Caucasian) South African primary school pupils with the same age distribution, (M_W 97.38; M_B 98.18; D/SE .32). Koh's Blocks, on the other hand, an equally important test, still regularly used for cross-cultural measurement, showed a highly significant difference in favour of the white group. (M_W 55.3; M_B 43.14; D/SE 2.97). For both tests we can construct an I.Q. The I.Q. from the one test will have a large, from the other no, heritability differential. What one do we prefer? And how can we permit a genetic component to play hide-and-seek in this way?

2. Heritability figures quoted for I.Q. variance are always obtained from relatively homogeneous environments. This is true for example of the frequently quoted study by Burt (1958) who attributed 88% to genetic factors. The figure would obviously rise to 100% if a completely homogeneous environment could be found and if the tests were perfectly reliable. Conversely the greater the environmental heterogeneity, the smaller the genetic component would become. A heritability ratio is therefore always relative, and the absolute value which tends to be given to it in relation to the I.Q. is accordingly unjustifiable. Though it is recognised that a heredity component in the within-group variance provides no proof of its involvement in the between-group variance, it constitutes an a-priori argument for its involvement and the higher the heritability index, the stronger the probability would appear to be. Hence the importance of appreciating its relativity.

3. The same criticism applies to the use Jensen makes of the concept of intelligence. Despite years of research, interpretation and polemics, we are still far from agreement on what behavioural function or functions are designated by the term. But Jensen treats it as if it had the same standing in psychology as "energy," or "mass" in physics. He describes it as the "causative element behind the consolidation of what has been learned into concept formation." This he thereupon identifies as g. From numerous factorial studies, we know that there is a good deal more to intelligence than that, and that I.Q. can consequently reflect many different things, differentially determined by genetics. Clearly "the I.Q." is not a suitable index for heritability analysis.

4. Jensen's treatment of "environment" is too coarse to establish the full range of causal relationships. Where so many influ-

ences, of such varied nature are involved, control would seem
to be the major consideration, and most investigations break
down in this respect. Jensen argues that if we control socioeconomic status (SES) we do in fact summarise the larger
part of those environmental factors that are most frequently
mentioned as the causes of racial I.Q. differences." He holds
that the subtler environmental influences, alleged to be over-
looked, have never been demonstrated to contribute significantly to multiple correlations, which remain persistently too
low to account for the interracial difference of one standard
deviation found in the literature. In broad outline, the arguments against the validity of this conclusion are as follows:

a. A socio-economic grading can be assumed to contribute
   large variances on such aspects as richness of material milieu,
   parental education, individuals education. These are the
   major determinants of the SES grading. But such aspects as
   parental solicitude and warmth of interpersonal relations,
   vary independently within the conventional SES grades.
   They can therefore not materially contribute to a multiple r
   in the usual SES research design. Groups specifically selected for these subtler variables would have to be used to
   assess their full impact. We would then still be left with the
   problem of assessing their interaction with the customary
   SES variables.

b. Jensen's view that there is no evidence that the subtler environmental factors can play a significant part by themselves is contradicted by a number of investigations. In a
   study reported many years ago by Bühler (1936) two
   groups of two-year-old children living in the same institution were segregated from each other and subjected to two
   divergent types of treatment. One group was given very
   little tenderness although adequately cared for in every
   other respect. In the other group a nurse was assigned to
   each child and there was no lack of tenderness and affection.

At the end of half a year the first group was mentally and physically retarded in comparison with the second. Similar results were reported by Gindl and Hetzer (quoted from Handbook of Child Psychology, Clark Univ. Press, Worcester, Mass., 1931, p. 422), on the contrast between children reared in an institution and in foster homes and by Skeels and Dye (1939) in their controversial study of feeble minded children transferred from an orphanage to an institution catering specifically for the feeble minded. Also relevant is the observation made in a number of large scale studies (Biesheuvel, 1952; Thomson, 1950; Burt, 1946, 1950; Cattell, 1950; Vernon, 1950), that regardless of socio-economic status, family rank order tended to have an effect on intelligence test performance, the earlier born putting up the better performance. Greater parental solicitude for the first born and the amount of time that could be devoted to them seemed the most likely explanation.

Jerome Kagan (1968) has shown that differences in the stimulation received by infants from their cultural environment have a bearing on the establishment of perceptual schemata as early as the 3rd and 4th months of postnatal life. The subjects were infants drawn from lower and upper middle class families. The stimuli were representations of a male face, photographic, schematic or three dimensional, with the features either normally arranged or scrambled.

Responses were measured in terms of the extent of cardiac deceleration, as a correlate of the process of attention. The children of poorly educated parents more frequently showed only small decelerations, or did not decelerate at all in response to the various presentations of the stimulus series. Kagan suggested that their schemata for the human face were more poorly articulated and that they were therefore less likely to perceive or to be surprised by discrepancies. This could be the result of more frequent face to face

contact with their children on the part of the better educated parents, which would make the parental countenance
a more distinctive stimulus. Kagan provided some empirical
support for this view by means of detailed day-long observational studies of mothers and their babies in their
homes. These studies also threw some light on differential
language development. Upper middle class mothers proved
less likely to ignore their infant daughters' vocalizations and
more likely to respond with distinctive vocalization accompanied by tactile and visual input, than lower class mothers.

This did not apply to sons and the precocity of language
development in upper middle class girls noted in many
studies is in all probability the outcome of this differential
maternal behaviour. The early establishment of schemata for
perceptual, motoric and linguistic development must inevitably influence the growth of more advanced structures, discriminative responsiveness to the environment, and the
efficiency of the learning process in general. To what extent observed intellectual differences between black and
white groups in the United States and elsewhere can be
accounted for by influences of this kind is a question for
future research to decide. The point is that right now, the
experimental evidence is not available, and Jensen's generali-
sations are therefore unwarranted at this stage. Jensen makes
much of the fact that in a nationwide survey, American Indians were lower than Negroes in all environmental categories deemed to have a causal relationship to intellectual
development, and that overall, Indians averaged further below Negroes than Negroes averaged below whites. Yet on
all intelligence tests, Indians scored higher than Negroes and
at approximately 6 years of age, the difference in non-verbal
I.Q. was 14 points. On the surface, this result argues strongly
against an environmental hypothesis, but unless the kind of
early childhood influences now believed to be most signifi-

cant were taken into account in applying environmental controls, it still does not prove genetic causation.

I know too little about Indian culture, child rearing practices and personality factors to be able to express an opinion on the significance of the results. For further information on the study, reference should be made to the Coleman Report (1966).

c. However, my major and most fundamental criticism of the way the environmental influences have been handled—and this applies to the majority of the sources on which Jensen relies for his estimates—is that control has been exercised cross-sectionally in time and not longitudinally. When nutritional status, or educational level, or socio-economic status etc. are equated as they are at the start of the investigation, these environmental factors are deemed to have been controlled, although the investigator may know nothing about how they varied during the preceding development period. This surely is decisive as virtually everything we are interested in under the heading of cognitive processes is the outcome of a long period of growth and maturation, from the prenatal stage onward. Adverse circumstances relating to health, nutrition, child rearing practices, mental stimulation, opportunities for interaction with the material and cultural environment, are all known to be relevant and the earlier their impact, the less reversible their effects appear to be.

The evidence suggests that for various functions there are critical maturational periods, during which physical well-being, mental stimulation, environmental interaction, have their optimum effect, and during which future deployment of potentialities can be permanently affected, either positively or negatively. Inability to take full advantage of later favourable opportunities (for example in the school) would be a consequence and cross-sectional environmental control would be particularly misleading in such cases.

5. In support of this general thesis, a longitudinal nutritional study conducted at the NIPR in Johannesburg is relevant. Successive generations of laboratory rats were reared on a protein deficient diet. Considerable deterioration occurred in their maze running ability and affective disturbances also made their appearance. When litters born from normal mothers were changed at birth to protein deficient lactating mothers and vice versa, both groups subsequently showed impairments, indicating that protein deficiency could exercise its effects both prenatally and during the neonate nursing period.

Electroencephalograms were abnormal and brain damage was confirmed in post mortems. Particularly significant was the fact that it took more than one generation to recover from the effects of chronic protein deficiency. Pups with protein deficient grandmothers, but born from mothers who had been weaned on to a normal diet, still continued to show a learning deficiency. (Cowley and Griesel, 1959, 1962, 1963, 1964, 1966; Griesel, 1965.)

Similar effects on the more complex brain of man could be even more enduring. In another investigation, again at NIPR, encephalograms were recorded from African infants suffering from acute kwashiorkor, a protein deficiency disease which tends to occur after weaning. Retardation in the normal pattern of brain rhythm development was noted, as well as a high frequency of focal disturbances in the temporal lobe. These findings suggest that protein deficiency may be responsible for persistent retardation of brain development and/or irreversible brain damage, at least in some cases. (Nelson, 1959, 1965). Jensen is aware of these and similar findings, but does not consider them relevant to the black-white intelligence test difference in the United States because "in negro communities where there is no evidence of poor nutrition, the average negro I.Q. is still about 1SD below the white mean." "When groups of Negro children with I.Q.'s below the general Negro average have been studied for nutritional status, no signs of malnutrition have been found." Whether or not they suffered from malnutrition at a much earlier and vulnerable stage one cannot tell from this kind of investigation, which aptly illustrates the inadequacy of the cross-sectional approach. Jensen discounts a longitudinal investigation by a team from Columbia (Harrell et al., 1956) which administered various combinations of vitamins to expectant mothers and right through the nursing period. A control group was given a placebo of inert tablets. One group of participants was drawn from the lowest socio-economic stratum in Norfolk, Virginia and 80% of the group was Negro. The other group were Kentucky rural families of equally low socio-economic status, but mostly of old American stock. When the offspring of the participating mothers were tested at ages 3 and 4, the Norfolk group showed various gains depending on the type of supplement, the optimum gain, involving the Vitamin B complex treatment, being 8.1 I.Q. points. The Kentucky group, who were generally able to supplement their diet with what they produced in their own gardens, showed no significant gain. The mean I.Q. of the two groups after treatment turned out to be the same. Without the nutritional therapy the largely negro town group would presumably have been 8 I.Q. points below the white country group.

Jensen considers this study to be inconclusive "as to whether any lasting effects on I.Q. were derived from the dietary supplement during pregnancy" because both the treatment *and the placebo groups* suffered a decline of about 3 I.Q. points between the ages of 3 and 4. This is a strange argument, besides being irrelevant. The nutritional gain is just as liable to erosion during early childhood as the I.Q. considered as a whole and the fact that both the experimental and control groups were similarly affected, presumably by their cultural milieu, proves this.

6. There are two further points made by Jensen which require comment:

a. Jensen discounts the effect of poor motivation on the test performance of blacks, claiming that there is no consistent evidence that they are less well motivated than other groups toward being tested. This may well be so, and fits in with my own experience with African subjects. What may occur, however, is a kind of affective blockage, perhaps due to overkeenness to do well, or to an anxiety reaction in a critical situation. A paper presented at the recent cross-cultural measurement conference held at Istanbul showed that a test difference between a lower and higher SES Group disappeared when the test situation was made less threatening to the former. (Gitmez, A. S., 1971.)

An experiment on the measurement of a differential threshold for brightness in African students, reported at the same conference, likewise illustrated the significance of attitudinal factors. The performance of the women students was consistently worse than that of the men, whilst no sex difference was found in a white student group. It is extremely unlikely that a real difference in visual discriminative capacity exists between sexes, nor was there any noticeable difference in motivation. The explanation would seem to lie in a lesser adaptability on the part of the black African women to the test situation. (Poortinga, 1971.) The operation of some similar process in the case of negroes, in view of their position as a minority group, subject to discrimination and disparaging attitudes, cannot be excluded.

b. Lastly, there is Jensen's statement that negroes put up a very much inferior performance to whites in psychomotor tests, such as rotor pursuit or two-hand co-ordination.

Learning experiments were conducted at NIPR involving this psychomotor function, in which race and sex of tester, intelligence, age, education, industrial experience, previous experience of performing similar tests, motivation and ethnic group were all controlled in a complex design. Though Jensen believes this function to have "a very high heritability," it was shown that a number of environmental factors significantly affected performance, and there was a clear implication that those with the closer and earlier association with Western culture learned more rapidly and achieved a better end performance. (Biesheuvel, 1963.)

7. I believe that Jensen has failed to establish a valid case in support of the hypothesis he has put forward. It is not possible to test this hypothesis by means of the type of cross-cultural or cross-sectional group comparisons, or the correlational studies that are usually undertaken. I consider that the establishment of adequate controls for representative samples is impracticable. Instead it is recommended that the problem be attacked by means of intragroup longitudinal studies in which we attempt to determine the limits of modifiability of behaviour in relation to a number of factors, varied both singly and in various combinations. This type of research is tedious, costly, and unlikely to yield conclusive answers for some time to come.

Either one must accept these conditions, or leave the problem alone. Meanwhile, the scientific evidence available at this stage on the genetic determination of race differences does not justify categorical statements which could have a major impact both on public policy and on race relations.

NOTES

1. The reader who is not familiar with Prof. Jensen's argument is referred to his principal article in the *Harvard Educational Review*, 1969, 39, 1-123: "How much can we boost I.Q. and scholastic achievement?"

REFERENCES

1. Biesheuvel, S. (1949). Psychological tests and their application to non-European peoples. In: *The Yearbook of Education*, Ch. IV. London, Evans.
2. Biesheuvel, S. (1952). The nation's intelligence and its measurement. *S. Afr. J. Sci.*, 49, 3-4.
3. Biesheuvel, S. (1963). The growth of abilities and character. *S. Afr. J. Sci.*, 59, 375-394.
4. Bühler, C. (1936). *From Birth to Maturity*. London, Kegan Paul.
5. Burt, Sir Cyril (1946). *Intelligence and Fertility*. London, Hamish Hamilton for The Eugenic Society.
6. Burt, Sir Cyril (1950). The trend of Scottish intelligence. *Br. J. educ. Psychol.*, 20, 1, 55-61.
7. Burt, Sir Cyril (1958). The inheritance of mental ability. *Am. Psychol.*, 13, 1-15.
8. Cattell, R. B. (1950). The fate of national intelligence—test of a thirteen year prediction. *Eugen. Rev.*, 42, 3, 136-148.
9. Coleman, J. S. et al. (1966). *Equality of Educational Opportunities*. Washington, U.S. Department of Health, Education and Welfare.
10. Cowley, J. J. and R. D. Griesel (1959). Some effects of a low-protein diet on a first filial generation of white rats. *J. genet. Psychol.*, 95, 187-201.
11. Cowley, J. J. and R. D. Griesel (1962). Pre- and post-natal effects of a low-protein diet on the behaviour of the white rat. *Psychol. Afr.*, 9, 216-225.
12. Cowley, J. J. and R. D. Griesel (1963). The development of second-generation low-protein rats. *J. genet. Psychol.*, 103, 233-242.
13. Cowley, J. J. and R. D. Griesel (1964). Low protein diet and emotionality in the albino rat. *J. genet. Psychol.*, 104, 89-98.
14. Cowley, J. J. and R. D. Griesel (1966). The effect of rehabilitating first and second generation low protein rats on growth and behaviour. *Anim. Behav.*, 14, 506-517.
15. Cowley, J. J. and R. D. Griesel (1965). The electroencephalogram in low protein rats. *Psychol. Afr.*, 11, 14-19.
16. Gitmez, A. S. (1971). Instructions as determinants of performance. *Paper read at Conference on Cultural Factors in Mental Test Development, Application and Interpretation, sponsored by the NATO Advisory Group on Human Factors and the Turkish Scientific and Technical Research Council*, Istanbul, July.
17. Harrell, R. F., Woodyard, E. R. and A. I. Gates (1956). The influence of vitamin supplementation on the diets of pregnant and lactating women on the intelligence of their offspring. *Metabolism*, 5, 555-562.
18. Kagan, J. (1968). On cultural deprivation, pp. 211-265. In: Glass, D. C., ed. *Environmental Influences. Proceedings of the Conference.* New York, Rockefeller University Press and Russell Sage Foundation.
19. Nelson, G. K. (1959). The electroencephalogram in kwashiorkor. *Electroenceph. clin. Neurophysiol.*, 11, 1, 73-84.
20. Nelson, G. K. (1965). Electroencephalographic studies in sequelae of

kwashiorkor and other diseases in Africans. *Proceedings of the Central African Science Medical Congress.* Oxford, Pergamon Press.

21. Poortinga, Y. H. (1971). Cross-cultural comparison of maximum performance tests: Some methodological aspects and some experiments with simple auditory and visual stimuli. *Psychol. Afr., Monogr. Supple.* No. 6.

22. Skeels, H. M. and H. B. Dye (1939). A study of the effects of differential stimulation on mentally retarded children. *Proceedings of the American Association of Mental Deficiencies.*

23. Thompson, Sir G. H. (1950). Intelligence and Fertility. *Eugen. Rev.,* 41, 4, 163–170.

24. Vernon, P. E. (1950). Psychological studies of the mental quality of the population. *Br. J. educ. Psychol.,* 20, 1, 35–42.

8

AN AFFLUENT SOCIETY'S EXCUSES FOR INEQUALITY: DEVELOPMENTAL, ECONOMIC, AND EDUCATIONAL

Edmund W. Gordon
with Derek Green

Those of us who are committed to the pedagogical enterprise note with interest, and often frustration, the recurring themes that challenge the conduct and advancement of our undertaking. Unlike the historian or sociologist, who might view these themes with interest but with some detachment, we are called upon to re-examine, clarify, and perhaps justify the presuppositions, methods, and goals that provide the framework within which education and development are carried on. Indeed this perhaps is as it should be, in view of the ambivalence with which these concerns are treated by a society that, on the one hand appears to value the perceived outcomes of the educational process, while on the other is often reluctant to invest the resources necessary to improve it, particularly when benefits seem likely to accrue to those who are on the lower end of the ethnic and socio-economic status scales.

Recent publications by several writers have reintroduced no-

From the *American Journal of Orthopsychiatry* 44 (1), January 1974, pp. 4–18. Copyright © 1974, the American Orthopsychiatric Association, Inc. Reprinted by permission.

tions that demand critical examination, particularly with reference
to the processes of education, schooling, and upward mobility of
people of low status in our society. These works have been the
basis of recent attempts to use educational and behavioral science
data to support the assertion that schooling can make little difference in the efforts of low-status people—Blacks, Chicanos, Native Americans, Puerto Ricans, and poverty stricken whites—to
achieve equality or a fair chance at survival. Two primary lines of
argument have been advanced:

1. It is asserted that some ethnic groups or races are genetically
inferior to others and thus are incapable of benefiting from schooling to the same extent as are others. Among the scholars whose
work has been used to support this position are Eysenck, Herrnstein, Jensen, and Shockley.

2. It is asserted that schools make little difference and are not
effective forces in changing the life chances of the pupils who
pass through them. Among the scholars whose work has been used
to support this position are Coleman and Jencks.

In the debate that has emerged around these two issues, considerable energy has been directed at attacking the individuals
whose work has been used, and some have even objected to the
scientific study of the questions as being immoral or politically
dangerous. I want to disassociate myself from any of the arguments directed at limiting free research inquiry and serious discussion of the issues. I believe that the pursuit of knowledge and
discussion must be uncensored, and I shall not use this platform to
join the argument concerning the individuals or their motives.
However, there are differences among these scholars, and some
can be clearly identified as more democratic and humane in their
convictions than others. What is more important than how these
scholars feel and what may be their motives is what the media try
to tell us about the meaning of this work and what the society
decides to do about the problems at which their work is directed.

It should be of particular significance to readers of this Journal that those scholarly or not so scholarly pronouncements that support the racist convictions prevalent in the society get a better press than those that do not. Statements and findings that support our preference not to spend money on the poor or to help low-status minorities are given prominence, while findings that could lend support to more humanistic developmental interventions somehow seem to be ignored.

For example, when Jensen's work was being published by the Harvard Educational Review and picked up by the press all across this country, there were already major works on the subject that had been ignored. About a year and a half prior to the attention given Jensen's speculations, Margaret Mead and several equally distinguished scholars published, through the Columbia University Press, the proceedings of the American Association for the Advancement of Science Symposium on Science and the Concept Race. Neither the minority press nor the so-called liberal white press ran major stories on that contribution to scientific understanding. Could that work have been ignored because it did not come to the popular conclusion that blacks are genetically inferior to whites? And why was that work not highlighted when the press picked up Jensen's work, even if Jensen was not a meticulous enough scholar to have included it and similar works in his own review of existing research on the subject?

In 1972, Arthur R. Jensen's book, *Genetics and Education*[12] was published both by Methuen in London and Harper & Row in the United States. It is the first of a series of three volumes, the second of which has recently become available,[13] with a third volume to be published shortly. In *Genetics and Education*, the author has collected a series of articles together with a preface that chronicles the events that led up to the writing and publication in the Harvard Educational Review of the article, "How Much Can We Boost IQ and Scholastic Achievement," and also documents the reactions, both academic and political, that its publication provoked. This article, with some minor corrections, forms the basis and perhaps *raison d'être* of the book.

The republication of this article in book form indicates to some degree the importance it has assumed, and will serve to broaden the audience already reached through the Harvard Educational Review publication. These factors—together with the continuing debate it has fostered, and the subsequent contributions of other scholars, which seem to lend support to Jensen's views—make further discussion appropriate and necessary.

Jensen, from an examination of the evidence for the success of compensatory education programs for the disadvantaged, concludes that such programs have failed, the measure of their failure being the extent to which they have been able to boost for any appreciable length of time the IQs of the participating students. From this examination he goes on to theorize that the reason for the ineffectiveness of such programs lies in the total environmentalist approach to the problem of IQ differences. Jensen advocates that we examine the possibility of the genetic determination of such differences, and offers evidence from a number of studies to support the view that a large portion of IQ variability, perhaps as much as 80%, can be accounted for by genetic factors. From this line of argument, the author suggests that the differences consistently found between groups (*e.g.*, the fifteen point difference between the mean IQ of whites and the mean IQ of blacks) may in fact be genetically based and that attempts to decrease these differences may necessitate the employment of biological techniques rather than those of psychology or education.

Differences in IQ scores between social or ethnic groups may indicate different patterns of ability, and Jensen has, from his own researches, identified two levels of learning that appear to be differentially associated with class differences among children. Level I ability (learning through association) is found more frequently among low-SES children (including most members of certain ethnic minorities), while children from high-SES families (largely white) are endowed with Level II ability, which permits learning through conceptualization and is highly correlated with IQ.

Jensen discusses the educational implications of this theory and indicates possible teaching strategies and educational emphases that take these into consideration. Among his recommendations are the following:

1. Educators should teach skills directly to Level I learners, rather than attempt to increase overall cognitive development.

2. IQ tests should be deemphasized as a method for determining instructional outcomes.

3. Research in education should be aimed toward the discovery and implementation of teaching methods based on a knowledge of the pattern of functional ability which specific student groups possess.

The logic of these arguments for the customizing of learning experiences has been largely ignored in the responses to Jensen's claim that the patterns themselves are genetically determined. When that debate has been adequately dealt with, if not resolved, the problems involved in matching individual learning patterns to individually prescribed learning experiences will still confront us. Hopefully these problems will not have to wait for the nature-nurture controversy to be settled.

In the second of Jensen's three volume set, *Educability and Group Differences*, he repeats the earlier theses and presents a more detailed account of the issues and evidence concerning "race differences in intelligence." Without retreating from his earlier conclusions, Jensen treats the issues with greater precision, and in his elaborations leaves considerably less room for distortions or exaggerated misapplications of his position. His central thesis as reflected in this work is that individuals and groups differ along a number of physical and behavioral dimensions, including intellectual ability and mental function. After review of most of the relevant research, he is convinced that environmental and genetic factors are involved in the average disparity between blacks and whites in the United States on measures of intelligence and educability. Of that disparity, represented by a mean score for blacks that is about fifteen points lower than the mean score for whites, between 50% and 75% of the difference appears to be best accounted for by genetic factors, with the remainder attributed to environmental factors and their interaction with the genetic differences.

This latest work reflects the seriousness with which Jensen has approached the positions of some of his critics. Except for the more polemical arguments advanced against him, he addresses most of the issues around which his position has been challenged. He discusses issues related to within and between group heritability, equating for socioeconomic variables, motivation, culture-biased tests, teacher expectancy, environmental inequalities, health and nutrition, intelligence of "racial hybrids," and other issues. His treatment of these issues is variable but this is unimportant since they bear only tangential relations to the central issue. In a sense, it is unfortunate that concern with ethnic differences in the quality of intellectual function has claimed so much of Jensen's attention as well as that of the public. For although the author makes much of the consistent findings of difference and the weight of available evidence on the side of genetic explanations, when it comes to what we are to do for groups, and particularly for individuals, good educational programming, wholesome and purposeful developmental conditions, greater diversity of curricula and goals, and greater attention to the needs of individual learners are indicated.

These are Jensen's recommendations. They are also the hallmark of effective pedagogy. But Jensen is concerned with more. He believes that to generate effective educational treatments we must first generate better knowledge of the mechanisms of effective learning. He sees the disparity in intellectual function and educational achievement between blacks and whites as a major national problem to which simple notions of equalizing educational opportunity are insufficient. He sees his work in support of concepts of group and individual differences (genetically based) as providing the impetus for greater attention being given to diversity of educational opportunity. To the extent that such diversity is not seen as placing (or is not utilized to place) arbitrary limits on the options available to learners because of ethnic group or social class from which they come, the concept can provide a progressive force in education.

On the whole, Eysenck's *Race, Intelligence and Education*[6] can be taken as a more simply written version of Jensen's work. However, Eysenck deals much more adequately with the concept of race, and places the hereditarian view in a more scientific perspective. It is advanced as one of two major hypotheses put forward to account for certain observed conditions, and as the one that he believes the "facts" favor at the present time. He goes beyond Jensen's earlier work in providing substantial evidence to support his position, nevertheless continually cautioning his readers that hypotheses are not proofs. This concern for relating the issues at hand to the ways of science is one of the distinctive features of the work. Eysenck pays particular attention to the process of theorizing and the elimination of rival hypotheses, arguing quite soundly that those critics who maintain that circumstantial evidence is insufficient to support an hereditarian hypothesis regarding IQ differences, fail to acknowledge that this is consonant with the way in which science operates. Disparate pieces of evidence that can be assimilated into a particular theoretical framework do in fact lend support to it. This is especially true where competing hypotheses cannot adequately account for the evidence.

Eysenck challenges critics of this position to "account" for the fact that when whites and Negroes are matched on education, socioeconomic status, and living area, differences are only slightly reduced as far as IQ is concerned: or the even more damaging fact that higher-class Negroes, when compared with lower-class whites, are still inferior in IQ. In posing this question, he obviously does not deal with the argument that matching for education, SES, and living area in racist societies does not result in groups exposed to similar or equal conditions of life. Nor does he fail to avoid repeating the error that Jensen and most investigators have made when they have neglected to control for intergenerational effects of economic, ethnic, and social status.

In a second general theme, Eysenck deals with the practical application of scientific discoveries to educational practice. Effective programs, Eysenck argues, can be implemented only when relevant facts are known, and this can be accomplished only through unfettered and adequately supported research programs. In response to the expressed belief that if IQ is largely a matter of genes then all programs of education aimed at those with low abilities are inevitably doomed to failure, the author points to the oft cited example of phenylketonuria and indicates how a knowledge of the mechanism through which genetic action affects a condition can lead to effective environmental control. Thus he argues that an understanding of the way in which intelligence may be influenced by heredity is a prime requisite for any educational program geared toward helping individuals with low IQs.

Whereas Jensen emphasizes the importance of functional patterns, Eysenck speaks primarily to the importance of high IQ for education, especially higher education. Maintaining that the abilities associated with high intelligence are essential for higher academic success, he considers it unreasonable for any racial group to disregard the importance of IQ as a prerequisite to academic attainment. On this issue he states:

> It makes no sense to reject the very notion of such abilities as being important . . . and at the same time demand access to institutions closely geared to the view that such abilities are absolutely fundamental to successful study. . . . any lowering of

standards of admittance with respect to IQ would demonstrably
lead to a disastrous lowering of standards of competence. . . .

For this reason as well as others, policies aimed at providing proportionate racial representation in colleges and universities without regard for IQ are in his view misguided.

Although virtually all the evidence presented relating racial differences to IQ differences is drawn from studies involving black
samples, Eysenck emphasizes that the issue is not simply one of
black versus white. He points out that the tested intelligence of
the Irish population is quite similar to that of the black American
population. (Interestingly the author suggests some possible mechanisms through which these "deficient" populations might have
emerged as non-random selections from a larger group. It is con-
jectured that selective migration of high IQ members of the Irish
population may have left a gene pool for low IQ in the home
country, while he claims it may have been Africans of low intellectual ability who were shipped as slaves. Eysenck also presents
an argument similar to that advanced by informed students of
Afro-American history, which holds that if the alleged low quality of inherited aspects of intellectual function are the culpable
agents in the performance of blacks in the United States, it may
be a function of genocide practiced against the most able and
rebellious slaves rather than the capture of the less able.) Speaking
again to the necessity for dealing with the issue in a non-racial
fashion Eysenck writes:

> . . . even if there were no Negroes or other minority groups in a
> country, there would still be bright and dull children, and the
> problems posed by their existence would be equally great, al-
> though the emotion invested would perhaps be less.

William Shockley,[19] Professor of Engineering Science at Stanford University, has asked us to consider, as "thinking exercise,"
the possibility of eugenic control to limit the production of such

individuals through a voluntary, remunerated sterilization program. Shockley, basing his arguments on the same data that Jensen used to determine the heritability of IQ arrives at the same conclusions, namely that IQ has a heritability of 80% and also that the average IQ difference between black and white populations in the United States is genetic in origin. This, together with the fact that those members of the population who are most deficient in IQ tend also to be more prolific breeders than those more well endowed genetically, raises the specter in Shockley's mind of a "down breeding" of the total population in intellectual ability. His fears for the continuation of society if this dysgenic trend is allowed to continue, are expressed in the following:

> With the advent of nuclear weapons, man has in effect reached the point of no return in the necessity to continue his intellectual evolution. Unless his collective mental ability can enable him reliably to predict consequences of his actions, it is possible that he may provoke his own extinction. . . .

Shockley leaves no doubt as to the source from which the main threat arises. For although, in theory, any voluntary sterilization program would include the genetically inferior of any race or class, he writes:

> Nature has color-coded groups of individuals so that statistically reliable predictions of their adaptability to intellectually rewarding and effective lives can easily be made and profitably be used by the pragmatic man in the street.

The criticisms of Jensen's position have come from a number of sources and have emphasized different aspects of his argument. The most general criticism comes from those who see in Jensen's work the recurring attempt to deal with the "nature-nurture" problem, which some see as a futile exercise based on a naive conception of the interplay between genetic and environmental factors in behavior.

Birch,[2] although writing in a context not directly related to the debate ensuing from Jensen's work, highlights this problem. (Indeed Birch's article antedates Jensen's and forms part of a collection of papers edited by Margaret Mead and others. This book represents the end products of a symposium held under the auspices of the American Association for the Advancement of Science to examine the concept of race as it is elucidated by scientific study.) Thus Birch argues that the nature-nurture controversy stems primarily from a confusion between the concepts "genetic" and "determined," and that while all aspects of an organism may be thought to be 100% genetic, they are not 100% determined. Phenotypic expression is the result of a continuous biochemical and physiological interaction of gene complex, cytoplasm, internal milieu, and external environment throughout the life span of the organism. In as much as IQ is a phenotypic characteristic it is virtually meaningless to attempt to determine the relative proportions of environmental and genetic influences that contribute to its expression.

Theodosius Dobzhansky,[4] the eminent geneticist, has leveled criticism at several aspects of Jensen's thesis. Two of these bases for disagreement will be examined, first the limitations of the genetic-IQ studies used to support the heritability estimates, and secondly the limitations of the concept of "heritability" itself. The data on which the determination of the heritability of IQ is based are derived from studies that compare the IQs of identical twins reared together and apart (this provides the most direct evidence on which the effects of environments are determined, since monozygous twins have identical genes). Other more indirect evidence is supplied by studies of fraternal twins, comparison of the IQs of adopted children with those of their biological and adoptive parents, and the relationship between the IQs of various generations within a family group. Dobzhansky indicates that, with respect to these studies, they predominantly concern Caucasian, middle-class samples, thus making questionable their applicability to other populations. Furthermore, "neither the twins nor siblings reared apart, nor the adopted children have been exposed to the full range of environments which occur in the societies in which they live." In effect, then, a true sampling of the effects of the environment has not been obtained. Dobzhansky emphasizes the several postulates concerning heritability:

1. Heritability is a property of a population and not an intrinsic property of a trait, in this instance, intelligence.

2. Heritability depends upon the extent to which genetic and environmental factors are uniform or heterogeneous.

3. The estimation of heritability between different populations is much more complex than that within populations.

4. Differences found in the average IQ scores between races and social classes, need not be genetically conditioned to the same extent as are the individual differences within groups.

On this last point Jensen is firmly criticized for invalidly using the heritability of IQ differences that are found within a particular population, and are thereby limited by the specific conditions prevailing in that population, to measure the heritability of population means.

Other scholars have similarly addressed themselves to the problems of the determination of heritability and its limited applicability. Hirsch[10] writes:

> Such measurement naturally requires a perfectly balanced experimental design—all genotypes (or their trait-relevant components) measured against all environments (or their trait-relevant components). Few, if any, behavioral studies have been so thorough, and certainly not any human studies.
>
> Only when we consider the number of possible genotypes and the number of potential environments that may influence trait expression do we begin to realize how narrowly limited is the range of applicability for any obtained heritability measure (pp. 42–43).

One further aspect of the heritability question merits consideration here. This concerns the possible interactions between genotype and environment.

In determining the heritability of IQ, Jensen includes an estimate of the interaction of genetic and environmental factors but indicates that the contribution this interaction makes to the overall variability among IQ scores is rather insignificant. Goldstein[8] cautions however that such interactive effects need not always be insignificant, and points to recent advances in medical science to indicate the dramatic interactive effects that environments can exert on genetically determined physical disorders:

> The discovery of insulin, the isolation of vitamin D, the production of tuberculostatic drugs, the uncovering and control of phenylketonuria are all those exceptional environmental changes which will make this interaction term significant. They indicate that environments everywhere are not merely supportive of hereditary potentialities, but can, at times, reverse deleterious effects. The great achievements of mankind lie in making that interaction term significant. Indeed it could almost be a maxim for schools of education, psychology, public health and medicine: "Make that interaction significant" (p. 20).

Perhaps then Jensen may be too pessimistic in suggesting that differences in IQ if genetically determined will not be minimized via manipulations of the environment.

Another issue concerning ethnicity and genetics around which confusion seems to persist in all of these works is the interchangeable use of the same ethnic group labels to refer to biological race as well as to social race. Fried sheds interesting light on this issue. According to Fried,[7] the humanistic intentions of most investigators who have studied intelligence, ability, or achievement endowment among different races do not alter the fact that their studies have invariably been based on racial constructs that are destructive and antisocial, in addition to being unscientific. In almost all studies the so-called racial background of individual respondents and respondent populations has been derived in ways that show no resemblance to means used by genetic specialists. In those few cases where any information is given about criteria of assortment, one usually finds that skin color has been the sole or dominant criterion, and that as measured by the eye. In other words, the actual genetic background of the subjects is uncontrolled. The classic study by Shuey[20] on the testing of Negro intelligence illustrates the racist implications of investigations conceived in this mode. In fact, there is as yet no study on a so-called racial sample that adequately links intelligence, potential ability, educability, or even achievement to a specifiable set of genetic coordinates associated with an aggregate larger than a family line or perhaps lineage.

The most useful studies linking race and certain specified socially valued traits make no pretense of dealing with biogenetic race: rather, they openly work with categories of "social race." A case in point is the massive survey by Coleman,[3] which focused on psychological reactions of being identified and identifying oneself as a Negro in the United States. If race is to be treated as a sociocultural construct, it is important to get the individual's views on his own identification and the identification he applies to others. However, if race is to be treated as a biological construct, the lay individual's views of his own racial identity or that of anyone else are unqualified and immaterial.

In September 1971 an article appeared in *The Atlantic* magazine, titled simply, "IQ," under the authorship of Richard Herrnstein,[9] professor of psychology at Harvard University. In his extremely readable article, Professor Herrnstein describes the gropings of philosophers and scientists for a reasonable definition of the concept of intelligence and for ways of measuring this attribute. The triumph scored by Binet in Paris in developing the first usable intelligence test, and the subsequent rapid spread of the techniques and instruments throughout the Western world, are described. The author deals with many of the problems often encountered in discussions of intelligence and its measurement. In treating the controversy surrounding the nature of intelligence he concludes:

> Even at best, however, data and analysis can take us only so far in saying what intelligence is. At some point, it becomes a matter of definition . . . at the bottom subjective judgement must decide what we want the measure of intelligence to measure.

With regard to the predictive validity of IQ scores, Herrnstein is also careful to indicate the cautions that must be observed both in dealing with evidence derived correlationally, and also the other factors that must be taken into account as contributing to, say, school success or other outcomes. Some minimum IQ, Herrnstein argues, seems to be prerequisite for a large number of successes, but it is never the sole requirement for any practical endeavor.

In his treatment of the observed IQ score differences between social classes, Herrnstein writes:

> It is one thing to note the correlation between social class and IQ but something else to explain, or even interpret it. . . . Since a family's social standing depends partly on the breadwinner's livelihood, there might be further correlation between IQ and occupation.

Further support for the high predictive power of IQ scores is drawn from Terman's Genetic Studies of Genius. In this study, a sample of over 1,500 California children with an average IQ of around 150 was followed over the course of some 30 years. High IQ was found to correlate with a host of factors, including amount of schooling, high status occupations, and high income. To put it in Herrnstein's words:

An IQ test can be given in an hour or two to a child and from this infinitesimally small sample of his output, deeply important predictions follow—about schoolwork, occupation, income, satisfaction with life and even life expectancy.

"This infinitesimally small sample" of output does indeed seem to be extremely powerful. What is its source? Why do some people have more than others and can we manipulate the quantities within individuals? Herrnstein addresses himself to these questions indirectly by going into a considerably detailed discussion of Jensen's work on the heritability of intelligence, particularly the methods and the studies from which the heritability was obtained. He concludes that little doubt exists regarding the 80% genetic contribution to intelligence that Jensen found among North American and Western European whites. Concerning whether the differences found between the average IQs of whites and blacks in the United States is of genetic origin, Herrnstein believes that a neutral commentator would have to concede that, given the present state of knowledge, the case is not settled. In subsequent discussions, the author does not deal with racial differences but applies the 80% heritability estimate to the total US population and speculates on the possible social and political implications of the heritability of IQ differences as it applies to different social classes.

Given the possibility that differences in mental abilities are inherited, that success requires these abilities, and that earnings and prestige depend upon success, Herrnstein considers the possibility that the heritability of intelligence may tend to increase the stratification of society, precipitating, as he puts it, "a low-capacity (intellectually and otherwise) residue . . . most likely to be born to parents who have similarly failed." Such a situation is almost bound to arise where the environment presents less obstacles to the development of intelligence, thus increasing its heritability, and where social mobility becomes more possible as traditional barriers are toppled. In effect, then, "by removing arbitrary bar-

riers between classes, society has encouraged the creation of biological barriers." This holds equally well for IQ as for the other
traits that might contribute to success.

In Herrnstein's view, the course is well set. Attempts to invert
or equalize the income structure as it presently exists are futile
since these would merely create a channeling of high intelligence
individuals into the now newly "desirable" occupations on the
one hand, or introduce the peril of critical shortages in professions
that are crucial to the conduct of society and require high intelligence. Herrnstein asks what is to be the lot of those who are "unable to master the common occupations and cannot compete for
success and achievement?"

The question of unequal distribution of the resources of society,
which Herrnstein sees as being largely determined by the unequal
distribution of IQ, is again brought into focus by Jencks,[11] in his
book, *Inequality*. Here Jencks attempts to demonstrate, based on
his reanalysis of a variety of secondary data, that the process of
schooling has little effect upon the way in which income is distributed in the society. The author's basic concern is to demonstrate that if society really is concerned with the equalization of
income or economic status, it must go about it more or less directly rather than by attempting to do so by manipulating mar-
ginal institutions such as schools.

Considering the variety of factors that might contribute to differences in occupational statuses of males, Jencks concludes that,
at the most, such factors as amount of schooling, family background and test scores, account for only about one half. The other
50% of the variation must be accounted for by factors other than
those commonly considered to be most important or perhaps
those for which we have no measures.

These "other factors" are merely guessed at by Jencks. He suggests that personality variables and luck may play a part in determining occupational status. A consideration of the other pos-

sible determinants of success is also relevant to the argument presented by Herrnstein, for although he suggests that IQ is the paramount determinant of occupational status he recognizes that:

> . . . there may be other inherited traits that differ among people and contribute to their success in life. . . . The meritocracy concerns not just inherited intelligence, but all inherited traits affecting success, whether or not we know of their importance or have tests to gauge them.

In order for Herrnstein's hypothesized caste system to evolve, it would be first necessary for the other traits contributing to success to be heritable. Secondly they should be correlated with IQ within each individual and preferably increase in heritability at about the same rate as IQ. The likelihood of this seems rather remote. If Jencks's analysis is reasonably accurate, it appears that at the present time substantial numbers of individuals who have similar test scores, family background, and schooling, will find themselves in occupations that are unequal in status, thus ensuring some amount of crossbreeding between individuals having different intellectual abilities.

But let us return to the problems of education and the value of schooling. The data of the several studies that Jencks and his associates have reanalyzed use intelligence and achievement tests scores as their primary indicators of competence. None of these studies is concerned with happiness and social usefulness as outcome dimensions. Jencks acknowledges some of the limitations of intelligence and achievement testing and dismisses the affective domain with a four-page chapter in which he concedes that he knows little about this area and has not given attention to it in his reanalysis. Now there are several problems here.

1. There is no question but that if we look at intelligence and achievement test scores for large numbers of pupils and try to relate them to the characteristics of schools as we usually measure

them, we find little variation that can be attributed to the impact of differences in the quality of schooling. This was one of the major findings from the Coleman study.[3] However, even Jencks concedes that Coleman's findings and the other available data did not include assessments of teacher-pupil and pupil-pupil interaction. These and other interactions we call process variables probably make for differences when status variables such as number of books, age of building, and expenditure per pupil do not. Additionally, since Jencks was looking for gross effects, one of Coleman's findings probably seems less important to him. Coleman reported that, for the most disadvantaged children and for black children, quality of school does make a difference in terms of achievement. In other words, differences in the quality and quantity of schooling in the USA seem to make little difference in your achievement scores unless you are poor or black. If you are both, it seems that schooling might make a powerful difference in your scores and your life chances.

2. Many educators believe that teaching and learning transactions deeply involve the affective (emotional) domain—one's feelings, sense of happiness, satisfaction, purpose, belonging, etc. It is these variables that are hardest to measure and are usually omitted from these studies either as inputs or outcomes. In fact, from the Coleman data, we see that a little measure, crudely conducted, of sense of power or environmental control, was more powerfully associated with achievement than any other variable studied save family background. Jencks did not study the affective and process variables, as input or output of the schools.

3. There appears to be considerable confounding or contaminating of data in the kind of analysis Jencks has used to arrive at the conclusion that schooling makes little difference. He concludes, for instance, that if "all elementary schools were equally effective, cognitive inequality among sixth graders would decline less than 3 percent." Now the data upon which this estimate is arrived at are the same data that reflect the problems referred to

earlier. In addition, Jencks uses the term "equally effective." It would be interesting to know what direction his argument would take if we used my term, *maximally effective*. Schooling as a part of the process by which we facilitate development in our children must—though it never has—define its goals in terms of maximal effectiveness. This involves us in the process of predicting not what will happen if the child and the school continue to function at their present levels, but what happens if we put the two in orbit and free them from the restraints that probably are limiting both.

We must remember that Jencks was not concerned with what schooling can do to develop people, he was particularly concerned with what schooling can do to increase and equalize economic status. These are related but quite different processes. It is to the process of human development and learning that I have devoted my professional career. An examination of some of the factors that may complicate those processes in low-income and minority groups may help us to put into proper perspective the conflicting opinions we hear concerning the influence of schooling.

For almost 25 years, hanging near my desk has been a print of a beautiful Thomas Hart Benton drawing, which he aptly titled, "Instruction." This sensitive drawing shows an old black man, with his tattered books, papers, clothing, and surroundings, working at the task of helping a young black child to learn. It symbolizes an endeavor to which a host of persons, before and after this simple soul, have devoted their efforts—some enthusiastically and with skill, others reluctantly and with incompetence. Would that the problems of teaching and learning were as simple as the spirit Benton captures in this drawing. Too many black children fail to master the traditional learning tasks of schooling. Too many Puerto Rican, Chicano, and Native American (American Indian) children are failed in our schools. Children from minority groups

and low income families are overrepresented among our schools'
failures. Why?

The problems involved in the equalization of educational
achievement patterns across economic and ethnic groups continue
to defy solution. The attempts at describing, evaluating, and interpreting these problems and the efforts directed at their solution
are frequently confusing. Over the past several years a variety of
special programs have been developed to improve the educational
achievement of disadvantaged children. These programs have
spanned a range from preschool through college; their special
emphases have included special guidance services to experimental
curriculums; they have grown from a few special efforts in the
great cities to nation-wide, federally sponsored programs supported by the Office of Economic Opportunity and the Office of
Education under the Elementary and Secondary Education Act.
Thousands of special programs have been spawned. Ten billion
and more dollars have been spent over the past several years. Yet
despite all of this activity, there is little evidence to suggest that
we have come close to solving the problems of educating large
numbers of ethnic minority group and poor white children.

The relative lack of success of these efforts at upgrading academic achievement in the target populations has resulted in some
criticizing of the educational services provided, but has also resulted in a renewal of old arguments in support of the exploration
of differences in the level of intellectual function across ethnic
groups based on alleged inferior genetic traits in lower status
groups. Neither of the simplistic approaches to understanding the
problems or fixing the blame for our failure to make school
achievement independent of ethnic or social class is adequate.

The problems of educating black and other disadvantaged populations who have been accidentally or deliberately, but always,
systematically deprived of the opportunity for optimal development is far more complex. The problem of equalizing educational

achievement across groups with differential economic, political, and social status may confront us with contradictions that defy resolution. Adequate understanding and appropriate planning for an attack upon these problems will require that attention be directed to several issues. Among these are: (1) the problems related to differential patterns of intellectual and social function, as well as varying degrees of readiness in multivariant populations served by schools whose programs are too narrowly conceived and too inflexible to provide the variety of conditions for learning dictated by the characteristics of the children served; (2) the problems related to the conditions of children's bodies and the conditions of their lives that may render them incapable of optimal development and that may seriously interfere with adequate function; (3) the problems related to ethnic, cultural and political incongruencies between the schools and their staffs on the one hand, and the children and communities served on the other; and (4) the problems related to the public schools as social institutions that have never been required to assume responsibility for their failures and thus become accountable to the society and its specific members whom they serve.

DIFFERENTIAL CHARACTERISTICS
AND DIFFERENTIAL TREATMENTS

Despite the long history in education of concern with meeting the special needs of individual children and the highly respected status of differential psychology as a field of study, schools have made little progress in achieving a match between the developmental patterns, learning styles, and temperamental traits of learners and the educational experiences to which they are exposed. A great deal of attention has been given to differences in level of intellectual function. This is reflected in the heavy emphasis on intelligence testing and the placement, even "tracking" of pupils based on these tests. This tradition has emphasized quantitative measurement, classification, and prediction to the neglect of qualitative measurement, description, and prescription. These latter processes are clearly essential to the effective teaching of children who come to the schools with characteristics different from those of their teachers and the children with whom most teachers are accustomed. Our research data indicate wide variations in patterns of intellectual and social function across and within sub-populations. These variations in function within privileged populations may be less important because of a variety of environmental factors that support adequate development and learning. Among disadvantaged populations, where traditional forms of environmental support may be absent, attention to differential learning patterns may be crucial to adequate development.

Some workers in the field have given considerable attention to differential patterns of language structure and usage. For example, importance has been attached to "black English" or the dialects of black peoples as possibly contributing to low academic achievement. These indigenous language forms are viewed by some as obstacles to be overcome. Others view them as behavioral phenomena to be utilized in learning. Workers holding the former position stress the teaching of "standard English" or English as a second language. Those holding the latter view emphasize the adaptation of learning experiences and materials to the indigenous language of the child. The debate is probably not important except as it may reflect respect or lack of respect for the language behavior of the learner. What may be more important than the fact of language difference is the role that language behavior plays in the learning behavior of the specific child. To understand and utilize that relationship in the education of the child requires more than teaching him how to translate "black English" into standard English and requires more than making him a more proficient utilizer of the indigenous language.

Understanding the role of one set of behaviors as facilitators of more comprehensive behaviors is at the heart of differential analysis of learner characteristics and differential design of learning experiences. Schooling for black children, indeed for all children in our schools, comes nowhere near to meeting these implied criteria. Assessment technology has not seriously engaged the problem. Curriculum specialists are just beginning to, in some of the work in individually prescribed learning.

LIFE CONDITIONS: HEALTH, NUTRITION, AND LEARNING

Contemporary research provides evidence of a variety of behaviors and conditions that are encountered in children from economically disadvantaged backgrounds with sufficient frequency to justify the conclusion that they are either induced by or nurtured by conditions of poverty. The excellent studies by Knobloch and Pasamanick[14, 18] of the relationships between health status and school adjustment in low-income Negro children in Baltimore, by Lashof [15] of health status and services in Chicago's South Side, and by Birch[1] of the health status of children from indigent families in the Caribbean area, provide mounting evidence in support of the hypothesis that there exists a continuum of reproductive errors and developmental defects significantly influenced by level of income. According to this hypothesis, the incidence of reproductive error or developmental defect occurs along a continuum in which the incidence of error or defect is greatest in the population for which medical, nutritional, and child care are poorest and the incidence least where such care is best.

These studies point clearly to the facts that: (1) nutritional resources for the mother-to-be, the pregnant mother and fetus, and the child she bears are inadequate; (2) medical care—prenatal, obstetrical, and postnatal—is generally poor; (3) the incidence of subtle to more severe neurologic defects is relatively high in low-income children; (4) case finding, lacking systematic procedures, is hit or miss, leaving the child not only handicapped by the disorder but frequently with no official awareness that the condition exists; and (5) family resources and sophistication are insufficient to provide the remedial or compensatory supports that can spell the difference between handicap and competent function.

These health-related conditions are thought to have important implications for school and general social adjustment. We know that impaired health or organic dysfunction influences school attendance, learning efficiency, developmental rate, personality development, etc. Pasamanick[17] attributes a substantial portion of the behavior disorders noted in this population to the high incidence of subtle neurologic disorders. Several authors relate a variety of specific learning disabilities to mild to severe neurologic abnormalities in children. Clearly, adequacy of health status and adequacy of health care in our society are influenced by adequacy of income, leading to the obvious conclusion that poverty results in a number of conditions directly referrable to health and indirectly to development in general, including educational development.

CULTURAL, ETHNIC, AND POLITICAL INCONGRUENCIES

Ethnic and economic integration in education appeared for a brief while to be a possible solution to underachievement in lower-status children. The data seem to indicate that academic achievement for black children improves when they are educated in middle-class and predominantly white schools. It is not at all clear that ethnic mix makes the difference. However, the evidence overwhelmingly supports an association between separation by economic group and school achievement with low economic status being associated with low school achievement. Consistently, poor children attending school in poor neighborhoods tend to show low level school achievement.

Before-and-after studies of desegregated schools have also tended to show that achievement levels rise with desegregation, although the exact interplay of reactions leading to this result has not yet been conclusively defined. For example, the process of desegregation may, by improving teacher morale or bringing about other changed conditions, result in an overall increase in the quality of education throughout the system. There have been a number of studies examining the possible relationship of integration (along racial or status group lines) and achievement, and the overall results of these efforts appear to demonstrate that children from lower-status groups attending schools where pupils from higher-status families are in the majority attain improved achievement level, with no significant lowering of achievement for the higher-status group. However when children from higher-status groups are in the minority in the school, there tends not to be an improvement in the achievement of the lower-status group.

Although these findings are generally supported in mass data compiled from large-scale populations, studies of minority group performance under experimental conditions of ethnic mix suggest a need for caution in making similar observations for smaller populations and individual cases. From these findings it becomes clear that the impact of assigned status and perceived conditions of comparison (that is, the subjects' awareness of the norms against which their data will be evaluated) results in a quite varied pattern of performance on the part of the lower status group subjects. Thus, it may be dangerous to generalize that across-the-board economic ethnic and social class integration will automatically result in positive improvement for the lower-status group.

To further complicate the picture, a new renaissance in cultural nationalism among all disadvantaged ethnic minorities has brought into question our assumptions concerning ethnic integration and education. In a society that has alternately pushed ethnic separation or ethnic amalgamation and that has never truly accepted cultural and ethnic pluralism as its model, blacks, Chicanos, Puerto Ricans, and Native Americans are insisting that the traditional public school is guilty not only of intellectual and social but of cultural genocide of their children. For many members of these groups the problem in education for blacks is that they have been subjected to white education, which they see as destructive to black people. When one views this argument in the context of the current stage in the development of craft unionism in education, the position cannot be ignored. The conditions and status of professional workers in education are justly the concern of their unions but blacks increasingly view the union concern as being in conflict with their concern for their children's development. That in New York City the workers are predominantly white makes it easy for the conflict to be viewed as ethnic in origin unless one looks at the situation in Washington, D.C., where Negroes are heavily represented in the educational staff, but some of the problems between professionals and clients are no less present.

There are class and caste conflicts to which insufficient attention has been given in the organization and delivery of educational services. If cultural and ethnic identification are important components of the learning experience, to ignore or demean them is poor education. If curriculum and delivery systems do not take these factors into account, inefficient learning may be the result. One would hope that black education by black educators is not the only solution, yet we are being pressed to no longer ignore it as a possible solution.

Would that the problems ended even there. It may well be that what has surfaced as cultural nationalism may be only the wave crest of a more important issue. Public schools as social institutions have never been required to assume responsibility for their failures. They, nonetheless, eagerly accept credit for the successes of their students. This may be related in part to the functions that schools serve in modern societies. The noted anthropologist, Anthony Wallace,[22] has discussed the differential attention given to training in technique or skills education for morality, and the development of intellect in societies that are revolutionary, conservative, or reactionary. For more than one hundred years the United States has been a conservative society—liberal in its traditions but essentially conservative in its functions. Some of us fear that that conservatism has given way to a reactionary stance. According to Wallace, the conservative society places highest emphasis on training in techniques and skills, with secondary attention to morality (correct behavior), and least attention to the development of the intellect. Societies in the reactionary phase place greatest emphasis on morality (now defined as law and order), second emphasis on techniques and skills, and only slight or no attention to the development of intellect. He sees society in its revolutionary phase as placing greatest emphasis on morality (humanistic concerns), with second-level interest on the development of intellect, and the least attention given to training in technique. Schools may not have developed a tradition of accountability because techniques and skills may be the least difficult of the learning tasks to master, if the conditions for learning are right. For large numbers of children who have progressed in the mastery of technique, their status in the society has facilitated technique mastery. Those who have not mastered the skills, our society has been able to absorb into low-skill work and non-demanding life situations. But by the mid-20th Century, entry into the labor force and participation in the affairs of the society increasingly require skills and techniques mastery. Those who would move toward meaningful participation and the assertion of power are increasingly demanding that the schools be accountable not only for pupils' mastery of skills, but also for the nurturance of morality and the development of intellectuality. In fact, with the rapidly increasing demand for adaptability and trainability in those who are to advance in the labor force, Du Bois's[5] concern with the liberating arts and sciences (the development of intellect) moves to the fore. Yet we must remember that the schools are at present instruments of a conservative (possibly reactionary) society, but blacks, other minority groups, and poor people increasingly see revolution (radical change) as the only ultimate solution to the problems and conditions in which their lives are maintained. As such, their concern with schooling may more sharply focus on issues related to morality and intellectual development, broadly defined—concerns that the schools have never been competent to meet. If circumstance has converted these concerns to educational needs, the schools then, in their present form, are ill prepared to educate these young people whose ideals and goals should be revolutionary, not conservative, and certainly not reactionary.

But this does not mean that schooling cannot be effective in the development of young people. To insure that our schools effectively educate is one of our tasks. To reduce or eliminate economic inequality is a related but separate task. It is from the accidental or deliberate confusing of these tasks, along with the distortion of the meaning of possible genetically based differences in the intellectual functioning of ethnic groups, that the threat to adequate support for educational and other human welfare programs is perceived. Jencks is correct, we do not equalize income by making schooling equally available or equally effective for all people. We equalize income, if that is our goal, by redistributing income and by eliminating the opportunity to exploit the wealth producing labor of others and to hoard capital. But that does not mean that there are not good reasons for a democratic and humane society to make schooling equally available and optimally effective for all people. Similarly, Jensen is correct. People do differ individually and by groups (races, if you will). It is quite likely that his assertion that groups of people differ with respect to qualitative aspects of intellectual function will find further support. Even before Jensen's work gained prominence, Lesser,[16] Zigler,[21] and others were reporting data and advancing postulates indicating ethnic group and social class differences in the character of intellectual function. That genetic factors influence mental function and in part account for individual and group differences does not mean that schooling and other environmental conditions have no effect, nor does it mean that these differences are not useful. Rather, the fact of difference, no matter what the source, in the interest of human development requires *diversity* of facilitative treatments and *sufficiency* of the resources to deliver them.

REFERENCES

1. Birch, H. 1966. Research needs and opportunities in Latin America for studying deprivation in psychobiological development. *In* Deprivation in Psychobiological Development. Pan American Health Organization (WHO), Scientific Publication No. 134, Washington, D.C.
2. Birch, H. 1968. Boldness of judgment in behavioral genetics. *In* Science and the Concept of Race, M. Mead et al., eds. Columbia University Press, New York.
3. Coleman, J. et al. 1966. Equality of Educational Opportunity. U.S. Office of Education, Washington, D.C.
4. * Dobzhansky, T. 1973. Genetic Diversity and Human Equality. Basic Books, New York.
5. Du Bois, W. 1968. The Autobiography of W. E. B. Du Bois (1st ed.) International Publishers, New York.
6. * Eysenck, H. 1971. Race, Intelligence, and Education. Temple Smith, London.
7. Fried, M. 1968. The need to end the pseudoscientific investigation of race. *In* Science and the Concept of Race, M. Mead et al., eds. Columbia University Press, New York.
8. Goldstein, A. 1969. A flaw in Jensen's use of heritability data. ERIC/IRCD Bull. 5(4):5–7, 14.
9. * Herrnstein, R. 1971. I.Q. The Atlantic. Sept.: 43–58, 63–64.
10. Hirsch, J. 1968. Behavior-genetic analysis and the study of man. *In* Science and the Concept of Race, M. Mead et al., eds. Columbia University Press, New York.
11. * Jencks, C. et al. 1972. Inequality: a Reassessment of the Effect of Family and Schooling in America. Basic Books, New York.
12. * Jensen, A. 1972. Genetics and Education. Harper and Row, New York.
13. * Jensen, A. 1973. Educability and Group Differences. Harper and Row, New York.
14. Knobloch, H. and Pasamanick, B. 1959. Distribution of intellectual potential in an infant population. *In* Epidemiology of Mental Disorder, B. Pasamanick, ed. American Association for the Advancement of Science, Washington, D.C.
15. Lashof, J. 1965. Unpublished report to the Department of Public Health, City of Chicago.
16. Lesser, G. and Stodolsky, S. 1967. Learning patterns in the disadvantaged. Paper prepared for the Information Retrieval Center on the Disadvantaged. Teachers College, Columbia University, New York. (Apr.)
17. Pasamanick, B. 1956. The epidemiology of behavior disorders in child-

hood. Neurology and Psychiatry in Childhood. Res. Publ. Ass. Nerv. Ment. Dis. Williams and Wilkins, Baltimore.

18. Pasamanick, B. and Knobloch, H. 1958. The contribution of some organic factors to school retardation in Negro children. J. Negro Educ. 27:4–9.

19. Shockley, W. 1972. Phi Delta Kappa. Jan. (special supplement): 297–307.

20. Shuey, A. 1966. The Testing of Negro Intelligence (2nd ed.) Social Science Press, New York.

21. Zigler, E. 1966. Mental retardation: current issues and approaches. *In* Review of Child Development Research, vol. 2, Hoffman and Hoffman, eds. Russell Sage Foundation, New York.

22. Wallace, A. 1968. Schools in revolutionary and conservative societies. *In* Social and Cultural Foundations of Guidance. Holt, Rinehart and Winston, New York.

* These publications were reviewed within this work.

9

NATURE WITH NURTURE:
A REINTERPRETATION OF
THE EVIDENCE

Urie Bronfenbrenner

Although Jensen's (1969a, 1969b) argument claiming genetically-based race differences in intelligence has been repeatedly and forcefully attacked (e.g., Scarr-Salapatek, 1971a), his thesis that 80 percent of the variation in intelligence is determined by heredity has been generally accepted (e.g., Scarr-Salapatek, 1971b). Since Jensen takes this thesis as the foundation both for his argument for innate differences in ability between the races, and for his contention that intervention programs with disadvantaged groups have little hope of success, it becomes important, both from the point of view of science and of social policy, to examine the evidence and line of reasoning that underlie his initial thesis. Jensen's argument rests on inferences drawn primarily from three sets of data:

1. Studies of resemblance between identical twins reared apart.
2. Studies of resemblance between identical vs. fraternal twins reared in the same home.

This article is an extension and further elaboration of an earlier paper entitled "Is 80% of Intelligence Genetically Determined?" published in U. Bronfenbrenner, *Influences on Human Development*, Hinsdale, Ill., Dryden Press, 1972.

3. Studies of resemblance within families having own children vs. adopted children.

Identical twins reared apart. The findings for this group are generally regarded as making the strongest case for genetic influence primarily because of the striking similarities in abilities, temperament, and other characteristics shown by twins separated from each other early in life. The most important index of this similarity, because it can be interpreted in terms of the proportion of variation accounted for, is the *intraclass r.* First proposed by R. A. Fisher, this measure differs from the conventional correlation coefficient in being interpretable in percentage terms. The smaller the difference between the two members of a twin pair, the closer r_i will come to its maximal value of 1.00. In the four published studies of identical twins reared apart the interclass r's were as follows: .66 (Juel-Nielsen, 1964), .67[1] (Newman, Holzinger, and Freeman, 1937), .77 (Shields, 1962), and .87 (Burt, 1966). Taking .75 as an average figure, Jensen draws the following conclusion:

> Since MZ twins develop from a single fertilized ovum and thus have exactly the same genes, any difference between them must be due to nongenetic factors. And, if they are reared apart in uncorrelated environments, the difference between a perfect correlation (1.0) and the obtained correlation (.75) gives an estimate of the proportion of the variance in IQs attributable to environmental differences: $1.00 - 0.75 = 0.25$. Thus, 75 percent of the variance can be said to be due to genetic variation (this is the heritability) and 25 percent to environmental variation (Jensen, 1969a, p. 50).

The conclusion drawn by Jensen rests on two fundamental assumptions. The first is acknowledged in the foregoing passage by the short but critical qualifying phrase: "in uncorrelated environments." *This condition requires that there be no relation between the quality of the environment into which one twin is placed and that into which the other twin is placed.* Otherwise any psychological resemblance between the twins would be due not only to their identical genetic endowment but also to their similar environments both before and after separation. By the same token, any tendency to place twins in similar environments would reduce the environmental variation between them, and, hence, any corresponding intra-pair difference in ability, which is the only variance attributed to environment in Jensen's model. It is therefore a matter of considerable importance whether the stipulated condition of "uncorrelated environments" is actually met.

The second assumption is necessary if one is to generalize, as Jensen and others do, from findings derived from samples of twins to the general population. To make this generalization, *one must assume that the range of environments into which separated twins are placed is as great as that for unrelated children of the same sex and age.* For, if the settings into which separated twins go are in fact restricted to some segment of the total environment in which families are found, then the power of the environment to effect variation in abilities is also restricted in proportionate degree. Such environmental restriction would arise if there were some selection of foster families, for example, in terms of social status, educational resources, age of parents, family structure, or values and practices of child rearing. Under such circumstances, the possible contribution of differences in environment to variability among foster children (including separated twins) would necessarily be smaller than among children in the general population distributed across the full range of existing environments.

Although the two basic assumptions are theoretically independent, their relevance for the issue at stake can be summarized in a single principle: for identical twins reared apart, the intraclass r can be interpreted as the proportion of variance attributable to genetic influence for the general population, *if, and only if, the variability of environments into which twins are separated is as great as that for unrelated children of the same sex and age.*

To what extent does the foregoing assumption hold for the

samples on the basis of which Jensen and others draw their conclusions? The data most relevant to this issue come from the
first and, from a number of points of view, the most carefully
analyzed study of identical twins reared apart, that of Newman,
Holzinger, and Freeman (1937) conducted at the University of
Chicago. In their study, ratings of educational, social, and physical
environmental differences for each twin pair were made by five
judges. Although the reliability of ratings was "highly satisfactory" (.90 or above in each of the three areas), the majority of
the differences were very low. Intraclass r's cannot be computed
for these ratings, since they were published only in difference
form. The individual case reports, however, provided information
on the number of years of schooling for each twin. The intraclass
r for this variable was .55. Taken as a whole, these data indicate a
definite tendency for the members of a twin pair to be placed in
somewhat similar social, educational, and health settings. The consequences of this fact are emphasized by the original authors:

> These distributions [of differences] have a very important bear-
> ing on the comparisons which follow because the effect of each
> type of environment on the whole group of twins will not be so
> pronounced as if each pair had marked differences in environ-
> ment (Newman, Holzinger, and Freeman, 1937, p. 337).

It necessarily follows that the obtained intraclass r for the separated twins reflects not only the influence of identical genetic
endowment but also of some similarity of environment. The magnitude of this environmental component would be reflected by the
correlations between ratings of the environment and the child's
IQ. Unfortunately, neither such correlations nor the data necessary for calculating them are cited by Newman, Holzinger, and
Freeman, or any other investigator of identical twins reared apart.
Some indication of the magnitude of the relationship is provided,
however, by correlations reported in the Chicago study between
differences in IQ for each pair of identical twins and differences in

their social and educational milieus. The two coefficients were .51 and .79 respectively. Had the differences in the environment not been reduced by the tendency to place the separated twins in similar settings, the obtained values would presumably have been even higher. In the words of the original investigators, "Since the environmental difference was not great for a majority of the separated cases, its relative effect could have been much greater for twins all reared under widely different conditions" (p. 347).

The psychological significance of such correlations becomes more readily apparent in concrete form. For example, of the 19 pairs of separated twins in this study, there were 8 pairs who had the same number of years of school; the average IQ difference for this group was 1.45. The remaining 11 pairs differed in amount of schooling for an average of 5 years; the corresponding average difference in IQ points was 10.4. The greatest single pair-difference in schooling was 14 years with an IQ difference of 24 points. Since all of these are identical twins, these differences in score cannot be genetic in origin and are therefore the product of varying educational environments. Accordingly, Newman, Holzinger, and Freeman (1937) conclude from their data that "differences in education and social environment produce undeniable differences in intelligence" (p. 341).

Turning to the remaining studies, Juel-Nielsen (1965) unfortunately provides no quantitative data bearing on the issue of differences in environment among separated twins. Shields (1962), in his study of 44 identical twins reared apart, reports that 30 of them were "brought up in different branches of the same family" (p. 47). In addition, he points out:

> Large differences in social class do not often occur in the present material. While the social and cultural level of the branches of a family tend to be similar, the same is also generally true of adoptive parents who obtain children from the same Children's Home (Shields, p. 48).

Jensen gives special weight to the Burt study (1966), primarily because in this English sample there was no significant correlation between social class ratings of environments for separated twins. Again, the problem is one of restricted environmental variability, since over two-thirds of Burt's cases fell in the lowest two of five social class groups. Similarly, correlations between differences in IQ and rated "differences in cultural conditions" were relatively low (.26 for an individual intelligence test and .43 for a group test of intelligence). But neither the parents' social class nor their cultural background constitute the only or the most influential ecological factors that can both affect intellectual development and become the basis for environmental correlation. For example, in the Chicago study, differences in the level and quality of the child's own education were the most productive of differences in IQ ($r = .79$), and there was a clear correlation between the educational environments of the separated twins. This correlation represents a specific instance of the more general phenomenon of *selective placement* observed in the assignment of children to foster homes (Skodak and Skeels, 1949). The phenomenon is manifested in a relation between the characteristics of the child and his family and social background on the one hand, and, on the other, the characteristics of the foster home into which he was placed, particularly in terms of such variables as religion, ethnicity, family structure, and—above all—values and practices of child rearing. The selective placement is brought about by a variety of factors, including the initiative and sophistication of the child's parents and relatives, systematic differences in clientele served by different agencies (both in terms of families *from* and *to* which children are referred), and, in particular, the desire of the staff members, often mandated by agency policy, to achieve some kind of a match between the child's background and his foster home.

The phenomenon of selective placement not only produces a

correlation between the environments in which children of similar family backgrounds are placed, but also restricts significantly the range of these environments. Thus, in a comprehensive survey of the research literature on adoption both in the United States and Great Britain, Kellmer-Pringle (1966) reports "a surprising uniformity among adoptive parents" (p. 15). The implications of this fact for studies of identical twins reared apart has been pointed out by Fehr (1969):

> The selection of foster homes by agencies gives preference to families who have sufficient financial resources to adequately care for the child and who show signs of intellectual and emotional understanding of the child's needs and the problems of adoption. Consequently, separated MZ twins placed for adoption through a professional agency are placed in selective and relatively homogeneous home environments as compared to the diversity that would result from random placement (p. 575).[2]

It is significant that all of Burt's separated twins were apparently placed through professional agencies of the London County Council. According to available information (Kellmer-Pringle, 1966; Shields, 1962), the practices of English placement agencies are not dissimilar to those of the United States.

The importance of degree of environmental variation in influencing the correlation between identical twins reared apart, and hence the estimate of heritability based on this statistic, is revealed by the following examples:

a. Among 35 pairs of separated twins for whom information was available about the community in which they lived, the correlation in Binet IQ for those raised in the same town was .83; for those brought up in different towns, the figure was .67.

b. In another sample of 38 separated twins, tested with a combination of verbal and non-verbal intelligence scales, the correlation for those attending the same school in the same town was .87; for those attending schools in different towns, the coefficient was .66. In the same sample, separated twins raised by relatives showed a correlation of .82; for those brought up by unrelated persons, the coefficient was .63.

c. When the communities in the preceding sample were classified as similar vs. dissimilar on the basis of size and economic base (e.g. mining vs. agricultural), the correlation for separated twins living in similar communities was .86; for those residing in dissimilar localities the coefficient was .26.

d. In the Newman, Holzinger, and Freeman study, ratings are reported of the degree of similarity between the environments into which the twins were separated. When these ratings were divided at the median, the twins reared in the more similar environments showed a correlation of .91 between their IQ's; for those brought up in less similar environments, the coefficient was .42.

The foregoing examples by no means exhaust the environmental variables in terms of which selection can occur in the placement of separated twins. As a result, the possible contribution of environment to differences between separated twins is considerably less than it would be in a population of unrelated children.

In view of these facts, the correlation of .75 or higher between IQ's of identical twins reared apart cannot be interpreted as reflecting the proportion of variance attributable solely to heredity. There is no question that genetic factors play a significant role in the determination of intelligence. Witness the fact that the correlation in IQ between identical twins reared apart is greater than that for fraternal twins raised in the same home. But, for the reasons given, the conclusion that 70 to 80 percent of the variance in mental ability is due to heredity represents an inflated estimate.[3]

In summary, the data from studies of identical twins reared apart lead to the following conclusions relevant to our concern. First, contrary to the assumption made by Jensen and others, the environments of separated twins are not uncorrelated. Second, as evidenced by the influence of ecological factors in producing differences between identical twins reared apart, the presence of correlated environments for such twins could make a significant contribution to their similarity in IQ. Hence the intraclass r for separated identical twins reflects environmental as well as genetic variance. To obtain a true estimate of the proportion of variance attributable to genetic factors among twins reared apart, one would have to partial out the correlation between the average IQ for a pair of twins and the degree of similarity in all aspects of their environment affecting intellectual development. This partialing would clearly reduce the estimate below the 75 percent figure claimed by Jensen. Finally, even though the reduced figure might be valid for a population of identical twins reared apart, it would not be generalizable to the population of children at large because of the restricted range of environments into which identical twins are separated as compared with the possibilities existing for unrelated children of the same age and sex. The effect of this restriction is to reduce variance attributable to environment and increase the relative influence of genetic factors compared to what it would be in the general population. For all these reasons, the interpretation of the intraclass r for separated identical twins as representing the proportion of variance attributable to heredity among children in general is unwarranted. While, as we shall see, there can be no question of the substantial role of genetic factors in the development of intelligence, the conclusion that they account for as much as 75 to 80 percent of the variance cannot be sustained on the basis of the evidence.

Own vs. adopted children. Because they similarly focus on the critical factor of the separation of the child from his biological parents, we come next to evidence from studies of resemblance within families having own vs. adopted children. Taking as his point of departure the correlation in IQ between unrelated (i.e., adopted) children raised in the same home (median intraclass r from five studies is cited as .24), Jensen (1969a) argues as follows:

Now let us go to the other extreme and look at unrelated children reared together. They have no genetic inheritance in common, but they are reared in a common environment. Therefore the correlation between such children will reflect the environment . . . this correlation is 0.24. Thus, the proportion of IQ variance due to environment is .24; and the remainder, 1.00 − .24 = .76 is due to heredity. There is quite good agreement between the two estimates of heritability (pp. 50–51).

Once again, the conclusion is based on an untenable assumption, in this instance, rather glaring in character. Jensen's argument requires that any difference between two children reared in the same home be due only and entirely to differences in heredity and not at all to possible differences in treatment or experience at home, in school, in the neighborhood, or elsewhere. Clearly this assumption is unwarranted.

Jensen and his colleagues also lean heavily on the consistently higher magnitude of parent-child correlations for true vs. adoptive parents (Burks, 1928; Honzik, 1957; Lawrence, 1931; Leahy, 1935). Particular emphasis is placed on the widely cited conclusions of Honzik, based on an investigation conducted a decade earlier by Skodak and Skeels (1949). These investigators had carried out a longitudinal study with a sample of 100 children who had been placed in foster homes because of the psychological and social inadequacy of their parents. In their original study, Skodak and Skeels related the characteristics of true mothers and foster mothers to the intellectual level of the child, who had been separated from his true mother under six months of age. The correlations between the child's IQ and the IQ and educational level of his true mother rose gradually over successive testings from two to thirteen years reaching maxima of .44 and .32 respectively. The corresponding coefficients for foster mothers were essentially zero. On the basis of the correlational data, Honzik concluded that "the education of the parents per se is not an environmentally important factor" and that the results "reflect individual differences that are largely genetically determined" (p. 227).

Although Jensen cites the above correlations he fails to mention what is perhaps the most striking finding obtained by the original investigators and also mentioned by Honzik; namely, the average IQ of the children's true mothers was 86, whereas the mean IQ for their children was 106. Skodak and Skeels confronted this apparent contradiction posed by their data in the following terms.

> . . . it is possible to throw the weight of interpretation in the direction of either genetic or environmental determinants. If the former point of view is accepted, then the mother's mental level at the time of her examination is considered to reflect her fundamental genetic constitution, and ignores the effects of whatever environmental deprivations or advantages may have influenced her own mental development. Thus it would be assumed that the children of brighter mothers would in turn be brighter than the children of less capable mothers regardless of the type of foster home in which they were placed. The increasing correlation might be interpreted to support this point of view, since the occupational differences between foster parents are not large. It is, however, inconsistent with the evidence that the children's IQ's substantially exceed those of their mothers and that none of them are mentally defective even though a number of the mothers were institutional residents (p. 111).

In their effort to resolve the dilemma, the original investigators compared the characteristics of those foster homes in which children had shown significant gains in IQ over a ten-year period, and those in which the IQ had remained relatively constant. Neither the education nor the occupational background of the foster parents discriminated between the two sets of homes. Instead, two other critical factors emerged.

The first was selective placement. The children ending up in the "better" foster homes had true mothers with higher IQ's and more education. As the original investigators point out, such selective placement would have tended to produce correlations between the child's IQ and the IQ and education of his true mother; hence the observed significant relationships "cannot be attributed to genetic determinants alone" (Skodak and Skeels, 1949, p. 114).

Second, the "better" foster homes differed markedly from the others in the type of atmosphere and social interaction that took place within the family. This same difference was even more striking when all the foster homes as a group were contrasted with the family situation typical of the homes into which the children had been born. Skodak and Skeels describe the key elements as follows:

> There is considerable evidence for the position that as a group these children received maximal stimulation in infancy with optimum security and affection following placement at an average of three months of age. The quality and amount of this stimulation during early childhood seemed to have little relation to the foster family's educational and cultural status (p. 111).

In their conclusions, the original investigators weigh the relative importance of genetic vs. environmental factors in the development of this group of adopted children born of inadequate parents, and emphasize what they view as the major theoretical and practical implications of their findings:

> Judging from the trend of correlations between mother's and child's IQ's, one might conclude that a relationship exists which became increasingly apparent with age. This is complicated by the evidence of selective placement, yet without a parallel relationship between foster parent education and child IQ. This one set of figures must not be permitted to overshadow the more significant finding that the children are consistently and unmistakably superior to their natural parents and in fact, follow and improve upon the pattern of mental development found among own children in families like the foster families. . . .
>
> The intellectual level of the children has remained consistently higher than would have been predicted from the intellectual, educational, or socioeconomic level of the true parents, and is equal to or surpasses the mental level of own children in environments similar to those which have been provided by the foster parents.

The implications for placing agencies justify a policy of early placement in adoptive homes offering emotional warmth and and security in an above average educational and social setting (pp. 116-117).

It is noteworthy that none of the foregoing conclusions drawn by the original investigators is noted by Honzik in her article based primarily on Skodak and Skeels' work, nor are they mentioned by Jensen or other authorities dealing with the specific issue, even though they claim familiarity with the primary data. For example, in two highly respected textbooks on human genetics (Lerner, 1968, pp 159-160; Stern, 1973, p. 709) reference is made to Skodak and Skeels' work as supporting the interpretation that the intelligence of adopted children has a high genetic component virtually uninfluenced by characteristics of the foster home.

In summary, a re-examination of data from studies of own vs. adopted children leads to the same conclusion indicated by research on identical twins reared apart. While there is clear evidence for the importance of genetic factors in the development of intelligence, the data do not support the claim that as much as 75 to 80 percent of the variance in mental ability is genetically determined.

Identical vs. fraternal twins. The most widely employed method for estimating the proportions of variance attributable to genetic factors is based on the comparison of within-pair differences for identical vs. same-sex fraternal twins, both groups reared in their own homes. The basic argument runs as follows. Differences between identical twins can be attributable only to environment since their genetic endowments are the same. Differences between fraternal twins, however, reflect both environmental and genetic effects, and are larger for that reason. Accordingly, if one subtracts the former variance from the latter, the resulting difference is the amount of variance attributable to heredity. By expressing this variance as a fraction of total variance of individuals in the sample of same-sex fraternal twins, one obtains an estimate of the proportion of total variation attributable to genetic factors. This ratio is referred to as *heritability*, and is usually designated as h², after Holzinger (1929), who first developed the index. The value of h² can also be calculated from intraclass r's for identical vs. fraternal twins through application of the following formula: [4]

$$h^2 = \frac{r_i - r_f}{1 - r_f}$$

According to published summaries of kinship correlations (Erlen-meyer-Kimling and Jarvik, 1963; Burt, 1966), the median intraclass r for identical twins reared together (14 studies) is approximately .89; for same-sex fraternals (11 studies), .56. Substituting these values in the formula yields an h² of .75. Jensen (1969a) presumably working from the same data, reports a coefficient of .80.[5]

As with identical twins reared apart, an estimate of genetic variance (represented in this case by the heritability coefficient) derived from a comparison of identical and fraternal unseparated twins also rests on certain assumptions. The first is analogous to the assumption of uncorrelated environments made in the case of separated twins; namely, *genetic differences are assumed to be randomly distributed in the environment so that there is no tendency, for example, for better genes to end up in better environments, or vice versa.* Newman, Holzinger, and Freeman, in discussing the relative contributions of nature and nurture, acknowledge that this assumption is not entirely warranted with the result that measures of heritability "probably weight the nature influences somewhat too heavily" (1937, p. 115).

In contrast, Jensen, although going even farther in acknowledging a substantial correlation between genetic ability and the quality of the environment, ends up crediting the effects of this correlation completely to genetic influences:

Such covariance undoubtedly exists for intelligence in our society. Children with better than average genetic endowment for intelligence have a greater than chance likelihood of having parents of better than average intelligence who are capable of providing environmental advantages that foster intellectual development. Even among children within the same family, parents and teachers will often give special attention and opportunities to the child who displays exceptional abilities. A genotype for superior ability may cause the social environment to foster the ability, as when parents perceive unusual responsiveness to music in one of their children and therefore provide more opportunities for listening, music lessons, encouragement to practice, and so on. A bright child may also create a more intellectually stimulating environment for himself in terms of the kinds of activities that engage his interest and energy. And the social rewards that come to the individual who excels in some activity therefore reinforce its further development. Thus the covariance term for any given trait will be affected to a significant degree by the kinds of behavioral propensities the culture rewards or punishes, encourages or discourages. For traits viewed as desirable in our culture, such as intelligence, hereditary and environmental factors will be positively correlated. . . .

In making overall estimates of the proportions of variance attributable to hereditary and environmental factors, there is some question as to whether the covariance component should be included on the side of heredity or environment. But there can be no "correct" answer to this question. To the degree that the individual's genetic propensities cause him to fashion his own environment, given the opportunity, the covariance (or some part of it) can be justifiably regarded as part of the total heritability of the trait. But if one wishes to estimate what the heritability of the trait would be under artificial conditions in which there is absolutely no freedom for variation in individuals' utilization of their environment, then the covariance term should be included on the side of environment. Since most estimates of the heritability of intelligence are intended to reflect the existing state of affairs, they usually include the covariance in the proportion of variance due to heredity (1969a, pp. 38, 39).

A second assumption underlying the interpretation of the heritability coefficient is generally acknowledged as not entirely valid, but this fact is not accorded much importance. Specifically, *the*

*greater similarity of identical over fraternal twins is interpreted
as due only and entirely to their greater genetic similarity (i.e.,
they have 100 percent rather than 50 percent of their genes in
common).* This means that the environments for identical twins
are presumed to be no more or less alike than they are for same-
sex fraternal twins. Almost all investigators concede that this is not
in fact the case, since identical twins are more likely to be placed
in similar environments and to be treated more alike. For example,
Burt (1966) states:

> Now it is well known that identical twins tend to keep together
> far more than fraternal twins, particularly since about half the
> fraternal twins are of different sex. The environmentalist there-
> fore naturally argues that the higher correlation for intelligence
> found in the case of identical twins can be fully explained by the
> greater similarity in their life-histories (p. 139).

Nevertheless, neither Burt nor any other investigators who have
relied on the heritability coefficient as a measure of genetic influence have taken this confounding factor very seriously. The general view is that the difference in environmental context for the
two groups of twins is so small as to be negligible in its consequences. For example, Newman, Holzinger, and Freeman assert
that the environmental variance for fraternal twins will be only
"slightly" larger than that for identical twins (1937, pp. 114, 121).

There is evidence to indicate, however, that the confounding
factor is considerably more important than has been acknowledged. This evidence comes from three sources: (1) data on the
differential experiences of identical vs. fraternal twins; (2) comparisons of heritability coefficients for different abilities and traits;
and (3) variations in heritability coefficients for different groups
(sexes, socioeconomic classes, and races).

(1) *Differential socialization of identical vs. fraternal twins.*
Over twenty-five years ago, Jones (1946), in a comprehensive
review of twin research, stated:

Several studies have shown that identical twins spend more time together, enjoy more similar reputations, are more likely to be in the same classroom . . . and in many other respects share a more common physical and social environment than that ordinarily experienced by fraternal twins (p. 613).

Subsequent research (Husen, 1959; Koch, 1966; Scarr, 1968; Shields, 1954) has both confirmed and strengthened this conclusion. For example, Koch found that identical twins are more likely to be dressed alike and are less often separated. More general findings along this same line are reported in the study by Scarr, who found that fraternal twins were perceived and treated more differently by their mothers than identical twins. In addition, she demonstrated that these differences in treatment were operative even when the mothers had misclassified their twins (i.e., thought them to be identical when they were really fraternal, and *vice versa*). In other words, identical twins tend to be treated more alike because they look more alike. Here is another instance of correlation between heredity and environment; specifically, a greater degree of genetic homogeneity evokes increased homogeneity in environmental reactions.

To what extent does the environmental difference thus engendered give rise to differences in the psychological development of identical vs. fraternal twins? We turn next to an examination of this question.

(2) *Variation in heritability coefficients for different abilities and traits.* If the greater similarity in treatment of identical twins results in greater psychological similarity between them, then the effects of this should be more marked for certain psychological variables than for others. Specifically, similarity between identical twins should be greatest for those characteristics in relation to which twins are most likely to have common experiences, especially in the context in which they are most likely to be treated alike—namely, the family. From this point of view, we should ex-

pect the greater similarity of identical twins to be more pronounced, for example, in verbal as against non-verbal abilities.

Available data are in accord with this expectation. Thus, Husen
(1959), in a study of 900 twin pairs located through the Swedish
draft system found that, in contrast to fraternal twins, identicals
were more alike in verbal than in non-verbal group tests of intelligence. The median value of h^2 calculated from Husen's samples
was .49 for verbal tests and only .23 for the non-verbal Matrices
test. Independent confirmation comes from data on an American
White middle class sample of 280 twin pairs (Scarr-Salapatek,
1971b). Heritability coefficients for verbal and non-verbal tests of
intellectual aptitude were .52 and .25 respectively.

Turning to the realm of personality traits, one would again
expect the greater similarity of identical twins to be maximized
for those characteristics which are most likely to be the product
of common experiences in the family. The principal kind of experience that twins are likely to share within the family is social
interaction. From this point of view, one would predict that
coefficients of heritability should be higher for personality variables reflecting social orientations, such as introversion-extraversion, or dominance-submissiveness, than for emotional or intra-
personal qualities such as anxiety or self-control. Again, the
expectation is confirmed, this time in a number of independent
investigations. For example, Gottesman (1966), using a series of
personality questionnaires, obtained substantially higher heritability coefficients for such variables as Dominance (.49) and Sociability (.49) than for Flexibility (.15), Self-control (.27), or Intellectual Efficiency (.18). Similarly, Loehlin (in press) found that
twin studies of introversion-extraversion had higher median heritability coefficients than studies of any other personality characteristics. Scarr (1969), using both questionnaires and observational
measures, reported that "social introversion . . . was estimated to
be more heritable than any other trait (e.g., activity, curiosity,

intelligence) in this population" (p. 826). She then cited nine other twin studies yielding confirmatory results.

It is of course possible that the foregoing pattern of results is the product solely of genetic factors uninfluenced by genetically-induced environmental reactions. If so, one must be prepared to conclude that the genetic component is greater in verbal intelligence than in non-verbal, in social personality characteristics than in emotional traits. Moreover, at least as yet, genetic theory provides no basis for anticipating such a pattern or explaining how it comes about. In contrast, an interactive hypothesis, which views the genetically-determined similarity of twins as a stimulus for setting in motion patterns of environmental treatment which are selective in "homogenizing" certain twin behaviors but not others, does provide a basis for anticipating and testing the emergence of differentiated patterns of similarity in identical twins. Moreover, the hypothesis predicts differences in similarity not only as a function of psychological content but also of the social context in which the twins are brought up.

(3) *Variations of heritability coefficients in different social contexts.* From an interactive perspective, it would follow that identical twins are most likely to be similar in those traits which parents select out for special attention. Or, to put it in another way, parents are most likely to treat identical twins similarly with respect to those behaviors and characteristics which they regard as important. The findings already reported are consistent with this principle. We can now carry the argument one step further. It is a well-established fact that parents view different experiences, behaviors, and abilities as appropriate for the two sexes (for a general summary see Mussen, 1969; Mischel, 1970). Thus boys are expected to do well in mathematics, girls in English. In terms of personality traits, the socialization of boys, at least in America, focuses around problems of aggression, competition, and dominance, whereas for girls the emphasis is on nurturance and social adaptation. Accordingly, in line with our guiding hypothesis,

heritability coefficients for the two sexes should differ along the lines indicated above with male identical twins being especially similar in one set of characteristics and female identical twins the other. Data most directly relevant to these predictions are available from two studies. Nichols (1965a, 1965b) analyzed performance on the National Merit Scholarship Test for a sample of over 1500 sets of twins. Heritability coefficients for the test as a whole were virtually identical for the two sexes ($h^2 = .72$ for boys, .74 for girls). Two of the five sub-tests, however, showed marked sex differences. Heritability on the English Usage test was substantially higher for girls (.67) than for boys (.27); a reverse trend appeared in the test for Mathematics Usage with a coefficient of .80 for boys and .65 for girls. Gottesman (1966), in his study of heritability of personality traits in a Boston sample, reported markedly higher heritability coefficients for females than males in Sociability, whereas males emerged as more heritable in Dominance and Self-acceptance.

The same line of reasoning may also be applied to predict differences in heritability coefficients by social class. Thus, at a general level, one can argue that identical twins brought up in different social contexts are likely to vary in similarity as a function of the intensity of the socialization process in that context. More specifically, identical twins will be most alike in those settings in which parent-child interaction is most frequent, sustained, and actively focused on the child's development. Studies of social class differences in child rearing reveal that it is precisely in these respects that middle class families differ from those in lower class. (For a summary of the evidence see Hess, 1970.) As one descends the social class ladder, parent-child interaction becomes both less frequent, less consistent, and more diffuse. Moreover, because the disorganizing forces of lower class status are most severe for Black families, the disruption of the socialization process is likely to be more marked in Blacks than in Whites. Our general hypothesis would therefore predict decreasing heritability coefficients for groups of twins as one moved from upper to lower class and from White to Black populations.

Data bearing precisely on this two-dimensional hypothesis is provided in a study by Scarr-Salapatek (1971b). Working with a sample of over 1500 twin pairs in the Philadelphia public schools, she computed heritability coefficients separately by race and two social class levels (above and below the median). Consistent with our expectations, intra-pair similarity for all types of twins was greater among White than among Black families, and in the upper as against the lower half of the social class distribution. The general pattern of results showed consistently higher measures of heritability for White than for Black families and for advantaged as against disadvantaged groups of both races. Indeed, the observed genetic effects in the lower socioeconomic groups were so small as to prompt Scarr-Salapatek to conclude that ". . . genetic factors cannot be seen as strong determinants of the aptitude scores in the disadvantaged groups of either race" (p. 1292).

Scarr-Salapatek's interpretation of her results focuses on the impact of suppressive environments on genetic expression. She takes as an analogue for her own study with human subjects Henderson's (1970) ingenious experiment with mice reared in standard cages vs. enriched environments. The percent of genetic variance for the former group was one-fourth that for the latter. In addition, mice from the enriched environment performed far better in a learning task than did the deprived group. In other words, to find expression, genetic differences require an appropriately complex and stimulating environment (as in Skodak and Skeels' foster homes). In the absence of such an environment, genetic potential remains undeveloped both in terms of absolute level of ability and of individual differences. It is for this reason, Scarr-Salapatek argues, that both lower class and Black groups, who in our society live in suppressive environments, exhibit both lower levels of ability and reduced genetic variability as reflected in low heritability coefficients.

Our own interpretation is fully consistent with this view, but goes one step further in describing the environmental mechanism whereby genetic potentials find expression in the particular case of identical twins. The argument holds that the degree of similarity between identical twins is *substantially* a function of the extent to which they are actively treated alike; that is exposed to the same stimulating and complex environments. If the environments are impoverished, inconsistent, and diffuse, the similarity between the twins will be much reduced. Scarr-Salapatek's data provide strong support for this argument. Presumably, identical twins are equally identical genetically whether they are Black or White and whether they grow up in advantaged or disadvantaged homes. Yet the heritability coefficient for general aptitude in Scarr-Salapatek's data was .40 for middle class Whites and .25 for middle class Blacks. The contrasts for advantaged vs. disadvantaged children, both Black and White, were even more pronounced. Obviously, such marked variations, in the expression of genetic variance, are a function of environmental factors. Thus Scarr-Salapatek concludes: ". . . the major finding of the analysis of variance is that advantaged and disadvantaged children differ primarily in what proportion of variance in aptitude scores can be attributed to environmental sources" (p. 1292).

In the light of the foregoing analysis, the explanation and remedy for observed differences in intellectual performance by race and class would seem to lie far more in the direction indicated by Scarr-Salapatek's demonstration of the role of the environment in realizing genetic potential, than in the more simplistic theories of Jensen and others who, with no evidence to support them, posit unequal allocation of genetically-rooted capacities among different races and social groups.

With respect to race differences in intelligence, independent confirmation of the decisive role of environmental factors comes from recent studies of intellectual development in children of mixed Black-White marriages. From the point of view of genetic theory, which parent is of which race should make no difference for the child's mental capacity. The research results indicate, however, that the IQ of the child correlates more with the race of the mother than that of the father. Since it is the mother who is a primary agent of child rearing, this finding is consistent with the conclusion that the suppressive environment in which Blacks grow up in our society disrupts the process of socialization with the result that the child of the impoverished environment fails to realize his genetic potential.

We have now offered several sets of facts and arguments for calling into question the second major assumption critical to Jensen's estimate of genetic influence from the comparison of identical and fraternal twins. This is the assumption that the greater similarity in the environment of identical twins is a negligible factor in producing their psychological similarity.

As we have seen, this influence is in fact substantial. A similar conclusion has been reached by Loehlin (in press), who, on the basis of an empirical analysis, concluded that the within-family environmental variance for identical twins was about 62 percent that of fraternal pairs. Schoenfeldt (1968), relying on Loehlin's empirical work, developed a formula for heritability which adjusts for this inequality. Estimates of heritability for a test of general aptitude in a large sample of twins ranged from .60, on the basis of the conventional formula, to .26, using Schoenfeldt's adjustment. On this and other grounds, Schoenfeldt concluded that:

> . . . *genetic components are not as large a proportion of the total variance as previously believed.* Since up to the present time virtually all heritability estimates from twin samples have been computed using procedures shown to be inadequate, it should be no surprise that psychologists have been overestimating the genetic component for a long time (p. 17).

But serious problems of interpretation remain even if Schoenfeldt's corrected values are taken as the estimates of genetic effect.

First of all, as Scarr-Salapatek's data indicate, the impact of environmental similarity for identical twins varies across social contexts and is substantially greater among families in upper as against lower socioeconomic strata. But even if this variation were taken into account, a major problem still remains. Before we can generalize any estimate of heritability from a population of twins to people at large, a third critical assumption must be met. As in the case of identical twins reared apart, the generalization is valid only if the *environmental differences that occur between twins are as great as those that occur for unrelated children of the same sex and age.* Obviously, the realities of life do not accord with this condition. In view of this fact, values of h² cited by Jensen and other investigators, to the extent that they are valid measures of genetic influence, reflect the relative contribution of heredity and environment in accounting for individual differences *between children of the same sex and age being raised in the same family.*

The implications of these restrictions are rather far-reaching. It is obvious, for example, that, within the same family, children of the same sex but of different ages are just as alike genetically as same-sex fraternal twins, but experience far more varied environments in the course of growing up. The importance of this greater environmental difference for estimates of genetic influence can be illustrated by computing a heritability coefficient from the comparison of IQ similarity between siblings and between unrelated children reared together. The respective median intra-class r's, as given by Jensen, are .55 and .24. Applying Jensen's (1967) formula for computing heritability from any two kinship correlations yields a value for h² of .56, compared to .80 computed by the same formula from twin data.

Even more consequential is the environmental restriction imposed by the fact that the children are brought up in the same home. As Shields (1962, p. 8) has pointed out, the coefficient of heritability computed from data on twins is based on the environmental variance that occurs within families but not between them.

Yet, most of the environmental variation affecting human development that does or could occur takes place precisely between families rather than within them. It is difficult for children growing up in the same family to experience, as unrelated children do, widely differing environments—one enriched, and the other impoverished. But if this were to happen, the heritability coefficient would obviously be reduced.

This important point was recognized by Newman, Holzinger, and Freeman in their pioneering research. After pointing out that h^2 in their study could have been "of the order of .50 or smaller" for more varied environments, they concluded, "The relative role of heredity and environment is thus a function of the type of environment" (1937, p. 347).

Although few other twin researchers have been aware of this limitation, ironically enough it was acknowledged by Jensen (1969). In his theoretical discussion of heritability, he stated "H [the heritability coefficient] will be higher in a population in which environmental variation relevant to the trait in question is small, than in a population in which there is great environmental variation" (p. 43). Unfortunately, Jensen did not take this important principle into account in interpreting empirical values of heritability coefficients based on the relatively limited environmental variations that occur within families. In particular, he failed to consider the implications of this restriction for estimating the probable impact of social and educational programs designed to reduce intellectual differences *among* families living in *widely differing environments*.

We have now concluded our re-examination of evidence and assumptions underlying the thesis of Jensen and others that 80 percent of the variation in human intelligence is genetically determined. The results of our analysis lead to rejection of this thesis both on theoretical and empirical grounds. But what of the fundamental question to which Jensen was so ready to supply an answer? What can be said about the relative contributions of heredity and environment to psychological development? On the basis of the analysis we have undertaken, several conclusions appear to be in order:

1. There can be no question that genetic factors play a substantial role in producing individual differences in mental ability. Many findings summarized in this account testify to the validity of this statement. Perhaps the most impressive is the fact that the similarity of identical twins reared apart (median r_I = .75) was clearly greater than that of fraternal twins reared together (median r_I = .56).

2. It is impossible to establish a fixed figure representing the proportion of variation in intelligence, or any other human trait, independently attributable to heredity vs. environment. Even if one assumes the absolute degree of genetic variation to be a constant, the fact that the contribution depends on the degree of variability present in a given environment and its capacity to evoke genetic potential means that the relative contribution of genetic factors will vary from one environmental context to another. Moreover, any attempt to establish the range of the relative contribution in terms of existing environments cannot predict what might occur in some new environment that might come about or be deliberately constructed.

3. It follows from the above principle that, contrary to Jensen's contention, a high heritability coefficient for a particular ability or trait cannot be taken as evidence that the ability or trait in question cannot be substantially enhanced through environmental intervention. An instructive example is cited by Gage (1972) in a reply to Shockley and Jensen. Gage calls attention to the striking gain in stature exhibited by adults in Western countries over the past 200 years as a function of improved conditions of health and nutrition.[6] He notes further that the heritability of height as determined from twin studies is about .90—higher than that for IQ. "If this high heritability index had been derived in the year 1800, would it then have been

safe to conclude that height cannot be increased through environmental influences? If that conclusion had been drawn, it would have been wrong" (Gage, 1972, p. 422).

4. Any attempt to identify the independent contribution of heredity and environment to human development confronts the fact of a substantial correlation between these two factors. Moreover, the relation is not unidirectional. It is true, as Jensen points out, that parents of better genetic endowment are likely to create better environments for their children, and that the child as a function of his genetic characteristics in fact determines the environment that he experiences. The genetic similarity of identical twins is a case in point. But Scarr-Salapatek's research on this same phenomenon provides dramatic evidence that the environment can also determine the extent to which genetic potential is realized. This reverse relationship calls into question the legitimacy of including covariance between heredity and environment in the proportion of variance due solely to genetic factors. The impossibility of assigning this covariance unequivocally to one or the other source is further ground for the conclusion that a fixed figure representing the proportion of variance attributable to genetic factors cannot be established.

5. For genetic potential to find expression, both in terms of level and diversity, requires an appropriately complex and stimulating environment. This fact leads to a new and somewhat ironic interpretation of measures of heritability. Since heritability coefficients are lowest in environments that are most impoverished and suppressive, and highest in those that are most stimulating and enriched, *the heritability coefficient should be viewed not solely as a measure of the genetic loading underlying a particular ability or trait, but also as an index of the capacity of a given environment to evoke and nurture the development of that ability or trait.*

6. Finally, with respect to the problem posed by the substantial

differences in intellectual performance exhibited across class and race, our refutation of Jensen's thesis also argues against reliance on methods of selective mating and population control and in favor of measures aimed at improving, and even creating, environments better suited to evoke and nurture the expression of genetic potential.

Thus, our analysis has brought us to a paradoxical conclusion. An inquiry into the heritability of inborn capacities has shed new light on the power and potential of the environment to bring about the realization of genetic possibilities.

NOTES

1. Jensen reports this correlation as .77 (Jensen, 1969a, p. 52). This figure is never cited in Newman, Holzinger, and Freeman's published work, but appears in a table presented by Burt with the comment: "Raw figures were corrected for age and range by McNemar, and the slight changes this involves have been accepted by Holzinger" (Burt, 1966, pp. 145–146).

2. The restricted range of environments into which separated twins are placed should presumably be reflected in some reduction in variability of IQ's for this group as compared with the population as a whole. Since the standard deviation of the Stanford-Binet is reliably established as 16.4 points (Terman and Merrill, 1937, p. 37), it is possible to test this expectation in the two studies which employed that instrument as the measure of intelligence. Newman, Holzinger, and Freeman report a standard deviation of 13.0 for their sample of 38 twins (1937, p. 336). Burt, in a private communication, reports a standard deviation of 14.7. This conflicts with the value of 15.3 cited in his published paper (1966, p. 144), but a computation from the original data (N = 35 pairs) generously provided to the author by Burt confirms the 14.7 figure.

3. Similar considerations apply to the interpretation of data on adopted vs. own children. The fact that intrafamilial correlations in IQ tend to be higher for families with own than with adopted children is in part a function of the greater homogeneity of adoptive parents as a group both in terms of social background characteristics and values. Hence the greater similarity among blood related vs. adoptive family members cannot be attributed solely or even primarily to genetic factors.

4. This is the formula developed by Holzinger and used in most of the published studies. There are other formulas for h^2 based on somewhat different assumptions about the amount of assortative mating in the pop-

ulation (Jensen, 1967; Nichols, 1965a; Scarr-Salapatek, 1971a), but all are subject to the difficulties of interpretation discussed below.

5. The higher value is due primarily to the fact that "the correlations from which this heritability estimate was derived were corrected for unreliability" (Jensen, 1969a, p. 51). This procedure involves estimating how much higher the correlations would have been if the intelligence tests employed had been perfectly reliable. In general, the higher the correlation, the greater the effect of correcting for unreliability. According to Newman, Holzinger, and Freeman, such correction formulas "overestimate the corrected coefficient for high correlations" (p. 118). If correction for unreliability is not introduced, the application of Jensen's own formula (Jensen, 1967), which takes into account assortative mating, yields a value for h² of .72. Following a similar procedure, Jensen applied his heritability formula to all the kinship correlations cited above, this time obtaining a value of .81 (again corrected for unreliability) which he describes as "probably the best single overall estimate of heritability of measured intelligence that we can make." Unfortunately, this estimate rests on the same questionable assumptions (see below) as that derived from data on twins alone.

6. Jensen's (1969b) argument that "the variance in *adult* height may be almost entirely attributable to genetic factors" has been specifically refuted by two geneticists (Cavalli-Sforza and Bodmer, 1971, pp. 609–610).

REFERENCES

Burks, B. S. The relative influence of nature and nurture upon mental development: A comparative study of foster parent-foster child resemblance and true parent-true child resemblance. 27th Year Book of the National Society for the Study of Education, 1928. (I), 219–316.

Burt, C. The genetic determination of differences in intelligence: A study of monozygotic twins reared together and apart. *British Journal of Psychology*, 1966, *57*, 137–153.

Cavalli-Sforza, L. L. and Bodmer, W. F. *The genetics of human population*. San Francisco· W. H. Freeman, 1971.

Erlenmeyer-Kimling, L. and Jarvik, L. F. Genetics and intelligence: A review. *Science*, 1963, *142*, 1177–1179.

Fehr, F. S. Critique of hereditarian accounts. *Harvard Educational Review*, 1969, *39*, 571–580.

Gage, N. L. I.Q. heritability, race differences, and educational research. *Phi Delta Kappan*, January, 1972, 297–307.

Gottesman, I. I. Genetic variance and adaptive personality traits. *Journal of Child Psychology and Psychiatry*, 1966, *7*, 199–208.

Henderson, N. Genetic influences on the behavior of mice can be obscured by laboratory rearing. *Journal of Comparative and Physiological Psychology*, 1970, Vol. 72, No. 3, 505–511.

Hess, R. D. Social class and ethnic influences on socialization. In P. H. Mussen (Ed.), *Carmichael's Manual of Child Psychology*. New York: John Wiley, 3rd edition, 1970, Vol. 2, 457–558.

Holzinger, J. The relative effect of nature and nurture influences on twin differences. *Journal of Educational Psychology*, 1929, *20*, 241–248.

Honzik, M. P. Developmental studies of parent-child resemblance in intelligence. *Child Development*, 1957, *28*, 215–228.

Husen, T. *Psychological twin research*. Stockholm: Almqvist & Wiksell, 1959.

Jensen, A. R. Estimation of the limits of heritability of traits by comparison of monozygotic and dizygotic twins. *Proceedings of the National Academy of Sciences*, 1967, *58*, 149–157.

Jensen, A. R. How much can we boost I.Q. and scholastic achievement? *Harvard Educational Review*, Winter, 1969, 1–123. (a)

Jensen, A. R. Reducing the heredity-environment uncertainty: A reply. *Harvard Educational Review*, 1969, *39*, 449–483. (b)

Jones, A. G. Environmental influences on mental development. In Earl Carmichael (Ed.), *Manual of Child Psychology*. New York: Wiley & Sons, 1946, 582–632.

Juel-Nielsen, N. *Individual and environment*. Copenhagen: Munksgaard, 1965.

Kellmer-Pringle, M. T. *Adoption—facts and fallacies*. London: Longmans, Green, 1966.

Koch, H. L. *Twins and twin relations*. Chicago: University of Chicago Press, 1966.

Lawrence, E. M. *An investigation into the relation between intelligence and inheritance*. Cambridge, England: Cambridge University Press, 1931.

Leahy, A. M. Nature-nurture and intelligence. *Genetic Psychology Monographs*, 1935, *17*, No. 4, 241–305.

Lerner, I. M. *Heredity, evolution, and society*. San Francisco: W. H. Freeman, 1968.

Loehlin, J. C. Psychological genetics, from the study of human behavior. In R. B. Cattell (Ed.), *Handbook of modern personality theory*. New York: Aldine, in press.

Mischel, W. Sex-typing and socialization. In P. H. Mussen (Ed.), *Carmichael's Manual of Child Psychology*. New York: John Wiley, 3rd edition, 1970, Vol. 2, 3–72.

Mussen, P. H. Early sex-role development. In D. A. Goslin (Ed.), *Handbook of socialization theory and research*. Chicago: Rand McNally, 1969, 707–732.

Newman, H. H., Freeman, F. N., Holzinger, K. J. *Twins: A study of heredity and environment*, Chicago: University of Chicago Press, 1937.

Nichols, R. C. The inheritance of general and specific abilities. *National Merit Scholarship Corporation Research Reports*, 1965, *1*, 1–13. (a)

Nichols, R. C. The National Merit twin study. In G. Vandenberg (Ed.), *Methods and goals in human behavior genetics*. New York: Academic Press, 1965, 231–245. (b)

Scarr, S. Environmental bias in twin studies. *Eugenics Quarterly*, 1968, *15*, 34–40.

Scarr, S. Social introversion-extraversion. *Child Development*, 1969, *40*, 823–833.

Scarr-Salapatek, S. Unknowns in the IQ equation. *Science*, 1971, *174*, 1223–1228. (a)

Scarr-Salapatek, S. Race, social class and IQ. *Science*, 1971, *174*, 1185–1295. (b)

Schoenfeldt, L. F. An empirical comparison of various procedures for estimating heritability. Paper read at the symposium on "Methodological Considerations Determining the Relative Roles of Heredity and Environment." Annual meeting of the American Psychological Association, August 31, 1968.

Shields, J. Personality differences and neurotic traits in normal twin school children. *Eugenics Review*, 1954, *45*, 213–247.

Shields, J. *Monozygotic twins brought up apart and brought up together.* London: Oxford University Press, 1962.

Skodak, M. and Skeels, H. M. A final follow-up study of one hundred adopted children. *Journal of genetic psychology*, 1949, *75*, 85–125.

Stern, C. *Principles of human genetics.* San Francisco: W. H. Freeman, 3rd edition, 1973.

Terman, L. M. and Merrill, M. A. *Measuring intelligence.* Boston: Houghton Mifflin, 1937.

10

RACIST ARGUMENTS
AND IQ

Stephen Jay Gould

Louis Agassiz, the greatest biologist of mid-nineteenth-century America, argued that God had created blacks and whites as separate species. The defenders of slavery took much comfort from this assertion, for biblical proscriptions of charity and equality did not have to extend across a species boundary. What could an abolitionist say? Science had shone its cold and dispassionate light upon the subject; Christian hope and sentimentality could not refute it.

During the Spanish-American War, a great debate raged over whether we had the right to annex the Philippines. Imperialists again took comfort from science, for social Darwinism proclaimed a hierarchy in racial ability. When antiimperialists cited Henry Clay's contention that God would not create a race incapable of self-government, Rev. Josiah Strong answered: "Clay's contention was formed before modern science had shown that races develop in the course of centuries as individuals do in years, and that an underdeveloped race, which is incapable of self-government, is no more of a reflection on the Almighty than is an underdeveloped child, who is incapable of self-government."

I cite these examples not merely because they expose science at its most ridiculous, but because they illustrate a far more important point: statements that seem to have the sanction of science have been continually invoked in attempts to equate egalitarianism with sentimental hope and emotional blindness. People who are unaware of this historical pattern tend to accept each recurrence at face value: that is, they assume each such statement arises from the "data" actually presented rather than from the social conditions that truly inspire it.

We have never, I shall argue, had any hard data on genetically based differences in intelligence among human groups. Speculation, however, has never let data stand in its way; and when men in power need such an assertion to justify their actions, there will always be scientists available to supply it.

The racist arguments of the nineteenth century were primarily based on craniometry, the measurement of human skulls. Today, these contentions stand totally discredited. What craniometry was to the nineteenth century, intelligence testing has been to the twentieth. The victory of the eugenics movement in the Immigration Restriction Act of 1924 signaled its first unfortunate effect—for the severe restrictions upon non-Europeans and upon southern and eastern Europeans gained much support from the results of the first extensive and uniform application of intelligence tests in America—the Army Mental Tests of World War I. These tests were engineered and administered by psychologist Robert M. Yerkes, who concluded that "education alone will not place the negro race [*sic*] on a par with its Caucasian competitors." It is now clear that Yerkes and his colleagues knew no way to separate genetic from environmental components in postulating causes for different performances on the tests.

The latest episode of this recurring drama began in 1969, when Arthur Jensen published his article entitled, "How Much Can We Boost I.Q. and Scholastic Achievement?" in the *Harvard Educational Review*. Again, the claim was made that new and uncom-

fortable information had come to light, and that science had to
speak the "truth" even if it refuted some cherished notions of a
liberal philosophy. But again, I shall argue, Jensen had no new
data; and what he did present was flawed beyond repair by inconsistencies in the data themselves and by illogical claims in his
presentation.

Jensen assumes that I.Q. tests adequately measure something we
may call "intelligence." He attempts to tease apart the genetic
and environmental factors causing differences in performance on
these tests. He does this by relying upon the one natural experiment we possess: identical twins reared apart—for here the differences can only be environmental. The average difference in
I.Q. for such twins is less than the difference for two unrelated
individuals raised in similarly varied environments. From the data
on twins, he obtains an estimate of the magnitude of environmental influence and estimates the genetic component from the additional differences in I.Q. between unrelated individuals. He concludes that I.Q. has a heritability of about 0.8 (or 80 percent)
within the population of American and European whites. The
average difference between American whites and blacks is 15 I.Q.
points (one standard deviation). He asserts that this difference
is too big to attribute to environment, given the high heritability
of I.Q. Lest anyone think that he writes in the tradition of abstract scholarship, I merely quote the first line of his famous
work: "Compensatory education has been tried, and it apparently
has failed."

I believe that this argument can be refuted in a "hierarchical"
fashion—that is, we can discredit it at one level and then show
that it would fail at a more inclusive level even if we allowed
Jensen's argument for the first two levels:

Level 1: The equation of I.Q. with intelligence. Who knows
what I.Q. measures? It is a good predictor of "success" in school,
but is such success a result of intelligence, apple polishing, or the
assimilation of values that the leaders of society prefer? Some

psychologists get around this argument by defining intelligence as the scores attained on "intelligence" tests. A neat trick. But at this point, the technical definition of intelligence has strayed so far from the vernacular that we no longer can define the issue. But let me allow (although I don't believe it), for the sake of argument, that I.Q. measures some meaningful aspect of intelligence in its vernacular sense.

Level 2: The heritability of I.Q. Here again, we encounter a confusion between vernacular and technical meanings of the same word. "Inherited," to a layman, means "fixed," "inexorable," or "unchangeable." To a geneticist, "inherited" refers to an estimate of similarity between related individuals based on genes held in common. It carries no implication of inevitability or of immutable entities beyond the reach of environmental influence. Eyeglasses correct a variety of inherited problems in vision; insulin can check diabetes.

Jensen insists that I.Q. is 80 percent heritable. Princeton psychologist Leon J. Kamin has recently done the dog-work of meticulously checking through details of the twin studies that form the basis of this estimate. He has found an astonishing number of inconsistencies and downright inaccuracies. For example, the late Sir Cyril Burt, who generated the largest body of data on identical twins reared apart, pursued his studies of intelligence for more than forty years. Although he increased his sample sizes in a variety of "improved" versions, some of his correlation co-efficients remain unchanged to the third decimal place—a statistically impossible situation. Other studies did not standardize properly for age and sex. Since I.Q. varies with these properties, an improper correction may produce higher values between twins not because they hold genes for intelligence in common, but simply because they share the same sex and age. The data are so flawed that no valid estimate for the heritability of I.Q. can be drawn at all. But let me assume (although no data support it), for the sake of argument, that the heritability of I.Q. is as high as 0.8.

Level 3: The confusion of within- and between-group variation. Jensen draws a causal connection between his two major assertions—that the within-group heritability of I.Q. is 0.8 for American whites, and that the mean difference in I.Q. between American blacks and whites is 15 points. He assumes that the black "deficit" is largely genetic in origin because I.Q. is so highly heritable. This is a *non sequitur* of the worst possible kind —for there is no necessary relationship between heritability within a group and differences in mean values of two separate groups.

A simple example will suffice to illustrate this flaw in Jensen's argument. Height has a much higher heritability within groups than anyone has ever claimed for I.Q. Suppose that height has a mean value of five feet two inches and a heritability of 0.9 (a realistic value) within a group of nutritionally deprived Indian farmers. This high heritability simply means that short farmers will tend to have short offspring, and tall farmers tall offspring. It says nothing whatever against the notion that proper nutrition could raise the mean height to six feet (taller than average white Americans). It only means that, in this improved status, farmers shorter than average (they may now be five feet ten inches) would still tend to have shorter than average children.

I do not claim that intelligence, however defined, has no genetic basis—I regard it as trivially true, uninteresting, and unimportant that it does. The expression of any trait represents a complex interaction of heredity and environment. Our job is simply to provide the best environmental situation for the realization of valued potential in all individuals. I merely point out that a specific claim purporting to demonstrate a mean genetic deficiency in the intelligence of American blacks rests upon no new facts whatever and can cite no valid data in its support. It is just as likely that blacks have a genetic advantage over whites. And, either way, it doesn't matter a damn. An individual can't be judged by his group mean.

If current biological determinism in the study of human intelligence rests upon no new facts (actually, no facts at all), then why has it arisen from so many quarters of late? The answer must be social and political—and the sooner we realize how much of science is so influenced, the sooner we will demythologize it as an inexorable "truth-making machine." Why now? The 1960s were good years for liberalism; a fair amount of money was spent on poverty programs and relatively little happened. Enter new leaders and new priorities. Why didn't the earlier programs work? Two possibilities are open: (1) we didn't spend enough money, we didn't make sufficiently creative efforts, or (and this makes any established leader jittery) we cannot solve these problems without a fundamental social and economic transformation of society; or (2) the programs failed because their recipients are inherently what they are—blaming the victims. Now, which alternative will be chosen by men in power in an age of retrenchment?

I have shown, I hope, that biological determinism is not simply an amusing matter for clever cocktail party comments about the human animal. It is a general notion with important philosophical implications and major political consequences. As John Stuart Mill wrote, in a statement that should be the motto of the opposition: "Of all the vulgar modes of escaping from the consideration of the effect of social and moral influences upon the human mind, the most vulgar is that of attributing the diversities of conduct and character to inherent natural differences."

11

INTELLIGENCE, IQ, AND RACE

Ashley Montagu

What is "intelligence"? The answer most people would give to that question would be, "What IQ tests measure." But as we shall see, IQ tests, whatever their proponents may claim, do not measure intelligence. The truth is that no one really knows what the *structure* of intelligence is, and therefore there cannot be anything even approximating a quantitative measure of intelligence, this abstraction of abstractions, that IQ tests purport to quantify. What is quite clear, except to IQ testers, is that many conditions enter into the making of the capabilities we call intelligence, and that without taking these factors into consideration such tests are quite valueless in providing a measure of "intelligence."

Psychologists have tried hard to reach some consensus as to what is to be understood by intelligence, but without success. Like myself, since my days as a student, in the early twenties, of Charles Spearman and his book on the nature of intelligence,[1] others have also found the unravelling of the structure of intelligence unaccomplished to the present day. The cumulative research during the last sixty years suggests that it would be a good working hypothesis to regard intelligence as constituted of a large assembly of highly varied, overlapping adaptive abilities or skills, rather than as a single faculty; that it is, indeed, largely the summation of the learning experiences of the individual.

As for the relation of the brain to intelligence, many a scientific reputation has been compromised when unsupportable racial differences were claimed to have been found in weight, size, convolutions, and other structures of the brain, and which were held sufficient to account for differences in racial intelligence. Though such claims have repeatedly been shown to be wholly unsound and have been thoroughly discredited over the last hundred years, they still go on. Within the normal range of variation in brain weight, size, convolutions, and its various structures, there is no demonstrable relation whatever to intelligence. Furthermore, the brain as an organ is vastly more than a physical structure. Indeed, it is the most complex and at the same time the most functionally educable system of structures of the body. Made up of trillions of neurons and associated entities in an amazingly complicated network of environmentaly educable interconnections, as well as a remarkable hormonal secretory activity and chemistry which it manages on its own,[2] it is the domain of the learned part of the environment. As functioning human beings, everything we know and come to do as human beings we have had to learn from others.

The evidence drawn from innumerable relevant researches is now overwhelming that *individual experience* literally shapes the developing brain and subsequent behavior.[3] The quality of that experience is fundamentally important for the development of the problem-solving behavior we call "intelligence" or "thinking," the ability to make the appropriately successful response, rather than "reaction," to the challenges of the environment. Just as the differences in cultural development between different societies may be explained by the differences in the history of their experience, so may the differences in intelligence between individuals be explained, for the most part, by the history of their experience; the parenthetic "for the most part" allowing for any genetic factors that may be involved.

The culture of IQ testing over the last seventy years has become so routinized, and its influence upon education so powerful, that what was once a byproduct of education has become a determinant of education as well as of social action. Schools often tailor their curricula to the measure of IQ results. Accordingly, narrow test skills are taught to the neglect of the development of the natural potentialities of the child—the tests being, for the most part, tests of information, not of the ability to think. Information is important, but it is not a measure of intelligence.[4]

There are so many influences entering into the individual's learning experiences that, unless these factors are evaluated for the role they may have played in the development of intelligence, IQ advocates will vainly continue their search in a dark room for a black cat which is not there. Such variables as the stimulation of maternal care, parental qualities, parental education, socioeconomic status, pre- and perinatal birth experiences, childhood—where the child's losses are, where his or her gains may also be—schooling, indeed, mental and physical health in all formative periods, are never considered in IQ testing. Without the consideration of these conditions, no matter what the innate predispositions of the individual may be, all tests of intelligence, and especially the most popular, the IQ tests, are worthless as measures of intelligence.

A predisposition is inborn, an ability is a trained predisposition or potentiality, which by learning, that is, the increase in the strength of any act by repetition, becomes an ability. Among the innate prenatal and perinatal undeveloped predispositions are the basic behavioral needs. In any test of intelligence it would be necessary, at the very least, to know that such needs exist, and that the understanding of the history, the satisfaction of those needs is indispensably necessary before one is able to arrive at a relatively true estimate of an individual's intelligence.

A basic behavioral need is an urge or drive toward satisfaction of that need. The thwarting of an expected satisfaction, especially the need for love during childhood, generally leads to serious disorders of physical and mental development, to aggressive or dysfunctional behavior, or so-called "failure to thrive," and may even lead to death.[5] Satisfaction of the basic behavioral needs leads to healthy behavioral growth and development. By healthy growth and development we mean here the ability to love, to work, to play, and to think soundly. Satisfaction of the basic behavioral needs is requisite also for the healthy growth and development of the body as well as the mind.[6]

The basic behavioral needs are the need for love, which means not only to be loved but also to love others, for curiosity, creativity, imagination, learning, explorativenes, experimental-mindedness, open-mindedness, speech, sound-thinking, flexibility, joyfulness, play, laughter, weeping, work, music, song, and dance.[7] These basic behavioral needs have never been recognized as playing a role in the development of intelligence, largely because the whole subject of the development of intelligence has been approached in too intellectualistic a manner.

Furthermore, the failure to consider the roles that religious, spiritual, and emotional influences may have played in the development of intelligence, has been to neglect among the most dominant influences in evaluating the intellectual development of the individual. It is a great error to approach the investigation of human intelligence as if, for the purpose of IQ testing, every individual were a product of a purely informational conditioning. Yet intelligence testers repeatedly commit that egregious error, thus simultaneously forfeiting any understanding of some of the most critical influences which enter into the shaping of intelligence.

Since the acronym "IQ" has entered the language as a scientific measure of intelligence as if indeed it were a real thing, it has done a great deal of damage to untold numbers of human beings. Lured into a belief in the false estimate of their capacities, the victims of IQ tests have frequently suffered a loss of self-esteem, of confidence in their abilities, and only too often a devastating hopelessness which has marred many a life. The psychometricians of humanity involved in such pernicious activities have rarely exhibited the slightest concern for the victims of their labors, but have often claimed, as in the latest case by the authors of *The Bell Curve*,[8] that their findings are for the good of us all.

The reprehensible thing about these taxonomists of the mind is the cluster of traits they generally display which disqualifies them from having any opinion on the nature of intelligence, especially when it affects blacks. Their obvious bias, their general insensitivity, their closed-mindedness, their failure to consider the evidence opposing their views, their citation of views, though long discredited, favorable to their kinds of arguments their abysmal ignorance of biological and cultural anthropology, and worst of all, their ignorance of *genetics*, has evoked innumerable rejections of both their methods and their conclusions.

Beginning with Walter Lippmann's[9] devastating attacks in 1923 on the work and findings of the leading IQ testers on World War I army recruits,[10] to the most recent of these on the flaws and failures of IQ testing, the criticisms have been unceasing. Outstanding among these are Stephen Jay Gould's *The Mismeasure of Man* (1981),[11] Professor Albert Jacquard's *In Praise of Difference* (1984),[12] and Elaine and Harry Mensh's *The IQ Mythology* (1991),[13] three works which should have given the authors of *The Bell Curve* plenty of time to deal with their critiques. However, the authors of that book, like so many of their predecessors, have been determinedly uninterested in pursuing such a course, a course that every genuine scientist follows as part of the normal procedure of checking the validity of one's work. Professor William Tucker in his book *The Science and Politics of Racial Research* (1994),[14] published just one month after the appearance of *The Bell Curve*, has shown pointedly and unequivocally that the authors of such works have not been interested in the facts or the most reasonable interpretation of their findings, but rather in the use of such devices as IQ tests to represent social and political inequality as the unavoidable and ineradicable consequences of natural differences. One wonders why these so-called scientists have never tried standing the argument on its head and considered the possibility that, far from being due to natural differences, the differences are largely due to social and political inequalities. And why they refuse to consider that "race" is a product of history, not of nature.

One wonders why these so-called scientists never seemed to have regarded it as possibly irresponsible to publish views in the name of science which have repeatedly been shown to be unsound, and disastrous for millions of people. Why is it that in the face of the Holocaust, "ethnic cleansing," and the endemic social and political inequalities that exist in the United States between whites and blacks, they have persisted in perpetuating demonstrably unsound views as an explanation for those inequalities and the evils to which they lead?

It is not a blindness of some sort from which these enemies of humanity suffer, but an attitude of mind, however acquired, which causes them to perceive members of "other" groups, identifiable as of different "race," as inferior, and therefore a threat to the continued integrity and welfare of society. I have called this viewpoint "man's most dangerous myth."[15] Hitler, by organizing the murder of millions of Jews,[16] Gypsies, and other targeted victims in the name of "race," proved indeed that the belief in "race" *is* man's most dangerous myth.

In America the myth of "race" has been endemic for several centuries, and remains America's number-one public-health problem.[17] It is therefore hardly surprising that the tide of passion whipped up by American public figures and windy writers should have overflowed its banks and surfaced on many a foreign shore. Indeed, the ideas and writings of many American "scientists" and writers on "race" were widely influential in contributing their support and often their endorsement of the ideologies of foreign reactionary politicians and demagogues. This was the case most notably in Germany, whose leaders found in the racist works of the Americans an encouragement and reinforcement for their extreme racist programs. Racism in Germany had been deeply entrenched long before the advent of Hitler and Naziism. With the defeat of Germany in the first World War in 1918, and the forced signing of the debasing Versailles peace treaty in 1919, there followed a catastrophic national depression, anarchy in the streets, and the pressing necessity for an explanation, a target upon which to blame it all. The populace was easily led to believe that Germany had lost the war because it had been betrayed—as the saying went, "stabbed in the back." A convenient scapegoat for their frustration was readily available: the Jews. The first prominent victim of the racist nationalists was Walther Rathenau, foreign minister and a Jew, who had served his country nobly and with great ability during the war and after. Rathenau, a charming man, who believed in conciliation rather than confrontation, was assasinated in June 1922.

In November, 1923 the failure of Hitler's Munich *putsch* found him in gaol, where over the course of five months he wrote *Mein Kampf.* It was here that he read an account of the passage of the United States Immigration Restriction Act of 1924. In *Mein Kampf* he wrote of it with the greatest enthusiasm, saying that it would serve as a model for his program of racial purification. Not only that, having read the American Madison Grant's *The Passing of the Great Race,*[18] the popular racist tract of its time, in which Grant spoke of Jews with especial malevolence, Hitler, who called his deep-seated hatred of Jews "the granite-firm foundation" of his ideology, wrote Grant to thank him, saying that the book was his "Bible."[19]

In passing it may be noted that this was the period in which America was pioneering the sterilization of the "unfit," with the aid of IQ tests, the propaganda of the eugenists, the invention of the "feeble-minded," and the passage of state laws legalizing their sterilization. By the mid-thirties some twenty thousand sterilizations had been performed. The legalization of these laws was widely reported in the world press. In 1933 Hitler's cabinet promulgated a Eugenic Sterilization Law.

Grant's book, published in 1916, was well-written and very readable, widely reviewed, enlarged, and reprinted over several years. Grant was a New Yorker, a bachelor, and a socialite who traced his ancestry back to colonial America. He was the founder of the New York Zoological Society, and also of the Galton Society, an exclusive group which met monthly in the American Museum of Natural History and which, as its name implies, was chiefly interested in eugenic issues. Grant was also an officer of the American Eugenics Society, a vice-president of the Immigration Restriction League; and, with Harry Laughlin, a perfervid advocate of sterilization.

Grant's book spawned many others which followed in rapid succession, and which were greeted with enthusiasm in Germany, especially by German anthropologists.[20] The German sociologist Stefan Kûhl has shown in his book *The Nazi Connection: Eugenics, American Racism, and German National Socialism*[21] that not only did the German anthropologists welcome the contributions of American authors to the cause of National Socialism, but they were in fact in regular contact with many of them. Some Americans served on the editorial board of well-known German racist journals, while others traveled to Germany to accept honorary degrees from Nazi-controlled German universities, among them Henry Fairfield Osborn, president of the American Museum of Natural History. Harry Laughlin, the instigator and drafter of the U.S. Restrictive Imigration Act of 1924, and assistant director of the Eugenics Record Office, was unable to travel to receive a similar award.[22]

In 1916 Osborn wrote an adulatory preface for the first edition of Madison Grant's *The Passing of the Great Race* in which he stated the function of "the modern eugenics movement in relation to patriotism, namely, the conservation and multiplication for our country of the best spiritual, moral, intellectual, and physical forces of heredity," and that "thus only will the integrity of our institutions be maintained in the future," concluding with the words, "If I were asked: What is the greatest danger which threatens the American republic today? I would certainly reply: The gradual dying out

among our people of those hereditary traits through which the principles of our religious, political, and social foundations were laid
down, and their insidious replacement by traits of less noble character."[23]

In the German translation of Grant's book the word for "insidious" in Osborn's preface is *"hinterlistig,"* meaning "crooked," "un-
derhanded," "stealthy." One can well imagine what an amenable
impression these words made upon Hitler. Unlike Osborn, who
lacked the courage to name explicitly who these "insidious" crea-
tures might be, Grant left no doubt in the reader's mind who they
were. They were the "the Slovak, the Italian, the Syrian and the
Jew." "The man of the old stock," Grant wrote, "is being crowded
out of many country districts by these foreigners just as he is today being literally driven off the streets of New York City by the
swarms of Polish Jews . . . the Polish Jew, whose dwarf stature, peculiar mentality, and ruthless concentration on self-interest are being engrafted upon the stock of the nation."[24]

In December, 1917 Osborn, while allowing his original preface
to remain, added a completely new one for the 1918, enlarged, new
edition of Grant's book. With the recent entry of the United States
into World War I in mind Osborn opened with the following ring-
ing words: "History is repeating itself in America at the present time
and incidentally is giving a convincing demonstration of the central
thought in this volume, namely, that heredity and racial predisposition are stronger and more stable than environment and education." This portentous announcement was followed by an extended
paen to "this strain of Anglo-Saxon life which has played so large a
part in American history."[25]

To bring Osborn's history up to date, it may seem ungracious to
add the fact that in world history the "strain of Anglo-Saxon" American racist authors played a significant role in providing the Nazis,
both before and during the Second World War, with the support
for a regime that was responsible for the monumental evil of the
Holocaust, and the perpetration of many other genocides and acts

of ruthlessness. It is estimated those evils resulted in the deaths of more than fifty million human beings.

It is generally held that anyone who cries "Fire" in a crowded theatre should be held responsible for the consequences of his conduct. The same rule should apply to anyone who, motivated by racism, publishes or utters inflamatory falsehoods concerning others, whether they be individuals, groups, or populations; they should by law be held responsible for their conduct. More than 200 years of racism, of libel and slander, are enough, and so it is with the use of IQ tests, which in a very real sense represent demeaning falsehoods, whether they be maliciously intended or not. In the final analysis, what is involved is the matter of responsibility, the welfare of human beings, the balancing of moral integrity with scientific responsibility.

It is important to understand that the whole concept of IQ is an arbitrary social invention, which has been given a spurious reality and an equally spurious quantification, which has no justification whatever for its continuing existence. It is upon the bedrock of the great diversity of humankind that the future of humanity depends, not upon the categorization of humanity by IQ tests, for it is in that diversity that the great riches of humanity are stored, in the wonder of our individual differences seeking expression for the benefit of us all. At birth we are born into a continuing social relationship;[26] that relationship is the love shared between mother and child. It is a bond and a relationship which is designed to grow and develop throughout our lives, and by extension to the whole of humanity. One recalls the words of Terence, "I am a man: nothing human is alien to me." Next to homicide the greatest crime one person can commit against another is to stand in the way of that other person's development, to deprive society of the fulfillment of his or her unique individuality and humanity.

The history of the concept of "race" is a dreadful one; from its beginning the term by its very existence served to narrow the definition of humanity, through the establishment of an hegemonic hierarchy of discrete entities. These entities, the so-called "races," were primarily based on differences in physical traits. Such physical traits were soon linked with cultural or social differences, with educability and intelligence. During the Victorian period, scientists were busily engaged in classifying the races of man, just as they had been classifying the races of animals.[27] Books were published showing typical members of the races of mankind well into the twentieth century. The display of the different types of man together with maps of their distribution were often beautifully colored, and served to reinforce a view of the differences between the races of man, thus further serving to confirm the classifiers as well as the reader in their belief in the actuality of physical races.

What the classifiers saw as they surveyed the peoples of the earth was a great deal of variability which, on the basis of the presenting physical differences, enabled one to fit the races into the appropriate taxonomic pigeonhole already available to them. In the pregenetic age in which they lived and worked, the scientists of the day could hardly have done anything else. With the development of genetics early in the twentieth century it gradually became quite clear where they had gone wrong: it was in treating populations as if they were composed of complexes of physical traits, rather than by the distribution of the gene frequencies for the various traits they presented. When such gene frequencies at last began to be investigated it was found that by far the greater proportion of genes for various traits was shared by every people. In short, the gene differences between human populations were found to be very few indeed, and that such differences contributed to the welfare of us all, mentally as well as physically. The traditional classificatory ardor had gone on to the point of virtually excluding some peoples from the community of humankind, and like nationalism created a scale of physical and mental differences where they in fact did not exist. Furthermore, given a "scientific" validation the idea of "race" led to the increased polarization between ethnicities within nations as well as between nations.[28] Social stratifications of caste and class within nations were also given a biological meaning. In Europe throughout the nine-

teenth century—especially during the kletptomaniac period of imperialism, slavery in America, and its offshoot, "manifest destiny"—
it was customary to speak of "higher" and "lower races." It is a
mark of some progress that there has been decline in the use of such
terms.

The work of anthropologists during the last two hundred years
among the indigenous peoples of the earth has incontrovertibly established the truth that if some groups of humanity are culturally
more advanced in some respects than others, it is because the challenges of their environments have been more complex, demanding
different adaptive social and technologic responses and inventions.
Socially, the levels of complexity of a society have everywhere elic-
ited much the same kinds of responses, adapted to the requirements
of environmental pressures.[29] All human populations under similar
kinds of environmental challenges make similar responses to them.

Every culture can be regarded as the historic result of a people's
effort to adjust itself to the environment. Before the advent of the
twentieth century that environment was usually narrowly circum-
scribed. Today the boundaries which formerly divided people are
crumbling before our eyes. Humankind is moving, in spite of occasional appearances to the contrary, toward greater understanding,
toward the condition in which the differences that today separate
people will be regarded, not as causes for suspicion, fear, discrimination, or pegs upon which to hang our prejudices, but as no more
important than the differences which separate members of the same
family, in a setting in which everyone is given the opportunity and
encouragement to become a fully realized human being.

In 1922 H. G. Wells wrote in his *Outline of History*, "History is
a race between education and catastrophe." Looking at the world
that men have created since Wells wrote, it is clear that catastrophe
has been winning out over education. Looking at education today,
Wells would have been appalled by what passes for education,
for he thought of education as *humanitas*, the concern for, and
the involvement in, humanity. What passes for education in our

time is not education at all, but instruction, a training in the traditional three "r's," as it were. Genuine education has been technologized by the technocrats of education into practical skills and techniques.

Our love affair with technology, which was to have been our slave, has, instead, made willing slaves of us.[30] We pride ourselves on having created machines that think like human beings, and have failed to understand that what we have done is to create human beings who think like machines. By any operative definition that is what we tend to call education. The result has been that we have turned our world into a technological disaster. We have a citizenry that thinks in stereotypes, in clichés, who have become the prisoners of their vocabularies. Never having been taught what thinking really is, they have little respect for those who do think.

As Sir Joshua Reynolds (1723–1792), the great self-taught painter, put it, few have been taught to any purpose who have not been their own teachers. Thinking is a skill which can be taught as a searching and delightful exercise which grows to be an immense, and vitally important, pleasure. Thinking can be taught in our schools, at all levels. That, however, does not appear to be one of the functions of our educational institutions, for there the rule is to teach *what* to think, rather than *how* to think. The result has been catastrophic, with the result that we have become the most self-endangered species on earth, surrounded as we are by so many ignorant minds, who in a very real sense hold us captive. As Henry Adams wrote in his luminous *Education*, "nothing in education is so astonishing as the amount of ignorance it accumulates in the form of inert facts." Prejudice and confusion feed upon the credulity of the ignorant.

We have a great task before us, namely, the complete revision of "education" and its replacement by a system of education which meets the basic behavioral needs of humanity. In the name of education our schools have become institutions for the promotion of illiteracy in the most important of all the arts: the art of being a warm, loving human being, one who cares, who thinks of the world not as full of strangers, but as full of friends, friends we have not yet met.

To love one's neighbor as oneself is not enough; one must love others more than one loves oneself, for that is the true measure of what love is.[31] In a world in which there is so much unloving love behind the show of love, it is more than ever necessary to understand that racism, in whatever form it may take, represents the dehumanizing loss of involvement in the welfare of our neighbors. How does one express a truth deeper than the words themselves, or find the word which does not exist for the meaning one wishes to express? By action. The meaning of a word is the action it produces. There are the words "race" and "racism," and there is the word "love." For most people, what they think and do about these words is what they mean, and what they mean or do, or fail to do, is for the most part thoroughly dehumanizing.

If we are ever to extricate ourselves from the slough of despond into which we have fallen, we must recognize that the central sum of all education is love, love defined as the deep involvement in the welfare of others in a creatively enlarging manner. It is only through learning to love that we find our true identity, and in giving it unconditionally that we fulfill ourselves and enable others to fulfill themselves. And when everything has been said and done, and all our scientific works have been published, and all our truths have been proven, we will not have made much more headway in dealing with racism than we have in the past unless we clearly understand the root cause and the cure of the disorder which racism is. It is because scientists have shied away from the study of love that I have devoted so much attention to it. A scientist is one who believes in proof without certainty, while most other people believe in certainty without proof. Scientists are generally specialists, and have often made invaluable contributions in their fields which have led to the better understanding of wider issues than their own. Scientists are not usually called upon to see the wood for the trees; however, their contributions, when seen through the eyes of the generalist, make the view of the wood highly rewarding.

It is largely through the investigations of anthropologists among the great and illuminating diversity of the peoples of the earth that we have come to learn, and to understand, the meaning of humanity. The discovery of the common bond that unites us all, in sharing a kinship of wondrous variety and creativity, confirming the heart's profound feeling that every human is incomparable, unique, universal, and fundamentally alike in all those qualities, is what make us human. It is this discovery, cumulatively and repeatedly authenticated by anthropologists during the last seventy years, that should encourage us to work in the belief that with improvement of the environment heredity offers no barrier, for the news from both anthropology and genetics is heartening. Finally, we need to understand that our genetic richness comes from diversity, that, as Saint-Exupery wrote in *A Letter to a Hostage*, "If I am different from you, I enrich rather than diminish you." Or to put it as a universal principle: you are precious to me because you are different, as I am to you.

NOTES

1. C. Spearman, *The Nature of Intelligence and the Principles of Cognition* (London & N.Y.: Macmillan, 1922).
2. S. Rose, *The Conscious Brain* (N.Y.: Knopf, 1973); S. Rose, *Molecules and Minds* (Phila.: Open University Press, 1987); M. C. Diamond, *Enriching Heredity: The Impact of the Environment on the Anatomy of the Brain* (N.Y.: Free Press, 1988); J. Boddy, *Brain Systems and Psychological Concepts* (N.Y.: Wiley, 1978).
3. M. Cynader. "Mechanisms of Brain Development and Their Role in Health and Well-Being." *Daedalus* 123: 4 (1995): 155–165; C. Hertzman, "The Lifelong Impact of Childhood Experiences: A Population Health Perspective." *Daedalus* 123: 4 (1995) 167–180.
4. R. Fuller, *In Search of the IQ Correlation* (Stony Brook, N.Y.: Ball-Stick-Bird Publications, 1977).
5. R. G. Patton and L. I. Gardner, *Growth Failure in Maternal Deprivation* (Springfield, Il.: C. C. Thomas, 1963); G. F. Powell, J. A. Brasel, and R. Blizzard, "Emotional Deprivation and Growth Retardation: Simulating Idiopathic Hy-

popituitrism." *New England Journal of Medicine* 276 (1967): 1271–1278; J. B. Reinhart and Allan A. Drash, "Psychosocial Dwarfism: Environmentally Induced Recovery." *Psychosomatic Medicine*, 31 (1969): 165–72; A. Montagu, ed., *Culture and Human Development: Insights Into Growing Human* (Englewood Cliffs N.J.: Prentice-Hall, 1974).

6. R. H. Munroe, R. L. Munroe, and B. B. Whiting, eds., *Handbook of Cross-Cultural Human Development* (New York: Garland STM Press, 1981); A. Peiper, *Cerebral Function in Infancy and Childhood* (N.Y.: Consultants Bureau, 1963).

7. A. Montagu, *Growing Young* (Westport, Ct.: Bergin & Garvey, 1989).

8. R. Herrnstein and C. Murray. *The Bell Curve* (N.Y.: Free Press, 1994).

9. W. Lippmann, "A Future for the Tests." *New Republic* (Nov. 29, 1922): 9–11; "The Mental Age of Americans." *New Republic* (Oct. 25, 1922): 213–225; "Mr. Burt and the Intelligence Tests." *New Republic* (May 2, 1923): 263–264; "The Mystery of the 'A' Men." *New Republic*, (Nov. 1, 1922): 246–248; "The Reliability of Intelligence Tests." *New Republic*, (Nov. 8, 1922): 275–277; "Tests of Hereditary Intelligence." *New Republic* (Nov. 22, 1922): 328–330; N. J. Block, and Gerald Dworkin, eds., *The IQ Controversy* (N.Y.: Random House, 1976).

10. R. M. Yerkes, "Psychological Examining in the United States Army." *Memoir of the National Academy of Sciences* 15: 1 (1922).

11. S. J. Gould, *The Mismeasure of Man* (N.Y.: Norton, 1981).

12. A. Jacquard, *In Praise of Difference: Genetics and Human Affairs* (N.Y.: Columbia University Press, 1984).

13. E. and H. Mensh, *The IQ Mythology* (Carbondale, Ill.: Southern University Illinois Press, 1991); C. G. Liungman, *What Is IQ?* (London: Gordon Cremonesi, 1975).

14. W. H. Tucker, *The Science and Politics of Racial Research* (Urbana: University of Illinois Press, 1994); R. Lewontin, S. Rose, and L. Kamin, *Not In Our Genes* (N.Y.: Pantheon Books, 1984).

15. A. Montagu, *Man's Most Dangerous Myth: The Fallacy of Race* (San Francisco: Altamira Press, 6th ed. 1997. First published in 1942 by Columbia University Press).

16. Report of the Joint Commission on Mental Health of Children, *Crisis in Child Mental Health*. New York: Harper & Row, 1970, pp. 216–249; C. V. Willie, B. M. Kramer, and B. S. Brown, *Racism and Mental Health*. Pittsburgh: University of Pittsburgh Press, 1973.

17. M. Gilbert, *The Holocaust: A History of the Jews of Europe during the Second World War* (N.Y.: Holt, Rinehart & Winston, 1985); L. S. Dawidowicz, *The War Against the Jews: 1933–1945* (N.Y.: Holt, Rinehart & Winston, 1975).

18. M. Grant, *The Passing of the Great Race* (N.Y.: Scribner's, 1916), vii–ix, 14–15, 80–81.

19. S. Kühl, *The Nazi Connection: Eugenics, American Racism, and German National Socialism* (N.Y.: Oxford University Press, 1994), 85–88.

20. Grant, *The Passing of the Great Race* (new edition, 1919, 89–92.)

21. S. Kühl, *The Nazi Connection: Eugenics, American Racism, and German National Socialism.*

22. Kühl, op. cit.; R. Proctor, From *Anthropologie* to *Rassenkunde* in the German Anthropological Tradition," in G. W. Stocking, Jr., ed., *Bones, Bodies, and Behavior* (Madison, Wi.: University of Wisconsin Press, 1988), 138–179; also R. Proctor, *Racial Hygiene: Medicine Under the Nazis* (Cambridge: Harvard University Press, 1988); B. Muller-Hill, *Murderous Science* (N.Y.: Oxford University Press,

1988). The Final Solution: A History of European Racism. George L. Mosse, Toward *The Passing of the Great Race*

23. A. Montagu, *The Direction of Human Development* (N.Y.: Harper & Row, 1955); A. Montagu, "The Origin and Significance of Neonatal Immaturity in Man," *Journal of the American Mediocal Association* 178 (1961): 156–157.
24. Grant, *The Passing of the Great Race*, (1916, p. 14.)
25. Osborn, H. F. in Grant, *ibid.*, pp xi–xiii.
26. C. Bolt, *Victorian Attitudes to Race* (London: Routledge, 1971).
27. F. von Bernhardi, N, *Germany and the Next War* (N.Y.: Longmans, Green & Co., 1914).
28. T. Dobzhansky, and A. Montagu, "Natural Selection and the Mental Capacities of Mankind." *Science* 105 (1947): 587–590. See 000–00.
29. A. Montagu, "Education, Technology, and Humanity," in Jarice Hanson ed., *Advances in Telematics* (Norwood, N.J.: Ablex Publishing Co., 1994) vol. 2, 1–15.
30. A. Montagu, *Growing Young.* 2nd ed. (Westwood, Ct., Bergin & Garvey, 1989).

REFERENCES

Birke, L. L., and J. Silvertown, eds. 1984. *More Than the Parts: Biology and Politics.* London.

Bolt, C. 1971. *Victorian Attitudes to Race.* London: Routledge.

Dumont, Louis. 1970. *Homo Hierarchicus.* Chicago: University of Chicago Press.

Greenspan, S. I. 1979. *Intelligence and Adaptation.* N.Y.: International Universities Press.

Kevles, D. J. 1985. *In the Name of Eugenics.* N.Y.: Knopf.

Liungman, C. 1975. *What is IQ?* London: Gordon Cremonesi.

Staub, E. 1989. *The Roots of Evil.* N.Y.: Cambridge University Press.

Stocking, Jr., G. W. 1987. *Victorian Anthropology.* N.Y.: Free Press.

Trent, Jr., J. W. 1994. *Inventing the Feeble Mind.* Berkeley: University of California Press.

Wiener, N. 1950. *The Human Use of Human Beings.* Boston: Houghton, Mifflin.

12

ON CREEPING JENSENISM

C. Loring Brace and
Frank B. Livingstone

Concern about the meaning of the physical differences between human populations dates back to before the dawn of written history, but it did not really become a major issue until the Renaissance, when the revolution in ocean-going transportation brought large numbers of diverse people physically face to face. The superior technology of the Europeans enabled them to coerce and exploit the peoples encountered, many of whom were forcibly uprooted and relocated as slaves. While one could argue that this was one of the most extraordinary examples of barbarism in the annals of "civilization," it was justified at the time, not so much on the basis of race, but because the people being enslaved were "heathens." Actually the "Christianity" of the unprincipled and largely illiterate slaving crews was often a convenient fiction, and the real reasons why the slave trade continued were greed and the force of firearms.

The phenomenon of the Christianized (and even literate) slave removed the initial rationale, but, needless to say, the institution persisted. Economics and the established social order in the

From *Race and Intelligence*, edited by C. L. Brace, G. R. Gamble, and J. T. Bond, 1971, pp. 64–75. Reprinted by permission of the American Anthropological Association.

American South assured its perpetuation while the Calvinistic fatalism of the North tended to maintain the status quo with little question. For example, in 1706 that godly Puritan, Cotton Mather, heartily supported the Christianization of "the Negro" on the one hand, while arguing on the other that baptism does not entitle a slave to liberty (Osofsky, 1967:389). Although Quakers publicly and repeatedly extended Christian principles to the extreme of condemning slavery from the latter third of the seventeenth century on, this did not become a matter of general concern until the winds of "enlightenment" ushered in the Age of Reason, complete with elegant statements on the nature of man and human rights, and culminating in the American Revolution. Backlash followed the excesses of the revolutions in Santo Domingo and France, and it was more than half a century before the momentum of the Enlightenment was regained and slavery was finally abolished—in name, at least. (For excellent and detailed historical treatment, see Jordan, 1968, and Stanton, 1960.)

The intellectual legacy from late eighteenth century idealism, however, is apparent in the continuing debate concerning the meaning of human physical differences. Clouding this debate has been another legacy of considerably less exalted origins. This legacy survives in the wretched social and environmental surroundings that continue to characterize the living conditions of Negroes in the United States. Quite recently there has been an explicit recognition of this situation—witness the belated extension (in 1954 and 1969) of eighteenth century Constitutional guarantees to Americans of African ancestry—but, at the same time, there has also been a continuation of the attempts to justify bloc differences in human treatment that began when slavery was already an accomplished fact.

Enforced inferior status—slavery was initially justified by the heathen state of African peoples. All the other attributes of Negroes were automatically stigmatized and, although the justification changed through time, their association with inferiority has remained a continuing item of faith. Black skin color was regarded as the result of the curse placed on Ham and all his descendants. Negroes then were identified with the Biblical Canaanites, their servitude was considered justified by Noah's curse, and their attributes were regarded as visible evidence of the Lord's displeasure. With the rise of a rational world view in the latter part of the eighteenth century, this became an increasingly unsatisfactory explanation to thoughtful men. Separate creations—separate and unequal—were suggested, although this was offensive to the faithful who preferred something which remained compatible with the Biblical original pair. The result was a pre-Darwinian development of a form of evolution by means of a crudely conceived kind of natural selection (Smith, 1965). Inevitably, however, vested interests of a social and political nature clouded all efforts at objectivity, as they continue to do. The record of published attempts to justify existing social inequalities on the basis of innate or biological differences extends unbroken from the Renaissance era of exploration and subsequent colonization (Jordan, 1968) through the nineteenth century (Barzun, 1965; Stocking, 1968) to the present day. The association with events that maximize human misery (epitomized in the American Civil War and World War II for instance) is so clear that each new attempt to justify differential treatment of large numbers of human beings, often prejudged en masse, should be examined with the greatest of care.

We offer this cautionary preamble because yet another such attempt has been made, this time couched in the language of modern science, published in circumstances which tend to enhance its prestige, and given widespread if uncritical publicity. The presentation we refer to is Jensen's (1969a) monograph-length article in the *Harvard Educational Review*. Pointing up the obvious seriousness of its implications is the fact that the very next issue of the *Review* (Vol. 39, Spring 1969) contained responses from more than a half-dozen scholars. Many of the

points raised are well-taken, but, in the haste of immediate reaction, documentation was incomplete, important aspects were
missed entirely, and organization suffered.[1] Adding further to
this unfortunate confusion is the treatment it has been given in
the popular press. The discussion in the prestigious *New York
Times Magazine* (Edson, 1969), attempting journalistic imparti-
ality, presents the various arguments and rebuttals as though
they were all of equal probability. The result has been the widespread circulation of conclusions which are possibly pernicious,
and certainly premature, to a readership which, though highly
literate, is largely unable to make a reliable independent evaluation.

Seen in perspective, "jensenism, n. the theory that IQ is largely
determined by the genes" (Edson, 1969), is the extreme if logical
outcome of the preoccupation which the field of behavior genetics
has had with the "defeat" of the environmentalists heritage of
Watsonian behaviorism (Hirsch, 1967b:118–119). The extreme
of the environmentalist position is best expressed in Watson's
(1924:82) famous dictum:

> Give me a dozen healthy infants . . . and I'll guarantee to take
> any one at random and train him to become any type of specialist
> I might select—doctor, lawyer, artist, merchant-chief and, yes,
> even beggar-man and thief, regardless of his . . . abilities . . .
> [and] race of his ancestors.

Fulminations against this position by committed racists, who
anathemize it as "equalitarian doctrine," are well known (Putnam, 1961). Objections to extreme environmentalism have also
been repeatedly offered by students of behavior genetics, one of
whom, Hirsch, has variously characterized it as a "counterfactual
assumption" (1961:480), a "counterfactual dogma" (1963), and
a "counterfactual . . . postulate" (1967a), based on "fallacious
reasoning" and "excessively anti-intellectual" (1967b). Both these
positions, the racist and the behavior geneticist, represent reac-

tions to the emotionally based humanitarianism in much of recent social science.

Leaving the racists out of it for the moment, it is evident that the advances in behavior genetics and ethology must be considered of prime importance among the recent major developments in biological, psychological, and anthropological science. This has led to the organization of many symposia and fostered the production of a series of popular books such as those by Lorenz (1966), and Ardrey (1966), Morris (1968, 1969), and Tiger (1969). Questions being asked include "Why are men aggressive?" "Does man have a pair bond?" and "Is there such a thing as male bonding?" The interest in basic human biology is apparent, and much of this new questioning is concerned with supposed "species-specific" characteristics of man, although there is a tendency to postulate a genetic cause for human behavioral differences—Lorenz's (1966:236) discussion of Ute aggression, for example. Given these recent trends, it seems inevitable that attention would be focused on intelligence differences and that genetic causation should be stressed.

In the general picture, caution should be urged on two accounts, and Jensen's work illustrates what can happen when neither problem is adequately considered. First, the distinction between individual and population performance should be clearly perceived; and, second, if genetic differences are to be the object of concern, thorough control of the environmental component of observed variation should be achieved.

Considering the first issue, one of the roots of the problem is the inability of Western science—and biological science in particular—to recognize and differentiate between individual and populational phenomena. Certainly birth rates, death rates, or intelligence levels are the result of individual performances, but their variability among human populations is not primarily due to individual genetic differences, however much these may be involved. Many of the recent discussions of incest, inbreeding, and sexual behavior demonstrate the same inability to differentiate populational and individual phenomena (Roberts, 1967; Livingstone, 1969). Ironically, Hirsch, one of the people most responsible for the trend of research which Jensen has carried to something of an extreme, has apparently sensed the fact that the approach he has promoted is being carried too far and has recently articulated a brief critique which could be applied to Jensen's work (Hirsch, 1968:42):

> What is the relative importance of genetic endowment and of environmental milieu in the development of the intelligence of *an* individual? The answers given to that question . . . have nothing to do with *an* individual, nor are they based on the study of development. The answers have been based on the test performance of a cross-section of a *population* of individuals at a single time in their lives.

In his critical comment, Kagan (1969) in fact notes that Jensen makes no effort to resolve this issue.

Turning to the environmental component in observed behavior, we see that again Jensen has made little effort to grapple with the problem. Admittedly, the thrust of recent work in behavior genetics has been to discount the environmental contribution, but, again, Hirsch, who has been a major part of this thrust, has recently provided a warning against excesses in this direction. While he refers to the heredity-environment question as "a pseudo-question to which there is no answer" (1968:42), he goes on to warn that

> it should also be noted that one cannot infer from a high heritability value that the influence of environment is small or unimportant, *as so many people try to do* [1968:43, italics Hirsch's].

To illustrate the unwarranted extreme of what Medawar (1961:60) has called "geneticism," Hirsch refers to the controversial pronouncements of William B. Shockley, Nobel laureate in physics. (For excerpts of Shockley's speech, see Birch 1968:49, and for a responsible rebuttal, see Crow, Neel, and Stern, 1967). Mention of Shockley in this regard is particularly important since Jensen was apparently much impressed by Shockley when he was visiting Stanford in 1966–67. The result was what has been called his "most unfortunate speech" illustrating "the dangers of inappropriate use of both the concept of heritability and that of race by the biometrically unsophisticated" (Hirsch, 1967a:434). Jensen's speech, in turn, provided the background for the article which is the focus of our concern here.

The first half of Jensen's article is a comprehensive review of quantitative genetics. He concludes this review with the statement (1969a:65) that

> the question of whether heritability estimates can contribute anything to our understanding of the relative importance of genetic and environmental factors in accounting for average phenotypic differences between racial groups (or any other socially defined group) is too complex to be considered here.

Since heritability estimates are specific to the population studied —at the time studied—and since they vary considerably with environmental circumstances, Jensen, as quoted, correctly expresses the problem and should have stopped there. He does not stop, however, and proceeds under the assumption that there is a definite intelligence heritability of .8. Not only is this the highest found, but it is based on twin data, which are most unlikely to differentiate the environmental component.[2] This estimate he then generalizes to all humanity.

Despite his statement that the matter is "too complex," his further discussion of racial differences apparently implies that the preceding review of quantitative genetics supports his view. It does not. Furthermore, we fail to see how, after pointing out that environment can change IQ by as much as 70 points, he can make the statement that "in short it is doubtful that there is any significant environmental effect on IQ."

For purposes of comparison, let us take the case of stature. As a "trait," it is sufficiently complex to warrant the expression of doubts concerning simplistic treatment, although it is somewhat less of a "typological reification" (Hirsch, 1968:44) than intelligence. Treating them for the moment as though they were comparable traits, it is evident that both are under polygenic control. Proceeding with this in mind, Kagan (1969), in his initial reaction to Jensen's article, cites the difference in stature between rural and urban populations in Latin America to show the effect of environment on an inherited trait. Hunt (1969), on his part, makes casual mention of stature in colonial Jamestown, Plymouth, and during the American Revolution, noting the radical changes that have taken place since that time.[8]

Other examples are well known and documented, but perhaps the changes in Sweden and the Low Countries in the past 100 years constitute a better example (Chamla, 1964). Stature certainly has a major genetic component. Estimates concerning its heritability vary widely, although they average about .5, comparable to the average for IQ despite what Jensen claims. For example, Kagan and Moss (1959) have found an average of .43 between parents and offspring for IQ, and an average correlation of .36 for stature. In the past 100 years, or about four generations, very little genetic change could have occurred, particularly when one considers the lack of evidence for strong selection. However, in that time, the stature of the average adult male in many European countries has changed 4-5 in., or almost two standard deviations. Since populational differences in IQ are at most about one standard deviation, we do not see why anyone would maintain that the same amount of nongenetic change could not occur where IQ is concerned—particularly when the trend of IQ increase is not only known but, in some cases, even greater than the trend for increase in stature.

The principal reason for the observed increase in stature appears to be a change in nutrition, particularly an increase in the amount of protein in the diet. A similar increase in stature is occurring in Japan (Kimura, 1967), and there is a strong correlation between stature and protein intake (Takahashi, 1966). Recently evidence has been accumulating to suggest that mental development can be markedly influenced by nutritional inadequacy—particularly where protein-calorie malnutrition occurs during the period in development when the brain is growing most rapidly (Cravioto, DeLicardie, and Birch, 1966; Davison and Dobbing, 1966; Eichenwald and Fry, 1969).

Brain weight, amount of brain protein, and RNA increase linearly during the first year of human life—all being directly proportional to the increase in head circumference. The amount of brain DNA is regarded as a good indication of cell number and, although it largely ceases to increase at six months, it too maintains a direct relation to head circumference during the first year of life (Winick and Rosso, 1969). With this in mind, it is of grim interest to note that in cases of severe malnutrition, head circumferences have been recorded that were two standard deviations below the mean for normal children of the same age. Brain weight and protein were reduced proportionately, while DNA content was reduced at least as much and in some cases more (Winick and Rosso, 1969:776). In one instance, rehabilitation was tried on malnourished children and behavioral recovery was measured by the Gesell method. Children who were under six months of age on admission retained their deficit, leading to the conclusion (Cravioto and Robles, 1965:463) that "there is a high possibility that at least the children severely malnourished during the first six months of their lives might retain a permanent mental deficit." In another instance, recovery of head circumference following early malnutrition lagged way behind other aspects of growth recovery (Graham, 1968, esp. Fig. 3).

The studies cited above deal principally with the consequences of malnutrition in Latin America, but the record from Africa is equally clear: small fetal and neonatal brain sizes among the starving people of Biafra (Gans, 1969), decreased cranial circumference and reduced brain weight among the malnourished of Uganda (Brown, 1965, 1966), reduced cranial circumference and lower intelligence test scores in the Cape Coloured of South Africa. In the latter case, the reduction in circumference and test score was in comparison with a control population, also of Cape Coloured, but one which was not suffering from severe malnutrition. The differences were statistically significant ($P = < .01$) but, interestingly enough, there was no significant difference between the parents of the two groups (Stoch and Smythe, 1963, 1968).

One could argue that the works we have mentioned deal principally with extremes of malnutrition, and, in fact, Jensen does so, claiming that there is little extreme malnutrition in the United States. Yet with substantially more than half of the American black population living at or below the poverty level as defined by the US Department of Health, Education, and Welfare, with the shocking deprivation recently and belatedly brought to the attention of the US Congress (Javits, 1969; Hollings and Jablow, 1970), and with the obstacles to survival facing the American poor so graphically depicted by Coles (1969), it would be most surprising if malnutrition did *not* contribute something to the lowering of intelligence test scores in American Negroes —all other things being equal, which, of course, is not the case.

Before leaving strictly biological matters, we should note that deprivation need not be extreme for its consequences to show. Admittedly, these data are derived from studies on experimental animals rather than on human beings, but this can hardly justify ignoring their implications. Inadequate nutrition delays development of the myelin nerve sheaths in rats, and the deficit is not completely made up. The importance of this particular study is to be seen in the fact that the deprivation was that of the lower end of the "normal" range and did *not* constitute "starvation" (Dobbing, 1964:508). Demonstration of the reduction in cell number of other brain tissues following early deprivation is equally clear (Dickerson, 1968:335; Dobbing, 1968:195). Not surprisingly, the behavioral consequences are also apparent (Eichenwald and Fry, 1969:646):

> Protein deprivation in early life not only causes . . . behavioral changes but also reduces the capacity of the experimental animal to learn at a later age. Furthermore, rats born of and suckled by malnourished mothers are similarly deficient in their learning capacity.

So far we have stressed the role of nutrition—particularly protein-calorie malnutrition—in the stunting of mental development. Vitamin deficiency, illness susceptibility, and chronic ill-health all contribute to a malnutrition-disease syndrome (see Scrimshaw and Gordon, 1968) which, given nothing else, should certainly lower performance levels on intelligence tests. These factors alone can go a long way towards accounting for the differences in the tested intelligence of the world's populations, but they constitute only a part of the nongenetic background of testable mental performance. However, strictly experiential factors can have an even more pronounced effect on intelligence test performance and may completely mask the nutritional and genetic factors.

Obviously there are many problems associated with estimating the heritability of behavioral traits. Data on IQ tests derived from family studies do indicate a genetic component, although this may in fact be somewhat less than the heritability for physical traits. The heritable component is extremely difficult to separate from the nonheritable component in assessing the results of most tests of complex behavior, and it is apparent that Jensen really does not make the effort to do so. The cumulative interaction of particular types of experience with facets of biological maturation produces an elaboration that is extremely difficult to assess in terms of what percentage of which part is represented in the end-product. This is what Hirsch meant when he referred to the nature-nuture problem as a "pseudo-question to which there is no answer," but if Jensen expects to demonstrate the credibility of his conclusions, it is a question to the solution of which he must direct research efforts more carefully planned and better controlled than any that have yet been undertaken or even proposed.[4]

Studies on the heritability of behavioral traits in *Drosophila* are frequently cited to bolster estimates on behavioral heritability in man, but, even ignoring the enormous phylogenetic gap, recent research has shown the heritability of the oft-mentioned geotactic and phototactic responses to be quite low. Richmond (1969), for example, found the heritability of both to be less than .2 in all cases and not significantly different from .0 in one instance. Dobzhansky and Spassky (1969) found realized heritabilities for these traits to be below .1.

We should like to make it quite clear that we do not deny the existence of a genetic component that contributes to differences in performance on IQ tests—*within* a single population, where conditions of early experience and education are relatively similar. The differences, however, are less important than implied by Jensen.[5] For example, he has noted that there are significant correlations between the IQ scores of adopted children and their real parents, while correlations with their foster parents tend to be nonsignificant. However, he does not mention the fact that adopted children consistently display a substantially higher IQ than their biological parents. Skodak and Skeels (1949) found that the average IQ of the real mothers was 86 while that of their children adopted into other families was 106—well over a whole standard deviation higher. Surely this indicates that, with an improved socioeconomic background, one can accomplish in one generation a change that is greater than any difference between racial or religious groups in the United States. The overwhelming component of this difference is certainly environmental.

In their review of behavior genetics, Spuhler and Lindzey (1967) come to much the same conclusion with regard to racial differences in IQ. While citing many cases of behavioral differences among humans which have a known genetic basis, they show that there is a very significant relationship between IQ and educational expenditure. They conclude (1967:405): that "we do not *know* whether there are significant differences between races in the kinds and frequencies of polygenes controlling general intellectual ability." In our turn, we do not see how anyone would disagree with this statement, but would go further. We suggest that it is possible to explain all the measured differences among major groups of men primarily by environmental factors, while noting, on the other hand, that it is not possible to provide genetic explanations which are evolutionarily plausible for most of these differences.

Within a given population there certainly is a spectrum of the inherited component of "intelligence," and there may be some association between this and certain demanding occupations, but from the perspective of biological evolution, the time depth of the professions in question is so shallow that little change in the genetic structure of the population can have occurred. Furthermore, Jensen's reaffirmation of the time-honored assumption that there are average differences in innate intelligence between social classes is also without demonstrable foundation and is very probably incorrect. At the top end of the social scale in America, the initial establishment of position may have had some relationship to ability, although demonstrable unprincipled ruthlessness was at least as important (Lundberg, 1968). Once established, position is retained with little relation to the continuing presence of ability in the families in question and reproductive behavior is notoriously unrelated to the *intellectual* attributes of the partners chosen.

At the bottom of the social hierarchy there is one outstanding factor that makes suspect any claims concerning inherited ability. This factor is poverty. It is not unexpected that "in most settings there is a positive association between poor nutrition and poor social conditions" (Richardson, 1968:355). And if this itself does not assure retardation in the development of mental ability, an atmosphere of social impoverishment certainly does. Inculcation into the ways of "the culture of poverty" (Lewis, 1966) does not train people to perform well on IQ tests. Nor has ability or its lack had much to do with recruitment into the ranks of the extremely poor. Mere possession of a black skin was sufficient until quite recently and, with the addition of certain geographic provisos, still is.

One of Jensen's basic assumptions is made explicit in the comment printed with his approval in *The New York Times Magazine* (Sept. 21, 1969, p. 14). In this he clearly regards "intelligence as the ability to adapt to civilization," adding that "races differ in this ability according to the civilizations in which they live." Building on this, he further assumes that "the Stanford-Binet IQ test measures the ability to adapt to Western civilization," an ability in which he claims American Negroes to be inferior to "Orientals," with the clear implication that, as a blanket category, they are far less well-endowed than American whites. For an educated man to hold such beliefs is regrettable, but for a presumed "scientist" to be allowed to publish them in a popular journal without informed editorial supervision is an example of the unfortunate failure of intellectual responsibility.

First of all, "Western civilization," if this is indeed a valid category in this context, is largely a product of the Industrial Revolution and has a maximum time depth of little more than two centuries. Even if natural selection had been operating at maximum efficiency during this time, it would have been hard put to change a polygenic trait as much as a full standard deviation for an entire population. In terms of actual reproductive performance, there is little reason to believe that the intellectually highly endowed were in fact favored to such an extent. If it is fair to make such sweeping judgments, we can make a case for the fact that most of the labor roles which were created by and ensured the success of the Industrial Revolution—and, hence, Western civilization—required relatively little learning and no creative decision-making on the part of their occupants. This, of course, is why child labor was practical until it was outlawed. In terms of the kind of folk knowledge and unwritten tradition necessary for survival, it is perhaps fair to claim that the average European (i.e., peasant) of the sixteenth century lived a life that had more elements of similarity with that of the average West African than it did with that of the descendents of either one in the Europe or America of the twentieth century.

Obviously in saying this we are making a value judgment that cannot be proven one way or the other, but, nevertheless, it would appear to square with the data of both anthropology and history rather better than Jensen's suggestion that races differ in intelligence "according to the civilizations in which they live." Considering the fact that, with a few numerically unimportant exceptions, all human populations now live under conditions characterized by cultural adaptations—"civilizations" in Jensen's terms—that are radically different from those of their lineal predecessors only a few thousand years ago (and often much less), it is reasonable to conclude that *no* races are really adapted to the "civilizations in which they live."

The time is not so long past when instructing Negroes in the mechanics of reading and writing was contrary to law in parts of the American South. Educational opportunities remain drastically substandard, and there is scarcely a rudimentary form of the tradition in child-rearing, so characteristic of the middle and upper-middle classes, which promotes literacy as the key to worldly success. When used to compare groups with different cultural backgrounds, the Stanford-Binet IQ test is less a com-

parative measure of ability than an index of enculturation into
the ways of the American middle class. Since Negroes have been
systematically (see the account in Woodward, 1966) denied en-
trance to the middle-class world, it is not surprising that their
learned behavior is measurably different from that on which the
IQ test is based. Certainly before the results of IQ tests can be
taken as indicating inherited differences in ability, some cogni-
zance should be taken of the effect of tester expectation on performance (Rosenthal, 1966), or motivation in its various aspects
(Katz, 1967), and of the results of nonverbal tests where conceptual styles of the groups being studied are markedly different
(Cohen, 1969).

Finally, Jensen's assertion that intelligence or brain differences
must exist among the "races" of man is an argument by analogy
which ends up assuming what he presumably was trying to
demonstrate. As he notes, separate breeding isolates will very
likely show differences on some genetic characteristics which will
be due to the various evolutionary forces. In most cases, these
differences, if at all considerable, will coincide with differences
in selective forces to which the populations are subject. To conclude from this perfectly reasonable genetic statement, as Jensen
does, that it is "practically axiomatic" that two populations
will be different in *any* characteristic having high heritability
(1969a:80) and, ergo, that the races of man differ in their genetic
capacities for intelligence or in the genetic properties of their
brains is simply a non sequitur. Certainly it is contrary to all we
have learned from evolutionary biology. All human populations
have 10 fingers, 10 toes, 2 eyes, and 32 teeth per individual. These
all have high heritability and some variability within human isolates, but are constant between isolates. This is primarily due to
the operation of natural selection, a factor which Jensen de-
emphasizes.

Behavior or brain function is obviously under the control of
many loci, and, equally obviously, it is subject to the influence

of natural selection. If differences exist at these loci among human populations, these differences would be correlated with differences in the forces of selection. These in turn would be reflected in the cultural and behavioral attributes designed to counteract them. Within any continent there are as many differences in cultural and behavioral adaptation as there are between continents.

However, implicit and even explicit in much of behavior genetics is the assumption that cultural differences are caused by genetic differences. The anthropological findings that cultural differences represent responses to varying environmentally imposed selective forces are simply ignored. Selective force distributions do not neatly coincide as a rule. Some may covary in some areas, some may show crosscutting distributions, and others may vary completely at random with respect to each other. Given this situation, we have elsewhere suggested that, in order to make sense out of human biological variation, the typological gestalt of the race concept be abandoned and human adaptation be studied trait by trait in the contexts where the relevant selective forces have been at work (Livingstone, 1962, 1964; Brace, 1964a, b). We cannot resist adding the comment that this approach, if taken seriously, can completely defuse the potentially explosive situation which Jensen has created.

Jensen (1969a:89) cites the Harlows (Harlow and Harlow, 1962) to the effect that if the average IQ were lower and thus fewer geniuses were produced, then there would be fewer people to make inventions and discoveries and thus cultural evolution would have been slower. We suggest that, just as mutation rate does not control the speed of biological evolutionary change, neither does the frequency of the occurrence of genius have anything to do with the rate of cultural evolution. We can even offer a converse suggestion and raise the suspicion that levels of cultural complexity are inversely related to IQ. Survival takes less innate wit for the socially and economically privileged than it does for those to whom culture does not offer ready-made solu-

tions for most of life's problems. It is possible that the average
level of intelligence is highest among populations where culture is
least complex. Post-Pleistocene food preparation techniques, including, especially, pots in which boiling was easy and common,
have rendered the human dentition of far less importance to
survival than before. The sharp reductions in the Post-Pleistocene
human face are concentrated in the dentition and have proceeded
farthest in just those people whose forebears have been longest
associated with "high civilization" (Brabant and Twiesselmann,
1964:55). Is it not possible that supraregional political and economic organization increased the survival chances of any given
individual without regard for his inherited ability? Why then
should we not expect an average lowering of basic intelligence
to accumulate under such circumstances? We offer this solely as
an hypothesis for possible testing. Jensen, on the other hand, feels
that failure to test the hypothesis that Negroes are intellectually
inferior for genetic reasons may constitute "our society's greatest
injustice to Negro Americans" (1969b:6). Unless there is a latent
racist bias to the kind of research Jensen feels is urgent,[6] it is difficult to see why the testing of the hypothesis we have outlined
above is not considered at least of equal importance with the
testing of its converse, and yet the possibility is not even mentioned, let alone seriously entertained. Ironically, the possible
consequences of our failure to take this issue seriously will be
enormous for *all* Americans, but particularly for non-Negro
Americans, i.e., "whites."

Knowledge of both cultural and biological dimensions is required for a full understanding of the human condition. The
stress on "geneticism" (to use Medawar's word again) should
be tempered by an insistence that the environmental component
be thoroughly controlled. Certainly as much effort and sophistication should be devoted to this task as to comparative performance
assessments. Jensen's work is conspicuously lacking in this regard.
As such, it is the logical antithesis to the old environmentalist

thesis. Perhaps the synthesis will contain the reasonable parts of each.

Finally, in the words of Jensen (1969:78), "If a society completely believed and practiced the ideal of treating every person as an individual, it would be hard to see why there should be any problems about 'race' per se." Unfortunately Jensen ignores this ideal in practice and, in the absence of adequate control, insists on treating a substantial portion of the American population as though a stereotype were sufficient and as though the individual could be ignored. In effect this guarantees that there *will* continue to be problems about race per se and that Jensen and his like will only intensify them.

NOTES

1. Since the preparation of this manuscript (for the November 1969 Annual Meeting of the American Anthropological Association), another paper by Jensen has appeared (1969b) in conjunction with more thoroughly documented critiques in the summer issue of the *Harvard Educational Review*. Some of the points we raise are discussed in greater detail than in our presentation, but since other important ones are not even mentioned we have decided to let our paper stand substantially as originally written.

2. For an elegant demonstration of the inappropriateness of Jensen's use of twin data, see the critique by Light and Smith (1969). Fehr (1969) also shows the inaccuracy of Jensen's use of twin data to arrive at his assumed heritability level.

3. Jensen (1969b) offers a rebuttal to the somewhat anecdotal accounts of Kagan and Hunt but, again, uses a single debatable account to generalize for all mankind.

4. This criticism of Jensen's approach has been eloquently and forcefully made by Stinchcombe (1969) and Deutsch (1969).

5. The interaction of heredity and environment in the development of a trait has been brought into focus by Stinchcombe (1969), but an even more important point is made by Gregg and Sanday in their contribution to this present volume. They note that heritability figures for given traits will vary in inverse proportion to the similarity of the environments of the populations being considered. This illustrates the generalization offered some time ago by Lerner (1958:63, italics his): "The heritability of a given trait may differ from one population to another, or vary in

the same population at different times . . . *strictly speaking, any intra-generation estimate of heritability is valid only for the particular genera-tion of the specific population from which the data used in arriving at it derive.*" As Hirsch (1969:138) has phrased it, "Heredity is a property of populations and not of traits."

6. The regretful comment made by a collaborator and admirer of Jensen's experimental research is worth quoting here: "I believe the impact of Jensen's article was destructive; that it has had negative implications for the struggle against racism and for the improvement of the educational system. The conclusions he draws are, I believe, unwarranted by the existing data and reflect a consistent bias toward a racist hypothesis" (Deutsch, 1969:525).

REFERENCES

Ardrey, R. 1966. The Territorial Imperative. New York: Delta.

Bajema, C. J. 1963. Estimation of the Direction and Intensity of Natural Selection in Relation to Human Intelligence by Means of the Intrinsic Rate of Natural Increase. Eugenics Quarterly 10:175–187.

Barzun, Jacques. 1965. Race: A Study in Superstition. New York: Harper Torchbooks.

Birch, Herbert G. 1968. Boldness and Judgment in Behavior Genetics. *In* Science and the Concept of Race. M. Mead, T. Dobzhansky, E. Tobach, and R. Light, eds. New York: Columbia University Press.

Brabant, H., and F. Twiesselmann. 1964. Observations sur l'Evolution de la Denture permanente humain en Europe Occidentale. Bulletin du Groupe-ment International pour la Recherche scientifique en Stomatologie 7:11–84.

Brace, C. L. 1964a. The Concept of Race. Current Anthropology 5:313–320. 1964b. A Non-Racial Approach Toward the Understanding of Human Diversity. *In* The Concept of Race. M. F. A. Montagu, ed. New York: Free Press.

Brown, Roy E. 1965. Decreased Brain Weight in Malnutrition and Its Im-plications. East Africa Medical Journal 42:584–595. 1966. Organ Weight in Malnutrition with Special Reference to Brain Weight. Developmental Medicine and Child Neurology 8:512–522.

Chamla, M-C. 1964. L'accroisement de la Stature en France de 1800 à 1960; Comparison avec les pays d'Europe Occidentale. Bulletins et Mémoires de la Société d'Anthropologie de Paris, Série 11, 6:201–278.

Cohen, Rosalie A. 1969. Conceptual Styles, Culture Conflict, and Nonverbal Texts of Intelligence. American Anthropologist 71:828–856.

Coles, Robert. 1969. Still Hungry in America. Cleveland: North American Library.

Cravioto, J., E. R. DeLicardie, and H. G. Birch. 1966. Nutrition, Growth and Neuro-Integrative Development: An Experimental and Ecologic Study. Pediatrics 38:319–372.

Cravioto, J., and B. Robles. 1965. Evolution of Adaptive and Motor Be-havior During Rehabilitation from Kwashiorkor. American Journal of Orthopsychiatry 35:449–464.

Crow, James F., James V. Neel, and Curt Stern. 1967. Racial Studies: Academy States Position on Call for New Research. Science 158:892-893.

Davison, A. N., and J. Dobbing. 1968. Myelination as a Vulnerable Period in Brain Development. British Medical Bulletin 22:40-44.

Dickerson, J. W. T. 1968. The Relation of the Timing and Severity of Undernutrition to Its Effect on the Chemical Structure of the Central Nervous System. *In* Calorie Deficiencies and Protein Deficiencies. R. A. McCance and E. M. Widdowson, eds. London: J. A. Churchill.

Dobbing, J. 1964. The Influence of Nutrition on the Development and Myelination of the Brain. Proceedings of the Royal Society of London, Series B, Biological Sciences 159:503-509. 1968. Effects of Experimental Undernutrition on Development of the Nervous System. *In* Malnutrition, Learning and Behavior. N. S. Scrimshaw and J. E. Gordon, eds. Cambridge: MIT Press.

Dobzhansky, T., and B. Spassky. 1969. Artificial and Natural Selection for Two Behavioral Traits in *Drosophila pseudoobscura*. Proceedings of the National Academy of Sciences 61:75-80.

Edson, Lee. 1969. jensenism, n. the theory that IQ is largely determined by the genes. The New York Times Magazine, August 31, pp. 10-11, 40-41, 43-47.

Eichenwald, Heinz F., and Peggy Crooke Fry. 1969. Nutrition and Learning. Science 163:644-648.

Gans, Bruno. 1969. A Biafran Relief Mission. The Lancet 1969-I:660-665.

Graham, G. G. 1968. The Later Growth of Malnourished Infants: Effects of Age, Severity and Subsequent Diet. *In* Calorie Deficiencies and Protein Deficiencies. R. A. McCance and E. M. Widdowson, eds. London: J. A. Churchill.

Hirsch, Jerry. 1961. Genetics of Mental Disease Symposium, 1960: Discussion: The Role of Assumptions in the Analysis and Interpretation of Data. American Journal of Orthopsychiatry 31:474-480. 1963. Behavior Genetics and Individuality Understood: Behaviorism's Counterfactual Dogma Blinded the Behavioral Sciences to the Significance of Meiosis. Science 142:1436-1442. 1967a. ed. Behavior Genetic Analysis. New York: McGraw-Hill. 1967b. Behavior-Genetic, or "Experimental," Analysis: The Challenge of Science Versus the Lure of Technology. American Psychologist 22:118-130. 1968. Behavior-Genetic Analysis and the Study of Man. *In* Science and the Concept of Race. M. Mead, T. Dobzhansky, E. Tobach, and R. Light, eds. New York: Columbia University Press.

Hollings, Ernest F., as told by Paul Jablow. 1970. We Must Wipe out Hunger in America. Good Housekeeping, January, pp. 68-69, 144-146.

Hunt, J. McV. 1969. Has Compensatory Education Failed? Has It Been Attempted? Harvard Educational Review 39:278-300.

Javits, Jacob. 1969. Hunger in America. Playboy, December, p. 147.

Jensen, Arthur R. 1969a. How Much Can We Boost IQ and Scholastic Achievement? Harvard Educational Review 39:1-123. 1969b. Arthur Jensen Replies. Psychology Today 3:4, 6.

Jordan, Winthrop D. 1968. White over Black: American Attitudes Toward the Negro, 1550-1812. Chapel Hill: University of North Carolina Press.

Kagan, Jerome S. 1969. Inadequate Evidence and Illogical Conclusions. Harvard Educational Review 39:274-277.

Kagan, J. S., and H. A. Moss. 1959. Parental Correlates of Child's IQ and Height: A Cross-Validation of the Berkeley Growth Study Results. Child Development 30:325-332.

Katz, Irwin. 1967. Some Motivational Determinants of Racial Differences in Intellectual Achievement. International Journal of Psychology 2:1-12.

Kimura, K. 1967. A Consideration of the Secular Trend in Japanese for Height and Weight by a Graphic Method. American Journal of Physical Anthropology 27:89-94.

Lewis, Oscar. 1966. The Culture of Poverty. Scientific American 215:19-25.

Livingstone, Frank B. 1962. On the Nonexistence of Human Races. Current Anthropology 3:279-281. 1964. On the Nonexistence of Human Races. *In* The Concept of Race. Ashley Montagu, ed. New York: Free Press of Glencoe. 1969. Genetics, Ecology and the Origins of Incest and Exogamy. Current Anthropology 10:45-61.

Lorenz, Konrad. 1966. On Aggression. New York: Bantam.

Lundberg, Ferdinand. 1968. The Rich and the Super-Rich: A Study in the Power of Money Today. New York: Lyle Stuart.

Medawar, P. B. 1961. The Future of Man. New York: Mentor.

Morris, Desmond. 1968. The Naked Ape. New York: McGraw-Hill. 1969. The Human Zoo. New York: McGraw-Hill.

Osofsky, Gilbert. 1967. The Burden of Race: A Documentary History of Negro-White Relations in America. New York: Harper and Row.

Putnam, Carleton. 1961. Race and Reason: A Yankee View. Washington: Public Affairs Press.

Richardson, Stephen A. 1968. The Influence of Social-Environmental and Nutritional Factors on Mental Ability. In Malnutrition, Learning and Behavior. N. S. Scrimshaw and J. E. Gordon, eds. Cambridge: MIT Press.

Richmond, R. C. 1969. Heritability of Phototactic and Geotactic Responses in Drosophila pseudoobscura. American Naturalist 103:315-316.

Roberts, D. F. 1967. Incest, Inbreeding and Mental Abilities. British Medical Journal 4:336-337.

Rosenthal, Robert. 1966. Experimenter Effects in Behavioral Research. New York: Appleton-Century-Crofts.

Scrimshaw, Nevin S., and John E. Gordon (eds.). 1968. Malnutrition, Learning and Behavior. Cambridge: MIT Press.

Skodak, M., and H. M. Skeels. 1949. A Final Follow-up Study of One Hundred Adopted Children. Journal of Genetic Psychology 75:85-125.

Smith, Samuel Stanhope. 1965. An Essay on the Causes of Variety of Complexion and Figure in the Human Species (reprint of the 1810 version). Winthrop D. Jordan, ed. Cambridge: The Belknap Press.

Spuhler, J. N., and G. Lindzey. 1967. Racial Differences in Behavior. In Behavior-Genetic Analysis. Jerry Hirsch, ed. New York: McGraw-Hill.

Stanton, William. 1960. The Leopard's Spots: Scientific Attitudes Toward Race in America, 1815-59. Chicago: University of Chicago Press.

Stoch, Mavis B., and P. M. Smythe. 1963. Does Undernutrition During Infancy Inhibit Brain Growth and Subsequent Intellectual Development? Archives of Diseases of Childhood 38:546-552. 1968. Undernutrition During Infancy, and Subsequent Brain Growth and Intellectual Development. In Malnutrition, Learning and Behavior. N. S. Scrimshaw and J. E. Gordon, eds. Cambridge: MIT Press.

Stocking, George W., Jr. 1968. Race, Culture and Evolution: Essays in the History of Anthropology. New York: Free Press.

Takahashi, E. 1966. Growth and Environmental Factors in Japan. Human Biology 38:112–130.

Tiger, Lionel. 1969. Men in Groups. New York: Random House.

Watson, J. B. 1924. Behaviorism. New York: W. W. Norton.

Winick, Myron, and Pedro Rosso. 1969. Head Circumference and Cellular Growth of the Brain in Normal and Marasmic Children. The Journal of Pediatrics 74:774–778.

Woodward, C. Vann. 1966. The Strange Career of Jim Crow. New York: Galaxy Book.

SUPPLEMENTARY REFERENCES

Deutsch, Martin. 1969. Happenings on the Way Back to the Forum: Social Science, IQ, and Race Differences Revisited. Harvard Educational Review 39:523–557.

Fehr, F. S. 1969. Critique of Hereditarian Accounts of "Intelligence" and Contrary Findings: A Reply to Jensen. Harvard Educational Review 39:571–580.

Harlow, H. F., and M. K. Harlow. 1962. The Mind of Man. In Yearbook of Science and Technology, pp. 31–39.

Hirsch, Jerry. 1969. Biosocial Hybrid Vigor Sought, Babel Discovered. Review of Genetics: Second of a Series on Biology and Behavior, edited by David C. Glass. Contemporary Psychology 14:138–139.

Jensen, Arthur R. 1969b. Reducing the Heredity-Environment Uncertainty: A Reply. Harvard Educational Review 39:449–483.

Lerner, I. Michael. 1958. The Genetic Basis of Selection. New York: John Wiley.

Light, Richard J., and Paul V. Smith. 1969. Social Allocation Models of Intelligence: A Methodological Inquiry. Harvard Educational Review 39:484–510.

Stinchcombe, Arthur L. 1969. Environment: The Cumulation of Effects Is Yet to be Understood. Harvard Educational Review 39:511–522.

13

RACE AND INTELLIGENCE

Richard C. Lewontin

In the spring of 1653 Pope Innocent X condemned a pernicious heresy which espoused the doctrines of "total depravity, irresistible grace, lack of free will, predestination and limited atonement." That heresy was Jansenism and its author was Cornelius Jansen, Bishop of Ypres.

In the winter of 1968 the same doctrine appeared in the "Harvard Educational Review." That doctrine is now called "jensenism" by the "New York Times Magazine" and its author is Arthur R. Jensen, professor of educational psychology at the University of California at Berkeley. It is a doctrine as erroneous in the twentieth century as it was in the seventeenth. I shall try to play the Innocent.

Jensen's article, "How Much Can We Boost I.Q. and Scholastic Achievement?" created such a furor that the "Review" reprinted it along with critiques by psychologists, theorists of education and a population geneticist under the title "Environment, Heredity and Intelligence." The article first came to my attention when, at no little expense, it was sent to every member of the National Academy of Sciences by the eminent white Anglo-Saxon inventor, William Shockley, as part of his continuing campaign to

From *Science and Public Affairs*, the Bulletin of the Atomic Scientists, March 1970, pp. 2–8. Copyright © 1970 by the Educational Foundation for Nuclear Science. Reprinted by permission.

have the Academy study the effects of inter-racial mating. It is little wonder that the "New York Times" found the matter newsworthy, and that Professor Jensen has surely become the most discussed and least read essayist since Karl Marx. I shall try, in this article, to display Professor Jensen's argument, to show how the structure of his argument is designed to make his point and to reveal what appear to be deeply embedded assumptions derived from a particular world view, leading him to erroneous conclusions. I shall say little or nothing about the critiques of Jensen's article, which would require even more space to criticize than the original article itself.

THE POSITION

Jensen's argument consists essentially of an elaboration on two incontrovertible facts, a causative explanation and a programmatic conclusion. The two facts are that black people perform, on the average, more poorly than whites on standard I.Q. tests, and that special programs of compensatory education so far tried have not had much success in removing this difference. His causative explanation for these facts is that I.Q. is highly heritable, with most of the variation among individuals arising from genetic rather than environmental sources. His programmatic conclusion is that there is no use in trying to remove the difference in I.Q. by education since it arises chiefly from genetic causes and the best thing that can be done for black children is to capitalize on those skills for which they are biologically adapted. Such a conclusion is so clearly at variance with the present egalitarian consensus and so clearly smacks of a racist elitism, whatever its merit or motivation, that a very careful analysis of the argument is in order.

The article begins with the pronouncement: "Compensatory education has been tried and it apparently has failed." A documentation of that failure and a definition of compensatory education are left to the end of the article for good logical and pedagogical reasons. Having caught our attention by whacking us over the head with a two-by-four, like that famous trainer of mules, Jensen then asks:

> What has gone wrong? In other fields, when bridges do not stand, when aircraft do not fly, when machines do not work, when treatments do not cure, despite all the conscientious efforts on the part of many persons to make them do so, one begins to question the basic assumptions, principles, theories, and hypotheses that guide one's offorts. Is it time to follow suit in education?

Who can help but answer that last rhetorical question with a resounding "Yes"? What thoughtful and intelligent person can avoid being struck by the intellectual and empirical bankruptcy of educational psychology as it is practiced in our mass educational systems? The innocent reader will immediately fall into close sympathy with Professor Jensen, who, it seems, is about to dissect educational psychology and show it up as a pre-scientific jumble without theoretic coherence or prescriptive competence. But the innocent reader will be wrong. For the rest of Jensen's article puts the blame for the failure of his science not on the scientists but on the children. According to him, it is not that his science and its practitioners have failed utterly to understand human motivation, behavior and development but simply that the damn kids are ineducable.

The unconscious irony of his metaphor of bridges, airplanes and machines has apparently been lost on him. The fact is that in the twentieth century bridges do stand, machines do work and airplanes do fly, because they are built on clearly understood mechanical and hydrodynamic principles which even moderately careful and intelligent engineers can put into practice. In the seventeenth century that was not the case, and the general opinion was that men would never succeed in their attempts to fly because flying was impossible. Jensen proposes that we take the same view of education and that, in the terms of his metaphor, fallen bridges be taken as evidence of the unbridgeability of rivers. The alternative explanation, that educational psychology is still in the seventeenth century, is apparently not part of his philosophy.

This view of technological failure as arising from ontological rather than epistemological sources is a common form of apology at many levels of practice. Anyone who has dealt with plumbers will appreciate how many things "can't be fixed" or "weren't meant to be used like that." Physicists tell me that their failure to formulate an elegant general theory of fundamental particles is a result of there not being any underlying regularity to be discerned. How often men, in their overweening pride, blame nature for their own failures. This professionalist bias, that if a problem were soluble it would have been solved, lies at the basis of Jensen's thesis which can only be appreciated when seen in this light.

Having begun with the assumption that I.Q. cannot be equalized, Jensen now goes on to why not. He begins his investigation with a discussion of the "nature of intelligence," by which he means the way in which intelligence is defined by testing and the correlation of intelligence test scores with scholastic and occupational performance. A very strong point is made that I.Q. testing was developed in a Western industrialized society specifically as a prognostication of success in that society by the generally accepted criteria. He makes a special point of noting that psychologists' notions of status and success have a high correlation with those of the society at large, so that it is entirely reasonable that tests created by psychologists will correlate highly with conventional measures of success. One might think that this argument, that I.Q. testing is "culture bound," would militate against Jensen's general thesis of the biological and specifically genetical basis of I.Q. differences. Indeed, it is an argument often used against I.Q. testing for so-called "deprived" children, since it is supposed that they have developed in a subculture that does not prepare them for such tests. What role does this "environmentalist" argument play in Jensen's thesis? Is it simply evidence of his total fairness and objectivity? No. Jensen has seen, more clearly than most, that the argument of the specific cultural origins of I.Q. testing and especially the high correlation of these tests with occupational status cuts both ways. For if the poorer performance of blacks on I.Q. tests has largely genetic rather than environmental causes, then it follows that blacks are also genetically handicapped for other high status components of Western culture. That is, what Jensen is arguing is that differences between cultures are in large part genetically determined and that I.Q. testing is simply one manifestation of those differences.

In this light we can also understand his argument concerning the existence of "general intelligence" as measured by I.Q. tests. Jensen is at some pains to convince his readers that there is a single factor, g, which, in factor analysis of various intelligence tests, accounts for a large fraction of the variance of scores. The existence of such a factor, while not critical to the argument, obviously simplifies it, for then I.Q. tests would really be testing for "something" rather than just being correlated with scholastic and occupational performance. While Jensen denies that intelligence should be reified, he comes perilously close to doing so in his discussion of g.

Without going into factor analysis at any length, I will point out only that factor analysis does not give a unique result for any given set of data. Rather, it gives an infinity of possible results among which the investigator chooses according to his tastes and preconceptions of the models he is fitting. One strategy in factor analysis is to pack as much weight as possible into one factor, while another is to distribute the weights over as many factors as possible as equally as possible. Whether one chooses one of these or some other depends upon one's model, the numerical analysis only providing the weights appropriate for each model. Thus, the impression left by Jensen that factor analysis somehow naturally or ineluctably isolates one factor with high weight is wrong.

"TRUE MERIT"?

In the welter of psychological metaphysics involving concepts of "crystallized" as against "fluid" intelligence, "generalized" intelligence, "intelligence" as opposed to "mental ability," there is some danger of losing sight of Jensen's main point: I.Q. tests are culture bound and there is good reason that they should be, because they are predictors of culture bound activities and values. What is further implied, of course, is that those who do not perform well on these tests are less well suited for high status and must paint barns rather than pictures. We read that "We have to face it: the assortment of persons into occupational roles simply is not 'fair' in any absolute sense. The best we can hope for is that true merit, given equality of opportunity, act as a basis for the natural assorting process." What a world view is there revealed! The most rewarding places in society shall go to those with "true merit" and that is the best we can hope for. Of course, Professor Jensen is safe since, despite the abject failure of educational psychology to solve the problems it has set itself, that failure does not arise from lack of "true merit" on the part of psychologists but from the natural intransigence of their human subjects.

Having established that there are differences among men in the degree to which they are adapted to higher status and high satisfaction roles in Western society, and having stated that education has not succeeded in removing these differences, Jensen now moves on to their cause. He raises the question of "fixed" intelligence and quite rightly dismisses it as misleading. He introduces us here to what he regards as the two real issues. "The first issue concerns the genetic basis of individual differences in

intelligence; the second concerns the stability or constancy of the
I.Q. through the individual's lifetime." Jensen devotes some three-
quarters of his essay to an attempt to demonstrate that I.Q. is
developmentally rather stable, being to all intents and purposes
fixed after the age of eight, and that most of the variation in I.Q.
among individuals in the population has a genetic rather than environmental basis. Before looking in detail at some of these arguments, we must again ask where he is headed. While Jensen argues strongly that I.Q. is "culture bound," he wishes to argue
that it is not environmentally determined. This is a vital distinction. The I.Q. is "culture bound" in the sense that it is related to
performance in a Western industrial society. But the determination of the ability to perform culturally defined tasks might itself
be entirely genetic. For example, a person suffering from a genetically caused deaf-mutism is handicapped to different extents
in cultures requiring different degrees of verbal performance, yet
his disorder did not have an environmental origin.

Jensen first dispenses with the question of developmental stability of I.Q. Citing Benjamin Bloom's survey of the literature,
he concludes that the correlation between test scores of an individual at different ages is close to unity after the age of eight.
The inference to be drawn from this fact is, I suppose, that it is
not worth trying to change I.Q. by training after that age. But
such an inference cannot be made. All that can be said is that,
given the usual progression of educational experience to which
most children are exposed, there is sufficient consistency not to
cause any remarkable changes in I.Q. That is, a child whose educational experience (in the broad sense) may have ruined his
capacity to perform by the age of eight is not likely to experience an environment in his later years that will do much to alter
those capacities. Indeed, given the present state of educational
theory and practice, there is likely to be a considerable reinforcement of early performance. To say that children do not change

their I.Q. is not the same as saying they cannot. Moreover, Jensen is curiously silent on the lower correlation and apparent plasticity of I.Q. at younger ages, which is after all the chief point of Bloom's work.

THE GENETIC ARGUMENT

The heart of Jensen's paper is contained in his long discussion of the distribution and inheritance of intelligence. Clearly he feels that here his main point is to be established. The failure of compensatory education, the developmental stability of I.Q., the obvious difference between the performance of blacks and whites can be best understood, he believes, when the full impact of the findings of genetics is felt. In his view, insufficient attention has been given by social scientists to the findings of geneticists, and I must agree with him. Although there are exceptions, there has been a strong professional bias toward the assumption that human behavior is infinitely plastic, a bias natural enough in men whose professional commitment is to changing behavior. It is as a reaction to this tradition, and as a natural outcome of his confrontation with the failure of educational psychology, that Jensen's own opposite bias flows, as I have already claimed.

The first step in his genetical argument is the demonstration that I.Q. scores are normally distributed or nearly so. I am unable to find in his paper any explicit statement of why he regards this point as so important. From repeated references to Sir Francis Galton, filial regression, mutant genes, a few major genes for exceptional ability and assortative mating, it gradually emerges that an underlying normality of the distribution appears to Jensen as an important consequence of genetic control of I.Q. He asks: ". . . is intelligence itself—not just our measurements of it—really normally distributed?" Apparently he believes that if intelligence, quite aside from measurement, were really normally distributed, this would demonstrate its biological and genetical status. Aside from a serious epistemological error involved in the question, the basis for his concern is itself erroneous. There is nothing in genetic theory that requires or even suggests that a phenotypic character should be normally distributed, even when it is completely determined genetically. Depending upon the degree of dominance of genes, interaction between them, frequencies of alternative alleles at the various gene loci in the population and allometric growth relations between various parts of the organism transforming primary gene effects, a character may have almost any uni-modal distribution and under some circumstances even a multi-modal one.

After establishing the near-normality of the curve of I.Q. scores, Jensen goes directly to a discussion of the genetics of continuously varying characters. He begins by quoting with approbation E. L. Thorndike's maxim: "In the actual race of life, which is not to get ahead, but to get ahead of somebody, the chief determining factor is heredity." This quotation along with many others used by Jensen shows a style of argument that is not congenial to natural scientists, however it may be a part of other disciplines. There is a great deal of appeal to authority and the acceptance of the empirically unsubstantiated opinions of eminent authorities as a kind of relevant evidence. We hear of "three eminent geneticists," or "the most distinguished exponent [of genetical methods], Sir Cyril Burt." The irrelevance of this kind of argument is illustrated precisely by the appeal to E. L. Thorndike, who, despite his eminence in the history of psychology, made the statement quoted by Jensen in 1905, when nothing was known about genetics outside of attempts to confirm Mendel's paper. Whatever the eventual truth of his statement turns out to be, Thorndike made it out of his utter ignorance of the genetics of human behavior, and it can only be ascribed to the sheer prejudice of a Methodist Yankee.

HERITABILITY

To understand the main genetical argument of Jensen, we must dwell, as he does, on the concept of heritability. We cannot speak of a trait being molded by heredity, as opposed to environment. Every character of an organism is the result of a unique interaction between the inherited genetic information and the sequence of environments through which the organism has passed during its development. For some traits the variations in environment have little effect, so that once the genotype is known, the eventual form of the organism is pretty well specified. For other traits, specification of the genetic makeup may be a very poor predictor of the eventual phenotype because even the smallest environmental effects may affect the trait greatly. But for all traits there is a many-many relationship between gene and character and between environment and character. Only by a specification of both the genotype and the environmental sequence can the character be predicted. Nevertheless, traits do vary in the degree of their genetic determination and this degree can be expressed, among other ways, by their heritabilities.

The distribution of character values, say I.Q. scores, in a population arises from a mixture of a large number of genotypes. Each genotype in the population does not have a unique phenotype corresponding to it because the different individuals of that genotype have undergone somewhat different environmental sequences in their development. Thus, each genotype has a distribution of I.Q. scores associated with it. Some genotypes are more common in the population so their distributions contribute heavily to determining the over-all distribution, while others are rare and make little contribution. The total variation in the population, as measured by the variance, results from the variation between the mean I.Q. scores of the different genotypes and the variation around each genotypic mean. The heritability of a measurement is defined as the ratio of the variance due to the differences between the genotypes to the total variance in the population. If this heritability were 1.0, it would mean that all the variation in the population resulted from differences between genotypes but that there was no environmentally caused variation around each genotype mean. On the other hand, a heritability of 0.0 would mean that there was no genetic variation because all individuals were effectively identical in their genes, and that all the variation in the population arose from environmental differences in the development of the different individuals.

Defined in this way, heritability is not a concept that can be applied to a trait in general, but only to a trait in a particular population, in a particular set of environments. Thus, different populations may have more or less genetic variation for the same character. Moreover, a character may be relatively insensitive to environment in a particular environmental range, but be extremely sensitive outside this range. Many such characters are known, and it is the commonest kind of relation between character and environment. Finally, some genotypes are more sensitive to environmental fluctuation than others so that two populations with the same genetic variance but different genotypes, and living in the same environments, may still have different heritabilities for a trait.

The estimation of heritability of a trait in a population depends on measuring individuals of known degrees of relationship to each other and comparing the observed correlation in the trait between relatives with the theoretical correlation from genetic theory. There are two difficulties that arise in such a procedure. First, the exact theoretical correlation between relatives, except for identical twins, cannot be specified unless there is detailed knowledge of the mode of inheritance of the character. A first order approximation is possible, however, based upon some simplifying assumptions, and it is unusual for this approximation to be badly off.

A much more serious difficulty arises because relatives are correlated not only in their heredities but also in their environments. Two sibs are much more alike in the sequence of environments in which they developed than are two cousins or two unrelated persons. As a result, there will be an overestimate of the heritability of a character, arising from the added correlation between relatives from environmental similarities. There is no easy way to get around this bias in general so that great weight must be put on peculiar situations in which the ordinary environmental correlations are disturbed. That is why so much emphasis is placed, in human genetics, on the handful of cases of identical twins raised apart from birth, and the much more numerous cases of totally unrelated children raised in the same family. Neither of these cases is completely reliable, however, since twins separated from birth are nevertheless likely to be raised in families belonging to the same socio-economic, racial, religious and ethnic categories, while unrelated children raised in the same family may easily be treated rather more differently than biological sibs. Despite these difficulties, the weight of evidence from a variety of correlations between relatives puts the heritability of I.Q. in various human populations between .6 and .8. For reasons of his argument, Jensen prefers the higher value but it is not worth quibbling over. Volumes could be written on the evaluation of heritability estimates for I.Q. and one can find a number of faults with Jensen's treatment of the published data. However, it is irrelevant to questions of race and intelligence, and to questions of the failure of compensatory education, whether the heritability of I.Q. is .4 or .8, so I shall accept Jensen's rather high estimate without serious argument.

The description I have given of heritability, its application to a specific population in a specific set of environments and the difficulties in its accurate estimation are all discussed by Jensen. While the emphasis he gives to various points differs from mine, and his estimate of heritability is on the high side, he appears to have said in one way or another just about everything that a judicious man can say. The very judiciousness of his argument has been disarming to geneticists especially, and they have failed to note the extraordinary conclusions that are drawn from these reasonable premises. Indeed, the logical and empirical hiatus between the conclusions and the premises is especially striking and thought-provoking in view of Jensen's apparent understanding of the technical issues.

The first conclusion concerns the cause of the difference between the I.Q. distributions of blacks and whites. On the average, over a number of studies, blacks have a distribution of I.Q. scores whose mean is about 15 points—about 1 standard deviation —below whites. Taking into account the lower variance of scores among blacks than among whites, this difference means that about 11 per cent of blacks have I.Q. scores above the mean white score (as compared with 50 per cent of whites) while 18 per cent of whites score below the mean black score (again, as compared to 50 per cent of blacks). If, according to Jensen, "gross socio-economic factors" are equalized between the tested groups, the difference in means is reduced to 11 points. It is hard to know what to say about overlap between the groups after this correction, since the standard deviations of such equalized populations will be lower. From these and related observations, and the estimate of .8 for the heritability of I.Q. (in white populations, no reliable estimate existing for blacks), Jensen concludes that:

> . . . all we are left with are various lines of evidence, no one of which is definitive alone, but which, viewed altogether, make it a not unreasonable hypothesis that genetic factors are strongly implicated in the average Negro-white intelligence difference. The preponderance of evidence is, in my opinion, less consistent with a strictly environmental hypothesis than with a genetic hypothesis, which, of course, does not exclude the influence of environment on its interaction with genetic factors.

Anyone not familiar with the standard litany of academic disclaimers ("not unreasonable hypothesis," "does not exclude," "in my opinion") will, taking this statement at face value, find nothing to disagree with since it says nothing. To contrast a "strictly environmental hypothesis" with "a genetic hypothesis which . . . does not exclude the influence of the environment" is to be guilty of the utmost triviality. If that is the only conclusion he means to come to, Jensen has just wasted a great deal of space in the "Harvard Educational Review." But of course, like all cant, the special language of the social scientist needs to be translated into common English. What Jensen is saying is: "It is pretty clear, although not absolutely proved, that most of the difference in I.Q. between blacks and whites is genetical." This, at least, is not a trivial conclusion. Indeed, it may even be true. However, the evidence offered by Jensen is irrelevant.

IS IT LIKELY?

How can that be? We have admitted the high heritability of I.Q. and the reality of the difference between the black and the white distributions. Moreover, we have seen that adjustment for gross socio-economic level still leaves a large difference. Is it not then likely that the difference is gentic? No. It is neither likely nor unlikely. There is no evidence. The fundamental error of Jensen's argument is to confuse heritability of a character within a population with heritability of the difference between two populations. Indeed, between two populations, the concept of heritability of their difference is meaningless. This is because a variance based upon two measurements has only one degree of freedom and so cannot be partitioned into genetic and environmental components. The genetic basis of the difference between two populations bears no logical or empirical relation to the heritability within populations and cannot be inferred from it, as I will show in a simple but realistic example. In addition, the notion that eliminating what appear a priori to be major environmental variables will serve to eliminate a large part of the environmentally caused difference between the populations is biologically naïve. In the context of I.Q. testing, it assumes that educational psychologists know what the major sources of environmental difference between black and white performance are. Thus, Jensen compares blacks with American Indians whom he regards as far more environmentally disadvantaged. But a priori judgments of the importance of different aspects of the environment are valueless, as every ecologist and plant physiologist knows. My example will speak to that point as well.

Let us take two completely inbred lines of corn. Because they are completely inbred by self-fertilization, there is no genetic variation in either line, but the two lines will be genetically different from each other. Let us now plant seeds of these two inbred lines in flower pots with ordinary potting soil, one seed of each line to a pot. After they have germinated and grown for a few weeks we will measure the height of each plant. We will discover variation in height from plant to plant. Because each line is completely inbred, the variation in height within lines must be entirely environmental, a result of variation in potting conditions from pot to pot. Then the heritability of plant height in both lines is o.o. But there will be an average difference in plant height between lines that arises entirely from the fact that the two lines are genetically different. Thus the difference between lines is entirely genetical even though the heritability of height is o!

Now let us do the opposite experiment. We will take two handsful from a sack containing seed of an open-pollinated variety of corn. Such a variety has lots of genetic variation in it. Instead of using potting soil, however, we will grow the seed in vermiculite watered with a carefully made up nutrient, Knop's solution, used by plant physiologists for controlled growth experiments.

One batch of seed will be grown on complete Knop's solution, but the other will have the concentration of nitrates cut in half and, in addition, we will leave out the minute trace of zinc salt that is part of the necessary trace elements (30 parts per billion). After several weeks we will measure the plants. Now we will find variation within seed lots which is entirely genetical since no environmental variation within lots was allowed. Thus heritability will be 1.0. However, there will be a radical difference between seed lots which is ascribable entirely to the difference in nutrient levels. Thus, we have a case where heritability within populations is complete, yet the difference between populations is entirely environmental!

But let us carry our experiment to the end. Suppose we do not know about the difference in the nutrient solutions because it was really the carelessness of our assistant that was involved. We call in a friend who is a very careful chemist and ask him to look into the matter for us. He analyzes the nutrient solutions and discovers the obvious—only half as much nitrates in the case of the stunted plants. So we add the missing nitrates and do the experiment again. This time our second batch of plants will grow a little larger but not much, and we will conclude that the difference between the lots is genetic since equalizing the large difference in nitrate level had so little effect. But, of course, we would be wrong for it is the missing trace of zinc that is the real culprit. Finally, it should be pointed out that it took many years before the importance of minute trace elements in plant physiology was worked out because ordinary laboratory glassware will leach out enough of many trace elements to let plants grow normally. Should educational psychologists study plant physiology?

Having disposed, I hope, of Jensen's conclusion that the high heritability of I.Q. and the lack of effect of correction for gross socio-economic class are presumptive evidence for the genetic basis of the difference between blacks and whites, I will turn to his second erroneous conclusion. The article under discussion began with the observation, which he documents, that compensatory education for the disadvantaged (blacks, chiefly) has failed. The explanation offered for the failure is that I.Q. has a high heritability and that therefore the difference between the races is also mostly genetical. Given that the racial difference is genetical, then environmental change and educational effort cannot make much difference and cannot close the gap very much between blacks and whites. I have already argued that there is no evidence one way or the other about the genetics of inter-racial I.Q. differences. To understand Jensen's second error, however, we will suppose that the difference is indeed genetical. Let it be entirely genetical. Does this mean that compensatory education, having failed, must fail? The supposition that it must arises from a misapprehension about the fixity of genetically determined traits. It was thought at one time that genetic disorders, because they were genetic, were incurable. Yet we now know that inborn errors of metabolism are indeed curable if their biochemistry is sufficiently well understood and if deficient metabolic products can be supplied exogenously. Yet in the normal range of environments, these inborn errors manifest themselves irrespective of the usual environmental variables. That is, even though no environment in the normal range has an effect on the character, there may be special environments, created in response to our knowledge of the underlying biology of a character, which are effective in altering it.

But we do not need recourse to abnormalities of development to see this point. Jensen says that "there is no reason to believe that the I.Q.'s of deprived children, given an environment of abundance, would rise to a higher level than the already privileged children's I.Q.'s." It is empirically wrong to argue that if the richest environment experience we can conceive does not raise I.Q. substantially, then we have exhausted the environmental possibilities. In the seventeenth century the infant mortality rates were many times their present level at all socio-economic levels.

Using what was then the normal range of environments, the infant mortality rate of the highest socio-economic class would have been regarded as the limit below which one could not reasonably expect to reduce the death rate. But changes in sanitation, public health and disease control—changes which are commonplace to us now but would have seemed incredible to a man of the seventeenth century—have reduced the infant mortality rates of "disadvantaged" urban Americans well below those of even the richest members of seventeenth century society. The argument that compensatory education is hopeless is equivalent to saying that changing the form of the seventeenth century gutter would not have a pronounced effect on public sanitation. What compensatory education will be able to accomplish when the study of human behavior finally emerges from its pre-scientific era is anyone's guess. It will be most extraordinary if it stands as the sole exception to the rule that technological progress exceeds by manyfold what even the most optimistic might have imagined.

The real issue in compensatory education does not lie in the heritability of I.Q. or in the possible limits of educational technology. On the reasonable assumption that ways of significantly altering mental capacities can be developed if it is important enough to do so, the real issue is what the goals of our society will be. Do we want to foster a society in which the "race of life" is "to get ahead of somebody" and in which "true merit," be it genetically or environmentally determined, will be the criterion of men's earthly reward? Or do we want a society in which every man can aspire to the fullest measure of psychic and material fulfillment that social activity can produce? Professor Jensen has made it fairly clear to me what sort of society he wants.

I oppose him.

14

HERITABILITY ANALYSES OF IQ SCORES: SCIENCE OR NUMEROLOGY?

David Layzer

The question, "To what extent can the development of basic cognitive skills be influenced by various kinds of environmental intervention?" is central to current discussions of educational and social policy. Much of the discussion has focused on one rather narrow, but comparatively well-defined, aspect of this question— the heritability of scores on standardized tests and the implications of heritability estimates. In 1969, A. R. Jensen (*1*) reviewed a large number of British and American studies of the broad heritability of IQ scores and concluded that, for representative British and American populations, it probably lies between 0.7 and 0.8, the best single estimate being close to 0.8. Jensen argued from these figures that inequalities in cognitive performance are largely genetic in origin and that comparatively little can be done to reduce them through practicable educational and social reforms, a thesis he has since developed further (*2*). He also argued that the reported difference in average IQ between black and white children in the United States probably has a substantial

From *Science*, Vol. 183, 29 March 1974, pp. 1259–66. Copyright 1974 by the American Association for the Advancement of Science. Reprinted by permission.

genetic component, another thesis elaborated later (3). From the same heritability estimates, R. J. Herrnstein has argued (4, 5) that the elimination of artificial barriers to social and economic mobility (such as those based on race, sex, income, and social class) must inevitably lead to the emergence of an hereditary meritocracy based on IQ.

After the publication of Jensen's 1969 article, Christopher Jencks undertook a detailed analysis of the available data on IQ. Devoting themselves to the broader question of how family and schooling affect social and economic, as well as cognitive, inequality, Jencks and his colleagues concluded (6, p. 315) that "the chances are about 2 out of 3 that [the heritability of IQ scores] is between 0.35 and 0.55." But Jencks' analysis also indicated that the purely environmental contribution to the IQ variance probably lies between 0.25 and 0.45—an estimate only mildly discordant with Jensen's estimate of 0.2 to 0.3. Jencks and his collaborators concluded, moreover, that educational inequalities accounted for only a minor part of the environmental variance.

From this brief summary, it is clear that two methodologically distinct kinds of issues are involved in current discussions of IQ heritability and its implications. Some of the issues are purely scientific: What are the limitations of conventional heritability analysis as applied to IQ scores? How reliable are heritability estimates like those quoted above? What inferences can legitimately be drawn from heritability estimates of various kinds? Of more widespread interest than these technical questions are those that involve social, political, educational, and philosophical considerations. Questions of the first kind can be discussed and resolved in a value-free context—or at least in a context of values agreed upon by members of the scientific community. Moreover, they must be resolved before the broader issues can be meaningfully debated. In this article I address myself to that task.

Although several illuminating discussions of IQ heritability have already appeared, it seems to me that some important aspects of the problem have not yet been adequately discussed. For example, nearly all the published discussions that I am aware of take it for granted that some meaningful estimate of IQ heritability—high or low, rough or accurate—can be extracted from the reams of published statistics and that refinements of current techniques for gathering and analyzing test data may be counted on to yield increasingly reliable estimates. These propositions are by no means self-evident, however, and one of my purposes here is to demonstrate that they are actually false.

This conclusion rests upon two arguments: One concerns the limitations of conventional heritability analysis, the other the validity of IQ scores as phenotypic measurements. Contrary to widely held beliefs, (i) heritability analysis does not require the genotype-environment interaction to be small, and (ii) a high phenotypic correlation between separated monozygotic twins does not, in general, imply that the genotype-environment interaction is small. If genotype-environment interaction does contribute substantially to the phenotypic value of a trait (as there are strong biological reasons for supposing in the case of phenotypically plastic traits), then a necessary and sufficient condition for the applicability of heritability analysis is the absence of genotype-environment correlation. This condition is rarely, if ever, met for behavioral traits in human populations. The second argument is that IQ scores contain uncontrollable, systematic errors of unknown magnitude.

LIMITATIONS OF THE HERITABILITY CONCEPT

Estimates of broad heritability (h^2) answer the question: What fraction of the variance of a phenotypic trait in a given population is caused by (or attributable to) genetic differences? A phenotypic value (P) that depends on a genotypic variable (or set of variables) (x) and an environmental variable (or set of variables) (y) may be expressed as the sum of a genotypic value $[G(x)]$, an environmental value $[E(y)]$, and a remainder $[R(x,y)]$ that depends jointly on x and y (see Eq. 4). Under certain conditions (which probably never obtain in natural human populations), there is a well-defined optimal additive decomposition of this kind—that is, a decomposition that minimizes the variance (Var) of R. Under these conditions, the quantities $h^2 = Var\{G\}/Var\{P\}$ and $e^2 = Var\{E\}/Var\{P\}$ (e^2 is the environmental fraction of phenotypic variance) are well defined.

Even when h^2 and e^2 are well defined, however, their practical significance may be obscure. Consider the hypothetical trait illustrated in Fig. 12.1. Note that the phenotypic value (P) cannot be expressed as the sum of a genotypic value $[G(x)]$ and an environmental value $[E(y)]$. Consider, for example, the pairs of points (A_1, A_2) and (B_1, B_2) in Fig. 12.1. Since ΔP (the difference between the phenotypic values) $= 0$ for each pair, the differences ΔG and ΔE would be equal and opposite if an additive representation were possible. But ΔG must have the same value for both pairs, and the values of ΔE must evidently be unequal [since they correspond to different increments (Δy)]. Hence an additive representation is impossible (7).

I show below that G and E can be unambiguously defined if, and only if, genotype-environment correlations are absent. Even then, however, a certain practical ambiguity persists. Genetic differences may influence the development of a trait in qualitatively distinct ways. For example, the curves labeled x_1, x_2, and x_3 in Fig. 12.1 have different thresholds, different slopes, and different final values. Heritability estimates do not take such qualitative distinctions into account. Thus, if the environmental variable y is distributed in a narrow range about the value y_1, as illustrated in Fig. 12.1, h^2 is close to unity. Yet in these circumstances the phenotypic variance could reasonably be considered to be largely environmental in origin since it is much greater than the phenotypic variance that would be measured in an environment ($y = y_2$) that permitted maximum development of the trait, consistent with genetic endowment. This point has been elaborated by R. C. Lewontin (*8*).

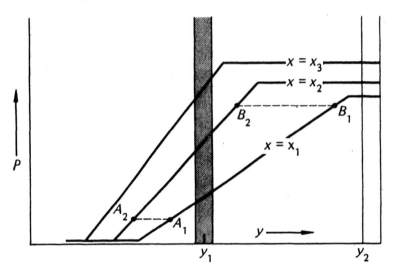

Fig. 12.1. Phenotypic value (P) of a hypothetical metric trait as a function of an environmental variable (x) for three values of a genotypic variable (y). A_1 and A_2 (also B_1 and B_2) indicate individuals with a common phenotypic value but distinct genotypes x_1 and x_2, respectively.

The conventional definitions of G (genotypic value) and E (environmental value) have specific mathematical advantages in the context of a specific mathematical theory. Other ways of assessing the effects of environment on phenotypically plastic traits may, however, be more useful in other contexts. In particular, certain kinds of intervention studies may provide more direct and more useful information about the effects of environment on IQ than conventional studies of IQ heritability.

CONVENTIONAL HERITABILITY ANALYSIS AND ITS LIMITATIONS

Three mathematically and biologically distinct effects complicate conventional heritability analysis: genotype-environment correlation, genotype-environment interaction, and gene-gene interaction. I now consider the theoretical limitations imposed by these effects.

Let $P(x,y)$ denote the value of a phenotypic character that depends on n genotypic variables $x_1, \ldots, x_n$, denoted collectively by x, and m environmental variables $y_1, \ldots, y_m$, denoted collectively by y. The x_i and y_j (where i and j are integers) are random variables whose joint-frequency distribution is specified by the function $\Phi(x,y)$; P is a random function of these random variables. $\mathcal{E}\{f\}$ is the expectation value of a function $f(x,y)$:

$$\mathcal{E}\{f\} = \int \ldots \int f(x,y)\, \Phi(x,y)dxdy \tag{1}$$

where $dx = dx_1 \ldots dx_n$, $dy = dy_1 \ldots dy_m$, and the integration extends over the ranges of all the variables.

The genotypic value G and the environmental value E are defined as follows (9):

$$G(x) = \int \ldots \int P(x,y)\, \Phi(y|x)dy \tag{2a}$$

$$E(y) = \int \ldots \int P(x,y)\, \Phi(x|y)dx \tag{2b}$$

where the conditional frequency functions $\Phi(x|y)$ and $\Phi(y|x)$ are defined by

$$\Phi(x,y) = \Phi(x|y)\, \Phi_2(y) = \Phi(y|x)\, \Phi_1(x) \tag{3a}$$

$$\Phi_1(x) = \int \Phi(x,y)dy, \quad \Phi_2(y) = \int \Phi(x,y)dx \tag{3b}$$

One can then write P in the form

$$P(x,y) = G(x) + E(y) + R(x,y) \tag{4}$$

(this equation defines R), whence

$$Var\{P\} = Var\{G\} + Var\{E\} + 2\,Cov\{G,E\} + I \tag{5}$$

where

$$I = 2\,Cov\{G + E, R\} + Var\{R\} \qquad (6)$$

Here Cov denotes the covariance and I the contribution of genotype-environment interaction to the phenotypic variance.

More generally, consider two subpopulations between whose members a 1-to-1 correspondence, defined by some genetic or environmental relationship, has been established. For example, the two subpopulations might consist of children and their respective mothers or of foster children and their respective foster siblings. For each subpopulation, one may write an equation with the form of Eq. 4. Using variables without primes to refer to the first subpopulation and variables with primes to refer to the second, multiplying the two equations together, and averaging the resulting equation, one obtains

$$Cov\{P,P'\} = Cov\{G,G'\} + Cov\{E,E'\}$$
$$+ Cov\{G,E'\} + Cov\{G',E\} + J \qquad (7)$$

where

$$J = Cov\{G + E, R'\} + Cov\{G' + E', R\} + Cov\{R,R'\} \qquad (8)$$

where J represents the contribution of genotype-environment interaction to the phenotypic covariance.

The phenotypic variance, along with phenotypic covariances referring to certain pairs of subpopulations, may be estimated from appropriate phenotypic measurements. From these data one must try to estimate the individual components of the phenotypic variance that appear on the right side of Eq. 5. In what circumstances is this possible?

If either E or G is negligible, the problem has a trivial solution. Otherwise, it is insoluble unless the genotype-environment covariances on Eqs. 5 and 7 are negligible. For if these terms are not negligible and their structure is not known a priori, the number of unknowns exceeds the number of conditions. One cannot even derive an upper bound for the genetic variance under these circumstances. For suppose one were to equate all genotype-environment correlations (*Cor*) in Eqs. 5 and 7 to their theoretical upper limits, $Cor\{G,E\} = Cor\{G',E'\} = 1$ and $Cor\{G,E'\} = Cor\{G',E\} = Cor\{G,G'\}$. The number of unknowns would still exceed the number of conditions because there is no a priori information about the magnitude, or even the sign, of the terms *I* and *J*.

The genotype-environment covariances are negligible if, and only if, the genotypic and environmental variables are statistically independent to a high degree of approximation. If this is true, then the joint-frequency function (Φ) assumes the form

$$\Phi(x,y) = \Phi_1(x)\, \Phi_2(y) \tag{9}$$

In these circumstances, not only do all genotype-environment covariances vanish, but so do the covariances $Cov\{G,R\}$, $Cov\{G,R'\}$, $Cov\{E,R\}$, and so forth in Eqs. 6 and 8 (*10*). Equations 5 and 7 then reduce to

$$Var\{P\} = Var\{G\} + Var\{E\} + Var\{R\} \tag{10a}$$
$$Cov\{P,P'\} = Cov\{G,G'\} + Cov\{E,E'\} + Cov\{R,R'\} \tag{10b}$$

This remarkable simplification of the terms *I* and *J* in Eqs. 5 and 7 is a consequence of Fisher's definitions of *G* and *E* (*9*). It does not occur for other definitions. An equally important consequence of these definitions is that they minimize the expectation of R^2 (*11*). That is, they provide the best possible additive representation of the phenotypic value. Both properties hold only so long as the genotypic and environmental variables are independent of one another.

The term $Cov\{R,R'\}$ in Eq. 10b vanishes if either the genotypes or the environments of the two subpopulations are statistically independent. It vanishes, in particular, for monozygotic twins reared in uncorrelated environments and for genetically unrelated individuals reared in identical environments. For these two special cases, respectively, the equations are

$$Cov\{P,P'\} = Var\{G\} \tag{11a}$$
$$Cov\{P,P'\} = Var\{E\} \tag{11b}$$

If all the subpopulations under consideration are fair samples of the parent population, then Eqs. 10a, 11a, and 11b are three equations for three unknowns, and $Var\{G\}$, $Var\{E\}$, and $Var\{R\}$ can all be estimated. If only the phenotypic variance and the variance for separated monozygotic twins are known, their difference provides an upper limit for the environmental variance.

Under certain assumptions, the genotypic covariance between related individuals can be related to the genotypic variance. Consider an equilibrated population of randomly mating diploids, effectively infinite in size so that inbreeding may be neglected, and assume that the trait under consideration is specified by an arbitrary number of unlinked genes, each of which may exist in an arbitrary number of statistically independent allelic states. Under these assumptions, G may be written in the form

$$G = \sum_{r,s} G(r,s) \tag{12}$$

where r and s, in the sum indicated by Σ, take on all integer values (and the value zero) consistent with the condition $r + s \leq n$, the number of pairs of homologous loci specifying the trait. The ordered pair (r,s) specifies a configuration consisting of r alleles at nonhomologous loci and s pairs of alleles at homologous loci. $G(r,s)$ denotes the sum of all contributions to G resulting from allelic configurations of the type (r,s):

$$G(r,s) = \Sigma g(i_1, \ldots, i_r; j_1, \ldots, j_s) \tag{13}$$

where g is a random variable depending on the indicated loci and the sum runs over all sets of indices specifying distinct configurations of the type (r,s). In particular, $G(1,0) \equiv G_A$ is the so-called additive contribution to G, a sum of $2n$ individual allelic contributions (each represented by a random variable); $G(0,1) \equiv G_D$ is the dominance contribution, a sum of n contributions from pairs of homologous loci; $G(2,0)$ is an epistatic contribution, made up of contributions from pairs of nonhomologous loci; and so on. By virtue of the assumptions concerning statistical independence of allelic states, all the random variables that figure in the decompositions (Eqs. 12 and 13) are statistically independent. The variance of G is accordingly given by

$$Var\{G\} \equiv \sigma_G^2 = \sum_{r,s} \sigma_{rs}^2$$

$$\sigma_{rs}^2 \equiv Var\{G(r,s)\}$$

$$= \sum Var\{g(i_1, \ldots, i_r; j_1, \ldots, j_s)\} \qquad (14)$$

where σ_{rs} denotes the variance of the random variable $G(r,s)$. The genotype covariance between individuals related in a known way is given by

$$Cov\{G,G'\} = \sum_{r,s} P(r,s)\sigma_{rs}^2 \qquad (15)$$

where $P(r,s)$ is the probability of coincidence between homologous allelic configurations of type (r,s) in the related individuals. In particular, $P(1,0)$ is the probability that a given allele in genome 1 also occurs (at one of the two corresponding loci) in genome 2; $P(0,1)$ is the probability that a given pair of alleles at homologous loci in genome 1 also occurs in genome 2; and so on. From the assumptions about statistical independence, it follows at once that

$$P(r,s) = P_1^r P_2^s \qquad (16)$$

where

$$P_1 \equiv P(1,0) = \frac{1}{2}(\phi + \phi')$$

$$P_2 \equiv P(0,1) = \phi\phi' \qquad (17)$$

Here ϕ and ϕ' denote the probability of receiving the same gene at a given locus by way of the father and the mother respectively. These results were first obtained by Kempthorne (*12*).

If the two subpopulations are characterized by statistically independent environmental variables, Eq. 10b reduces to

$$Cov\{P,P'\} = \sum_{r,s} P(r,s)\sigma_{rs}^2 \qquad (18)$$

For the series in Eq. 14 to be useful in practice, one must be able to truncate it after a number of terms no greater than the number of distinct phenotypic covariances that can be measured. For example, it may be possible to represent the genotypic covariance between parent and offspring or between half-sibs by the leading term in Eq. 15 (in both cases $P_2 = 0$) and thereby estimate $\sigma_{10}^2 = \sigma_A^2$, the additive component of the genotypic variance. The ratio σ_A^2/σ_P^2, called the narrow heritability, determines the rate at which phenotypic changes can be achieved through artificial selection (13).

A CONVENTIONAL APPLICATION OF HERITABILITY ANALYSIS

Before considering the applicability of the theory just sketched to IQ scores, I will examine some conventional heritability estimates that, as was first pointed out by Lerner (14), have an important bearing on the analysis of IQ data. Figure 12.2 shows heritability estimates, derived from different kinds of correlations, for four commercially important traits in dairy cattle. The primary data show a high degree of internal consistency, in that investigators at different test stations report similar measured correlations. Nevertheless, heritability estimates derived for the same trait from different kinds of data differ substantially and systematically.

Heritability estimates derived from half-sib correlations calculated from field data (indicated by open circles in Fig 12.2) are systematically and substantially lower than estimates derived from half-sib correlations calculated from test-station data (indicated by ×'s in Fig. 12.2). Lerner (14) has pointed out that these differences afford a direct and striking illustration of the importance of genotype-environment covariance and genotype-environment interaction. The fact that environments at test stations are randomized (made random with respect to genotype) greatly reduces, if not entirely eliminates, both effects. (Genotype-environment correlation may be expected to reduce half-sib correlation because it tends to amplify the genotypic effects of the maternal contribution to the genotype of the calf; in dairy cattle, the maternal contributions to the genotypes of half-sibs are uncorrelated.)

For each of the four traits, the heritability estimate derived from separated monozygotic twins is close to unity. This finding can be reconciled with the comparatively low estimates derived from half-sib correlations in two ways:

1. If environmental randomization has, in fact, effectively eliminated correlations between genotypic and environmental variables, so that Eqs. 10a and 11a are applicable, the correlations between separated monozygotic twins are estimates of broad heritability, and the difference $1 - h^2$ provides an upper limit for e^2, the environmental fraction of the phenotypic variance. The half-sib correlations, on the other hand, yield estimates of narrow heritability, and the differences between these estimates and those derived from split monozygotic pairs represent the nonadditive genotypic contribution to h^2.

2. If, however, the environmental value (E) contains a sizable component correlated with the animals' genotype, Eqs. 10a and 11a do not apply. Such a component would be present if the environmental variables were imperfectly controlled, allowing the animals to exercise a modicum of environmental selection—with respect to diet, for example. To the extent that such selection was genetically determined, it would give rise to a "hidden" genotype-environment correlation. And since separated monozygotic twins would tend to select the same environments (to the extent permitted by the controls), their environments would be correlated. In these circumstances, a high phenotypic correlation between monozygotic twins would not entail a correspondingly low

value for the environmental component of the phenotypic variance. Hidden genotype-environment interaction would similarly
inflate estimates of other phenotypic covariances.

In the absence of additional information, it does not seem possible to choose unequivocally between these explanations, or even
to be sure that gene-gene interactions and hidden genotype-environment correlations are jointly responsible for the systematic
differences under discussion. Explanation 1 is perhaps the less
plausible of the two because it requires the nonadditive genotypic variance to be greatest when the additive genotypic variance is least and because it fails to explain why their sum is nearly
the same for traits whose narrow heritabilities span a wide range
of values. Until explanation 2 can be ruled out, it must be assumed that estimates of broad heritability based on phenotypic
correlations between separated monozygotic twins may be grossly
unreliable.

IQ SCORES AS MEASUREMENTS OF A PHENOTYPIC CHARACTER

Before examining the applicability of heritability analysis to IQ
scores, one must ask whether such scores can legitimately be assimilated to measurements of a phenotypic character. Tests of
IQ differ from measurements of conventional phenotypic characters in two important respects.

In the physical and biological sciences, every measurable quantity is defined in the context of a definite theoretical structure
that, in general, serves to generate a variety of distinct operational
definitions. For example, the physical geometry of rigid bodies
provides the basis for several operationally distinct ways of measuring length and distance. Electromagnetic theory provides a second set of operational definitions of distance and length; the
theory of sound a third set; and so on. The flexibility conferred
by the existence of operationally distinct ways of measuring the

same quantity is important because it makes possible the detection and eventual elimination of systematic errors; and the existence of distinct operational definitions implies an underlying theoretical structure.

The definition of IQ has no theoretical context or substratum. Tests of IQ measure what they measure. They are precisely analogous to physical readings made with a black box—a device whose internal working is unknown. Because we do not know what an IQ test or a black box is supposed to measure or how it works, we cannot know to what extent measurements carried out on different subjects are comparable or to what extent they are influenced by extraneous factors. Thus IQ scores contain uncontrollable, systematic errors of unknown magnitude.

This helps to explain why different investigators frequently report such widely differing estimates of the same IQ correlation. For example, reported estimates of the parent-child correlation range from .2 to .8, while estimates of the correlation between same-sex dizygotic twins range from .4 to .9 (*15*). According to Jensen (*16*), there are no objective criteria (other than sample size) for weighting discrepant estimates of the same correlation.

Because the definition of IQ is purely instrumental, it fails to confer the most essential attribute of a scientific measurement—objectivity. To measure a subject's Stanford-Binet IQ, one must administer a specific test in a specific way under specific conditions. By contrast, a well-equipped physics laboratory does not need to have replicas of the standard meter and the standard kilogram to measure length and mass, and the physicist or biologist is free to devise his own techniques for measuring such quantities. Systematic discrepancies between measurements of the same quantity are never ignored in the physical and biological sciences, because they signal the presence of unsuspected systematic errors or of defects in the theory underlying the measurements.

IQ scores also differ from conventional measurements in that they have no strict qualitative meaning. The IQ is an index of rank order on a standardized test, expressed according to a convenient but essentially arbitrary convention (*17*). In effect, the intervals of the IQ scale are chosen in such a way as to make the frequency distribution of test scores in a reference population approximately normal, but other methods of defining the scale could claim equal prior justification.

These considerations show that IQ scores are not phenotypic measurements in the usual sense. This is not to say that they have no scientific value or practical utility, or that certain aspects of intelligent behavior cannot, in principle, be adequately defined, quantified, and measured. It is even conceivable that valid measurements of some well-defined behavioral trait would rank subjects in roughly the same way as IQ tests and that they would turn out to be normally distributed. In these circumstances, IQ scores would indeed approximate valid measurements of a phenotypic trait, although they would continue to be afflicted by uncontrollable systematic errors of unknown magnitude. For the moment, however, I ignore these shortcomings of the primary data, and turn to the methods available for analyzing them.

HERITABILITY OF IQ

In applications of heritability analysis to metric (continuously variable) characters in plants and animals, at least some of the relevant genetic and environmental factors are under experimental control. In particular, plant and animal geneticists can minimize genotype-environment correlation by randomizing environments. As I have shown, this step is indispensable for the application of heritability analysis. Unless Eqs. 5 and 7 can be replaced by Eqs. 10a and 10b, there is no hope of disentangling the genotypic and environmental contributions to phenotypic variances. Recent discussions of the applicability of heritability analysis to IQ scores have failed to stress this point. The applicability of heritability analysis does not, as is commonly assumed, hinge on the smallness of the interaction term (R) relative to the terms G and E in Fisher's decomposition of the phenotypic value. In fact, one may reasonably assume on biological grounds that genotype-environment interaction makes a substantial contribution to the phenotypic value of every phenotypically plastic trait, except in populations where the ranges of genetic and environmental variation are severely restricted. Even so, heritability analysis can be applied to phenotypically plastic traits, provided that the relevant genetic and environmental variables are statistically uncorrelated. When this condition is not satisfied, the contributions of interaction to phenotypic variances and covariances cannot, in general, be separated from the contributions of genotype and environment, and heritability analysis cannot, therefore, be applied meaningfully.

In adult subpopulations, IQ and environment are well known to be more or less strongly correlated. Since differences in IQ are undeniably related to genetic differences (although not, perhaps, in a very simple way), one may safely assume that genotype-environment correlation is significant in adult subpopulations and in subpopulations composed of children reared by their biological parents or by close relatives. Hence, no valid estimate of IQ heritability can be based on data that refer to such subpopulations.

Yet data of precisely this kind make up the bulk of the available material, and many published heritability estimates have been based on them. Burt (*18*), Jensen (*1*), and Herrnstein (*4*), for example, all cite kinship correlation data as evidence for a high value of h^2.

These authors, among others, rely especially on IQ correlations between separated monozygotic twins. Such correlations, however, are highly sensitive to distortion by genotype-environment correlation. As I have shown, significant distortion may occur even under experimental conditions in which the controllable aspects of the environment have been randomized, because selection of "microenvironments" is genetically influenced. The development of human cognitive skills is presumably even more sensitive to such selection than the development of physiological characters of dairy cattle. In published studies of separated monozygotic twins, no serious attempts have been made to minimize the effects of genotype-environment interaction—something that would be very difficult to do under the best of circumstances. For example, in the largest and the most homogeneous of the four major twin studies, that of Burt (*18*), one member of each of the 53 pairs included in the study was reared by his or her natural parent (*19*).

Since reliable inferences about the heritability of behavioral traits cannot be drawn from data referring to subpopulations of adults or of children reared by their biological parents or by close relatives, one must turn to studies in which the subjects are adopted children. For example, phenotypic correlations between half-sibs reared in foster homes would yield estimates of narrow heritability analogous to those indicated by ×'s in Fig. 12.2— provided that there was no selective placement and that the range and distribution of relevant environmental factors was the same for the subpopulation of foster homes as for the reference population. Analogous data on siblings would be somewhat less useful, because gene-gene interactions—in particular, the dominance covariance—could contribute substantially to the phenotypic covariance. However, no suitable data for either siblings or half-sibs seem to exist (*6*).

Finally, the IQ correlation between unrelated, randomly selected children reared in the same foster home could, in principle, provide an estimate of e^2 (Eq. 11b). The phenotypic covariance might substantially underestimate e^2, however, because the environments of children reared together are never identical. Age differences may give rise to significant "macroenvironmental" differences, while differences in genotype may give rise to significant "microenvironmental" differences, as discussed above.

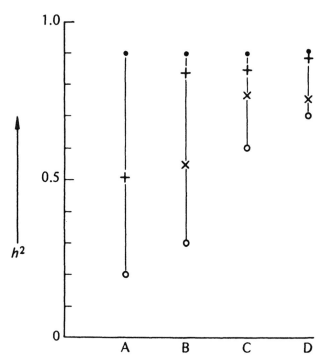

Fig., 12.2. Heritability estimates for four metric traits in dairy cattle: (A) calf weight and measure, (B) milk yield, (C) fat percentages, and (D) body weight and measure at 2 years. The estimates are derived from comparisons among separated monozygotic twins (closed circle), monozygotic and dizygotic twins (cross), half sisters at testing stations in which environment is randomized ($\times$), and half sisters at field stations (open circle). [Source: Donald (25), reproduced by Lerner (14, p. 412)]

Jencks *et al.* (6) cite four studies of pairs of unrelated foster children reared together. The reported IQ (Stanford-Binet) correlations, corrected for unreliability and restriction of range, are as follows: .17 (10 cases), .29 (21 cases), .46 (93 cases), and .72 (41 cases). Using Fisher's method (20) to combine these estimates, one arrives at the value $r = .5 \pm .05$. The differences between the individual estimates of r, although large, are not statistically significant, according to the test described by Fisher (20). For the reasons explained above, the environments of unrelated foster children reared together may be significantly different. On the other hand, selective placement may introduce a correlation between the genotypes of the foster children. The two effects work in opposite directions, and neither can be reliably estimated. Making the not-very-safe assumption that they cancel, one arrives at the highly tentative estimate, $e^2 \simeq .5 \pm .05$. This estimate refers to the purely environmental fraction of the phenotypic variance. Of greater relevance to the social and educational issues mentioned at the beginning of this article is the nongenetic fraction of the phenotypic variance, given by $1 - h^2 = e^2 + i^2$, where $i^2 = Var\{R\}/Var\{P\}$ is the fraction of the phenotypic variance relating to interaction. (As noted earlier, this decomposition of the phenotypic variance presupposes that genotype-environment correlations are absent.) Since there are no available data that would permit an independent estimate of the interaction contribution, the above estimate of e^2 provides only a lower limit for $1 - h^2$.

Thus the available data for unrelated foster children raised together yield the following, highly tentative estimate of the broad heritability:

$$0 \leq h^2 < .5 \tag{19}$$

It is important to notice that this estimate refers specifically to the subpopulation of unrelated foster children reared together. [For this subpopulation, it is consistent with the estimates of Jencks *et al.* (6).] It does not apply to populations composed of children reared by their biological parents or by near relatives, because, as shown above, both the conceptual and operational definitions of heritability break down in the presence of significant genotype-environment correlation. This explains why Jencks *et al.* (6) were unable to reconcile their heritability estimate based on unrelated foster children reared together with estimates derived from other kinds of IQ data. The present considerations show that the estimates based on other kinds of data are, in a strict sense, meaningless.

Systematic effects of genotype-environment correlation are by no means the only obstacles to meaningful analyses of IQ correlations. Additional serious difficulties arise from:

1. *Ignorance of the specific environmental factors affecting cognitive development.* Because social scientists have not yet identified the specific environmental factors most relevant to cognitive development, they are unable to assess environmental similarities or differences objectively, even at a qualitative level. For example, some authors (*1*, p. 52; *4*, p. 55) have assumed that the within-pair environmental differences between separated monozygotic twins in Burt's study (*18*) are representative of those between randomly selected subjects of the same age. This assumption is based on a reported lack of correlation between the occupational statuses of the biological and adoptive fathers. As far as I know, no evidence has been adduced to support the implied assumption that the occupational status of the father plays a crucial role in cognitive development. Current studies suggest that specific kinds of mother-child interaction during infancy and early childhood do play a significant role in cognitive development (*21*), but the study of such interactions is still in a primitive stage.

2. *Nonrandom mating.* If one wishes to analyze phenotypic correlations between related persons other than monozygotic twins, one must allow for assortative mating. This introduces two more unknowns into the analysis: the environmental and the phenotypic covariances between mates. In the absence of reliable assessments of relevant environmental factors, the environmental covariance is not measurable, so the only additional datum would be the phenotypic covariance. Thus assortative mating introduces a further unknown into an already top-heavy analysis. Moreover, Eq. 15 (for the genotypic covariance) applies only to populations with random mating, and an appropriate generalization of it

that allows for assortative mating has not yet, to my knowledge, been made.

3. *Gene-gene interactions.* The possibility of evaluating the narrow heritability of a trait hinges on how rapidly the series in Eq. 15 converges, the number of unknown components of the genotypic variance one can hope to estimate being limited by the number of measured kinship correlations. Now, for a trait specfied by n pairs of genes, $\sigma_{r_s}^2$ is made up of $2^r n!/r!s!(n-r-s)!$ separate contributions. This suggests that, as n increases, the relative importance of gene-gene interactions of a given kind also increases: the greater the number of genes contributing to the specification of a trait, the more likely it is that nonadditive genetic effects will play an important role. These considerations raise the possibility that human intelligence, however it may be defined, could depend on the total genotype in a manner too complex to permit the application of conventional heritability analysis. In any case, one may reasonably expect to find substantial differences between the broad and narrow heritabilities of cognitive traits (22).

In view of the difficulties discussed above, studies of unrelated foster children reared together and of half-sibs reared in foster homes seem to offer the only realistic prospects for estimating, respectively, the environmental fraction of the IQ variance and the narrow heritability.

ALTERNATIVE QUANTITATIVE APPROACHES

Heritability analysis was devised to help answer one of the central practical questions of plant and animal genetics: Under given environmental conditions, how rapidly can systematic changes in a metric character be produced by artificial selection? Fisher's "fundamental theorem of natural selection" (23) implies that the rate of evolution in question is proportional to the additive genotypic variance and hence to the narrow heritability of the character. For obvious reasons, this question—and, therefore, the value of the narrow heritability—is not of comparable importance for human behavioral traits. On the other hand, the phenotypic plasticity of human behavioral traits is of considerable interest both to geneticists and to students of human behavior. Estimates of the broad heritability—or, better still, of e^2—do tell us something about the sensitivity of a trait to environmental variation, but they throw little light on what are perhaps the most important questions: To what sorts of environmental changes are behavioral traits most sensitive? To what extent can cognitive performance be improved by appropriate forms of environmental intervention? How do genetic differences affect levels of cognitive performance attainable under optimal environmental conditions? These and similar questions are not of less scientific interest than those to which heritability estimates provide answers; and they are considerably more relevant to the educational, social, and political issues mentioned at the beginning of this article.

It may turn out to be less difficult to find semiquantitative or even quantitative answers to such questions than to obtain reliable heritability estimates. Notable progress along these lines has already been made. The remarkable achievements of the Milwaukee Project (*24*), to cite a single example, afford a direct and dramatic demonstration of the efficacy of appropriate environmental modifications in accelerating cognitive development. In this study, now in its sixth year, a comprehensive family intervention program produced a sustained, 30-point difference in IQ between an experimental group and a control group, each composed of 20 randomly selected children of mothers with tested IQ's of under 75. Over a 5-year period, the average IQ of the experimental group remained close to 125. Children in the experimental group were evaluated through independent tests administered by psychologists not connected with the study.

The methodological difficulties of intervention studies should not be minimized. Nevertheless, the nature of the questions such studies are trying to answer makes these difficulties inherently less formidable than those besetting the application of conventional heritability analysis to IQ scores. For example, the shortcomings of IQ as a phenotypic measurement, although they cast serious doubt on the meaningfulness of heritability estimates, do not impair the usefulness of IQ tests for assessing differences in cognitive performance between an experimental group and a control group in studies like that of Heber and his colleagues.

IQ AND RACE

Jensen (2) and others have argued that reported differences in average IQ between black and white children are probably attributable in part to systematic genetic differences. Jensen explicitly states the "rule of inference" used to draw this conclusion (16, p. 438): "The probability that a phenotypic mean difference between two groups is in the same direction as a genotypic mean difference is greater than the probability that the phenotypic and genotypic mean differences are in opposite directions." This rule fails, however, when systematic effects whose magnitude cannot be estimated are known to contribute to the phenotypic mean differences. (Unfortunately, these are the only circumstances in which the rule might be useful.) In order to estimate the probabilities mentioned in the rule, one would need to estimate the probability that the observed phenotypic mean difference exceeds the contribution of systematic effects—which, by assumption, is impossible.

Among the relevant systematic differences between blacks and whites are cultural differences and differences in psychological environment. Both influence the development of cognitive skills in complex ways, and no one has succeeded in either estimating or eliminating their effects. "Culture-free" tests deal with this problem only on the most superficial level, for culture-free and "culture-bound" aspects of cognitive development are inseparable. The difficulties cannot be overcome by refined statistical analyses. As long as systematic differences remain and their effects cannot be reliably estimated, no valid inference can be drawn concerning genetic differences among races.

Precisely the same arguments and conclusions apply to the interpretation of IQ differences between socioeconomic groups.

SUMMARY AND CONCLUSIONS

Estimates of IQ heritability are subject to a variety of systematic errors.

The IQ scores themselves contain uncontrollable, systematic errors of unknown magnitude. These arise because IQ scores, unlike conventional physical and biological measurements, have a purely instrumental definition. The effects of these errors are apparent in the very large discrepancies among IQ correlations measured by different investigators.

Genotype-environment correlations, whose effects can sometimes be minimized, if not wholly eliminated, in experiments with plants and animals, are nearly always important in human populations. The absence of significant effects arising from genotype-environment correlations is a necessary condition for the applicability of conventional heritability analysis to phenotypically plastic traits. When this condition fails, no quantitative inferences about heritability can be drawn from measured phenotypic variances and covariances, except under special conditions that are unlikely to be satisfied by phenotypically plastic traits in human populations.

Inadequate understanding of the precise environmental factors relevant to the development of specific behavioral traits is an important source of systematic errors, as is the inability to allow adequately for the effects of assortative mating and gene-gene interaction.

Systematic cultural differences and differences in psychological environment among races and among socioeconomic groups vitiate any attempt to draw from IQ data meaningful inferences about genetic differences.

Estimates based on phenotypic correlations between separated monozygotic twins—usually considered to be the most reliable kind of estimates—are vitiated by systematic errors inherent in IQ tests, by the presence of genotype-environment correlation, and by the lack of detailed understanding of environmental factors relevant to the development of behavioral traits. Other kinds of estimates are beset, in addition, by systematic errors arising from incomplete allowance for the effects of assortative mating and from gene-gene interactions. The only potentially useful data are phenotypic correlations between unrelated foster children reared together, which could, in principle, yield lower limits for e^2. Available data indicate that, for unrelated foster children reared together, the broad heritability (h^2) may lie between 0.0 and 0.5. This estimate does *not* apply to populations composed of children reared by their biological parents or by near relatives. For such populations the heritability of IQ remains undefined.

The only data that might yield meaningful estimates of narrow heritability are phenotypic correlations between half-sibs reared in statistically independent environments. No useful data of this kind are available.

Intervention studies like Heber's Milwaukee Project afford an alternative and comparatively direct way of studying the plasticity of cognitive and other behavioral traits in human populations. Results obtained so far strongly suggest that the development of cognitive skills is highly sensitive to variations in environmental factors.

These conclusions have three obvious implications for the broader issues mentioned at the beginning of this article.

1. Published analyses of IQ data provide no support whatever for Jensen's thesis that inequalities in cognitive performance are

due largely to genetic differences. As Lewontin (*8*) has clearly shown, the value of the broad heritability of IQ is in any case only marginally relevant to this question. I have argued that conventional estimates of the broad heritability of IQ are invalid and that the only data on which potentially valid estimates might be based are consistent with a broad heritability of less than 0.5. On the other hand, intervention studies, if their findings prove to be replicable, would directly establish that, under suitable conditions, the offspring of parents whose cognitive skills are so poorly developed as to exclude them from all but the most menial occupations can achieve what are regarded as distinctly high levels of cognitive performance. Thus, despite the fact that children differ substantially in cognitive aptitudes and appetites, and despite the very high probability that these differences have a substantial genetic component, available scientific evidence strongly suggests that environmental factors are responsible for the failure of children not suffering from specific neurological disorders to achieve adequate levels of cognitive performance.

2. Under prevailing social conditions, no valid inferences can be drawn from IQ data concerning systematic genetic differences among races or socioeconomic groups. Research along present lines directed toward this end—whatever its ethical status—is scientifically worthless.

3. Since there are no suitable data for estimating the narrow heritability of IQ, it seems pointless to speculate about the prospects for a hereditary meritocracy based on IQ.

REFERENCES

1. A. R. Jensen, *Harv. Educ. Rev. 39*, 1 (1969).
2. ———, *Genetics and Education* (Harper & Row, New York, 1972).
3. ———, *Educability and Group Differences* (Methuen, London, 1972).
4. R. J. Herrnstein, *Atl. Month. 228*, 43 (1971).
5. ———, *IQ and the Meritocracy* (Little, Brown, Boston, 1973).
6. C. Jencks *et al., Inequality: A Reassessment of the Effects of Family and*

Schooling in America (Basic Books, New York, 1972), appendix A, pp. 266–319.

7. A similar argument was given as long ago as 1933 by Hogben [cited by C. H. Waddington, *The Strategy of the Genes* (Allen & Unwin, London, 1957), pp. 92–94].

8. R. C. Lewontin, *Bull. At. Sci.* 26, 2 (March 1970); in *The Fallacy of IQ*, C. Senna, Ed. (Third Press, New York, 1973), pp. 1–17.

9. R. A. Fisher, *Trans. R. Soc. Edinb.* 52, 399 (1918). In this fundamental paper, Fisher expresses the genotypic value (G) of a trait as the sum of additive allelic contributions $(G_1, G_2, \ldots G_n)$ and dominance contributions $(G_{12}, G_{13}, \ldots)$ in such a way as to minimize the contribution of dominance to the genotypic variance (pp. 404, 415). The decomposition (Eq. 4) of the phenotypic value (P) into additive genotypic and environmental values $(G$ and $E)$ and a residual interaction term (R) is formally analogous: E (in the formula $E = E_1 + E_2 + E_{12}$) corresponds to P (in the formula $P = G + E + R$), E_1 to G, E_2 to E, and E_{12} to R. The formal analog of the requirement of statistical independence between genotype and environment (Eq. 9) is Fisher's assumption that genes assort independently. Thus the effects of linkage are formally analogous to those of genotype-environment correlation.

10. Consider first the case of a single genotypic variable $x \equiv x_{11}$ and a single environmental variable $y \equiv y_1$. That the covariances in question do indeed vanish follows immediately from the power-series representations of G, E, and R:

$$G = \sum_k \frac{1}{k!}(x^k - \mathcal{E}(x^k))P_{k,0}(0,0)$$

$$E = \sum_j \frac{1}{j!}(y^j - \mathcal{E}(y^j))P_{0,j}(0,0)$$

$$R = \sum_{r>1}\sum_{s>1} \frac{1}{(r+s)!}[x^r y^s - \mathcal{E}(x^r)\mathcal{E}(y^s)]P_{r,s}(0,0)$$

where

$$P_{r,s}(0,0) = \left[\frac{\partial^{r+s}}{\partial x^r \partial y^s}P(x,y)\right]_{x=y=0}$$

These formulas follow from the Taylor expansion of P (assumed to be valid for all x, y) and the defining conditions (2). In the general case, the proof is notationally more complex but essentially the same.

11. For notational simplicity, let $x \equiv x_1$, $y \equiv y_1$. The most general form of R (assuming that it has derivatives of all orders at $x = y = 0$) is

$$R = R^*(x,y) + f(x) + g(y)$$

where R^* is the expression for R given earlier (10), g is a random variable depending on the indicated loci, and $\epsilon\{f\} = \epsilon\{g\} = 0$. By expanding f and g, one finds that $\epsilon\{R^*f\} = \epsilon\{R^*g\} = 0$. Hence

$$\{R^2\} = \mathcal{E}\{R^{*2}\} + \mathcal{E}\{f^2\} + \mathcal{E}\{g^2\} \geq \mathcal{E}\{R^{*2}\}$$

12. O. Kempthorne, *Proc. R. Soc. Lond. Ser. B Biol. Sci.* *143*, 103 (1954).
13. Narrow heritability is also the kind of heritability that is relevant to Herrnstein's (*4*) meritocracy argument.
14. I. M. Lerner, *Evol. Biol.* *6*, 399 (1972).
15. L. Erlenmeyer-Kimling and L. F. Jarvik, *Science* *142*, 1477 (1963).
16. A. R. Jensen, *Cognition* *1*, 427 (1973); see also D. Layzer, *ibid.*, p. 453.
17. This point has been made by S. S. Stevens, *Science* *103*, 677 (1946).
18. C. Burt, *Br. J. Psychol.* *57*, 137 (1966).
19. Jencks *et al.* (*6*) recognized that estimates of h^2 derived from twin studies must make allowance for genotype-environment correlation, and they have, in fact, attempted to do this. However, once the effects of genotype-environment correlation are admitted to be significant, the problem of estimating h^2 becomes mathematically indeterminate: the number of unknowns exceeds the number of available conditions. The analysis of Jencks *et al.*, although considerably more elaborate and realistic than previous analyses of the same data, depends on plausible but ad hoc assumptions to close the gap between the number of unknowns and the number of conditions.
20. R. A. Fisher, *Statistical Methods for Research Workers* (Oliver & Boyd, Edinburgh, ed. 13, 1958), p. 204.
21. U. Bronfenbrenner, *Is Early Intervention Effective?* (Cornell Univ. Press, Ithaca, N.Y., 1974).
22. Thus Jensen's estimate of broad heritability, whatever its validity, is not directly relevant to the argument by which Herrnstein (*4*) predicts the emergence of an hereditary meritocracy. This is not to say that the argument is free from other serious defects.
23. R. A. Fisher, *The Genetical Theory of Natural Selection* (Dover, New York, ed. 2, 1958), p. 22.
24. R. Heber, H. Garber, S. Harrington, C. Hoffman, "Rehabilitation of families at risk for mental retardation" (unpublished research report). Some writers [for example, Jensen (*16*, p. 427)] have expressed skepticism concerning the reported gain of IQ because of its size. Recent findings by R. B. McCall, M. I. Appelbaum, and P. S. Hogarty [*Monographs of the Society for Research in Child Development 38*, 1 (1973)] may help to put those of Heber and his colleagues in perspective: "Normal home-reared middle-class children change in IQ performance during childhood, some a substantial amount . . . the average individual's range of IQ between 2½ and 17 years of age was 28.5 IQ points, one of every three children displayed a progressive change of more than 30 points, and one in seven shifted more than 40 points. Rare individuals may alter their performance as much as 74 points" (p. 70).
25. H. P. Donald, in *Proceedings of the Tenth International Congress of Genetics* (Univ. of Toronto Press, Toronto, 1959), vol. 1, pp. 225–235; reproduced by Lerner (*14*, p. 412).
26. I am indebted to L. Cavalli-Sforza, E. R. Dempster, and I. M. Lerner for helpful comments, criticism, and suggestions.

15

ON THE CAUSES OF IQ DIFFERENCES BETWEEN GROUPS AND IMPLICATIONS FOR SOCIAL POLICY

Peggy R. Sanday

. . . Unnecessary difficulties arise when we allow the scientific question to become mixed up with its possible educational, social, and political implications. The scientific question and its solution should not be allowed to get mixed up with the social-political aspects of the problem, for when it does we are less able to think clearly about either set of questions. The question of whether there are or are not genetic racial differences in intelligence is independent of any questions of its implications, whatever they may be

(Jensen, 1971:25).

As William F. Brazziel (1969) eloquently demonstrates in his "A Letter from the South," written in response to Arthur Jensen's original article (1967), the question of whether or not there are genetic racial differences in intelligence cannot be independent of any questions of educational, social, and political implications. Five days after Jensen made headlines in Virginia papers

From *Human Organization*, Vol. 31 (4), Winter 1972, pp. 411-24. Reprinted by permission of the Society for Applied Anthropology.

"regarding the inferiority of black people as measured by IQ tests" (Brazziel, 1969:200), a suit was fought in the Federal District Court to integrate the Greensville and Caroline County schools. The argument presented by the defense quoted heavily from the work of Jensen and concluded that "white teachers could not understand the Nigra mind" and that black children who did not make a certain score on standardized tests should be assigned to all black remedial schools where "teachers who understood them could work with them" (Brazziel, 1969:200).

This incident, and the others like it (see Deutsch, 1969), raises complex ethical issues for social scientists working in areas which are inextricably linked with controversial social policy questions. At present, there are no enforceable standards—similar to the standards which have been developed to protect the public against many of the other products of an advanced technology—for examining the validity of the claims of social science research. It is doubtful whether any such standards could be found, since for every social scientist claiming a certainty there is invariably another social scientist whose research demonstrates the opposite. This is particularly the case in the area of IQ and race where, as Scarr-Salapatek (1971b) and Light and Smith (1969) demonstrate, dissimilar explanatory models—one genetic and the other environmental—can be used to generate the reported racial differences.

Jensen is right in stating (1971) that there are grave educational and social problems that need to be solved and that we must first understand the causes of problems if we are to be effective in solving them. With respect to the causes of the average mean difference in intelligence and scholastic achievement scores between blacks and whites in the United States, Jensen is wrong in implying (in such a way that others take it as a certainty) that such differences have a genetic basis, because, as this paper will demonstrate, the question has by no means been resolved.

The purpose here will be to present an analysis supported by recently published data which raises further doubts concerning the imputation that racial differences in IQ might be genetic. An alternative approach to the analysis of IQ differences between racial groups will then be presented which can be extended to the analysis of similar differences in the test performances of other nonmainstream groups. In the furor following Jensen's original article, little attention has been given to the fact that other groups —namely orphanage children, mountain children, and deaf children in the United States as well as nonmainstream groups in other countries (Cronbach and Drench, 1972)—exhibit a score differential similar to that which has been reported for blacks and lower socioeconomic white children. Finally, this paper will discuss the contribution of anthropology to social policy research.

THE ARGUMENT FOR A GENETIC BASIS OF RACIAL DIFFERENCES IN IQ

Jensen's article (1969), which attributes IQ differences to genetic factors, is devoted to a lengthy exposition of how the relative roles of heredity and environment can be determined. His major conclusions are that heredity has a far greater role to play than environment and that the reported mean differences in the IQ of blacks and whites may result from different gene pools. He bases his argument on the concept of heritability and on the fact that the heritability estimates for the white population (the only group we have an estimate for) are quite high (.80). One implication drawn from this argument is that since very little of the variance can be attributed to environmental factors, compensatory programs such as Headstart will be doomed to failure if their goal is to boost IQ.

Gregg and Sanday (1971) discuss the meaning of the concept of heritability and take issue with Jensen's interpretation. Light and Smith (1969) question the components of the variance model underlying Jensen's estimate of heritability. Fehr (1969) raises questions concerning the formula Jensen uses to arrive at an empirical estimate of heritability and proposes an alternative formula. The formula used by Jensen will be presented below and discussed in connection with heritability estimates of numerical and spatial ability which have been reported in the literature for a sample of black and white twins. The results raise serious questions concerning the use of the formula on which Jensen bases his argument.

Jensen buttresses his argument, based on the .80 heritability estimate for a white population, by reporting a number of results which seem to confirm his position. For example, he states (1971:17) that if race differences in IQ are due to environmental factors, it should be possible to reduce the racial correlation with IQ to zero by holding constant the truly causal factors only incidentally correlated with both race and IQ. According to him, no one has been able to do this in black-white comparisons, and every combination of environmental variables selected has always yielded some significant correlations between race and IQ. Four recent studies, three on IQ and the fourth on scholastic achievement, do exactly what Jensen says no one has been able to do. These studies will be discussed below. The fourth study, a reanalysis of the Coleman data (first presented by Coleman et al., 1966), also places in question Jensen's (1971:13) statement (which he based on the data presented in the original Coleman report) that American Indians score higher than blacks on scholastic achievement tests even though they are considerably more impoverished than blacks.

THE MEANING AND ESTIMATION OF HERITABILITY

The meaning of the concept of heritability is discussed in detail by Gregg and Sanday (1971). Briefly, their argument is that heritability is not a measure of the magnitude of the genetic contribution to a given trait (as Jensen leads us to believe) but a

measure of the extent to which the variability in a trait is due to
genetic factors relative to environmental factors. For example, in
a uniform environment the heritability estimate will be high.
Correspondingly, in a population which is uniform genetically
(i.e., is homozygous for the trait in question), the environmental
estimate will be high. In neither case do we gain information on
the magnitude of the genetic nor the environmental contribution
to the development of the trait itself.

The magnitude of the genetic contribution to a given polygenic trait, such as IQ, cannot be estimated with the methods
currently available to geneticists. The complexity of the problem
is discussed by Bodmer and Cavalli-Sforza (1970) who point out
that there are probably many genes influencing the expression of
intelligence which are polymorphic in character. Furthermore,
the expression of any one of these genes may be profoundly influenced by the environment. The position taken by these authors,
with respect to efforts to assess the genetic contribution, is similar to the position adopted by the National Academy of Science
in 1967. According to this position, it is fruitless to try to disentangle the relative roles of heredity and environment with present methods since the results of such research would be unclear
in meaning and would invite misuse. Even greater difficulties,
according to the Academy's statement, are encountered when
the goal is to assess the relative role of these factors in determining differences between populations.

Gregg and Sanday make a clear distinction between the magnitude of the genetic contribution to a given trait (which cannot be measured for intelligence) and the extent to which the
variability in a trait is due to genetic factors relative to environmental factors (which is supposedly measured by heritability estimates). Jensen seems to be aware of this distinction when he says
that the estimates of heritability

> . . . will be higher in a population in which environmental
> variation relevant to the trait in question is small, than in a

population in which there is great environmental variation. Similarly, when a population is relatively homogeneous in genetic factors but not in the environmental factors relevant to the development of the characteristic, the heritability of the characteristic in question will be lower. In short, the value of H is jointly a function of genetic and environmental variability in the population (1969:43).

Jensen, however, does not follow through with the logical implications of this statement when he says in the same article that the control of highly heritable characteristics is usually in the organism's internal biochemical mechanisms and that traits of low heritability are usually controlled by external environmental factors. Jensen also confuses estimates of the variance in IQ scores with the magnitude of the genetic contribution when he rejects the hypothesis of genetic equality between black and white samples reported by Kennedy, Van de Riet, and White (1963) on the basis of an analysis of the variances in the distribution of IQ scores for the two samples (Jensen, 1971:20–21). The rationale for rejecting the hypothesis of genetic equality between the two samples is based on the ubiquitous heritability estimate of .80 for the white population.

The formula Jensen uses for empirical estimates of heritability and the data on which the .80 estimate is based were not presented in his 1969 article, probably because both are discussed by him in a paper written in 1967. In the latter paper, he presents a new formula for computing heritability estimates from twin data. Jensen then uses this formula to extract the .80 estimate from data presented by Erlenmeyer-Kimling and Jarvik (1963). The salient points of this method will be presented below and applied to data reported by Osborne and Miele (1969) and by Osborne and Gregor (1968) on racial differences in the heritability of numerical and spacial ability. The purpose of this exercise will be to demonstrate the problems with Jensen's formula in computing heritability estimates.

Heritability (h^2) is defined (Jensen, 1967:149) as the proportion of phenotypic variance attributable to genotypic variance and can vary between 0 and 1 as follows:

$$1.00 = h^2 + E^2 + e^2 \qquad (1)$$

or

$$h^2 = 1.00 - (E^2 + e^2) \qquad (2)$$

where:

h^2 = heritability (the proportion of total variance due to heredity)
E^2 = between family variance
e^2 = within family variance

The formulae for computing each of these variance components are:

$$h^2 = \frac{r_{MZ} - r_{DZ}}{1 - \rho_\infty} \qquad (3)$$

$$e^2 = 1 - r_{MZ} \qquad (4)$$

$$E^2 = 1 - (h^2 + e^2) \qquad (5)$$

where:

r_{MZ} = correlation between identical twins reared together
r_{DZ} = correlation between fraternal twins reared together
ρ_∞ = genetic correlation between siblings or fraternal twins

As can be seen from these equations, the formula for estimating heritability rests on the correlation between identical and fraternal twins and the estimation of the parameter ρ_∞ which is defined as the genetic correlation between siblings or fraternal twins (Jensen, 1967:151). This parameter is estimated from the genetic correlation between unrelated parents. The formula for estimating ρ_∞ is:

$$\rho_\infty = \frac{1 + \rho PP}{2 + \rho PP}$$

where

ρPP = the genetic correlation between unrelated parents

Since, according to Jensen (1967:151), there is known to be assortive mating for intelligence (which means that the genetic correlation between unrelated parents will be greater than zero on tests of intelligence), the best estimates of h^2 would be obtained from values of ρ_∞ (sibling genetic correlation) close to .55, resulting from a genetic correlation of 0.25 between parents. Jensen applies his formula for h^2 (see equation 3 above) to the data summarized by Erlenmeyer-Kimling and Jarvick (1963) which give the median values of all the twin studies reported in the literature. Estimating ρ_∞ as .55, taking the median twin correlations presented by these authors ($r_{MZ} = .92$; $r_{DZ} = .56$), and plugging these values into equation 3, we get one of the several sets of values for h^2, E^2, and e^2 which Jensen (1969:51) reports:

$$h^2 = \frac{.92 - .56}{.45} = \frac{.36}{.45} = .80$$
$$e^2 = 1 - .92 = .08$$
$$E^2 = 1 - (.80 + .08) = .12$$

Jensen concludes that "according to these data—the average of all the major twin studies—four times as much of the variance in measured intelligence is attributable to heredity as to environment" (1967:151).

Before discussing this formula in connection with recently reported heritability estimates of black and white twins, several additional points mentioned by Jensen concerning the calculation of heritability need to be introduced. The first concerns the importance of determining the significance of the F ratio which compares the within-pair variance of DZ (fraternal) twins with the within-pair variance of MZ (identical) twins. The determination of the variance ratio F is "an essential step prior to computing h^2; if F is not statistically significant, h^2 cannot be presumed to differ significantly from zero" (Jensen, 1967:149). The heritability estimates for intelligence, scholastic performance, and physical characteristics reported by Jensen (1967:152) are all

supported by values of F significant beyond the 0.01 level. This
is not the case for the heritability estimates of numerical and
spatial ability in black twins to be reported below.

The second point concerns what Jensen (1967:154) refers to
as "impossible" values of h^2 and E^2. An impossible value results
when (1) h^2 is negative as happens when the correlation between
DZ twins on a trait is greater than the correlation between MZ
twins; or, (2) when E^2 is negative which happens when the sum
of h^2 and e^2 is greater than one. The latter case can occur frequently depending on the value of ρ_∞. Of the 50 heritability estimates for intelligence, scholastic performance, and physical characteristics reported by Jensen (1967:152) for ρ_∞ values set at .50
or .55 (for random and some positive assortative mating), there
are four "impossible" values for h^2 and E^2. Three of these values
result from heritability estimates greater than one, and one results
from a negative value for E^2. According to Jensen (1967:156),
impossible values set the upper limit of the estimation of ρ_∞. In the
data discussed below on black twins, an unusual number of impossible values result even when the upper limit of ρ_∞ is set at
zero, which means that the genetic correlation between parents
is −1.00, which occurs under conditions of complete negative
assortative mating (i.e., no genes contributing to the population
variance are shared between parents).

Some additional restrictions in the estimation of the components of genetic and environmental variation, which were not
stressed by Jensen, concern the importance of sample size in the
efficient detection of these components and the amount of information which can be gained from relying on twin data. Classical twin studies, such as the studies supplying the data in Jensen's estimation of heritability, are often based on samples of
fewer than 100 twin pairs. Eaves (1972:152) found that a much
larger sample than those generally employed is necessary in order
to go beyond the mere demonstration that variation has a heritable component. He states, however, that the desirability of larger

sample sizes in twin studies of the classical kind is questionable since little further information about gene action can be derived from studies based solely on twin data. Such studies are probably adequate only to estimate the within-family environmental variance from MZ twins reared together and to provide a test of the significance of within-family genetic influences (Eaves, 1972: 151).

Osborne and Gregor (1968) and Osborne and Miele (1969) have reported heritability estimates for black and white twins on tests of spatial and numerical ability. These authors use Jensen's formula along with the formulae which were traditionally in use. Their work is important because estimates are reported for black twins and it provides evidence of how the misuse of Jensen's formula can lead to drawing unsubstantiated conclusions. For example, basing an argument on the conclusions and estimates reported by Osborne, Gregor, and Miele, a eugenicist writing in the *Atlantic Monthly* states that the heritability estimates reported by these authors

> . . . lend further support to a genetic interpretation of the mean differences observed between U.S. whites and U.S. Negroes on intelligence test performance. (Swan, 1971:106)

The sample reported by these authors consisted of 172 pairs of identical twins and 112 pairs of like-sexed fraternal twins from two southeastern states. Forty-three twin pairs were "disadvantaged" black (32 identical and 11 fraternal) and 241 twin pairs were "advantaged" white (140 identical and 101 fraternal). The number of black twins is far too small for efficient estimation. This may explain the fact that most of the F values reported for black twins are nonsignificant.[1] This is not the case for the values reported for the white twins. If we accept Jensen's interpretation, noted above, this means that the corresponding h^2 estimates for the black twins cannot be presumed to differ significantly from zero. Furthermore, if Osborne, Gregor, and Miele (1968:663) are correct in their theoretical interpretation of the source of the within-pair variance of identical twins and fraternal twins, the nonsignificant F ratios indicate that the environmental differences confronting the black MZ twins are as large as the environmental plus genetic differences confronting the black DZ twins. This could mean that either (1) the genetic potential in both types of twins has not developed and hence there is no variability from that source and the only variability is environmental; and/or (2) the tests given to the two sets of twins were culturally biased and both sets responded only to those items which were familiar to their semantic domains.

A second interesting result that can be noted in these data is that most of the within-family variances[2] (e^2) are larger for black twins than for white twins, and most of these values for the black twins are larger than the .20 figure suggested by Jensen for the total amount of environmental variance. According to Jensen (1971:41), within-family environmental variance is due to prenatal effects related to a mother's age, health, accidental prenatal factors, ordinal position among other siblings, and random stochastic development processes in the first weeks after conception. Which of these factors are most important, if any of them are, is a matter of speculation. Two recent studies indicate that the equal availability of prenatal and postnatal medical care (Scarr-Salapatek, 1971a) and the size of family (Mercer, 1971) are two of several factors which, when controlled, result in equivalent IQ test performance of large samples of black and white children. The large within-family variance for the black twins could possibly be due to inadequate prenatal and postnatal care, resulting in one twin being prenatally favored over the other, and/or to the ordinal position of the twins in a family, resulting perhaps in one twin receiving more attention than the other.

The third point, particularly in evidence in the data presented by Osborne and Gregor (1968:738), concerns the number of "impossible" h^2 and E^2 values which result when $\rho PP \geqslant 0$.[8] The number of impossible values is similar to the number of impossible values Jensen (1967:154) finds when estimating heritability for personality scales. For most of the measures of personality traits "impossible" values of h^2 and E^2 result when $\rho PP > 0$, that is when there is positive assortative mating. Jensen speculates that this may well mean that the genetic additive model is grossly inappropriate for dealing with heritability of personality traits. His conclusion is:

> In terms of the present formulation of h^2, there are obviously serious difficulties in making sense of the twin data on personality scales. Precisely where the trouble lies is not understood, but the present formulation at least highlights the problem. (1967:154)

In terms of Jensen's formulation of h^2, there are similar difficulties in making sense out of the black twin data on the scales reported by Osborne, Gregor, and Miele. These authors used Jensen's 1967 article and must have been aware of most of the points which have been stressed here. Their conclusions however provide no evidence of this awareness. Osborne and Gregor conclude with the following statement:

> The primary purpose of this study was to test the hypothesis of differential heritability ratios for white and Negro children on tests of spatial ability. In Table I the two groups are compared on eight spatial ability tests by four different heritability estimates. On the basis of these data the hypothesis of a lower heritability ratio for Negro than for white children must be rejected. The h^2 differences are not remarkable but on seven of the eight spatial tests h^2 was higher for Negroes than for whites suggesting more rather than less genetic or biological contributions for Negro children than for white children on spatial test performance. Environment does not play a more significant role in the mental development of spatial ability of the disadvantaged (Negro) than of the culturally disadvantaged (1968:738–39).

Osborne and Miele (1969:538) come to the same conclusion that "environment does not play a significantly greater role in the development of numerical ability among disadvantaged (Negro) children than among culturally advantaged white children." Even if the heritability estimates presented by these authors were acceptable and did not violate all the restrictions presented above, their conclusion concerning the meaning of a higher heritability estimate is valid. A higher heritability estimate for black children would indicate that they are exposed to a more uniform environment. Gregg and Sanday (1971) suggest, in fact, that heritability estimates for black children will probably be higher than for white children. This is the case for heritability estimates reported by Scarr-Salapatek (1971b) for a black sample (see below for further discussion of this point).

The above analysis supports the growing disillusionment, reported by Scarr-Salapatek (1971a), with the concept of heritability and those who would like to eliminate h² from human studies. I would not go so far as to suggest complete elimination of efforts to measure heritability since, if computed correctly, it can be a very useful measure of the degree of homogeneity of the environment which various groups are exposed to with reference to a particular trait (for a similar argument see Scarr-Salapatek, 1971a). However, it should be stressed that the current formulae are not adequate measures of heritability, and some research effort should be put into finding an adequate measure. An appropriate measure, however, cannot be confused, as was argued above, with measures of the magnitude of the genetic contribution to a given trait.

IQ TEST EQUIVALENCE CONTROLLING FOR ENVIRONMENTAL FACTORS

Until there is some reliable means for estimating the magnitude of the genetic contribution, the question of genetic differences between groups can be only indirectly researched. One research approach might be to assume that the distribution of intelligence due to the genetic component alone is the same for all groups of a population and to analyze reported mean differences in test performance between racial groups as possible effects of qualitative environmental differences. Note that this statement does not imply that there is no genetic variation in intelligence *within* these groups. It simply places the emphasis on searching for the *determinable* causes of IQ differences *between* such groups. Such an approach would also have the value of focusing the serious effort on looking for manipulable environmental factors. This kind of research would be of use to the developers of social and educational policy who are committed to the concept of equality of educational opportunity.

According to Jensen (1971:17), if group differences in IQ are due to environmental factors alone it should be possible to reduce the group membership correlation with IQ to zero by holding constant the causal environmental factors. Referring to black children, Jensen states that so far no one has succeeded in finding the environmental conditions which, when held constant, result in comparable IQ scores between black and white children (1971:24). He notes further, referring to the work of Shuey (1966), that when black children are grouped by their parents' socioeconomic status those in the highest SES level still score two to three IQ points below white children in the lowest SES level (1971:24).

Recent studies provide contradictory evidence. Referring to data presented in a doctoral thesis written at the University of Minnesota by P. L. Nichols in 1970, Scarr-Salapatek (1971a:1228) reports that the seven-year Wechsler Intelligence Scale for Children (WISC) IQ scores yielded the same means and distributions for two large samples of black and white children when social class variables were equated. Prenatal and postnatal medical care was equally available to blacks and whites in these samples, which,

according to Scarr-Salapatek (1971a:1228), may have contributed
to the relatively high IQ scores of the black children.

Golden et al. (1971) found that the range in the mean Stanford
Binet IQ scores of a sample of black children classified by social
class is almost identical to the range reported by Terman and
Merrill for their standardization sample classified by social class.
The range reported by Golden et al. (1971:42) for black children
from middle-class to lower-class/welfare families was 116 to 93.
The range reported by Terman and Merrill (see Golden et al.,
1971:42) for white children whose father's occupation was classified from a "professional" to "unskilled labor" was 116 to 94.

Mercer (1971), in a study of Chicago, black, and white elementary school children, found that when five "modal" sociocultural characteristics were held constant there was no difference between the measured intelligence (using the full-scale
WISC) of Chicano, black and Anglo children. The five modal
characteristics which were important for the Chicano sample
were: coming from less crowded homes (less than 1.4 per room);
having mothers who expected them to be educated beyond high
school; living in a home where the head of the household had
more than a ninth grade education; living in a home where
English was spoken all or most of the time; living in a family
which was buying or owned its home. The five modal characteristics which were important for the black sample were: living
in a family with five or fewer members; having mothers who
expected them to be educated beyond high school; living in a
family where the head was married; living in a family which was
buying or owned its home; living in a family where the head
had an occupation rated 30 or higher on the Duncan Socioeconomic Index (Mercer, 1971:15-16).

When each of these five characteristics are successively held
constant in each group, the results are dramatic. The average IQ
for the entire Chicano sample (N = 598) is 90.4, approximately
two-thirds of a standard deviation below the mean for the

standardization group. The average IQ for the subsample of Chicano children (N = 127) from backgrounds least like the modal sociocultural configuration of the community (i.e., having o or only one modal characteristic) is 84.5. The average IQ for the subsample (N = 146) with two of the modal characteristics is 88.1; for those with three modal characteristics (N = 126) the mean is 89.0; for those with four modal characteristics (N = 174) the mean is 95.5; for those with all five modal characteristics (N = 25) the mean is 104.4, which is 4.4 points above the mean of the white standardization sample (Mercer, 1971:17).

Mercer reports similar trends for the black sample. The average IQ for the entire black sample (N = 339) is 90.5. The average IQ for the subsample of black children (N = 47) from backgrounds least like the modal configuration of the community is 87.1. The average IQ for the subsample (N = 101) with two modal characteristics is 87.1; for those with three modal characteristics (N = 106) the mean is 95.5; and for those with five modal characteristics (N = 17) the mean is 99.5, which is the national norm for the test. Thus, according to Mercer (1971:21), "black children who came from family backgrounds comparable to the modal pattern for the community did just as well on the Wechsler Intelligence Scale for Children as the children on whom the norms were based. When sociocultural differences were held constant, there were no differences in measured intelligence."

Mayeske (1971), using the data tapes of the Coleman et al. (1966) study, also controls on a number of sociocultural characteristics in a study of racial-ethnic differences in scholastic achievement. Mayeske comes to the same conclusions for scholastic achievement differences as Mercer for IQ differences. Mayeske shows that for sixth grade students, 24% of the total differences among students in their composite achievement scores is the maximum national value that can be associated with membership in one of the six racial-ethnic groups studied by Coleman et al. (1966). This relationship prevails *before* sociocultural factors are taken into consideration. When a variety of social condition variables are controlled, this percentage drops to 1.2.

Mayeske finds (1971:12) that the differences among the racial-ethnic groups in their composite achievement scores approach zero as more and more considerations related to differences in their social conditions are taken into account. When the racial-ethnic group achievement means are adjusted for social background conditions, the differences are reduced from 15 points to four points. The rank order of the mean achievement scores for each ethnic group after all conditions are controlled from highest to lowest is Oriental Americans, whites, blacks, American Indians, Mexican Americans, and Puerto Ricans.

The social conditions which were important were: social and economic well being of the family, the presence or absence of key family members, the students' and parents' aspirations for schooling, their beliefs about how the student might benefit from an education, the activities that they engaged in to support those aspirations, the region of residence, and the achievement and motivational levels of the students one goes to school with. From these results, Mayeske concludes that "no inferences can be made about the 'independent effect' of membership in a particular racial-ethnic group on academic achievement, for that membership, as it related to academic achievement, is almost completely confounded with a variety of social conditions" (Mayeske, 1971:21).

These results are interesting in light of Jensen's statement (1971:13) that "American Indians, though considerably more impoverished than Negroes in the United States, score higher than Negroes on tests of intelligence and scholastic achievement." Jensen (1969:85) based these remarks on the reported Coleman data, while Mayeske's analysis is based on the full set of data which can be brought by interested researchers from the Office of Education. Utilizing these tapes, I looked at the verbal achievement scores (based on the number of verbal rights) of American

Indians and blacks by geographical region in a random sample (N = 7,908) of all twelfth graders in Coleman's sample. I found that while the overall mean verbal achievement of American Indians is slightly larger than that of blacks, the means by geographical region are virtually the same with the exception of the southeast where American Indians score four points higher.

The points made by John (1971:39) concerning Indian life, in her response to Jensen's comparison of black and Indian children, might be appropriate for explaining the score differential between American Indians and blacks in the southeast region. Referring to Indian children in general, John (1971:39) points out that many Indian children are not in school which may bias the selection of children who are sent to school. She also states that fewer brain-damaged children survive in Indian than in black communities because of the lack of roads and hospital facilities on the reservations. The results of my comparison of the verbal achievement scores of American Indian and black children suggest that John's explanation may apply primarily to American Indian children in the southeast region. Finally, it should be pointed out that the highest mean verbal achievement score in the two ethnic samples occurs for black twelfth graders in the Great Lakes region. The highest for American Indian twelfth graders is three points less and occurs in the Far West-Rocky Mountain region.

The data presented in this section support the simulated results of the social allocation model presented by Light and Smith (1969) as an alternative to Jensen's reasoning with respect to the mean differences between blacks and whites. Social allocation is the "process whereby members of different racial groups are assigned to environments nonrandomly" (Light and Smith, 1969:487). Using a simulation procedure based on Jensen's variance estimates and census data on the percentage allocation of blacks and whites in 12 socioeconomic categories, Light and Smith (1969:498) conclude that the large difference between black and white mean IQs may be explained by "the nongenetic differences in the allocation of blacks and whites to different environments, and environment-genetic combinations."

AN ALTERNATIVE MODEL FOR ANALYSIS OF
BEWEEN-GROUP DIFFERENCES IN IQ

In the United States a number of groups in addition to the racial and lower socioeconomic groups have been observed to exhibit lower IQ scores than the white middle and upper classes. Examples are orphanage children (Tyler, 1965), mountain children (Wheeler, 1942), rural children (Tyler, 1965), and deaf children (Graham and Shapiro, 1953). Such groups have some interesting common characteristics. They are isolated in varying degrees from the American cultural mainstream of the white middle and upper classes, and the mean and standard deviation of the IQ scores recorded for these groups are on the average lower than those recorded for the mainstream group.

The hereditarian would argue that genetic inferiority and selective migration explain the difference in means between rural, ethnic, and urban majority groups. *An alternative explanation is that these groups by virtue of their isolation are not exposed to the cultural elements related to the expression of IQ.* The hereditarian would argue that the homogeneity in measured intelligence in these groups (as indicated by a lower standard deviation) is due to inbreeding. If the latter were the case, then we might also expect a degree of homogeneity in other phenotypic characteristics which, to my knowledge, does not exist. *An alternative explanation is that these groups are exposed to an environment which is uniform in the absence of at least some of the relevant components which are important in IQ test performance.* The advantage of these alternative explanations is that they can be applied both to groups which may not represent different gene pools (such as orphanage and deaf children) and to groups which do (such as racial groups). The systematic development of these explanations is articulated in the conceptual model presented below. This development is based on the work of Davis (1948), Eells et al. (1951), Sanday (1972), and Scarr-Salapatek (1971a, 1971b).

The variation of IQ *within* groups is generally agreed to be largely a function of genetic and environmental components. The *expression* of genetic variation is a function of (1) prenatal and postnatal medical care, (2) diet, and (3) the actual genetic structure of individuals. Environmental variance is a function of (1) individual emotional, motivational factors and (2) degree and nature of contact with the mainstream culture. In the discussion below, prenatal and postnatal medical care and diet are included as environmental factors.

Given any two groups (such as blacks and whites in the United States or upper- and lower-class groups) where there is a reported mean difference in performance on tests measuring general intelligence, the problem is to explain these differences. If all of the factors contributing to the variation within groups were equally distributed across groups, group correlations with IQ would disappear. In the presence of significant differences in test performance between groups, those who argue that genotypes are unequally distributed across groups generally attempt to show that the other factors are not significantly related to test performance. Those who argue that the environmental factors are unequally distributed generally assume that the genotypic distribution is the same for all groups and that the remaining factors are unequally distributed.

It is assumed here that the distribution of intelligence due to the genetic component alone is similar for racial groups of a population and that reported mean differences in IQ scores are related to an unequal distribution of the remaining factors listed above. Each one of these factors will be discussed below.

The effects of biological environmental disadvantages on school performance and mental development have been reviewed by

Birch and Gussow (1970) and Brace and Livingstone (1971). The effect of such disadvantages on genetic variance and the expression of individual differences has been discussed by Scarr-Salapatek (1971b:1293). Briefly, the argument is that in an environment which does not provide adequate medical or nutritional care, the genetic potential of most genotypes cannot be realized. Such an environment can also affect motivational and emotional states. A biologically supressive environment can restrict the expression of genetic variability in performance, thereby reducing the total phenotypic variance and reducing mean performance scores.

Sanday (1972) argues that differences in the degree and nature of contact with the mainstream culture can also contribute to the reduction of phenotypic variability and mean performance scores. This statement is predicated on the following analysis: (1) there are a number of cognitive components which test developers seek to measure; (2) the locus of the components which test developers seek to measure resides in the mainstream culture; and (3) these components are diffused differentially to individuals who are peripheral or outside of the cultural mainstream. Davis (1948:63–65) has defined problem solving as a system of acts which are learned through cultural training and are interconnected with acts under genetic control and acts under control of the emotional system. Three types of acts—cultural, genetic, and emotional—comprise the mental system in operation. The cultural acts determine the goal of the total system's operation and direct the system toward solutions sanctioned by group consensus. The members of different groups often do not share the same set of cultural acts and culturally based cognitive components.

It is well known that the standard intelligence tests were developed to measure cognitive components which are highly correlated with doing well in school and teachers' evaluations of pupils (Davis in Eells et al., 1951:29–38; Jensen, 1969). An item analysis of some of these tests (see Eells et al., 1951) further demonstrates that the content of test items is often related to experience and learning which only middle- and upper-class children would be likely to be exposed to. It is on this basis that the process of diffusion is considered to be important in the under-standing of differential test performance between groups.

Diffusion, as used by anthropologists, refers to the process by which material objects or learned behaviors are relayed from a point of origin within a single society to any number of other societies. Diffusion used in this sense is a cross-cultural process. Diffusion as it is used here refers to an intracultural process by which behaviors are relayed from a point of origin within a society to other points in the same society.

Holding the biological factors constant, mean differences in test scores of groups within a given society can be seen as a function of the group's degree and nature of contact with the mainstream culture, the locus of the components being measured. Degree of contact is a combined measure of psychological, social, and geographical distances from the mainstream cultural unit. The weights assigned to these dimensions can vary depending on the non-mainstream units being considered in the empirical test of the model. Nature of contact is a measure of the type of af-fective interaction between members of the nonmainstream unit and the mainstream unit. Affective interaction can range from accepting to nonaccepting. The weights assigned to the distance and affective dimensions can be viewed as the parameters of the diffusion process (i.e., the rate of diffusion).

The above discussion primarily emphasizes two general factors which are hypothesized to reduce the mean performance in non-mainstream groups. These two factors are biologically related environmental disadvantages and lack of exposure to the cultural mainstream. Scarr-Salapatek (1971b) predicts that in a biologically suppressive environment the heritability estimates will be low reflecting the lack of expression of genetic potential. Based on the analysis of heritability presented in Gregg and Sanday, Sanday (in press) predicts that in an environment which is uniformly lacking the cognitive components which test developers seek to measure, heritability estimates will be higher than those recorded for the mainstream group since a small proportion of the variance will be accounted for by differences in the environment. These hypotheses appear to conflict, since a biologically suppressive environment is usually correlated with low exposure to the mainstream culture. An analysis of the two hypotheses indicates that both are partially correct and that together a more complete picture emerges.

The size of the h^2 estimate is a linear function of the size of the difference between identical and fraternal twin correlations. When this difference is low, the heritability estimate will be low, and when this difference is high, the heritability estimate will also be high. In a biologically suppressive environment, it is conceivable that one twin will be environmentally or prenatally favored over the other thus inhibiting the expression of the genetic potential of one twin. Another possibility is that the expression of the genetic potential in both fraternal and identical twins will be equally inhibited. In such a case the expression of genetic variability would be reduced, leaving only environmental variability. In the former case there would be some genetic variability but it would conceivably be the same for both types of twins. Both cases could result in similar correlation coefficients for the two types of twins and, consequently, a low heritability estimate. In either case, the h^2 estimates in a biologically disadvantaged environment are simply an artifact of malnutrition and general health and cannot be used to assess genetic variability relative to environmental variability.

The hypothesis suggested by the author applies only to non-mainstream groups receiving biologically related environmental advantages. In such groups the genetic variability will flourish, and the heritability estimates will be high. It is predicted that these estimates will be higher than in similarly advantaged mainstream groups due to the lack of exposure to the cognitive components being measured. The data reported by Scarr-Salapatek (1971b:1285–1295) are consistent with this hypothesis. The black group which she classifies as "advantaged" exhibit much higher heritability estimates than the "advantaged" whites in two out of three tests. In the third test, the heritability estimate for the "advantaged" blacks is similar, but lower, than that reported for the white "advantaged" group.

The diffusion hypothesis[4] can be tested first by controlling for the biological factors, as much as is possible given the available data, and then analyzing the nature and correlates of the test items where there is a significant difference between the percentage of right answers between a mainstream and a nonmainstream group. Conventional performance measures, according to Cohen (1971:49) are constructed to assess information repertoires and the ability to use analytic tools. An analysis of test items from some IQ tests (see Eells et al., 1951:81–304) indicates that many items are information loaded. If the diffusion hypothesis is correct, significant differences in correct answers between mainstream and nonmainstream groups should occur on items reflecting mainstream culture content.

Many items on the tests, however, involve the use of the analytic conceptual style and are not, at least obviously, tied to identifiable culture content. The relationship between a child's information repertoire and preferred conceptual style needs more thought and research in relation to the diffusion hypothesis. Whether there is an antecedent or a spurious relationship between a child's information repertoire and the ability to use the analytic style is an interesting research question. Cohen (1971:49) states that the use of analytic skills is an important determinant of school performance; however, she also indicates that when size of the information repertoire is held constant, nonanalytic style users achieve reasonably high scores on performance measures.

Stinchcombe's (1969) layer cake analysis of the cognitive styles that intelligence tests measure indicates that a child's ability to employ these styles is partially dependent on degree and nature of contact. He notes, as does Jensen, that black children's capacities decrease from a slight superiority to whites at early ages to inferiority at later ages. He suggests that this is due to the lower density and frequency of interaction of black children with people in their environment who will lead them from one cognitive style to the next. The hours of attention and the ability to motivate children to be attentive are two factors which Stinchcombe suggests are important in aiding a child to develop his full intellectual capacities. Factors like this may explain the frequently observed correlation between ordinal position in the family, size of the family, and IQ of teacher with the IQ of children.

Where the data do not permit analyzing the test items, another approach for evaluating the diffusion hypothesis would be to examine change in scores over time in a population of school children and to note correlated changes with increasing exposure to the mainstream culture. An empirical analysis which provides some interesting data with respect to this is the demonstration by Estes (1953, 1955) that while there was a significant difference in the mean WISC scores of a population of second grade upper- and lower-class children, there was no significant difference between these same children three years later, which, according to Estes, indicated the influence of the school. Depending on the school, of course, it can be seen as the major source of exposure to the mainstream culture for nonmainstream children. This is supported by the Coleman et al. (1966) report which suggested that the school environment has more influence on the performance of black children than it does on the performance of white children.

CONCLUSION: ANTHROPOLOGISTS AND SOCIAL POLICY

While anthropologists traditionally have not devoted much research and teaching attention to the study of their own national and social needs, there is evidence of an increasing interest within the profession to include the United States as a legitimate subject for basic and applied research. The importance of this new direction was underscored by Wallace (1972:11) in his presidential address at the Awards Luncheon of the 70th Annual Meeting of the American Anthropological Association. In his talk, Wallace raises the question of the ethical and intellectual propriety of American anthropologists who continue to engage in research in other cultures but ignore American national and social needs and the study of American communities.

The growth of this awareness corresponds and may be related to the growing tendency of federal agencies to fund research activities which promise to increase an understanding of the causes of the nation's problems and to provide solutions. At the same time there has been a growing conviction among policy makers in Washington that social science evidence can be used to seek solutions to social and economic problems (Cohen, 1970). Examples of this conviction are the reports prepared by Coleman et al. (1966) on equality of educational opportunity and by Moynihan (1965) on the black family, both of which were commissioned by Congress. The 1954 Supreme Court desegregation decision cited specific social science documents. The Court referred to a study conducted by Clark and Clark (1965) which showed that black children as young as three years old rejected black dolls as inferior to white dolls. Chief Justice Earl Warren wrote in his 1954 opinion:

> To separate (black children) from others of similar age and qualification solely because of their race generates a feeling of inferiority as to their status in the community that may affect their hearts and minds in a way unlikely ever to be undone.

With the holistic and dynamic approach to the study of man and the understanding of the interaction between culture and biology and between evolutionary and cultural adaptation, it would seem that anthropologists should be among the most, rather than the least, visible in domestic policy making circles. In view of the human costs of inadequately tested solutions to social problems, this lack of visibility may be a good thing. While anthropologists are generally well equipped to deal with substantive issues, they are usually unequipped with the appropriate methodological tools to carry a research problem to a convincing empirical conclusion which may lay the foundation for a given solution. Although the participant observer technique may render new insights and hypotheses, it is not enough to engage in ethnographic detailing when the interest is in seeking generalizations upon which to build a policy which affects a nation. The present emphasis on language requirements and foreign fieldwork to the almost total exclusion of research design and statistical methods in most Ph.D. programs is unlikely to prepare students to read with understanding the appropriate background studies, much less to carry out new and promising lines of social policy related research. In fact, an examination of many of the present Ph.D. programs and emphases in recruiting faculty indicates that anthropologists are training students who will be equipped solely to compete for a scarce number of university positions where the cycle will be perpetuated.

Unfortunately, it will be the students who must bear the cost of narrowly conceived training programs. With the expected decrease in the number of college-age people and the increase of the costs of education, it has been predicted (see D'Andrade, 1972:13) that there will be fewer employment opportunities for anthropologists unless jobs outside academic institutions can be obtained. Casagrande's (1971:6) proposal to develop programs in selected universities which would provide training for work in nonacademic fields will, hopefully, aid in breaking the traditional training emphasis.

As far as the substantive issues are concerned, anthropologists, when not overcome by emotion, can excel. Herrnstein (1971) might have revised his futuristic predictions had he consulted an anthropologist. Accepting Jensen's interpretation of the meaning of heritability estimates, Herrnstein finds himself thoroughly convinced that both individual and social class differences in IQ performance are, at present, primarily genetically determined. On the basis of this conviction, he predicts that the successful realization of the egalitarian goals of our society will give rise to a caste system based on inborn ability with the bright people at the top of the social structure and the "IQ dregs" at the bottom (Scarr-Salapatek, 1971a:1225). This might be the case if Herrnstein were correct in assuming that the mental abilities currently correlated with success, as now defined, will be the same mental abilities which will be correlated with success as it is defined in the future.

A totally different set of predictions emerge if one employs an evolutionary perspective. It is more than possible that the least adaptable are those who have been overtrained in narrow specialties and who depend on affluent conditions. Any exogenous influence which destroys these conditions (such as a U.S. based war, depletion of the present energy sources, or other influences) and wipes out the need for the present wide range of narrow specialties could render the "bright" people functionless, while the "IQ dregs" may exhibit the adaptive capacity necessary for survival.

Another point to be raised concerns Herrnstein's assumption that mental abilities are inherited. Mental ability, as measured by the IQ test, is not in itself an inherited trait but a function of the brain hardware which may be inherited. There are many different kinds of ability and the mental functioning so highly prized at present may not be rewarded in the future. Berg (1970), in fact, suggests that this is the case at the present. Universities are creating an oversupply of Ph.D.'s at a time when the evidence indicates that, for the roles available, education beyond a certain level tends to be negatively correlated to productivity and job tenure. According to Friendenberg (1971), a superior IQ in a highly bureaucratized society can be counterproductive because the certifiable schooling that usually goes with it may gain people a higher place than their contribution to production warrants.

To conclude, the detail provided here has been to inform, to point out the contradictions, and to indicate the amount and complexity of the research which remains before a complete understanding of the causes of differential performance on IQ and scholastic achievement tests can be understood. Such research is essential for the development of intervention strategies. The diffusion hypothesis is interesting because of its implications for school integration strategies. If the degree of contact with the mainstream culture is related to adopting the cognitive styles associated with occupational success, one would be tempted to propose a strategy of school integration with a certain ethnic composition. However, if nature of contact is also important then the frequent racial hostility occurring in integrated schools could offset the effects sought through integration, and the strategy might be to allocate more time, energy, and resources to the education of nonmainstreamers.

Whatever strategy is finally implemented, social scientists ought to find some way to resolve the following dilemma posed by Senator Walter Mondale in an address to the American Education Research Association's annual meeting in February 1971:

> I had hoped to find research to support or to conclusively oppose my belief that quality integrated education is the most promising approach. But I have found very little conclusive evidence. For every study, statistical or theoretical, that contains a proposed solution or recommendation, there is always another, equally well documented, challenging the assumptions or conclusions of the first. No one seems to agree with anyone else's approach. But more distressing: no one seems to know what works. As a result I must confess, I stand with my colleagues confused and often disheartened. (Light and Smith, 1971:430-431)

NOTES

1. In their presentation of the data, Osborne and Gregor (1968) and Osborne and Miele (1969) report the value of the F ratio but do not mention the level of significance. This was determined by the author using the .05 level with df calculated as $N_{DZ} - 1$, $N_{MZ} - 1$.
2. The values of e^2 and E^2 for these data were computed by the author using equations 4 and 5 presented in this paper. These values are not presented by Osborne, Gregor, and Miele.
3. Whenever the value of $h^2 + E^2 + e^2$ was greater than 1.00, the value of E^2 and h^2 was called impossible.
4. Some of the research discussed here has just been initiated by the author together with Anthony Boardman, William Morris, Daniel Rosen, and Richard Staelin.

REFERENCES

Berg, I. 1970. Education and Jobs: The Great Training Robbery. New York: Praeger.
Birch, H., and J. Gussow. 1970. Disadvantaged Children: Health, Nutrition and School Failure. New York: Harcourt, Brace, and World.
Bodmer, W. F., and L. L. Cavalli-Sforza. 1970. Intelligence and race. Scientific American 223:19-29.
Brace, C. L., and F. B. Livingstone. 1971. On creeping Jensenism. *In* Race and Intelligence, Anthropological Studies No. 8, C. L. Brace, G. R. Gamble, and J. T. Bond, eds. Washington, D.C.: American Anthropological Association.
Brazziel, W. F. 1969. A letter from the South. Harvard Educational Review 39:348-56.
Casagrande, J. B. 1971. Comment, Newsletter of the American Anthropological Association, Vol. 12, No. 5:6.
Clark, K. B., and M. P. Clark. 1965. Racial identification and preference in Negro children. *In* Basic Studies in Social Psychology, H. Proshansky and B. Seidenberg, eds. New York: Holt, Rinehart, and Winston.
Cohen, E. 1970. A New Approach to Applied Research: Race and Education. Columbus: Charles Merrill.
Cohen, R. 1971. The influence of conceptual rule sets on measures of learning ability. *In* Race and Intelligence, Anthropological Studies No. 8, C. L. Brace, G. R. Gamble, and J. T. Bond, eds. Washington, D.C.: American Anthropological Association.
Coleman, J. S. et al. 1966. Equality of Educational Opportunity. Washington, D.C.: Government Printing Office.
Cronbach, L., and P. Drenth, eds. 1972. Proceedings of the NATO Conference on Cultural Factors in Mental Test Development, Application and Interpretation. Mouton Press (in press).

D'Andrade, R. G. 1972. Comment. Newsletter of American Anthropological Association, Vol. 13, No. 6:13.

Davis, A. 1948. Social-Class Influences Upon Learning. Cambridge: Harvard University Press.

Deutsch, M. 1969. Happenings on the way back to the forum. Harvard Educational Review 39:523–57.

Eaves, L. J. 1972. Computer simulation of sample size and experimental design in human psychologenetics. Psychological Bulletin 77:144–52.

Eells, K. et al. 1951. Intelligence and Cultural Differences. Chicago: University of Chicago Press.

Erlenmeyer-Kimling, L., and L. F. Jarvik. 1963. Genetics and intelligence: a review. Science 142:1477–79.

Estes, B. 1953. Influence of socioeconomic status on Wechsler intelligence scale for children: an exploratory study. Journal of Consulting Psychology 17:58–62. 1955. Influence of socioeconomic status on Wechsler intelligence scale for children: addendum. Journal of Consulting Psychology 19:225–26.

Fehr, F. S. 1969. Critique of hereditarian accounts of "intelligence" and contrary findings: a reply to Jensen. Harvard Educational Review 39:571–80.

Friedenberg, E. Z. 1971. More about I.Q.: backtalk. Atlantic Monthly 228:104.

Golden, M., B. Birns, W. Bridger, and A. Moss. 1971. Social-class differentiation in cognitive development among black preschool children. Child Development 42:37–45.

Graham, E. E., and E. Shapiro. 1953. Use of the performance scale of the Wechsler intelligence scale for children with the deaf child. Journal of Consulting Psychology 17:396–98.

Gregg, T. G., and P. R. Sanday. 1971. Genetic and environmental components of differential intelligence. In Race and Intelligence, Anthropological Studies No. 8, C. L. Brace, G. R. Gamble, and J. T. Bond, eds. Washington, D.C.: American Anthropological Association.

Herrnstein, R. 1971. I.Q. Atlantic Monthly 228:43–64.

Jensen, A. E. 1967. Estimation of the limits of heritability of traits by comparison of monozygotic and dizygotic twins. In Proceedings of the National Academy of Sciences 58:149–56. 1969. How much can we boost I.Q. and scholastic achievement? Harvard Educational Review 39:1–123. 1971. Can we and should we study race differences? In Race and Intelligence, Anthropological Studies No. 8, C. L. Brace, G. R. Gamble, and J. T. Bond, eds. Washington, D.C.: American Anthropological Association.

John, V. 1971. Whose is the failure? In Race and Intelligence, Anthropological Studies No. 8, C. L. Brace, G. R. Gamble, and J. T. Bond, eds. Washington, D.C.: American Anthropological Association.

Kennedy, W. A., V. Van de Riet, and J. C. White. 1963. A normative sample of intelligence and achievement of Negro elementary school children in the southeastern United States. Monograph. Social Research Child Development 28 (6).

Light, R. J., and P. V. Smith. 1969. Social allocation models of intelligence:

a methodological inquiry. Harvard Educational Review 39:484–510. 1971. Accumulating evidence: procedures of resolving contradictions among different research studies. Harvard Educational Review 41:429–71.

Mayeske, G. W. 1971. On the Explanation of Racial-Ethnic Group Differences in Achievement Test Scores. Washington, D.C.: Office of Education.

Mercer, J. R. 1971. Pluralistic diagnosis in the evaluation of black and Chicano children: a procedure for taking sociocultural variables into account in clinical assessment. Paper presented at the meetings of the American Psychological Association, Washington, D.C.

Moynihan, D. P. 1965. The Negro Family: The Case for National Action. Washington, D.C.: Office of Policy Planning and Research, U.S. Department of Labor.

National Academy of Sciences. 1967. Racial studies: academy position on call for new research. Science 158:892–93.

Osborne, R. T., and A. J. Gregor. 1968. Racial differences in heritability estimates for tests of spatial ability. Perceptual and Motor Skills 27:735–39.

Osborne, R. T., A. J. Gregor, and F. Miele. 1968. Heritability of factor V: verbal comprehension. Perceptual and Motor Skills 26:191–202.

Osborne, R. T., and F. Miele. 1969. Racial differences in environmental influences on numerical ability as determined by heritability estimates. Perceptual and Motor Skills 28:535–38.

Sanday, P. R. 1972. A model for the analysis of the cultural determinants of variation in measured intelligence between groups. *In* Proceedings of the NATO Conference on Cultural Factors in Mental Test Development, Application, and Interpretation, L. Cronbach, and P. Drenth, eds. Mouton Press.

Scarr-Salapatek, S. 1971a. Unknowns in the I.Q. equation. Science 174: 1223–28. 1971b. Race, social class, and I.Q. Science 174:1285–95.

Shuey, A. M. 1966. The Testing of Negro Intelligence. New York: Social Science Press.

Stinchcombe, A. L. 1969. Environment: the cumulation of effects is yet to be understood. Harvard Educational Review 39:511–22.

Swan, D. A. 1971. More about I.Q.: backtalk. Atlantic Monthly 228:106.

Tyler, L. E. 1965. The Psychology of Human Differences. New York: Appleton-Century-Crofts.

Wallace, A. F. C. 1972. Shifts in conditions of anthropological practice. Newsletter of the American Anthropological Association 13:10–11.

Wheeler, L. R. 1942. A comparative study of the intelligence of east Tennessee mountain children. Journal of Educational Psychology 33:321–34.

16

RACE AND IQ:
THE GENETIC BACKGROUND

W. F. Bodmer

This essay is a review of the meanings of race and IQ, and the approaches for determining the extent to which IQ is inherited. The first question to consider is "What is race?" and then one must demonstrate how one can study the biological inheritance of mental ability as measured by IQ tests. These two aspects of genetics form the main underlying theme for this essay.

WHAT IS RACE?

In almost all the psychological studies carried out on racial groups, race is defined sociologically or culturally and not biologically. However, biological race boundaries often coincide with those that are culturally evident, though not always. An example of a sociological or cultural definition of race that is not strictly valid biologically is that of children of black-white marriages in the USA, who are still regarded as black.

To a biologist a race is just a group of individuals or populations which form a recognizable sub-division of the species. The

From *Race, Culture and Intelligence* (Penguin Edition, 1972), edited by Ken Richardson *et al.*, pp. 83–113. Copyright © Martin Richards, Ken Richardson & David Spears, 1972. Reprinted by permission of Penguin Books Ltd.

group is identified by the fact that the individuals within it share characteristics which distinguish them from other sub-groups of the species. The species itself is most simply defined as that set of individuals which includes all those who could produce fertile offspring if they mated with each other. This means, of course, that matings between members of different races are just as fertile as matings within races. The members of a race or a sub-group are however most likely to find their mates within their own group. This results in the groups becoming separated from one another as far as reproduction is concerned. Because such groups mate among themselves rather than with other groups, they tend, as we shall see, to become more and more different. The more different they become and the more they are separated from each other, the less likely it becomes that individuals marry outside their own group. This tends to make the groups become more and more distinguishable from each other.

The sorts of things that keep groups physically apart are, for example, mountain ranges, wide rivers, seas and deserts, and just distance alone. It took many thousands of years before Europeans crossed the Atlantic in significant numbers and came into contact with the American Indians. And even then, they hardly inter-married—it was mainly germs causing diseases like measles, which crossed the racial barriers. But even in a comparatively small country like England, distances are such that at least until quite recently, it was not very likely if you came from the north you would marry someone from the south. In fact, you would be most likely to marry someone from your own parish, or at least one quite nearby. Modern transport, of course, has scaled down the significance of distance as an isolating factor. Partly as a result of this, many of the differences that have accumulated in past years, even between neighbouring towns, are now rapidly disappearing. But most of the sub-divisions of man which are nowadays called races, originated long before the Industrial Revolution and modern transport. Greater mobility, as well as affecting local marriage

patterns, certainly has an enormous impact on the larger sub-
divisions of the human species by bringing together groups of
people who had previously lived more or less in isolation from
each other. This happened when slaves were taken over to the
Americas from Africa and more recently when American blacks
moved into the northern states and their cities, from the southern
states.

Major migrations have led also in the past, often in the form of
invasions, to new marriage patterns and the emergence of new
population groups. The bringing together of different peoples
should eventually bring about a blending of the differences between them, but at the same time it can be a cause of many of the
racial tensions that we see in the world today.

Groups of people who are geographically and reproductively
isolated from one another, tend to become different for a number
of reasons, all of which may interact with each other. The environment itself may have a direct effect, for example, a diet deficient in iodine leads to high frequencies of goitres, and sunlight
makes the skin darker. Environment factors may lead to different
patterns of living, adapted to differences in the climate for example, and these in turn may lead to cultural differences. Differences in the ways of living and in language can also, however,
arise simply by chance and historical accident. Cultures change
continuously at varying rates, and it is not necessary to suppose
that all the changes are adaptations to the prevailing environment
or way of life. Exactly the same is true of inherited or genetic
differences. In any population there are, as we shall see later, very
many genetic differences between individuals. People may differ
genetically, in such outwardly obvious features as their hair colour
or their eye colour, or in unseen "constitutional" characters, such
as their blood types. Geneticists call the makeup of an individual
his genotype. Thus people with blue eyes have a different genotype from those with brown or green eyes, at least as far as those
genes determining eye colour are concerned. The frequencies of

the various genotypes may be quite different in different populations. Thus the frequency of the blue-eyed genotype is, for example, much higher in Caucasian populations of European origin than in any other type of population. Genotype frequencies may change simply by chance, just like cultural differences, but such chance variations tend to be more important for small than for large populations.

Many, if not most, genetic changes are adaptive. By adaptive I mean that some one or more of those genotypes which are better suited to the environment leave more offspring or survive better, and so contribute relatively more to the next generation of individuals. This is the process of natural selection. Natural selection is the major agent of evolution because it is a major cause of changes in the genetic constitution of a population.

There are two major differences between cultural and inherited characteristics of populations. First, cultural characteristics tend to apply to all individuals of a population, whereas inherited differences are mostly measured by the frequency with which they occur in the population. Thus, while all members of a population will, for example, speak the same language and wear similar types of clothing, an inherited variation, such as blue versus green or brown eyes, may be found in a number of different populations, but it may occur with different frequencies in each of them. This means that a population is mostly characterized, not by being altogether of one or another genotype, but by the frequency with which the genotype is found in it. Blue eyes, for example, are certainly more common in northern than in southern Europe. But by no means all northerners are blue-eyed and some blue eyes will be found in the south. The second major difference between cultural and inherited characteristics, is in the way that they are transmitted from individual to individual. Inherited traits are passed on from parents to offspring in accordance with Mendel's laws of genetics. Changes in the frequency of inherited traits depend on differences in the rate at which people of the various genotypes reproduce relative to one another. Genetic changes like these always take many generations, even when fairly strong natural selection is involved. Cultural characteristics, on the other hand, are not only passed from parents to offspring, but may be passed on from any one individual to another by word of mouth or by writing. So some cultural changes may be adopted quite quickly by a whole population. Transmission of culture is rather like transmission of an infection. Flu and cold epidemics spread very quickly, especially with the large amount of contact that people of all countries of the world now have with each other. In the same way cultural habits such as pop music preferences and clothing fashions may spread very quickly nowadays especially through the media of radio and television. However, other deep-rooted cultural characteristics of races and racial subgroups are much more difficult to change. These are the cultural patterns that are so resistant to alteration that they have the appearance of being innate; indeed, the difficulties in changing attitudes to school performance and in changing IQ in deprived populations, reflect in part, the difficulty in changing a cultural pattern.

GENETIC POLYMORPHISM

Traditionally people have thought of human races in terms of outwardly obvious features such as skin colour, hair colour and texture, facial and other physical characteristics, whose inheritance cannot yet be explained in terms of simple gene differences whose pattern of occurrence in families follows Mendel's laws. Many common genetic differences are, however, known which are simply inherited but are not outwardly obvious and have no untoward effects. Most geneticists now would say that the only biologically valid approach to defining races is in terms of such simply inherited differences.

These simply inherited differences are mostly identified by laboratory tests on blood cells or serum. Perhaps the best known example of such differences, are the ABO blood types. Blood donors always have to have their blood ABO typed for transfusion, so as to match their potential recipients. There are four common ABO types, A, B, AB and O which are genetically determined. An individual's type is determined by which versions of the gene responsible for making A, B or O substances he carries. Thus one form of the gene makes A, another B, and the third form neither. For example, individuals both of whose ABO genes are of the third form, are type O, while those with one A and one B gene, are type AB. (Remember that genes occur in pairs, one from each parent.) Geneticists call different versions of a gene, like those for the A or B substances, alleles.

Apart from identical twins, all people look different. The outward physical features by which we distinguish people are paralleled by simple inherited differences such as the ABO blood types. Such genetic traits are called polymorphisms, when the alternative versions of the genes that determine them, or the alleles as the geneticist calls them, each occur within a population with a substantial frequency. In the case of the ABO blood types, the allele A occurs in Caucasian populations with a frequency of 28 per cent, the B allele in 6 per cent and the O allele in 66 per cent. Over thirty such polymorphic genetic systems, including the blood groups, in which alternative genetic forms of a trait occur are already known and new ones are being discovered all the time. These thirty polymorphisms alone are enough to identify almost everyone as unique.

What proportion of genes occurring with a substantial frequency are polymorphic? The answer seems to be at least 30 per cent and could be even more.

So, the thirty or so polymorphisms we now know are a minute fraction of the total of more than 300,000 that must exist, taking into account the total number of genes in the human genome. The potential for genetic differences between individuals is truly staggering. The numbers of genetically different types of sperm or eggs which any one single individual could in principle produce, is many millionfold more than the number of humans that have ever lived. The polymorphisms so far discovered concern mainly chemical substances in the blood. Among those still to be discovered must surely be many which affect the chemical substances of the brain and involve behavioural differences. It is clear that the extraordinary genetic uniqueness of human individuals applies not just to the blood but to all physical, physiological and mental attributes. This enormous genetic variety within a population seems to be a property of almost all species.

VARIATION IN GENE FREQUENCIES BETWEEN RACES

If we look at the blood types and other polymorphisms in races we find that the frequencies of polymorphic genes vary widely. Geneticists use these frequencies to define races. In Oriental populations, for instance, the frequency of the gene for the blood type B is 17 per cent while it is only 6 per cent in Caucasians (see figure 14.1). This means that type B individuals are generally three times as common in most of Asia than they are in Europe. All the known polymorphisms differ at least to some extent in their frequencies between different populations, though some are much more variable than others. One of the major tools in helping to work out the relationships between populations or races has been the analysis of the frequencies of genetic polymorphisms. In simple terms, the more similar are the polymorphic frequencies, the more closely related are the populations. A comparison of polymorphic frequencies in different races shows three very important features of the nature of genetic variation within and among them. Perhaps most important, the extent of variation *within* any population is usually far greater than the average difference *between* populations; in other words there is a great deal of overlap (for IQ see, for example, figure 14.5). Then, differences between populations and races are mostly measured by

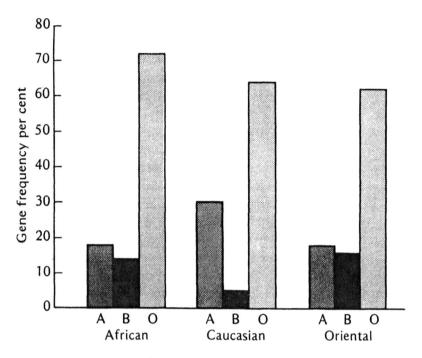

Figure 14.1 Frequencies of polymorphic genes among Africans. Caucasians and Orientals provide a means of differentiating these three races biologically. The columns represent the frequencies with which the genes of the A B O blood group system occur in these races.

differences in the frequencies of the various genetic polymorphisms. They are not measured by whether or not a given gene is present. Any particular genetic combination may be found in almost any race, but the *frequency* with which it is found will vary from one race to another. Some genetic differences may simply be present or absent and so are, to some extent, characteristic of a race. Genes like this are clearly very useful in helping to delineate the human races, but they are very much the exception rather than the rule. Most genetic differences between populations can only be measured on average. It is this fact which underlies the need to distinguish differences among *individuals* from differences among *populations*. The final point about the study of polymorphic frequencies is that the distinction between races is often quite blurred. This is mainly the result of interbreeding between races at their boundaries, and of the mixing effect of large migrations. Even in the United States, where marriage between American blacks and whites is still quite rare, it is estimated that up to 30 per cent of the genes of the average black American from the northern states can be traced to white ancestry. This, of course, represents the cumulative effect of a number of generations during each of which a small amount of interbreeding took place. The American blacks are now clearly a new population genetically, which has been formed from a mixture of black Africans and white Americans. The Jews provide another example of the blending of racial distinctions. They are all presumably derived from one population, or at most a few closely related populations, of biblical times. Gene frequency studies, however, show that now Jewish populations in different parts of the world tend to resemble their surrounding populations at least as much, if not more, than they do each other. Such genetic studies, when combined with historical information, and sociological ideas of race and culture, can be very useful in understanding the origin of modern populations. Still remembering that most of the psychological and sociological studies of race are based on cultural determination of the boundaries, the definition of race in terms of differences in the frequencies of genetic polymorphisms is fairly arbitrary. How much difference does there have to be between populations before we call them different races? After all, even the people of, say, Lancashire and Yorkshire are likely to differ significantly in the frequency of at least some polymorphisms, but we should hardly refer to them as different races. On the other hand, most people would agree that the differences between the indigenous peoples of the major continents, such as the differences between Africans, Orientals and Caucasians, are obvious enough to merit the label race. Between these two extremes, however, lie a multitude of possibilities and it is largely a matter of taste as to whether one is a splitter or a lumper of population groups into races.

INHERITANCE OF COMPLEX OR QUANTITATIVE CHARACTERS

Heredity refers to the transmission of characteristics from parent to offspring. The primary biological functional unit of heredity is the gene, and the human genome—the complete set of genes which characterizes the biological inheritance of an individual—may consist of as many as five to ten million genes. Some of these genes can be individually identified by their patterns of inheritance in families, and the expression of many of these analysed at the biochemical level. The inheritance of differences between individuals which are known to be determined by one or a few genes can thus be reliably predicted and, in some cases, the biochemical or physiological basis for the inherited differences clearly established. Intelligence is, however, a composite and complex character, the expression of which must be dependent on a combination of the effects of environmental factors and the products of many different genes, each gene probably only having a small effect on measured IQ. The tools for dealing with the inheritance of such complex characters are necessarily complicated and still relatively ineffective.

As we have noted, intelligence must be a complex characteristic under the control of many genes. However, extreme deviations from normal levels, as in the cases of severe mental retardation, can sometimes be attributed to single gene differences. Such deviations can serve to illustrate important ways in which genetic factors can affect behaviour. Consider the disease phenylketonuria (PKU). Individuals with this receive from both of their parents a mutated version of the gene controlling the enzyme that converts one amino acid, phenylalanine, into another, tyrosine. The mutated gene allows phenylalanine to accumulate in the blood and in the brain, causing mental retardation. The accumulation can, to some extent, be checked early in life by a diet deficient in phenylalanine.

The difference between the amounts of phenylalanine in the blood of people with PKU and that in the blood of normal people, which is closely related to the primary activity of the gene causing PKU, clearly creates two genetic classes of individuals. When such differences are compared with differences in IQ, there is a slight overlap, but individuals afflicted with PKU can be distinguished clearly from normal individuals. It is, indeed, routine today to test all babies for the tell-tale presence of ketane bodies with a nappy or urine test that reveals the phenylketonuric genotype, that is, the genetic constitution that leads to PKU which is associated with extreme mental retardation. If differences in head size and hair colour in phenylketonuric individuals and normal individuals are compared, however, they show a considerable overlap. Although it can be said that the phenylketonuric genotype has a statistically significant effect on both head size and hair colour, it is not, given the large variations of head size and hair colour among PKU individuals, an effect large enough to distinguish the phenylketonuric genotype from the normal one (see figures 14.2a and 14.2b). Thus the genetic difference between phenylketonuric and normal individuals contributes in a major way to the variation in blood phenylalanine levels but has only a minor, although significant, effect on head size and hair colour.

The phenylketonuric genotype is very rare, occurring with a frequency of only about one individual in 10,000. It therefore has little effect on the overall distribution of IQ in the population. However, among all the genes which are polymorphic must be included many whose effect on IQ is comparable to the effect of the phenylketonuric genotype on head size or hair colour. These genotype differences cannot be individually identified, but their total effect on the variation of IQ may be considerable.

The nature of PKU demonstrates another important point: the expression of a gene is profoundly influenced by environment. Phenylketonuric individuals show appreciable variation. This indicates that the genetic difference involved in PKU is by no means the only factor, or even the major factor, affecting the level of phenylalanine in the blood. It is obvious that dietary differences have a large effect, since a phenylalanine-deficient diet brings the level of this amino acid in the blood of a phenylketonuric individual almost down to normal. If an individual receives the phenylketonuric gene from only one parent, his mental development is not likely to be clinically affected. Nevertheless, he will tend to have higher than normal levels of phenylalanine in his blood. The overall variation in phenylalanine level is therefore the result of a combination of genetic factors and environmental factors. Measuring the relative contribution of genetic factors to the overall variation is thus equivalent to measuring the relative importance of genetic differences in determining this type of quantitative variation.

Characters determined by the joint action of many genes, like height and IQ, are often called quantitative characters because they are measured on a continuous scale. They are much more susceptible to environmental influences than are polymorphisms such as the blood groups which seem to be pretty well independent of all environmental factors. Because the contribution of individual genes to such characters cannot easily be recognized, one has to resort to complex statistical analyses to sort out the relative contributions of heredity and environment. These analyses try to assess the extent to which relatives tend to be more like each other than they are to unrelated or to more distantly related people.

The occurrence of identical and non-identical twins is a sort of natural experiment that illustrates very simply the way in which environmental and genetic factors can be separated. Identical (or monozygotic = MZ) twins are derived from a single fertilized

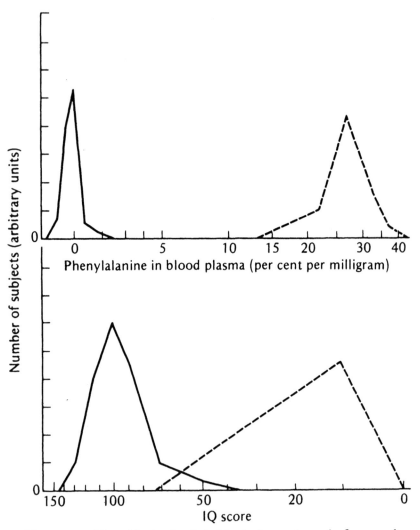

Figure 14.2a Phenylalanine levels in blood plasma shown in first set of curves (top) distinguish those who carry a double dose of the defective gene that causes high phenylalanine levels (broken curve), a condition called phenylketonuria, from those with normal phenylalanine levels (solid curve). Second set of curves (bottom) shows that this genotype has a direct effect on intelligence: phenylketonurics (broken curve) have low IQs because accumulation of phenylalanine and its by-products in blood and nerve tissue damages the brain. Individuals with functioning gene (solid curve) have normal I Qs.

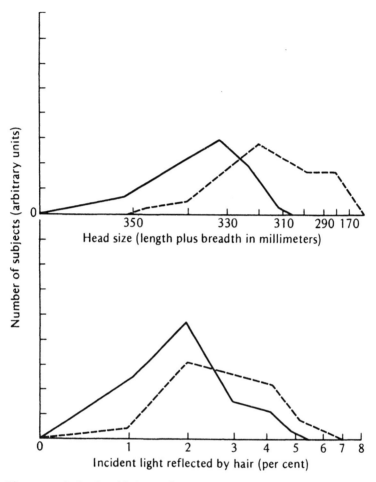

Figure 14.2b In the third set of curves (top) phenylalanine levels are related to head size (displayed as the sum of head length and breadth), and in the fourth set (bottom) phenylalanine levels are related to hair colour (displayed as the percentage of light with a wavelength of 700 millimicrons reflected by the hair). In both cases it is obvious that the phenylketonuric genotype has a significant effect on each of these characteristics: the reflectance is greater and the head size is smaller (broken curves) among phenylketonurics than they are among normal individuals (solid curves). Yet the distribution of these characteristics is such that they cannot be used to distinguish those afflicted with phenylketonuria from those who are not.

egg and so are identical genetically. Any differences between
them must, therefore, be due to the environment. Non-identical
(or dizygotic = DZ) twins come from two eggs fertilized at the
same time by different sperm and so are as different, or alike, genetically as any brothers or sisters. Both types of twins are usually
brought up within a family and so, on average, are subject to
more or less the same types of environmental variation. The extent to which non-identical twins differ more than identical twins
is thus an indication of the importance of genetic factors in differentiating the non-identical twins. Differences in IQ, among
non-identical pairs show a greater spread than those among identical pairs, indicating that the genetic diversity among the non-
identical pairs adds to the purely environmental differences which
differentiate the identical pairs of twins. A comparison of the
average difference between members of individual identical pairs
and the average difference between members of non-identical pairs,
could in principle be taken as a measure of the relative importance
of genetic and environmental factors. (For statistical reasons, it is
usually better to consider not the mean differences but their
squares. These are directly related to the *variance*, which is a well-
known statistical measure of the spread of a distribution.)

There are two major contrasting reasons why such a simple
measure is not entirely satisfactory. First, the difference between
members of a dizygous pair represents only a fraction of the
genetic differences that can exist between two individuals. Dizygous twins are related to each other as two siblings are; therefore
they are more closely related than two individuals taken at random from a population. This implies a substantial reduction
(roughly by a factor of two) in the average genetic difference
between dizygous twins compared with that between two randomly chosen individuals. Secondly the environmental difference
between members of a pair of twins encompasses only a fraction
of the total environmental differences that can exist between two
individuals, namely the difference between individuals belonging

to the same family. This does not take into account differences among families, which are likely to be large. Within the family the environmental differences between twins are limited. For instance, the effect of birth order is not taken into account. Differences between ordinary siblings might therefore tend to be slightly greater than those between dizygous twins. It also seems possible that the environmental differences between monozygous twins, who tend to establish special relations with each other, are not exactly comparable to those between dizygous twins. In short, whereas the contrast between monozygous and dizygous twin pairs minimizes genetic differences, it also tends to minimize environmental differences.

In order to take account of such difficulties one must try to use all available comparisons between relatives of various types and degrees, of which twin data are only a selected case. For technical reasons one often measures similarities rather than differences between two sets of values such as parent IQs and offspring IQs. Such a measure of similarity is called the correlation coefficient. It is equal to 1 when the pairs of values in the two sets are identical or, more generally, when one value is expressible as a linear function of the other. The correlation coefficient is 0 when the pairs of measurements are completely independent, and it is intermediate if there is a relation between the two sets such that one tends to increase when the other increases.

The mean observed values of the correlation coefficient between parent and child IQs and between the IQs of pairs of siblings, are close to 0.5. This is the value one would expect on the basis of the simplest genetic model in which the effects of any number of genes determine IQ and there are no environmental influences or complications of any kind. It seems probable, however, that the observed correlation of 0.5 is coincidental. Complicating factors such as different modes of gene action, tendencies for like to mate with like and environmental correlations among members of the same family must just happen to balance one another almost exactly to give a result that agrees with the simplest theoretical expectation. If we ignored these complications, we might conclude naively (and in contradiction to other evidence, such as the observations on twins) that biological inheritance of the simplest kind entirely determines IQ.

HERITABILITY OF IQ

We need a means of determining the relative importance of environmental factors and genetic factors, taking account of several of the complications. In theory this measurement can be made by computing the quotients known as heritability estimates. To understand what such quotients are intended to measure, consider a simplified situation. Imagine that the genotype of each individual with respect to genes affecting IQ can be identified. Individuals with the same genotype can then be grouped together. The differences among them would be the result of environmental factors, and the spread of the distribution of such differences could then be measured. Assume for the sake of simplicity that the spread of IQ due to environmental differences is the same for each genotype. If we take the IQs of all the individuals in the population, we obtain a distribution that yields the total variation of IQ. The variation within each genotype is the environmental component. The difference between the total variation and the environmental component of variation leaves a component of the total variation that must be accounted for by genetic differences. This component, when expressed as a fraction of the total variance, is one possible measure of heritability.

In practice, however, the estimation of the component of the total variation that can be accounted for by genetic differences (from data on correlations between relatives) always depends on the construction of specific genetic models, and is therefore subject to the limitations of the models. One problem lies in the fact that there are a number of alternative definitions of heritability depending on the genetic model chosen, because the genetic variation may have many components that can have quite different meanings. A definition that includes only those parts of the genetic variation generally considered to be most relevant in animal and plant breeding is often used. This is called heritability in the narrow sense. If all genetic sources of variation are included, then the heritability estimate increases and is referred to as heritability in the broad sense.

The differences between these estimates of heritability can be defined quite precisely in terms of specific genetic models. The resulting estimates of heritability, however, can vary considerably. Typical heritability estimates for IQ (derived from the London population in the early 1950s, with data obtained by Sir Cyril Burt) give values of 45 to 60 per cent for heritability in the narrow sense and 80 to 85 per cent for heritability in the broad sense.

A further major complication for such heritability estimates has the technical name "genotype-environment interaction." The difficulty is that the realized IQ of given genotypes in different environments cannot be predicted in a simple way. A given genotype may develop better in one environment than in another. In man there is no way of controlling the environment. Even if all environmental influences relevant to behavioural development were known, their statistical control by appropriate measurements and subsequent statistical analysis of the data would still be extremely difficult. It should therefore be emphasized that, because estimates of heritability depend on the extent of environmental and genetic variation that prevails in the population examined at the time of analysis, they are not valid for other populations or for the same population at a different time.

The investigation of the same genotype or similar genotypes in different environments can provide valuable controls over environmental effects. In man this can be done only through the study of adopted children. A particularly interesting type of "adoption" is that in which monozygous twins are separated and reared in

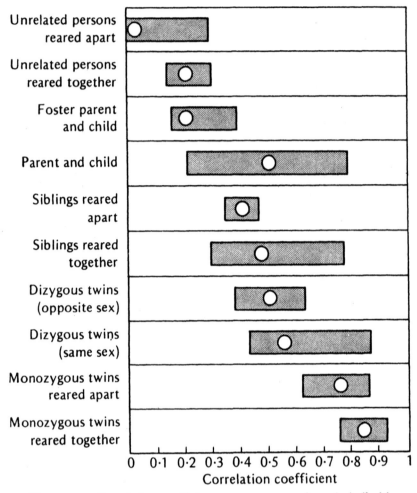

Figure 14.3 Correlation coefficients are representative of similarities and differences. A coefficient of 1 indicates that the two classes compared are identical. 0 indicates independence of one value from the other. The horizontal bars represent the range of differences in coefficients found in the relationships shown. The mean of each range is represented by the circle in each bar. A mean coefficient of 0.50 is that which would be expected if there were no environmental effects in IQ. As other evidence indicates that environment exerts a significant effect, these calculations must be further refined. These data are extracted from the work of Erlenmeyer-Kimling and Jarvik.

different families from birth or soon afterwards. The outcome is in general a relatively minor average decrease in similarity. Following the same line of reasoning, the similarity between foster parents and adopted children can be measured and contrasted with that between biological parents and their children (see figure 14.3). The results show that, though the correlation between foster parents and their children is significantly greater than 0, is undoubtedly less than that between biological parents and their offspring. However, a complete analysis of such data is difficult because children are not adopted at random and so even adoption does not provide a convincing control over the environment. Nevertheless, on the basis of all the available data and allowing for the limitations to its interpretations, the heritability of IQ is still fairly high. It must be emphasized however, that the environmental effects in essentially all the studies done so far are limited to the differences among and within families of fairly homogeneous sections of the British or United States populations. The results cannot therefore be extrapolated to the prediction of the effects of greater differences in environment or to other types of differences.

IQ AND SOCIAL CLASS

There are significant differences in mean IQ among the various social classes. One of the most comprehensive and widely quoted studies of such differences and the reasons for their apparent stability over the years was published by Burt in 1961 (see figure 14.4). His data come from schoolchildren and their parents in a typical London borough. Socio-economic level was classified, on the basis of type of occupation, into six classes. These range from Class 1, including "university teachers, those of similar standing in law, medicine, education or the Church and the top people in commerce, industry or civil service," to Class 6, including "unskilled labourers and those employed in coarse manual work." There are four main features of these data:

Figure 14.4 An English study by Burt indicates that intelligence and social class are closely related. The darker bars represent parental IQs for the social classes while the lighter bars indicate the IQs of their children. The phenomenon of children of above average parents having lower IQ scores is known as regression to the mean, and children of low-IQ parents exhibit an upward trend towards the population mean.

1. Parental mean IQ and occupational class are closely related. The mean difference between the highest and the lowest class is over 50. Although occupational class is determined mostly by the father, the relatively high correlation between the IQs of husband and wife (about 0.4) contributes to the differentiation among the classes with respect to IQ.

2. In spite of the significant variation between the parental mean IQs, the residual variation in IQ among parents within each class is still remarkably large. The mean standard deviation of the parental IQs for the different classes is 8.6, almost three-fifths of the standard deviation for the entire group. That standard deviation is contrived in test construction to be about 15.

3. The mean IQ of the offspring for each class lies almost exactly between the parental mean IQs and the overall population mean IQ of 100. This is expected because it is only another way of looking at the correlation for IQ between parent and child, which as we have already seen tends to be about 0.5 in any given population.[1]

4. The last important feature of the data is that the standard deviations of the IQ of the offspring, which average 13.2, are almost the same as the standard deviation of the general population, namely 15. This is another indication of the existence of considerable variability of IQ within social classes. Such variability is almost as much as that in the entire population.

The most straightforward interpretation of these data is that IQ is itself a major determinant of occupational class and that it is to an appreciable extent inherited (although the data cannot be used to distinguish cultural inheritance from biological). Burt pointed out that, because of the wide distribution of IQ within each class among the offspring and the regression of the offspring to the population mean, appreciable mobility among classes is needed in each generation to maintain the class differences with respect to IQ. He estimated that to maintain a stable distribution of IQ differences among classes, at least 22 per cent of the offspring would have to change class, mainly as a function of IQ in each generation. This figure is well below the observed intergenerational social mobility in Britain, which is about 30 per cent.

Fears that there may be a gradual decline in IQ because of an apparent negative correlation between IQ and fertility have been expressed ever since Francis Galton pointed out this correlation for the British ruling class in the second half of the nineteenth century. If there were such a persistent association, if IQ were at least in part genetically determined and if there were no counteracing environment effects, such a decline in IQ could be expected. The fact is that no significant decline has been detected so far. The existing data, although they are admittedly limited, do not support the idea of a persistent negative correlation between IQ and overall reproductivity.

IQ—RACE DIFFERENCES

The average frequency of marriages between blacks and whites throughout the US is still only about 2 per cent of the frequency that would be expected if marriages occurred at random with respect to race. This reflects the persistent high level of reproductive isolation between the races, in spite of the movement in recent years towards a strong legal stance in favour of desegregation. Hawaii is a notable exception to this separation of the races, although even there the observed frequency of mixed marriages is still 45 to 50 per cent of what would be expected if matings occurred at random.

Many studies have shown the existence of substantial differences in the distribution of IQ in US blacks and whites. Such data were obtained in an extensive study published by Wallace A. Kennedy of Florida State University and his coworkers in 1963, based on IQ tests given to 1800 black children in elementary school in five south-eastern states (Florida, Georgia, Alabama, Tennessee and South Carolina) (see figure 14.5). When the distribution these workers found is compared with a 1960 sample of the US white population, striking differences emerge. The mean difference in IQ between blacks and whites is 21.1, whereas

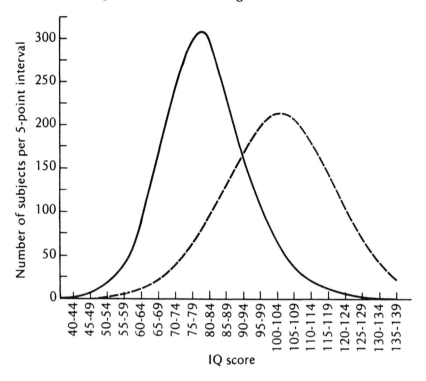

Figure 14.5 IQ difference between blacks and whites in the USA emerges from a comparison of the IQ distribution in a representative sample of whites (broken curve) with the IQ distribution among 1800 black children in the schools of Alabama, Florida, Georgia, Tennessee and South Carolina (black curve). Wallace A. Kennedy of Florida State University, who surveyed the students' IQ, found that the mean IQ of this group was 80.7. The mean IQ of the white sample is 101.3, a difference of 21.1 points. The two samples overlap distinctly but there is also a sizable difference between the two means. Other studies show a difference of 10 to 20 points, making Kennedy's result one of the most extreme reported.

the standard deviation of the distribution among blacks is some 25 per cent less than that of the distribution among whites (12.4 v. 16.4). As one would expect there is considerable overlap between the two distributions, because the variability for IQ within any population is (like the variability for most characteristics) substantially greater than the variability between any two populations. Neverthless, 95.5 per cent of the blacks have an IQ below the white mean of 101.8 and 18.4 per cent have an IQ of less than 70. Only 2 per cent of the whites have IQs in the latter range.

Reported differences between the mean IQs of blacks and whites generally lie between 10 and 20, so that the value found by Kennedy and his colleagues is one of the most extreme reported. The difference is usually less for blacks from the northern states than it is for those from the southern states, and it clearly depends heavily on the particular populations tested. One well-known study of army "alpha" intelligence-test results, for example, showed that blacks from some northern states achieved higher average scores than whites from some southern states, although whites always scored higher than blacks from the same state. There are many uncertainties and variables that influence the outcome of IQ tests, but the observed mean differences between US blacks and whites are undoubtedly more or less reproducible and are quite striking.

There are two main features that clearly distinguish IQ differences among social classes described above from those between blacks and whites. First, the IQ differences among social classes relate to the environmental variation within the relatively homogeneous British population. It cannot be assumed that this range of environmental variation is comparable with the average environmental difference between black and white Americans. Secondly, and most important, these differences are maintained by the mobility among occupational classes that is based to a significant extent on selection for higher IQ in the higher occupational classes. There is clearly no counterpart of this mobility with respect to the differences between US blacks and whites; skin colour effectively bars mobility between the races.

The arguments for a substantial genetic component in the IQ differences between the races assume that existing heritability estimates for IQ can reasonably be applied to the racial difference. These estimates, however, are based on observations within the white population. We have emphasized that heritability estimates apply only to the population studied and to its particular environment. Thus the extrapolation of existing heritability estimates to the racial differences assumes that the environmental differences between the races are comparable to the environmental variation within them. Let us consider a simple model example which shows that there is no logical connection between heritability as determined within races and the genetic differences between them. Suppose we take a bag of seed collected from a field of wheat and sow one handful on barren, stony ground and another one on rich, fertile ground. The seeds sown on fertile ground will clearly grow more vigorously and give a much higher yield per plant than that sown on barren ground. If we were to study the extent to which individual differences in yield between the plants grown on the fertile ground were genetically determined, we should expect to find comparable genetic differences to those which existed between the plants grown in the original wheat field from which our bag of seed was collected. The same would be true for the differences between the individual plants growing on the barren ground. The fact that there are genetic differences between these plants both on the fertile and on the barren ground clearly does not have anything to do with the overall differences between the two sets of plants grown in these two very different environments. This we know must be due to the differences in the soil. The genetic stock from which all the plants were derived was, after all, the same. It was the original one bag of seed. The same logic must apply to the human situation. How can we be sure that the different environments of US blacks and whites are not comparable to the barren and fertile soils? Our original bag of human genes may not be as uniform as the wheat field, but why should the differences between the original human samples, the Africans and the Caucasians, have anything to do with con-

ventional IQ measurements? Whether or not the variation in IQ
within either race is entirely genetic or entirely environmental has
no bearing on the question of the relative contribution of genetic
factors and environmental factors to the differences between the
races.

IQ AND ENVIRONMENT

A major argument given by Jensen, Eysenck and others in favour
of a substantial genetic component to the IQ difference is that it
persists even when comparisons are made between US blacks and
whites of the same socio-economic status. This status is defined in
terms of schooling, occupation and income, and so it is necessarily
a measure of at least a part of the environmental variation, comparable to the class differences we have discussed here.

Taken on face value—that is, on the assumption that status is
truly a measure of the total environment—these data would indicate that the IQ difference is genetically determined. It is difficult
to see, however, how the status of blacks and whites can be compared. The very existence of a racial stratification correlated with
a relative socio-economic deprivation makes this comparison suspect. Black schools are well known to be generally less adequate
than white schools, so that equal numbers of years of schooling
certainly do not mean equal educational attainment. Wide variation in the level of occupation must exist within each occupational class. Thus one would certainly expect, even for equivalent
occupational classes, that the black level is on the average lower
than the white. No amount of money can buy a black person's
way into a privileged, upper-class, white community, or buy off
more than two hundred years of accumulated racial prejudice on
the part of the whites, or reconstitute the disrupted black family,
in part culturally inherited from the days of slavery. It is impossible to accept the idea that matching for status provides an

adequate, or even a substantial, control over the most important environmental differences between blacks and whites.

Let us consider just two examples of environmental effects on IQ which show both how complicated is the environment and how large can be the effects of environmental differences. The first concerns a comparison of the IQs of twins and triplets as compared to single births. A number of studies have shown that twins have an IQ that is systematically about 5 points lower than non-twins. This reduction seems to be independent of socio-economic variables and of such other factors as parental age, birth order, overall family size, gestation time and birth weight as has been shown particularly convincingly by a recent study carried out in Birmingham, England, by Record, McKeown and Edwards. These authors based their study on the results of verbal reasoning tests given in the 11+ examinations during the period from 1950 to 1954. The average scores for 48,913 single births and 2164 twin births were 100.1 and 95.7 respectively. Furthermore the average score for 33 triplets was 91.6, another 4 points lower, while the average score for 148 twins, whose co-twins were stillborn or died within four weeks after birth was 98.8. This, they point out, is only very little lower than the score of 99.5, which is obtained by standardizing the data to the maternal ages and birth ranks observed for these 148 twins. The environmental factor involved in this remarkable effect on IQ must be post-natal and may well have something to do with the reduced attention parents are able to give each of two very young children born at the same time. This one subtle factor in the familial environment, which clearly is not reflected in standard measurements of socio-economic status, has an effect on IQ which is about one-third of the overall average difference between US blacks and whites. Measuring the environment only by standard socio-economic parameters, is a little bit like trying to assess the character of an individual by his height, weight and eye colour.

The second example of a major environmental effect comes from a well known study of adopted children. Skodak and Skeels studied the IQs of a series of white children placed into adopted homes through Orphans' Home Institutions in Iowa, mostly before the infants were six months old, and compared these IQs with the IQs of their foster parents and of their biological parents. As in other similar studies they found a higher correlation between the IQs of the adopted children and their biological parents than with their foster parents. Most strikingly, however, they found that while the mean IQ of the 63 adopted children who had been followed through until they were about thirteen to fourteen years old was 106, the mean IQ of the biological mothers of these 63 children was only 85.5, a difference of fully 20 points! Even if one assumes that the biological mothers came from a low socio-economic group and that their husbands had the population average IQ of 100 and that IQ is completely genetically determined, the expected average IQ of the children would be only one half $(100 + 85.5) = 92.75$. The difference between expected and observed is still $106 - 92.75 = 13.25$ points, which is just about the same as the average US black-white IQ difference. The adoptive homes were strongly biased towards the upper socio-economic strata. This study thus shows what a striking effect an improved home background can have on IQ. In Skodak and Skeel's own words "the implications for placing agencies justify a policy of early placement in adoptive homes offering emotional warmth and security in an above average educational and social setting."

WHY SHOULD THERE BE A GENETIC COMPONENT TO THE RACE–IQ DIFFERENCE?

Jensen has stated that because the gene pools of whites and blacks are known to differ and "these genetic differences are manifested in virtually every anatomical, physiological and biochemical comparison one can make between representative samples of identifiable racial groups . . . there is no reason to suppose that the brain should be exempt from this generalization." But there is no *a priori* reason why genes affecting IQ which differ in the gene pools of blacks and whites, should be such that on the average whites have significantly more genes increasing IQ than blacks do. On the contrary, one should expect, assuming no tendency for high IQ genes to accumulate by selection in one race or the other, that the more polymorphic genes there are that affect IQ and that differ in frequency in blacks and whites, the less likely it is that there is an average genetic difference in IQ between the races. The same argument applies to the differences between any two racial groups.

Since natural selection is the principal agent of genetic change, is it possible that this force has produced a significant IQ difference between American blacks and whites? Using the simple theory with which plant and animal breeders predict responses to artificial selection, one can make a rough guess at the amount of selection that would have been needed to result in a difference of about 15 IQ points, such as exists between blacks and whites. The calculation is based on three assumptions: that there was no initial difference in IQ between Africans and Caucasians, that the heritability of IQ in the narrow sense is about 50 per cent and that divergence of black Americans from Africans started with slavery about two hundred years, or seven generations, ago. This implies a mean change in IQ of about 2 points per generation. The predictions of the theory are that this rate of change could be achieved by the complete elimination from reproduction of about 15 per cent of the most intelligent individuals in each generation. There is certainily no good basis for assuming such a level of selection against IQ during the period of slavery.

Eysenck has actually suggested as one basis for genetic differences that significant selection might have taken place during the procurement of slaves in Africa. He proposes, for example, that the more intelligent were less likely to be caught or that the less intelligent were the ones that were sold off by their tribal chiefs. If one makes the extreme assumption that this initial selection is the sole cause of a 15 point IQ difference between US blacks and whites, then following the same lines of analysis that were used above, the slaves that were caught or sold must have been in the bottom 5 per cent as far as IQ is concerned. This would seem to indicate that the tribal chiefs knew how to administer and interpret IQ tests almost as well as we do today! It is clearly very difficult, if not impossible, to assess the role that natural selection might have played in accentuating IQ differences between the races. Certainly any hypothesis one chooses to put forward is in the realm of unsubstantiated speculation that cannot be claimed as even suggestive evidence for a substantial genetic component to the race–IQ difference.

One approach to studying this question that has been suggested by Shockley, Eysenck and others is to correlate IQ measurements with an assessment of the proportion of Caucasian genes in different samples of US blacks. The proportion of Caucasian genes in a sample of US blacks can be estimated from a comparison of the frequencies of polymorphic genes in Caucasians, African blacks and US blacks. This approach would mean that groups with different degrees of admixture of "white" and "black" genes would have to be studied for their IQ. It is known, however, that the degree of admixture varies from less than 10 per cent in some southern states to more than 30 per cent in some northern states. For this knowledge to be useful, one has to assume that the environment is the same for all these populations and that there is no correlation between differences in the environment and the extent of the black-white admixture. One example of data that shows quite clearly that this is not true has been analysed by Spuhler and Lindzey. They pointed out that for both blacks and whites, the mean values per state of US army alpha intelligence-test scores obtained during the First World War correlated precisely with the *per capita* state expenditure, at that time, on education. The states with a mean expenditure of less than $5 per head (Arkansas, Florida, Georgia, Kentucky, Louisiana, Mississippi, North and South Carolina, Tennessee, Texas and Virginia— *all* southern states) gave overall mean alpha scores of 50.2 for whites and 24.9 for blacks. The states with a mean expenditure of more than $10 (Illinois, Indiana, Kansas, New Jersey, New York, Ohio and Pennsylvania) gave mean alpha scores of 65.3 for whites and 44.9 for blacks. Southern whites hardly scored better than northern blacks, as pointed out long ago by J. B. S. Haldane, Any hope of using such data for genetic studies is clearly out of the question.

The only approach applicable to the study of the IQ difference between the races is that of working with black children adopted into white homes and vice versa. The adoptions would, of course, have to be at an early age to be sure of taking into account any possible effects of the early home environment. The IQs of black children adopted into white homes would also have to be compared with those of white children adopted into comparable white homes. To our knowledge no scientifically adequate studies of this nature have ever been undertaken. It is questionable whether or not such studies could be done in a reasonably controlled way at the present time. Even if they could, they would not remove the effects of prejudice directed against black people in most white communities. It therefore seems that the question of a possible genetic basis for the race–IQ difference will be almost impossible to answer satisfactorily before the environmental differences between US blacks and whites have been substantially reduced.

Jensen has stated on the basis of his assessment of the data (and Eysenck quotes him):

> so all we are left with are various lines of evidence no one of which is definitive alone, but which, viewed all together, make it a not unreasonable hypothesis that genetic factors are strongly

implicated in the average Negro-white intelligence difference. The preponderance of evidence is, in my opinion, less consistent with a strictly environmental hypothesis than with a genetic hypothesis, which of course does not exclude the influence of environment or its interaction with genetic factors.

My assessment of the evidence made together with my colleague Professor Cavalli-Sforza and published in an article in the *Scientific American*—and this is an assessment that we share with many of our geneticist colleagues—is that we simply do not have enough evidence at present to resolve the question. It seems to us that differences in IQ for instance, between American blacks and whites, could be explained by environmental factors, many of which we still know nothing about. This does not mean that we exclude the possibility that there might be a genetic component to such a mean IQ difference. We simply maintain that currently available data are inadequate to resolve this question in either direction and that we cannot see how the question could be satisfactorily answered using presently available techniques.

WHAT USE CAN BE MADE OF KNOWLEDGE CONCERNING GENETIC COMPONENTS TO RACE-IQ DIFFERENCES?

The Nobel prize-winning US physicist William Shockley has repeatedly asked for a major expenditure of funds directed specifically at finding the answer to the question of a genetic component to the race IQ difference and other similar questions, because of their practical importance. He has in fact said in this context:

> I believe that a nation that achieved its ten-year objective of putting a man on the moon can wisely and humanely solve its human quality problems once the objective is stated and relevant facts courageously sought.

No one surely should argue against the need for a better scientific understanding of the basis of intellectual ability and the benefits to society that might accrue from such an understanding. But why concentrate this effort on the genetic basis for the race–IQ difference? Apart from the intrinsic, almost insurmountable difficulties in answering this question at the present time, it is not in any way clear what practical use could be made of the answers. Perhaps the only practical argument is that, since the question that the difference is genetic has been raised, an attempt should be made to answer it. Otherwise those who now believe that the difference is genetic will be left to continue their campaigns for an adjustment of our educational and economic systems to take account of "innate" racial differences.

A demonstration that the difference is not primarily genetic could counter such campaigns. On the other hand, an answer in the opposite direction should not, in a genuinely democratic society free of race prejudice, make any difference. Our society professes to believe there should be no discrimination against an individual on the basis of race, religion or other *a priori* categorizations, including sex. Our accepted ethic holds that each individual should be given equal and maximum opportunity, according to his or her needs, to develop to his or her fullest potential. Surely innate differences in ability and other individual variations should be taken into account by our educational system. These differences must, however, be judged on the basis of the individual and not on the basis of race. To maintain otherwise indicates an inability to distinguish differences among individuals from differences among populations.

NOTES

1. We must note an important fallacy in Eysenck's (and others') argument that "regression presents strong evidence for genetic determination of IQ differences." In any multi-casual system, such as that involved in the determination of IQ, there will be many factors which will tend to increase performance, and others that work to decrease it. In the average

situation these will balance and give the mean IQ of 100. Less commonly they will not balance and we will get extreme IQs, well above or below the mean. These extreme cases arise from relatively rare interactions of genes and environment where (at least statistically) most of the causal factors are pushing in one direction. It is extremely unlikely that this situation will hold for children of very high or very low IQ parents. Things will tend to be more equal and causal factors more nearly balance, so the children's IQ will regress to the mean and the largest regression will be seen in the children of extreme IQ parents. All the presence of regression tells us is that the system is multi-causal. It says nothing about the origin of these causes. Indeed, it is theoretically possible to have regression to the mean in an entirely environmentally controlled system. [Eds.]

FURTHER READING

L. L. Cavalli-Sforza and W. F. Bodmer, *The Genetics of Human Population*, Freeman, 1971.

T. Dobzhansky, *Mankind Evolving*, Yale University Press, 1962.

I. M. Lerner, *Heredity, Evolution and Society*, Freeman, 1968. This book is particularly suitable for the non-biologist.

J. Maynard-Smith, *The Theory of Evolution*, Penguin, 1966. *Myths in Human Biology*, BBC Publications, 1971. A collection of transcripts from recent radio talks.

17

IS EARLY INTERVENTION EFFECTIVE? SOME STUDIES OF EARLY EDUCATION IN FAMILIAL AND EXTRA-FAMILIAL SETTINGS

Urie Bronfenbrenner

THE PROBLEM

Does early intervention have any enduring effects? The 1960's saw the widespread adoption in this country programs of early education aimed at counteracting the effects of poverty on human development. Although some of these programs produced dramatic results during the first few months of operation, the question of long-term impact has remained unanswered for lack of extended follow-up data. Recently, however, research results have become available which shed some light on five questions of considerable scientific and social import:

1. Do children in experimental early education programs continue to gain in intellectual development so long as the education continues, or at least do they maintain the higher level achieved in the initial phase?

This is a condensed version of a longer report: *Is Early Intervention Effective?* Washington, D.C.: Department of Health, Education and Welfare Office of Child Development, 1974.

2. Do children continue to improve, or at least to hold their own, after termination of the program, or do they regress to lower levels of function once the program is discontinued?
3. Is development enhanced by intervention at early ages, including the first years of life?
4. In terms of long-range impact, what kinds of programs are most effective?
5. Which children from what circumstances are most likely to benefit in the long run from early education programs?

THE NATURE AND LIMITATIONS OF THE DATA

Follow-up data are available from two types of early education projects: those conducted in group settings outside the home, and those which involve regularly scheduled home visits by a trained person who works both with the child and his parents, usually the mother. We have attempted to insure comparability in our analysis by reviewing only those studies which (1) include follow-up data for at least two years after the termination of intervention; (2) provide information on a matched control group; and (3) provide data which are comparable to results in other studies.

With respect to the third criterion, it is regrettable that the only comparable measures available from most studies are IQ scores (usually the Stanford-Binet) and, for older children, school achievement tests. This circumstance seriously qualifies the conclusions that can be drawn. Thus we have no systematic information about effects of intervention programs outside the cognitive realm, and even within that sphere standarized tests of intelligence and achievement are limited in scope and subject to a marked middle class bias. Not only are they typically administered by middle class professionals in middle class settings, but the kinds of objects, facts and activities with which the tests are concerned are far more common in middle class than in less-favored environments.

As a result, the scores obtained inevitably underestimate the potential of children from disadvantaged families.

Nevertheless, few scientists or citizens would dismiss as unimportant the demonstration that a particular strategy of early intervention had enabled children from disadvantaged backgrounds to solve problems of the type presented on tests of intelligence at a level of competence comparable to that of the average child of the same age. Wheras performance below the norm on tests of this kind cannot be taken as firm evidence that the child lacks mental capacity, attainment of the norm year after year does mean that the child both possesses intellectual ability and can use it. It is from this perspective that the present analysis was undertaken.

In this analysis, we review seven studies which meet the criteria mentioned above (summarized in Table 1) and draw from additional studies which, although they do not satisfy all requirements, add important clarifications.

METHODOLOGICAL PROBLEMS

Before turning to an interpretation of the results, several methodological complications must be noted.

1. If low IQ is used as a criterion for admission to the program (as in the Weikart and Hodges studies), the initial gains are appreciably inflated by regression to the mean. This phenomenon is responsible for the mistaken but often cited conclusion that the most deprived children are the ones who profit most from intervention programs. In fact, the opposite is the case (see below).

2. A child whose parents are interested in his development and are eager to take advantage of opportunities for him is likely to be more adavanced in and to gain more from an intervention program. Thus failure to control for differences in parents' motivation leads to spurious results.

TABLE 1

Identifying Data	Sample	Nature of Intervention	Experimental and Control Groups
Howard University Preschool Program Washington, D.C. Elizabeth Herzog (Herzog, Newcomb, and Cisin, 1973, 1972a, 1972b; Kraft, Fuschillo, and Herzog, 1968)	Black children in generally good health from families selected at random from four census tracts in Washington inner-city neighborhoods. All parents had to agree in advance to have their children attend the pre-school program if selected. No other requirements. Approximately 68% of families below poverty line; 18% on welfare, median income about $3,500 but extending up to $10,000. About 25% of parents graduated from high school, 90% unskilled labor, remainder skilled and semi-professional. 28% of the mothers worked, and apparently all of the fathers when present. No father in 40% of the homes. Median number of children in the family 4. The "no-show" rate was over 30% during the recruitment phase, but attrition was very low thereafter.	"A well-run middle class nursery school, with no specific 'enrichment' features." Children attended full day for 5 days a week. Each group of twelve had its own teacher and two or three teachers' aides. Weekly parent meetings were held at the university plus individual contacts with families, usually unscheduled. In the hope of consolidating any benefits . . . a series of special school situations was arranged for the 30 experimental children during the three years immediately following nursery school." These included being in the same class in kindergarten, extra teachers and aides, an enriched curriculum, special trips, and assignment of a social worker to the children's families.	30 children from one census tract were designated as the experimental group and 69 from the other three tracts as the control group. The experimental group ended up with a higher percentage of intact families (66% versus 16%), and slightly smaller families.

Identifying Data	Sample	Nature of Intervention	Experimental and Control Groups
Perry Preschool Project Ypsilanti, Michigan David P. Weikart (Weikart, D. P., *et al.*, 1970; Weikart, 1967)	Black children from disadvantaged homes residing in a city of 50,000 on the fringe of metropolitan Detroit. To qualify all children had to have IQ's between 50 and 85 with no discernible organic involvement. In addition, families had to fall below a low cutting point on a cultural deprivation scale based primarily on parents' education and occupation, and also number of persons per room in the home. Parents' education averaged below tenth grade; occupations over 70% unskilled; half the families are on welfare; no information on income; 14% of fathers unemployed. Average number of children in the family 4.8; 48% of the children have no father in the home; about 28% working mothers. There appears to have been little self-selection of families in the sample and attrition during the course of the project has been low.	Half-day classes, five days a week, from mid-October through May for two years. Curriculum derived mainly from Piagetian theory and focused on cognitive objectives. Four teachers for each of 24 children with emphasis on individual and small group activities. Teachers made weekly 90-minute home visit "to individualize instruction through a tutorial relationship with the student and to make parents knowledgeable about the educative process . . . mothers are encouraged to observe and participate in as many teaching activities as possible during the home visits."	Children from the total sample were divided at random into experimental and control groups with some adjustment to assure matching on social class, IQ, boy/girl ratio, and percent of working mothers. The groups appear to be well matched on other variables as well. Although there were 5 waves of experimental and control groups initiated over a period of years, the waves have been pooled in reporting follow-up data.

TABLE 1 (*continued*)

Identifying Data	Sample	Nature of Intervention	Experimental and Control Groups
Early Training Project Nashville, Tennessee Susan W. Gray (Gray and Klaus, 1970; Klaus and Gray, 1968)	Black children from families "considerably below" the poverty line. Selected on the basis of parents' occupation (unskilled or semi-skilled), education (average below eighth grade), income (average $1,500), and poor housing conditions. No data on welfare status or percent of parents unemployed; one-third of the homes with no father; median number of children per family 5. Both self-selection of families at entry in attribution over the course of the study appear to have been minimal.	In summer, daily morning classes emphasized the development of achievement motivation, perceptual and cognitive activities, and language. Each group of nineteen had a Black head teacher and three or four teaching assistants divided equally as to race and sex. In dealing with the children, staff emphasized positive reinforcement of desired behavior. The weekly home visit stressed the involvement of the parent in the project and in activities with the child. Home visits lasted through the year.	Sixty-one children from the same large city were divided at random into two, experimental groups (E_1 and E_2) and one control group (C_1). The remaining control group, (C_2), consisted of twenty-seven children from like backgrounds residing in a similar city 65 miles away. Group E_1 attended the ten-week intervention program for three summers plus three years of weekly meetings with a trained home visitor when preschool was not in session. Group E_2 began the program a year later with only two years of exposure.
Philadelphia Project Temple University E. Kuno Beller (1972)	Children from urban slum areas of North Philadelphia, 90% Black. Families in target mainly employed in unskilled or semi-skilled labor with median income of $3,400.	Nursery groups composed of fifteen children with one head and one assistant teacher for four half days a week, with a fifth day devoted to staff meetings, teacher training, and	A major purpose of the research was to examine the effect of age at entry into school by examining intellectual development of three comparison groups starting in

Children admitted to the nursery group were selected from families responding to a written invitation, who also met the following criteria: "dependency of family on public services, mothers working, and broken homes." Kindergarten group consisted of children from the same classroom attended by nursery children, but without prior nursery experience. First grade group was composed of children entering the same classrooms but without prior nursery or kindergarten experience. Attrition was 10% by the time the original groups reached fourth grade.

parent conferences. "The program was a traditional one" emphasizing "curiosity for discovery . . . creativity . . . warm, personalized handling of the child . . . balance of self-initiated instructed activities." Kindergarten and first grade classes consisted of twenty-five to thirty children, meeting five half days a week, with one head teacher and an aid or assistant teacher. Work with parents and home visits were conducted by a home-school coordinator.

nursery, kindergarten, and first grade respectively. Groups were matched on age, sex, and ethnic background. No data are available on comparability of the three groups in terms of education, socioeconomic status, or family structure. Comparison at time of entry into school, on three different tests of intelligence and on other psychological measures, however, revealed no significant differences. The children from all three groups attended the same classrooms through Grade II, but by Grade III children were dispersed over many schools.

Indiana Project
Indiana University
Bloomington, Indiana
Walter L. Hodges
(Hodges *et al.*, 1967)

Five year old children in good health, predominantly White from Bloomington and from small semi-rural Indiana communities, selected on the basis of low-rated "psycho-social deprivation," and Binet intelligence score between 50 and 85. Average length of schooling for parents just below tenth

Group E1 was exposed to a special "diagnostically-based curriculum" designed to remedy specific deficits of individual children through "an intensive, structured, cognitively-oriented" program. The children met daily for morning sessions. To increase the likelihood of adoption of the program by the

One experimental group (E1) and control group (C2) were constituted by random assignment. Group E1 attended one year of the specially-designed kindergarten program in Bloomington. C2 was composed of at-home controls from the same city. Children in Group C1 attended regular

TABLE 1 *(continued)*

Identifying Data	Sample	Nature of Intervention	Experimental and Control Groups
	grade. No information on welfare status or income. Fathers' occupation approximately 70% unskilled and 8% semi-skilled; 12% unemployed; one-third of the mothers work; 20% of the homes have no father present; average number of children in the family 5; no information is available on the degree of self-selection among sample families. There was only one slight attrition over the course of the study.	public schools, "the teacher to child ratio was smaller in the present study than that reported in the other pre-school projects . . . For the same reason, no work was done with the families of the subjects."	kindergartens newly established in several semi-rural Indiana towns. This was a "traditional kindergarten," providing facilities and equipment similar to those for C_2, but without the special "diagnostically-evolved" curriculum. Group C_3 consisted of at-home controls in these same localities. In general, the families in the experimental group were rated by investigators as more disadvantaged than those in the control group but this difference is not reflected in indices of socioeconomic status, family size, parents' education, or occupation.
Infant Education Research Project Washington, D.C. Earl S. Schaefer (Schaefer, 1972a, 1968; Schaefer and Aaronson, 1972; Infant Education Research Project, undated)	Fifteen month old Black male infants selected from door-to-door surveys of families in two low socioeconomic inner-city neighborhoods in Washington. To be accepted, families had to meet four criteria: (1) income under $5,000; (2) mother's education under twelve years; (3) occupation either unskilled	Trained tutors worked with each child in the home for one hour a day, five days per week, from the time the child was 15 months old until three years of age. The main emphasis was on development of verbal and conceptual abilities through the use of pictures, games, reading, and puzzles. "Partici-	Chosen from different neighborhoods to avoid contamination. "Comparisons between the groups revealed only small differences, many of which favored the control group, on the family variables that might be expected to influence the child's intellectual development."

or semi-skilled; and (4) willingness to have infant participate in either the experimental or control group. In addition, "an attempt was made to choose participants from relatively stable homes, not so noisy or overcrowded as to interfere with the home tutoring sessions." No other background information available. Of the 64 subjects in the original sample, 48 (equally divided between experimental and control group) were available for the final follow-up.

pation of the mother and of other family members in the education of the infant was encouraged but not required."

Verbal Interaction Project
Mineola, New York
Phyllis Levenstein
(1972a, 1970)

Infants 2 to 3 years of age, 90% Black, from disadvantaged families in three Long Island suburbs. To qualify, mothers had to be eligible for low income housing with an education not higher than high school graduation. About 25% of the families were on welfare. Average education of parents was eleventh grade; fathers apparently all employed; about 65% unskilled or semi-skilled. About 35% of mothers work; 30% of the fathers absent. Average number of children per family 3–4. Self-selection

Semi-weekly half-hour visits in the home for seven months each year by trained worker who stimulated interaction between mother and child with the aid of a kit of toys and books referred to as VISM (Visual Interaction Stimula Materials).

Randomized by housing project. The several experimental and control groups differ on age of entry into the program (2 vs. 3, see Table 3), length and intensity of intervention, and prior experience. Groups E1 and E2 had one year of the regular program at two years of age followed by a much abbreviated program in the second year as follows. Group E1 received seven visits in which the focus of attention was on the kit of materials with no involvement of the mother in interaction with

TABLE 1 *(continued)*

Identifying Data	Sample	Nature of Intervention	Experimental and Control Groups
	involved in willingness of mothers in experimental group to participate. Attrition especially high in untreated control groups. Average IQ of mothers of children in the experimental groups was 83; in the control group 88.		the child. Group E2 was given the regular program but with half as many visits as in the first year. Group E3 received the full program for two years beginning at two years of age. Groups E4 and E5 were both given one year of the regular program at age three, but Group E5 had served the previous year as a "placebo" control group which had received the semi-weekly visits but without exposure to the special kit of materials or encouragement of mother-child interaction. The visitor simply brought a gift and played records for the child. Seven of the eight groups are generally comparable on major background variables, but one control group (C2) was far out of line—with better educated mothers, smaller families, higher occupational status, no absent fathers, etc.

3. Recent evidence (Herzog *et al.*, 1972b) indicates that programs involving children from relatively less deprived homes are likely to achieve more favorable results. In comparing effects from different projects, this source of variation must be taken into account.

4. In evaluating results of intervention, other possible sources of confounding include children's age (the effects of deprivation increase as the child gets older), and diffusion effects from experimental to control group (i.e. the latter begins to adopt the practices of the former).

SOME EFFECTS OF PRESCHOOL INTERVENTION IN GROUP SETTINGS

The results of group intervention studies are summarized in Table 2. For each study, the table records the number of subjects, IQ's achieved in successive years by experimental and control groups, and the differences between them. The scores given first are those obtained by both groups before the program began. A double-line indicates the point at which intervention was terminated. At the bottom, major changes over time are summarized in terms of initial gain (before-after difference in the first year of treatment), gain two years after all intervention was terminated (shown because it permits a comparison of all seven studies), and overall gain (difference between initial IQ and last follow-up score three to four years after the children left the program). Also shown are differences between these gains for the experimental and control group. Finally, the bottom row records the average grade equivalent attained on a test of academic achievement administered in the final year of follow-up. Unless otherwise noted, significant differences between experimental and control groups for each year are designated by asterisks, one for the five percent level and two for one percent. The absence of asterisks indicates that the difference was not reliable. Ordinarily

TABLE 2
Effects on Later Intellectual Development
of Intervention Programs in Preschool Settings

	Herzog			Weikart			Gray					Beller			Hodges				
	1 E	2 C	3 E-C	4 E	5 C	6 E-C	7 E1	8 E2	9 G	10 G	11 Ē-G[b]	12 G	13 G	14 G	15 E	16 G	17 G	18 G	19 Ē-G[a]
N	66—61			58—13[a]			10	10	18	13		57—50	53—46	57—53	11	11	13	13	
Age 3																			
Before	81	85	−4	79.7	70.1	.6	87.6	92.5*	85.4	86.7	−1.4[e]								
After	91	85	6	93.8	83.4	11.4**	102.0	92.3*	88.1	87.4	11.8[ec]								
Age 4																			
Before	96	88	8**	94.7	84.7	11.0**	96.4	94.8	80.6	86.7	6.0	91.1							
After							97.1	97.5	87.6	84.7	9.7*								
Kindergarten																			
Before							93.8	96.6	81.9	80.1	13.3*	98.6	91.1		74.5	73.0	74.5	72.5	0
After							98.1	99.7	91.4	89.0	7.5*	98.4	94.4	80.9	93.8	87.5	80.0	81.3	11.0*
Grade I							91.1	96.0	87.0	84.6	5.7*				97.4	83.1	90.7	84.8	5.4
Grade II							86.7	90.1	84.0	77.7	3.5**	97.8	92.8	88.6	94.9	85.5	80.1	86.5	5.7
Grade III												97.6	91.1	80.3					
Grade IV												98.4	91.7	88.6					
Initial Gain	10	0	10	16.1	4.3	11.8	14.4	5.0	1.8	.7	6.0	6.5*	3.1	−1.3	10.3	11.5	6.4	8.8	11.0
Gain 2 Years After	14	4	10	11.5	4.2	7.3	3.6	3.5	1.5	−2.1	.7	6.3	1.6	−.6	10.4	10.5	14.7	11.0	5.7
Overall Gain	6		9	9.9	9.0	.9	−.9	−1.3	−.5	−9.0	1.1	6.3	.5	−1.3	1.1	2.0	1.8	1.5	.4
Achievement Level	no difference			1.1	.6	1.5*[f]	3.7	4.0	3.8	3.4	.1	—	—	—					

a. N's decrease because only earlier waves reached grade school (see Table 1).
b. Published significance level includes C_2.
c. Intervention began one year later in E_2; hence C_1 includes E_2 for this age group only.
d. Significance of difference not tested
e. Difference significant for the distal control group (C_2) only.
f. Difference significant for girls only.
g. A reduced parent intervention program was continued through grade one.
Note: Double line designates point at which intervention was terminated

no significance tests are available for gain scores, but these are shown in the few instances when they were computed by the original investigator.

Two striking patterns become apparent. First, early intervention produces substantial gains in IQ so long as the program lasts. But the experimental groups do not continue to make gains when intervention continues beyond one year, and, what is more critical, the effects tend to "wash out" after intervention is terminated. The longer the follow-up, the more obvious the latter trend becomes (Weikart, Gray). There appear to be some exceptions to the generally regressive trend, but these are faulted by methodological artifacts—regression to the mean in the Hodges and Weikart programs; inadequate control for parents' motivation in the non-random comparison groups of the Beller and Gray projects.

Additional support for our conclusion comes from DiLorenzo's evaluation of long term effects of preschool programs in New York State. Although DiLorenzo (1969) still found significant differences between experimental and control groups on achievement tests administered in first grade, these differences were no longer visible at the end of second grade.

The DiLorenzo study also adds some new evidence on the comparative effectiveness of different types of preschool programs. The data presented suggest that most significant differences between experimental and control groups were found in highly structured, cognitively oriented programs. Furthermore, these programs produced the most pronounced long-term effects. Karnes (1969) reports similar findings. In comparing Montessori programs to structured, cognitively oriented programs, she concludes that structure *per se* is not crucial. Rather, the greatest and most enduring gains are made in structured programs which include an emphasis on *verbal and cognitive training*.

The intervention programs reported above were carried out over one or two years' time. Deutsch (1971) reports results of more extended intervention conducted with severely disadvantaged inner city children over a five year period. After five years of the program, the difference between the experimental and control groups in the third grade was a non-significant four points.

These findings raise the important issue of the effect of program length. Of the programs reported in Table 2, four extended longer than one year. Of these, only one (Herzog) showed some rise after the first year. Two indicated no change (Weikart and Gray E_2) and the third (Gray E_3), like Deutsch's, exhibited a decline. It is significant, in light of Herzog's conclusion "The less they have the less they learn" (Herzog et al., 1972b), that the Gray and Deutsch samples were the most economically depressed of any included in the analysis.

The hope that group programs begun in the earliest years of life will produce greater and more enduring gains is also disappointed. In a project directed by Caldwell (Braun and Caldwell, 1973) children entering intervention programs before the age of three did no better than later entrants, with duration of participation held constant.

One ray of hope emanates from Follow-Through, a nationwide, federally sponsored program, which extends the basic philosophy of Head Start into the primary grades. Some early findings indicate that Follow-Through children made significantly larger fall-to-spring gains in achievement than did children in the control group. Furthermore, greatest gains were made by participants who were below the OEO poverty line and by children who had previously participated in Head Start. Finally, highly structured curricula produced the greatest gains. These findings, though encouraging, must be viewed with caution because of inadequate matching between experimental and control families in socioeconomic characteristics and parental motivation. Nevertheless, the possibility exists that the comprehensiveness of the Head Start and Follow-Through programs—including family services and health and nutritional care—accounted for the more enduring gains.

The long term effectiveness of Follow-Through is yet to be determined. Many of the declines apparent in Table 2 occurred after first grade. Other studies (Deutsch, Gray) report a drop in IQ occurring beyond the first grade level even while the program was still in operation. It has been fashionable to blame the schools for the erosion of competence in disadvantaged children after six years of age. The decline in Deutsch's experimental subjects, who were at the time in an innovative and enriched educational program, suggests that the fault lies in substantial degree beyond the doors of the school. Additional findings lend support to this conclusion. The children who profited least from intervention programs and who showed the earliest and most rapid decline were those who came from the most deprived social and economic backgrounds. Especially relevant in this regard were such variables as the number of children in the family, the employment status of the head of the household, the level of parents' education, and the presence of only one parent in the family.

The impact of such environmental factors is reflected in a study of school achievement by Hayes and Grether (1969). Rather than assessing academic gains from September to June, as is done conventionally, they looked at changes from June to September—that is, over the summer. They found that, during summer vacation, white children from advantaged families either held their own or continued to gain, whereas youngsters from disadvantaged and black families reversed direction and lost ground. Hayes and Grether conclude that differences over the summer months account for 80% of the variation in academic performance between economically advantaged whites and children from nonwhite families. Accordingly, they argue that intervention efforts are best directed at the home. Our analysis of home-based programs, however, did not lead to such a verdict. Rather, as indicated below, it suggested combining elements from both strategies in a sequential manner.

SOME EFFECTS OF HOME-BASED INTERVENTION

The form of Table 3 is the same as that of Table 2, but the substance is more encouraging. The experimental groups in most home-based programs not only made substantial initial gains but these gains increased and continued to hold up rather well three to four years after intervention had been discontinued. The fact that matched controls also exhibited gains in IQ over time is probably due to the special characteristics of the families who participated in home-based intervention: first, the parents were all volunteers who were then randomly assigned to experimental or control groups. Thus, all were motivated to provide educational experiences for their children and were willing to accept a stranger into their home. Second, participants in these programs were from relatively less disadvantaged backgrounds, thus providing some corroboration for Herzog's sobering verdict, "The less they have, the less they learn" (Herzog et al., 1974). But other important factors distinguish these home-based programs: they begin working with children at an earlier age, and they emphasize one-to-one interaction between the child and adult.

However, this one-to-one interaction appears to require special participants. For example, a tutor visiting on a daily basis produces only temporary gains (Schaefer, 1968; Kirk, 1969). From their analyses of the reasons for the failure of this type of program, Schaefer and Aaronson (1972) concluded that a necessary and crucial component was maternal interest and direct involvement in the teaching process. Schaefer's (1972) insistence on a "family-" rather than "child-centered" approach is exemplified in a project developed by Levenstein. She developed strategies to maximize mother-child interaction around educational materials which she provided. Viewed as a whole, the results from Levenstein's five differentially treated experimental groups suggest that the earlier and more intensely mother and child were stimulated to engage in communication around a common activity, the greater and more enduring the gain in IQ achieved by the child.

To facilitate this mother-child interaction, Levenstein trained home visitors, whom she called Toy Demonstrators. After first using professionals, she found that non-professional low income mothers were equally competent in this role. Their task was to demonstrate the use of the toys, but far more importantly, to "treat the mother as a colleague in a joint endeavor in behalf of the child" (Levenstein, 1970a, p. 429). Levenstein strongly emphasized that the Demonstrators "keep constantly in mind that the child's primary and continuing educational relationship is with his mother" (1970a, p. 429). The task of the Demonstrator was to enhance this relationship. Thus Levenstein not only created a structured-cognitive program, but directed it at the mother-child system. Furthermore, the mother, rather than a stranger-expert, is the primary agent of intervention.

The resulting reciprocal interaction between mother and child involves both cognitive and emotional components which reinforce each other. When this reciprocal interaction takes place in an interpersonal relationship that endures over time (as occurs between mother and child), it leads to the development of a strong emotional attachment which, in turn, increases the motivation of the young child to attend to, and learn from the mother. It is important, as demonstrated in the Levenstein project, that this process be reinforced when the child's dependency on the mother is greatest—that is, in the second year of life (Bronfenbrenner, 1968). In addition, Levenstein reports that neither a friend's visit with mother and child nor the provision of instructional materials alone was sufficient by itself to produce the major effect; the critical element involved mother-child interaction around a common activity.

This reciprocal process may explain the relatively enduring effectiveness of home intervention programs. Since the participants remain together after intervention ceases, the momentum of

TABLE 3
Effects on Later Intellectual Development of Home-based Intervention Programs

	Schaefer[a]			Lowenstein I[c]					Lowenstein II				
	1 E	2 C	3 $E-C$	4 E_1	5 E_2	6 E_3	7 C_1	8 $E-C_1$[d]	9 E_4	10 E_5	11 C_5	12 C_6	13 $E-C_2$
N	24	24		6	7	21	8		8	15	7	10	
Age 1 — Before	105.9	109.2	−3.3[b]										
Age 1 — After	95.3	89.4	5.9										
Age 2 — Before	99.6	90.2	9.4	81.8	82.6	90.1	91.4	−8.7					
Age 2 — After				101.8	101.1	101.8	89.8	11.6*					
Age 3 — Before	105.6	89.4	16.2	102.6	105.0	108.6			91.1	87.6	91.3	91.0	−3.5
Age 3 — After									101.3	102.4	95.8	—	6.4
Age 4 — Before	99.1	90.1	9.0	98.5	103.6	108.2	85.0	16.0[b]	106.6	103.8	101.1		
Kindergarten — Before	97.8	92.8	5.0										
Grade 1	100.9	96.9	3.7	98.8	100.6	107.2	88.8	10.9[b]	104.5	94.4	104.3	96.3	0
Initial Gain	−10.6	−19.8	9.2	19.0*	18.5*	11.7*	−1.6	20.4*	10.2	14.8*	4.5	—	8.7[b]
Gain 2 Years After	−8.1	−16.4	8.3	15.7*	21.0*	17.1*	−6.4	14.8[b]	15.5*				
Overall Gain	−5.3	−12.3	7.0	16.0*	18.0*		−2.6	19.6	13.4[b]	6.8[b]	12.9	5.3	2.2
Achievement Level	.7	.7	0	1.2	1.4	1.2	1.2	.1	2.1	1.5	1.6	.2	.2

a. Bayley Infant Scale was used for first three testing periods; Binet thereafter.

b. No significant tests available for this value and rest of column.

c. Cattel Test used at age 2.   d. $E = \frac{1}{2}(E_1 + E_2)$.

NOTE: Double line designates point at which intervention was terminated. Single broken line designates point of entry into school.

the system insures some degree of continuity for the future. As a result, the gains achieved through this kind of intervention strategy are more likely to persist than those gained in group preschool programs, which, after they are over, leave no social structure with familiar figures who can continue to reciprocate and reinforce the specific adaptive patterns which the child has learned. In emphasizing the primary role of the parent, and in carrying out the intervention at home, Levenstein maximizes the possibility that gains made by the child will be maintained.

But is it necessary to involve both the mother and child? Perhaps the same result can be obtained by working mainly with the mother? Karnes *et al.* (1969) developed a program which included home visits, but emphasized weekly group meetings of the mothers and lasted fifteen months instead of seven as in the Levenstein study. At the end of the program, the experimental group obtained a mean IQ of 106, 16 points higher than the comparison group. To control for factors associated with home and family, Karnes *et al.* also compared IQ scores of the experimental subjects with those that had been obtained by older siblings when they were of the same age. A 28 IQ point difference in favor of the experimental group was found.

Encouraged by these findings, Karnes and her colleagues sought to create an optimal intervention strategy by combining the mother-intervention with a preschool program for the children themselves. The results were disappointing, at least by comparison. The children entered the program at age four. After two years there were no differences in IQ between the experimental and control group, and the latter actually scored reliably higher in tests of language development. Why the marked difference in effectiveness? The authors cite one crucial change in the program: the introduction of a group preschool experience. This, combined with a reduction in the number of at-home visits, may have led the mothers to believe that they no longer played the critical role in furthering the development of their children.

The effectiveness of parent intervention also appears to vary as a function of age. Evidence from a number of studies (e.g. Gilmer *et al.*, 1970; Karnes, 1968, 1969b; Levenstein, 1970a) indicates that the greatest gains are obtained with two year olds, and tend to be smaller with older preschoolers, becoming negligible when children are not enrolled until five years of age. Further support for this conclusion comes from Gilmer *et al.* (1970) in an investigation of the effect of home-based intervention on siblings of the target child. Results indicated that younger siblings of those in the parent-intervention groups benefited even more from the program than did the target children.

In the same study, Gilmer and her colleagues also demonstrated a further complexity as a function of age. In addition to looking at effects on siblings, these investigators compared the relative effectiveness of group-, home- and combined programs with four and five year old participants. They found that the group program was most effective initially, but scores rapidly declined after discontinuation of the program. The parent intervention groups, while not exhibiting as dramatic gains, nevertheless sustained their advantage longer than the group-centered children. Thus, although parent intervention did not achieve as high gains in the later preschool period, it appeared to retain its power to sustain increases attained by whatever means, including group programs in preschool settings.

A SEQUENTIAL STRATEGY FOR EARLY INTERVENTION

Gilmer's results suggest the possibility of a phased sequence beginning with parent intervention in the first two years of life, followed by the addition of group programs in the late preschool and early school years. A program involving such a phased sequence is currently being conducted by Gordon (1971, 1972, 1973) with indigent families from twelve Florida counties. A weekly home visit is being conducted for the first two years of life, with a small group setting being added in the third year. About 175 children were randomly distributed into eight groups, systematically varied with respect to age at entry and length of exposure to the program, with one group receiving no treatment whatsoever.

Although no measures of intellectual level were obtained at the beginning of the program, Gordon (1973) has recently reported Binet IQ's for each group five years after intervention was started; that is, from two to four years after "graduation." Of the seven experimental groups, the only three that still differed from controls by more than five IQ points (with means from 95 to 97 in the last year of follow-up) were those that had received parent intervention in the first year of life and continued in the program for either one, or two consecutive years. Groups which started parent intervention later, whose participation was interrupted for a year, or who were exposed to parent and group intervention only simultaneously, did not do as well. Moreover, the addition of group intervention in the third year did not result in a higher IQ for those groups that had this experience. Indeed, in both instances in which parent intervention in the second year was followed by the addition of preschool in the third, the mean scores showed a drop over the two year follow-up period. In contrast, the two groups for whom parent intervention was continued for a second year without the addition of a group program either held their own or gained during the follow-up period, despite the fact that they were tested three rather than only two years after intervention had ended.

Taken as a whole, Gordon's results lend support to the following conclusions:

1. The generalization that parent intervention has more lasting effects the earlier it is begun can now be extended into the first year of life.

2. When parent intervention precedes group intervention, there

are enduring effects after completion of the program, at least throughout the preschool years.

3. The addition of a group program after parent intervention has been carried out for a one or two years period clearly does not result in additional gains, and may even produce a loss, at least when the group intervention is introduced as early as the third year of life.

But what if the preschool component is not added until the children are four or five years old?

A partial answer comes from the evaluation of a Supplementary Kindergarten Intervention Program (SKIP) developed by Weikart *et al.* (Radin, 1969). The program involved disadvantaged kindergarten children of high ability and consisted of two components in various experimental combinations: (1) a special class supplementing the regular kindergarten session with a Piagetian, cognitively oriented curriculum, and (2) a home visit program to plan similar activities with the mother which she subsequently carried out with her child. The children who experienced the full program—both group and home—exhibited higher IQ gains than those who experienced the supplementary program plus kindergatren, or kindergarten only. But, more importantly, an analysis comparing children who had attended a preschool program involving intensive parent intervention, with those who had not, revealed that children who had had the earlier parent involvement experience gained more in IQ during the SKIP program. Furthermore, children who experienced no parent intervention, either in preschool or school, but who spent a full day first in regular kindergarten and then in the SKIP Piaget course, fell six points in IQ during the kindergarten year. The impact of the classroom program was negative in the absence of any previous or concomitant parent intervention—particularly since it kept the child away from home for a full day.

Radin (1972) has replicated her findings in a second study designed to provide a direct test of the hypothesis that prior exposure to parent intervention enhances the impact of subsequent group programs. Three matched groups of 21–28 four-year-olds from lower class homes were exposed to a preschool program supplemented with bi-weekly home visits. In one group, the visitor worked directly with the child, the mother not being present. In a second group, the visitor employed the same activities as a basis for encouraging mother-child interaction. In the third group, mother-child intervention was supplemented by a weekly group meeting led by a social worker and focusing on child rearing practices conducive to the child's development. At the end of the first year, all three groups made significant gains in IQ but did not differ reliably from each other. In addition, the mothers in the two treatments involving parent intervention showed changes in attitude interpreted as more conducive to the child's development, with the greatest shift observed in the group receiving home visits supplemented by weekly meetings.

During the following year, when the children were attending regular kindergarten (with no parent intervention program), the children who had been tutored directly in the preceding year made no additional gains in IQ, whereas the two groups exposed to prior parent intervention achieved further increases of 10 to 15 points. Radin concludes:

> In general the findings of this study suggest that a parent education component is important if the child is to continue to benefit academically from a compensatory preschool program, although there may be no immediate effect on the youngsters. . . . A parent program does appear, however, to enhance the mothers' perception of themselves capable of independent thought. Thus, perhaps, new maternal behaviors are fostered which are conducive to the child's intellectual functioning (1363).

It is to be emphasized that Radin's parent program, like all the other effective parent strategies we have examined, focuses attention on interaction between parent and child around a common activity. This approach is to be distinguished from the widespread traditional forms of parent education involving courses, dissemination of information and counseling addressed only to the parent. There is no evidence for the effectiveness of such approaches (Amidon and Brim, 1972).

Radin's data indicate that the beneficial influence of parent intervention is substantial if it is introduced before the child enters school, but the effect is reduced if home visits are not begun until the kindergarten year. But what of the influence of parent intervention in the later school years? Smith (1968) demonstrated that parent involvement, in a slightly different form, continues to be effective through the sixth grade. Her project included 1000 children from low income housing projects, most of them Black. Smith asked parents to support the child's educational activities without being actively involved in teaching, as in the preschool programs. Support consisted of such things as insuring household quiet during homework time, reading books themselves in the presence of the children, and listening to children read. This program produced significant gain in scores on reading achievement in both the second and fifth grades. Once again the family emerges as the system which sustains and facilitates development, spurred by educational experience outside the home. These findings, however, do not displace our earlier conclusion: the optimal time for parent intervention is in the first three years of life.

In summary, intervention programs which place major emphasis on involving the parent *directly* in activities fostering the child's development are likely to have constructive impact at any age, but the earlier such activities are begun, and the longer they are continued, the greater the benefit to the child.

But one major problem still remains. Given that the optimal period for parent intervention is in the first three years of life, or at least before the child enters school, implementation of this strategy still requires the cooperation of the parents at home. But many disadvantaged families live under such oppressive circumstances that they are neither willing nor able to participate in the activities required by a parent intervention program. Inadequate health care, poor housing, lack of education, low income and the necessity for full-time work all continue to rob parents of time and energy to spend with their children. Does this mean that the best opportunity for the child must be foregone? Is there an alternative course? In our last section we turn to an examination of the problem and some possible solutions.

THE ECOLOGY OF EARLY INTERVENTION

One radical solution to this problem, which is being tried by Heber in his Milwaukee Project, involves removing the child from his home for most of his waking hours, placing him in an environment conducive to his growth and entrusting primary responsibility for his development to persons specifically trained for the job (Heber *et al.*, 1972). The sample for this study consisted of Black mothers with newborns who were living in a severely depressed area of Milwaukee and who had IQ's of 75 or less. The experimental group of children attended an intensive, cognitively structured program taught by paraprofessional-teachers selected from the children's own neighborhood. The children entered the program at the age of three months and stayed at the center from 8:45 in the morning until 4:00 in the afternoon. Each child remained with his primary teacher on a one-to-one basis until he reached 12 to 15 months of age. Later, children were placed in small groups of two to four per teacher.

A parallel program conducted for the mother involved two phases: job training and training in home economics and child-rearing skills. Mothers appear to have benefited from this program —particularly from the occupational rehabilitation.

With respect to the cognitive development of the children, the program has been astoundingly successful and will probably continue to be so long as intervention lasts. At age 5½, the control and experimental groups were separated by 30 IQ points, with a mean of 124 for the latter.

Given our frame of reference, the success is not unexpected since the program fulfills major requirements we have stipulated as essential or desirable for fostering the cognitive development of the young child. With one particular person remaining the primary agent of intervention, group experiences were gradually introduced emphasizing language and structured cognitive activities. The entire operation was carried out by a group of people sharing and reinforcing a common commitment to young children and their development.

But what will happen when intervention is distintinued remains an open question. In addition, the costs of the program are prohibitive in terms of large scale applicability. Nor have the ethical questions of removing a child from his home been dealt with. Is there another approach which does not entail these problems?

An affirmative answer to this question is suggested by Harold Skeels (1966) in his report of a follow-up study of two groups of mentally retarded, institutionalized children, who constituted the experimental and control groups in an experiment Skeels had initiated thirty years earlier (Skeels, Updegraff, Wellman, and Williams, 1938; Skeels and Dye, 1939). The average IQ of the children and of their mothers was under 70. When the children were about two years of age, thirteen of them were placed in the care of female inmates of a state institution for the mentally retarded with each child being assigned to a different ward. The control group was allowed to remain in the original—also institutional—environment, a children's orphanage. During the formal experimental period, which averaged a year and a half, the experimental group showed a mean rise of 28 points, whereas the control group dropped 26 points. Upon completion of the experiment, it became possible to place eleven of the experimental children in legal adoption. After 2½ years with their adoptive parents, this group showed a further nine-point rise to a mean of 101. Thirty years later, all of the original thirteen children, now adults, in the experimental group were found to be self-supporting, all but two had completed high school, with four having one or more years of college. In the control group, all were either dead or still institutionalized. Skeels concludes his report with some dollar figures on the amount of taxpayer's money expended to sustain the institutionalized group, in contrast to the productive income brought in by those who had been raised initially by mentally deficient women in a state institution.

The Skeels experiment is instructive on two counts. First, if Heber demonstrated that disadvantaged children of mothers with IQ's under 75 could, with appropriate intervention, attain an IQ well above the norm, Skeels showed that retarded mothers themselves can achieve the same gains for children under their care at substantially less expense. How was this accomplished? First, Skeels points out that almost every experimental child was involved in an intense, one-to-one relationship with an older adult. Not only did the children enjoy this close interpersonal relationship, but the girls and the attendants "spent a great deal of time with 'their children' playing, talking, and training them in every way" (Skeels, pp. 16–17). The grounds and house also afforded a wide range of toys and activities, and all children attended a nonstructured preschool program as soon as they could walk.

Thus three of the essential components of the sequential strategy we previously identified are included in the Skeels research: the initial establishment of an enduring relationship involving intensive interaction with the child; priority, status, and support for the "mother-child" system; the introduction, at a later stage, of a preschool program, but with the child returning "home" for half the day to a highly available mother substitute. The only element that is missing is the systematic involvement of the child in progressively more complex activities, first in the context of the mother-child relationship, and later, in the curriculum of the preschool program. Had these elements of cognitively challenging experience been present, it is conceivable that the children would have shown even more dramatic gains in IQ, approaching the levels achieved by Heber's experimental group.

Both the Skeels and Heber experiments demonstrate the effectiveness of a major transformation of the environment for the child and the persons principally responsible for his care and development. We shall refer to this kind of reorganization as *ecological intervention*. The aim is to effect changes in the *context* in which the family lives which enable the family as a whole to exercise the functions necessary for the child's development.

The need for ecological intervention arises when the conditions of life are such that the family cannot perform its childrearing functions even though it may wish to do so. Under these circumstances no direct form of intervention aimed at enhancing the child's development is likely to have much impact. For children living in the most deprived circumstances, the first step in any strategy of intervention must be to provide the family with adequate health care, nutrition, housing and employment. It is clear that ecological intervention is not being carried out today because it almost invariably requires institutional changes.

But even when the basic needs for survival are met, the conditions of life may be such as to prevent the family from functioning effectively in its childrearing role. As we have seen, an essential prerequisite for the child's development is an environment which provides not only the opportunity but also support for parental activity. Once this is established, the style and degree of parent-child interaction becomes a crucial factor.

Skodak and Skeels (1949) demonstrate this in a study of the effects of adoption on the development of 100 children whose true parents were both socioeconomically disadvantaged and mentally retarded. The children were placed in foster families who were above average in economic security and educational and cultural status. The average IQ of the children's true mothers was 86; by the age of 13 the mean IQ of their children placed in foster homes was 106. A thorough analysis revealed that among the group of adopted children, those who made the greatest sustained gains were those who had experienced "maximal stimulation in infancy with optimum security and affection following placement at an average of three months of age" (Skodak and Skeels, 1949, p. 111). These three investigations demonstrate the extraordinary effectiveness of massive ecological intervention. But two of them involved placing institutionalized children in foster homes. When the child remains a member of his family, such a course is problematic. Can anything be done for such disadvantaged families, whose basic needs for survival are being met but whose lives are so burdened as to preclude opportunity for effective fulfillment of the parental role?

No answers are available to this question from our analysis of the research literature, for, as we have indicated, ecological intervention is as yet a largely untried endeavor both in our science and in our society. It seems clear, however, that certain urgent needs of families will have to be met in ways which provide support and status for parents in their childrearing activities. Possibilities exist in four major areas:[1]

1. the world of work—part-time jobs and flexible work schedules
2. the school—parent apprentice programs in the schools to engage older children in supervised care of the young, involvement of the parents in work at school
3. the neighborhood—parent-child groups for mutual assistance, family centers for discussions and demonstrations
4. the home—pre-natal training in nutrition, medical care, etc.,

homemaker service, emergency insurance, television teaching Programs focused on these themes, addressed to both children and adults, would contribute to making parenthood a more attractive and respected activity in the eyes of children, parents, and the society at large.

SOME PRINCIPLES OF EARLY INTERVENTION: A SUMMARY

Although further research is needed to replicate results and eliminate alternative interpretations, some principles can be stated specifying the elements that appear essential for the effectiveness of early intervention programs.

First, the family seems to be the most effective and economical system for fostering and sustaining the child's development. Without family involvement, intervention is likely to be unsuccessful, and what few effects are achieved are likely to disappear once the intervention is discontinued.

Secondly, ecological intervention is necessary for millions of disadvantaged families in our country—to provide adequate health care, nutrition, housing, employment and opportunity and status for parenthood. Even children from severely deprived backgrounds of mothers with IQ's below 70 or 80 are not doomed to inferiority by unalterable constraints either of heredity or environment. But it is certain that ecological intervention will require major changes in the institutions of our society.

Thirdly, a long range intervention program may be viewed in terms of five uninterrupted stages:

1. preparation for parenthood—child care, nutrition and medical training

2. before children come—adequate housing, economic security

3. the first three years of life—establishment of a child-parent relationship of reciprocal interaction centered around activities which are challenging to the child; home visits, group meetings, to establish the parent as the primary agent of intervention

4. ages four through six—exposure to a cognitively oriented pre-school program along with a continuation of parent intervention

5. ages six through twelve—parental support of the child's educational activities at home and at school; parent remains pri-

mary figure responsible for the child's development as a person.

In completing this analysis, we reemphasize the tentative nature of the conclusions and the narrowness of IQ and related measures as aspects of the total development of the child. We also wish to reaffirm a deep indebtedness to those who conducted the programs and researches on which this work is based, and a profound faith in the capacity of parents, of whatever background, to enable their children to develop into effective and happy human beings, *once our society is willing to make conditions of life viable and humane for all its families.*

NOTES

1. For a more extensive discussion, see Bronfenbrenner, U. The origins of alienation. *Scientific American*, August 1974.

REFERENCES

Amidon, A. and Brim, O. G. What do children have to gain from parent education? Paper presented for the Advisory Committee on Child Development, National Research Council, National Academy of Science, 1972.

Bee, H. L., Van Egeren, L. F., Streissguth, A. P., Nyman, B. A., and Leckie, M. S. Social class differences in maternal teaching strategies and speech patterns. *Developmental Psychology*, 1969, *1*, 726–734.

Bell, R. Q. A reinterpretation of the direction of effects in studies of socialization. *Psychological Review*, 1968, 75, 81–95.

Beller, E. K. Impact of early education on disadvantaged children. In S. Ryan (Ed.), A Report on Longitudinal Evaluations of Preschool Programs. Washington, D.C.: Office of Child Development, 1974.

Beller, E. K. Personal communication, 1973.

Bereiter, C. and Engelmann, S. *Teaching disadvantaged children in the preschool*. Englewood Cliffs, N.J.: Prentice-Hall, 1966.

Bissell, J. S. *The cognitive effects of preschool programs for disadvantaged children*. Washington, D.C.: National Institute of Child Health and Human Development, 1971.

Bissell, J. S. *Implementation of planned variation in Head Start: First year report*. Washington, D.C.: National Institute of Child Health and Human Development, 1971.

Bloom, B. S. *Compensatory education for cultural deprivation.* New York: Holt, Rinehart and Winston, 1965.

Bogatz, G. A. and Ball, S. *The second year of Sesame Street: A continuing evaluation.* Vols. 1 and 2. Princeton, N.J.: Educational Testing Service, 1971.

Braun, S. J. and Caldwell, B. Emotional adjustment of children in daycare who enrolled prior to or after the age of three. *Early Child Development and Care,* 1973, *2,* 13–21.

Bronfenbrenner, U. The changing American child: A speculative analysis. *Merrill-Palmer Quarterly,* 1961, 7, 73–84.

Bronfenbrenner, U. Early deprivation: A cross-species analysis. In S. Levine and G. Newton (Eds.), *Early experience in behavior.* Springfield, Ill.: Charles C. Thomas, 1968. (a)

Bronfenbrenner, U. When is infant stimulation effective? In D. C. Glass (Ed.), *Environmental influences.* New York: Rockefeller University Press, 1968. (b)

Bronfenbrenner, U. *Two worlds of childhood: U.S. and U.S.S.R.* New York: Russell Sage Foundation, 1970.

Bronfenbrenner, U. The roots of alienation. In U. Bronfenbrenner (Ed.), *Influences on human development.* Hinsdale, Ill.: Dryden Press, 1972.

Bronfenbrenner, U. Developmental research and public policy. In J. M. Romanshyn (Ed.), *Social science and social welfare.* New York: Council on Social Work Education, 1973.

Bronfenbrenner, U. and Bruner, J. The President the children. *New York Times,* January 31, 1972.

Caldwell, B. M. and Smith, L. E. Day care for the very young—prime opportunity for primary prevention. *American Journal of Public Health,* 1970, *60,* 690–697.

Coleman, J. S. *Equality of educational opportunity.* Washington, D.C.: U.S. Office of Education, 1966.

Deutsch, M. Minority group and class status as related to social and personality factors in scholastic achievement. *Society for Applied Anthropology Monograph No. 2.* Ithaca, N.Y.: New York State School of Industrial and Labor Relations, Cornell University, 1960.

Deutsch, M., et al. *Regional research and resource center in early childhood: Final report.* Washington, D.C.: U.S. Office of Economic Opportunity, 1971.

Deutsch, M., Taleporos, E., and Victor, J. A brief synopsis of an initial enrichment program in early childhood. In S. R. Ryan (Ed.), *A report on longitudinal evaluations of preschool programs.* Washington, D.C.: Office of Child Development, 1972.

DiLorenzo, L. T. *Pre-kindergarten programs for educationally disadvantaged children: Final report.* Washington, D.C.: U.S. Office of Education, 1969.

Gardner, J. and Gardner, H. A note on selective imitation by a six-week-old infant. *Child Development,* 1970, *41,* 1209–1213.

Gilmer, B., Miller, J. O., and Gray, S. W. *Intervention with mothers and young children: Study of intra-family effects.* Nashville, Tenn.: DARCEE Demonstration and Research Center for Early Education, 1970.

Gordon, I. J. *A home learning center approach to early stimulation.* Institute for Development of Human Resources, Gainesville, Florida, 1971.

Gordon, I. J. *A home learning center approach to early stimulation.* Institute for Development of Human Resources, Gainesville, Florida, 1972.

Gordon, I. J. *An early intervention project: A longitudinal look.* Gainesville, Florida, University of Florida, Institute for Development of Human Resources, College of Education, 1973.

Gray, S. W. and Klaus, R. A. Experimental preschool program for culturally-deprived children. *Child Development,* 1965, *36*, 887-898.

Gray, S. W. and Klaus, R. A. The early training project: The seventh-year report. *Child Development,* 1970, *41*, 909-924.

Hayes, D. and Grether, L. The school year and vacation: When do students learn? Paper presented at the Eastern Sociological Convention, New York, 1969.

Hebb, D. O. *The organization of behavior.* New York: John Wiley, 1949.

Heber, R., Garber, H., Harrington, S., and Hoffman, C. *Rehabilitation of families at risk for mental retardation.* Madison, Wisc.: Rehabilitation Research and Training Center in Mental Retardation, University of Wisconsin, October, 1972.

Hertzig, M. E., Birch, H. G., Thomas, A., and Mendez, O. A. Class and ethnic differences in responsiveness of preschool children to cognitive demands. *Monograph of the Society for Research in Child Development,* 1968, *33*, No. 1.

Herzog, E., Newcomb, C. H., and Cisin, I. H. Double deprivation: The less they have the less they learn. In S. Ryan (Ed.), *A report on longitudinal evaluations of preschool programs.* Washington, D.C.: Office of Child Development, 1972. (a)

Herzog, E., Newcomb, C. H., and Cisin, I. H. But some are poorer than others: SES differences in a preschool program. *American Journal of Orthopsychiatry,* 1972, *42*, 4-22. (b)

Herzog, E., Newcomb, C. H., and Cisin, I. H. *Preschool and Postscript: An evaluation of the inner-city program.* Washington, D.C.: Social Research Group, George Washington University, 1973.

Hess, R. D., Shipman, V. C., Brophy, J. E., and Bear, R. M. *The cognitive environments of urban preschool children.* Chicago: University of Chicago Graduate School of Education, 1968.

Hess, R. D., Shipman, V. C., Brophy, J. E., and Bear, R. M. *The cognitive environments of urban preschool children: Follow-up phase.* Chicago: University of Chicago Graduate School of Education, 1969.

Hodges, W. L., McCandless, B. R., and Spicker, H. H. *The development and evaluation of a diagnostically based curriculum for preschool psychosocially deprived children.* Washington, D.C.: U.S. Office of Education, 1967.

Hunt, J. McV. *Intelligence and experience.* New York: Ronald Press, 1961.

Infant Education Research Project. Washington, D.C.: U.S. Office of Education Booklet #OE-37033.

Jonas, S. J. and Moss, M. A. Age, state, and maternal behavior associated with infant vocalizations. *Child Development,* 1971, *42*, 1039.

Kagan, J. On cultural deprivation. In D. C. Glass (Ed.), *Environmental influences.* New York: Rockefeller University Press, 1968.

Kagan, J. *Change and continuity in infancy.* New York: John Wiley, 1971.

Karnes, M. B., Studley, W. M., Wright, W. R., and Hodgins, A. S. An approach to working with mothers of disadvantaged preschool children. *Merrill-Palmer Quarterly,* 1968, *14,* 174–184.

Karnes, M. B. *Research and development program on preschool disadvantaged children: Final report.* Washington, D.C.: U.S. Office of Education, 1969.

Karnes, M. B. and Badger, E. E. Training mothers to instruct their infants at home. In M. B. Karnes, *Research and development program on preschool disadvantaged children: Final report.* Washington, D.C.: U.S. Office of Education, 1969. (a)

Karnes, M. B., Hodgins, A. S., and Teska, J. A. The effects of short-term instruction at home by mothers of children not enrolled in a preschool. In M. B. Karnes, *Research and development program on preschool disadvantaged children: Final report.* Washington, D.C.: U.S. Office of Education, 1969. (b)

Karnes, M. B., Hodgins, A. S., and Teska, J. A. The impact of at-home instruction by mothers on performance in the ameliorative preschool. In M. B. Karnes, *Research and development program on preschool disadvantaged children: Final report.* Washington, D.C.: U.S. Office of Education, 1969. (c)

Karnes, M. B., Teska, J. A., Hodgins, A. S., and Badger, E. D. Educational intervention at home by mothers of disadvantaged infants. *Child Development,* 1970, *41,* 925–935.

Karnes, M. B., Zehrbach, R. R., and Teska, J. A. An ameliorative approach in the development of curriculum. In R. K. Parker (Ed.), *The preschool in action.* Boston: Allyn and Bacon, 1972.

Kirk, S. A. *Early education of the mentally retarded.* Urbana, Ill.: University of Illinois Press, 1958.

Kirk, S. A. The effects of early education with disadvantaged infants. In M. B. Karnes, *Research and development program on preschool disadvantaged children: Final report.* Washington, D.C.: U.S. Office of Education, 1969.

Klaus, R. A. and Gray, S. W. The early training project for disadvantaged children: A report after five years. *Monographs of the Society for Research in Child Development,* 1968, *33* (4, Serial #120).

Kraft, I., Fushillo, J., and Herzog, E. Prelude to school: An evaluation of an inner-city school program. *Children's Bureau Research Report Number 3.* Washington, D.C.: Children's Bureau, 1968.

Levenstein, P. Cognitive growth in preschoolers through verbal interaction with mothers. *American Journal of Orthopsychiatry,* 1970, *40,* 426–432.

Levenstein, P. *Verbal Interaction Project.* Mineola, N.Y.: Family Service Association of Nassau County, Inc., 1972. (a)

Levenstein, P. But does it work in homes away from home? *Theory Into Practice,* 1972, *11,* 157–162. (b)

Levenstein, P. Personal communication, 1972. (c)

Levenstein, P. and Levenstein, S. Fostering learning potential in pre-schoolers. *Social Casework*, 1971, *52*, 74–78.

Levenstein, P. and Sunley, R. Stimulation of verbal interaction between disadvantaged mothers and children. *American Journal of Orthopsychiatry*, 1968, *38*, 116–121.

Moss, H. A. Sex, age, and state as determinants of mother-infant interaction. *Merrill-Palmer Quarterly*, 1967, *13*, 19–36.

Radin, N. The impact of a kindergarten home counseling program. *Exceptional Children*, 1969, *36*, 251–256.

Radin, N. Three degrees of maternal involvement in a preschool program: Impact on mothers and children. *Child Development*, 1972, *43*, 1355–1364.

Radin, N. and Weikart, D. A home teaching program for disadvantaged preschool children. *Journal of Special Education*, Winter 1967, *1*, 183–190.

Resnick, M. B. and Van De Riet, V. Summary evaluation of the Learning to Learn program. Gainesville, Florida. University of Florida, Department of Clinical Psychology, 1973.

Rheingold, H. L. The social and socializing infant. In D. A. Goslin, *Handbook of socialization theory and research*. Chicago: Rand McNally, 1969.

Schaefer, E. S. *Progress report: Intellectual stimulation of culturally-deprived parents*. National Institute of Mental Health, 1968.

Schaefer, E. S. Need for early and continuing education. In V. H. Denenberg (Ed.), *Education of the infant and young child*. New York: Academic Press, 1970.

Schaefer, E. S. Personal communication, 1972. (a)

Schaefer, E. S. Parents as educators: Evidence from cross-sectional longitudinal and intervention research. *Young Children*, 1972, *27*, 227–239. (b)

Schaefer, E. S. and Aaronson, M. Infant education research project: Implementation and implications of the home-tutoring program. In R. K. Parker (Ed.), *The preschool in action*. Boston: Allyn and Bacon, 1972.

Schoggen, M. and Schoggen, P. *Environmental forces in home lives of three-year-old children in three population sub-groups*. Nashville, Tenn.: George Peabody College for Teachers, DARCEE Papers and Reports, Vol. 5, No. 2, 1971.

Skeels, H. M. Adult status of children from contrasting early life experiences. *Monographs of the Society for Research in Child Development*, 1966, *31*, Serial #105.

Skeels, H. M. and Dye, H. B. A study of the effects of differential stimulation on mentally retarded children. *Proceedings and Addresses of the American Association on Mental Deficiency*, 1939, *44*, 114–136.

Skeels, H. M., Updegraff, R., Wellman, B. L., and Williams, H. M. A study of environmental stimulation: An orphanage preschool project. *University of Iowa Studies in Child Welfare*, 1938, *15*, #4.

Skodak, M. and Skeels, H. M. A final follow-up study of 100 adopted children. *Journal of Genetic Psychology*, 1949, *75*, 85–125.

Smith, M. B. School and home: Focus on achievement. In A. H. Passow (Ed.), *Developing programs for the educationally disadvantaged*. New York: Teachers College Press, 1968.

Soar, R. S. An integrative approach to classroom learning. NIMH Project Number 5-R11MH01096 to the University of South Carolina and 7-R11-MH02045 to Temple University, 1966.

Soar, R. S. Follow-Through classroom process measurement and pupil growth (1970–71). Gainesville, Florida: College of Education, University of Florida, 1972.

Soar, R. S. and Soar, R. M. Pupil subject matter growth during summer vacation. *Educational Leadership Research Supplement*, 1969, 2, 577–587.

Sprigle, H. Learning to learn program. In S. Ryan (Ed.), *A report of longitudinal evaluations of preschool programs.* Washington, D.C.: Office of Child Development, 1972.

Stanford Research Institute. Implementation of planned variation in Head Start: Preliminary evaluation of planned variation in Head Start according to Follow-Through approaches (1969–70). Washington, D.C.: Office of Child Development, U.S. Department of Health, Education and Welfare, 1971. (a)

Stanford Research Institute. Longitudinal evaluation of selected features of the national Follow-Through program. Washington, D.C.: Office of Education, U.S. Department of Health, Education and Welfare, 1971. (b)

Tulkin, S. R. and Cohler, B. J. Child rearing attitudes on mother-child interaction among middle and working class families. Paper presented at the 1971 meeting of the Society for Research in Child Development.

Tulkin, S. R. and Kagan, J. Mother-child interaction: Social class differences in the first year of life. *Proceedings of the 78th Annual Convention of the American Psychological Association*, 1970, 261–262.

Van De Riet, V. A sequential approach to early childhood and elementary education. Gainesville, Florida: Department of Clinical Psychology, University of Florida, 1972.

Weikart, D. P. *Preschool intervention: A preliminary report of the Perry Preschool Project.* Ann Arbor, Mich.: Campus Publishers, 1967.

Weikart, D. P. A comparative study of three preschool curricula. A paper presented at the Bi-annual meeting of the Society for Research in Child Development, Santa Monica, Calif., March 1969.

Weikart, D. P., et al. *Longitudinal results of the Ypsilanti Perry Preschool Project.* Ypsilanti, Mich.: High/Scope Educational Research Foundation, 1970.

Weikart, D. P., Kamii, C. K., and Radin, M. *Perry Preschool Progress Report.* Ypsilanti, Mich.: Ypsilanti Public Schools, 1964.

Weikart, D. P., Rogers, L., Adcock, C., and McClelland, D. *The cognitively oriented curriculum.* Washington, D.C.: National Association for the Education of Young Children, 1971.

18

BAD SCIENCE, WORSE POLITICS

Alan Ryan

The Bell Curve is the product of an obsession, or, more exactly, of two different obsessions. Richard Herrnstein—who died on September 24, 1994—was obsessed with the heritability of intelligence, the view that much the largest factor in our intellectual abilities comes in our genes. He was also convinced that there had been a liberal conspiracy to obscure the significance of genetically based differences in the intelligence of different races, social classes, and ethnic groups, and that all manner of educational and economic follies were being perpetrated in consequence. Charles Murray—who is energetically and noisily with us still—is obsessed with what he believes to be the destructive effects of the American welfare state.

The result of their cooperation is a decidedly mixed affair. The politics of *The Bell Curve* are at best slightly mad, and at worst plain ugly. Its literary tone wobbles uneasily between truculence and paranoia. Its intellectual pretensions are often ill founded. For all that, anyone who has an interest in the philosophy of science and a taste for public policy will enjoy much of *The Bell Curve*; it is full of interesting, if dubiously reliable, information, and it offers the always engaging spectacle of two practical-minded men firmly in the grip of irrational passion.

Richard Herrnstein's passion was the conviction that each person has a fixed or nearly fixed quantum of "cognitive ability," the intelligence whose quotient constitutes your IQ. Herrnstein began his career as a disciple of the behaviorist psychologist B. F. Skinner, and therefore as a devout environmentalist. Then he fell in love with "Spearman's g." Charles Spearman was a turn-of-the-century British Army officer and statistician who thought that people possess varying amounts of general intelligence—or "g"—and invented statistical techniques to discover which intelligence tests most directly tap into this basic ability.

Skeptics have always said that g explains nothing: the fact that the performance of individuals on different tests is closely correlated, and predicts their success in school work and some occupational settings, is important and interesting. Talk of g adds nothing to the fact of the correlation. Herrnstein, however, was no skeptic in this matter. At the first mention of g he confesses that "its reality . . . was and remains arguable." But eleven pages later, he claims that g sits at the center of the mind's capacities "as an expression of a core mental ability much like the ability Spearman identified at the turn of the century," while eight pages on, after a further bout with the skeptics, he announces that it is universally accepted that "there is such a thing as a general factor of cognitive ability on which human beings differ."

Does it matter? Only to the extent that it reinforced Herrnstein's fascination with ethnicity. The more you think that talk of IQ is talk of a mysterious something that possesses the same reality as visible qualities like skin color or the curliness of the hair, the more obvious it will seem that either groups that differ in such visible qualities must differ in intelligence too. By the same token, it bolsters the extraordinary fatalism that infuses *The Bell Curve*: once you discover that the average IQ of people in jail is 93, it's easy to believe that people with too little g are more or less doomed to social dysfunction. How other countries of the same ethnic composition as white America manage to commit fewer murders and jail far fewer of their citizenry remains for ever inexplicable. Conversely, a certain skepticism about what there is to IQ besides being good at certain sorts of tests may make us less superstitious about its importance.

Charles Murray is intoxicated by an apocalyptic vision of the American future nicely summarized as "The Coming of the Custodial State." The anxieties about the widening inequality produced by the American economy are ones that Mickey Klaus and Robert Reich long ago familiarized us with, but they are here run through Murray's wilder and darker imaginings to yield a vision of an incipient semifascist future that neither of them would recognize.[1] American society is increasingly partitioned into a high-IQ, ever more affluent upper caste, a hard-pressed middle class, and a cognitively underprivileged underclass, whose criminality threatens the rest of us and whose unchecked breeding threatens to dilute the pool of talent, and so alarmingly on. The well-off migrate to enclaves of comfortable housing, which are walled-off, well-policed, and equipped with decent schools; the underclass are shut away in urban slums. The struggling middle class feels trapped.

The elite may hold liberal views and they may be willing to pay for help to the poor, but they will not live among them. The middle class have neither the money to spend on the underclass nor tolerance of its ways. They will insist on coercive policing and a more punitive welfare system, and will want the underclass kept in whatever "high-tech and more lavish version of the Indian reservation" it takes to keep them from preying on the respectable. The end result, Murray argues, is catastrophe: a version of the welfare state in which the incompetent have their lives managed without their consent.

It is difficult to imagine the United States preserving its heritage of individualism, equal rights before the law, free people running their own lives, once it is accepted that a significant part of the population must be made permanent wards of the state.

This is a eugenicist, and not (in the usual sense) a racist, night-mare, for Murray believes that the bottom 10 percent of the white population is headed for the degradation that already afflicts the black urban underclass. The people he affectionately describes as "white trash" will need as much looking after as their black coun-terparts.

So far as I can see, none of Murray's anxieties about the direction of American domestic policy depends on the truth of Richard Herrnstein's ideas about the ontological status of g, and none of Herrnstein's claims about intelligence support Charles Murray's ideas about social policy. Murray himself seems to recognize this: "Like other apocalyptic visions, this one is pessimistic," he says, "perhaps too much so. On the other hand, there is much to be pessimistic about." That statement is a bit casual when it is used as the basis of social prophecy; there always has been much to be pes-simistic about, but not much of it licenses the expectation of the imminent extinction of American civil liberties. For all the scientific apparatus with which they are surrounded, Murray's fears are closer to the ravings of Rush Limbaugh's audience than to Tocqueville's anxieties about "soft despotism."

Herrnstein and Murray don't explicitly contradict each other, to be sure, but Murray was hostile to the welfare state long before he encountered Herrnstein; and Herrnstein's views on intelligence are in principle consistent with the politics of almost any persuasion from socialist to libertarian. Socialists might think that ineradicable differences in IQ should be met by making sure that the less clever were compensated with more education than the gifted, and with income supplements to make up for their difficulties in the com-petitive marketplace; libertarians might think we should treat such differences as the luck of the draw, no more worthy of treatment than the accident that makes some of us better baseball players than others. Between trying to obliterate their effects and letting them make whatever difference they make in the labor market, there are innumerable further alternatives.

Herrnstein and Murray have many common enemies—Head Start, open door immigration, unwed mothers, lax ideas about sexual morality, and the "dumbing down" of American secondary education—but *The Bell Curve* is very much not the work of one mind. Indeed, each of the authors is in more than one mind on more than one issue.

2

For all its oddities, *The Bell Curve* is a fluent piece of work. It is a still more fluent piece of publicity-seeking. The authors have tried to have their cake and eat it, and they have succeeded in a big way. They—and this is largely Murray's achievement—claim to be frightened that they will stir up terrible controversy, but they have advertised their fears in such a way as to do just that. They insist that they have no urge to stir up racial dissension or give comfort to racists, but then say that their findings only reflect what people already think in their heart of hearts—which is, that blacks and white trash are born irremediably dumb, that black Americans have been overpromised in the academy, that smarter white workers have been displaced by incompetent black ones at the behest of the federal government. A disagreeably wheedling tone is an unsurprising feature of such arguments.

There is a good deal of genuine science in *The Bell Curve*; there is also an awful lot of science fiction and not much care to make sure the reader knows which is which. What catches the eye of reviewers and reporters are Herrnstein's gloomy predictions about the declining intelligence of the American population, and Murray's prediction of imminent fascism. Fewer readers will notice the authors' throwaway admissions that these predictions are highly speculative, and only loosely rooted in the data they assemble. Take the connection between the fact that illegitimacy rises as IQ declines, and Murray's fears about the imminent collapse of the liberal state. It is, for a start, quite impossible—as is readily acknowledged by the authors—that the rising rate of illegitimate births to both the black and white American populations should in the first instance have had much to do with intelligence.

The rate remained almost stable between 1920 and 1960, at about 5 percent of all births, then took off sharply in the 1960s to reach 30 percent in 1990. Herrnstein and Murray say, "If IQ is a factor in illegitimacy, as we will conclude it is, it must be in combination with other things (as common sense would suggest), because IQ itself has not changed nearly enough in recent years to account for the explosive growth in illegitimacy." They then evade the obvious implication that their obsession with IQ is largely irrelevant. They say "some of these 'other things' that have changed in the last three decades—broken homes and the welfare system being prime suspects—interact with intelligence, making it still more likely than before that a woman of low cognitive ability will have a baby out of wedlock." True, but largely beside the point; the social pressures they mention make it more likely that women of *any* degree of cognitive ability will have a baby out of wedlock. If the pressures operate more powerfully on women of lower intelligence, we want to know why this is so.

The interesting question is not one of genetics but one of changes in the culture; it is not what has happened to the intelligence of the mothers that needs explaining, but what happened in the early 1960s that so altered the incentives to have babies later rather than earlier and in wedlock rather than out. (It must mean something that divorce rates rose at the same speed during the same years.) That is the sociologist's territory, not the psychometrician's, and too often *The Bell Curve* relies on Herrnstein's real distinction as a psychologist to prop up what is essentially armchair sociology. A sociologist would at least wonder why the welfare system should be one of the "prime suspects" in the rising rate of illegitimacy when it has been *decreasingly* generous over the past thirty years; and a sociologist would at least notice that other Western societies such as Britain and the Netherlands have experienced rising illegitimacy rates, too. None of this suggests we ought not to worry about the propensity of the less clever to get pregnant out of wedlock, but it does suggest that we ought to attend to the real complexities of the social environment in which all this takes place.

Again, all readers will grasp the authors' insistence that Head Start programs haven't worked; fewer will notice that those failures are more partial than the authors say, and that the failures provide a better argument for seeking programs that work than they do for *The Bell Curve*'s conclusion that we should abandon the attempt to raise the IQs of the disadvantaged and devote virtually all our attention to the highly intelligent. The fashion in which such programs have failed is not analyzed with the scrupulousness one might wish. In essence, *The Bell Curve*'s data suggest that Head Start and other preschool programs can raise children's IQs quite sharply for a short period; once the children are in a regular school, their IQ scores drift back to something like the level they began at. For a believer in g, this is evidence that in the long run the quantum of cognitive ability, whatever it might be, simply reveals itself.

Someone who wanted to draw the opposite conclusion might think that the data only show that there is no cheap, one-shot environmental fix for deprivation. Environmental fixes are possible, but they take much longer to work, or, where they work quickly, they need to be repeated so that they keep working. It may well be that a much more extensive transformation of the child's environment than Head Start and preschool programs can offer is needed to effect lasting changes in intelligence. There are suggestive data about the impact of adoption on the children of low-IQ mothers that might make one believe that is the case. If it is true, however, it provides an argument for affirmative action that renders *The Bell Curve* irrelevant from start to finish; for it suggests that one purpose in creating a larger black (or whatever) middle class is to create a better environment for the next generation and its descendants. The true beneficiaries of affirmative action on this view would be the children and the grandchildren of the people promoted today.

That could be quite wrong; it might be that the only effective environmental fix would be a national health service that gave babies a better prenatal and perinatal environment. It might even be that Charles Murray's "custodial state" would have to get into the act to insist that the mothers of children who are at risk should use such care. What one can certainly say is that the failure of Head Start to live up to its backers' most extravagant hopes is neither a knock-down argument for genetic determinism nor any sort of argument for abandoning the disadvantaged. Herrnstein and Murray argue elsewhere in *The Bell Curve* that American secondary education has "dumbed down" bright children and so imply—what they elsewhere admit—that bad environments at least have an effect. After several hundred pages of this, one begins to wonder just what Herrnstein and Murray do believe other than that any old argument against helping the disadvantaged will do.

3

The sheer repetitiveness of its tables, graphs, and bar charts eventually dulls *The Bell Curve*'s impact for the conscientious reader; but Herrnstein and Murray do not expect—and perhaps do not really want—most of their readers to work their way through all 845 pages of their text.[2] They say they want to make the reader's life easy. For readers whose minds go blank at the mention of multiple regression, they provide a wonderfully lucid appendix on "Statistics For People Who Are Sure They Can't Learn Statistics." For readers in a particular hurry, they summarize their claims in some forty pages of italicized text spread across their twenty-two chapters.

Their main claims can be boiled down further still. They are essentially these: America is today a "meritocracy" in the sense that the best predictor of success in life is IQ; the various institutions that pass children up the ladder to success increasingly select the brightest children to train for entry to the best colleges, the best professional schools, and the most rewarding occupations. Where once the alumni of Harvard and Princeton were socially rather than mentally smarter than their peers, the students of the best colleges are today almost off the scale—inside the top 1 percent of their age group. Nor does IQ represent the result of training, or parental advantage; the social standing of our parents is a less reliable predictor of our future economic success and failure than our IQ—it's good to have well-off parents *and* brains, but if you can only have one, take the brains.

More intriguingly, most indicators of our ability to function successfully in society correlate to a significant degree with IQ. Very few students with an average or above average IQ fail to complete high school; conversely, the students who fail to complete high school usually do so because they find it intellectually beyond them; unsurprisingly, they have higher levels of long-term unemployment, both when they are able-bodied and because they are more likely to be sick. Men with lower IQs show up disproportionately in prison, and that is not because the dim crooks get caught, since self-reported but otherwise undetected crime is also largely committed by the less bright. Crime, of course, is mainly a male activity, and *The Bell Curve* duly acknowledges that what IQ explains is which men are more likely to commit offenses, not why men do and women (generally) don't. Herrnstein and Murray's interest in women is mostly an interest in their propensity to produce children out of wedlock, to go on welfare, and to have difficult children. As ever, the less bright have higher rates of illegitimacy and less amenable children, and to nobody's surprise stay longer on welfare.

As for our relations with one another, the clever marry later, breed later, and stick together; the less bright marry in haste and repent in haste, or at any rate are twice as likely to get divorced within five years. One thing to remember in the face of all this—

and usefully insisted on by the authors—is that IQ differences do not account for *much* of the difference in the fate or behavior or people; in statistical terms, IQ rarely accounts for as much as a fifth of the difference between one person and another, and usually for much less. The only thing with which IQ correlates very closely is our performance on tests that measure the same skills that IQ tests measure—which in a world full of lawyers and economists and scientifically trained professionals is surely likely to create a high-IQ caste of what Robert Reich labeled "symbolic analysis." Intelligence tests test for just that kind of intelligence. To the extent that other personal characteristics are involved in what happens to us, the impact of IQ is less. The importance of *any* contribution of IQ to the causation of social problems, however, is that when we are dealing with very large numbers it makes a difference whether we think the population we are dealing with is averagely bright, especially bright, or rather dim.

For readers who are convinced that any discussion of the heritability of intelligence is fundamentally, if covertly, a discussion of the inferior mental capacities of black Americans. Herrnstein and Murray seem at first to provide some measure of reassurance. All these gloomy results about the damage done by having lower intelligence than the average come from an analysis of the experiences of white Americans in the 1980s. Most of the data which Herrnstein and Murray use come from the National Longitudinal Survey of Labor Market Experience of Youth (NLSY), a study of some 12,500 Americans who were between fourteen and twenty-two in 1979 when the survey began, and whose progress has been followed ever since.

Its usefulness to Herrnstein and Murray is that "only the NLSY combined detailed information on the childhood environment *and* parental socioeconomic status *and* subsequent educational and occupational achievement *and* work history *and* family formation *and*— crucially for our interests—detailed psychometric measures of cognitive skills." The sample was used by the federal government to reassess its intelligence tests, so it fortuitously provides data on measured intelligence as well as on everything else that correlates with success and failure in the labor market. The NLSY covers all ethnic groups, but the first twelve chapters of *The Bell Curve* stick to the distribution of intelligence across the white American population in that sample. Only then do Herrnstein and Murray turn to the discussion of ethnic differences in IQ.

Of course, as the hubbub in the press suggests, the reassurance is less than skin deep; as soon as ethnic differences have been identified—the one that swamps all others is that the mean IQ of African Americans is 85 as against 100 for white Americans—the reader is in for two hundred pages of familiar complaints against affirmative action policies. Before we move on to these, some other findings are worth a brief look. The most familiar will be the fairly well-confirmed discovery that, just as African Americans are one "standard deviation," i.e., 15 percent, less good than white Americans at tests of analytical and spatial intelligence, so East Asians—especially the Hong Kong Chinese—are anything up to one standard deviation better. If the white American average is set at 100, the black American average is 84, and the East Asian average is 111–115. Ashkenazi Jews have similar scores to East Asians, but the scores of Oriental Jews in Israel show an embarrassing contrast.

Herrnstein and Murray don't dwell at length on the implications of their views for the social difficulties of black Americans, but they hardly need to. Once they have piled up the statistics on the disadvantages attendant on having an IQ much below 100, the case is made. Where they concentrate their attention is on the two related questions, whether we can do anything to raise IQ, and whether affirmative action policies in education and employment are worth the candle. In brief, their answer to both questions is no.

The greater part of the argument against remedial education is their argument against Head Start and analogous programs. But that argument, as we have seen, can be used to suggest that the programs should be more intensive, not abandoned. They acknowledge the possibility in principle of eugenicist programs, but flinch at the thought of putting into the hands of government the power to dictate such matters as who may or may not produce children—William Shockley gets a passing mention as someone who enjoyed shocking people by suggesting that we might pay the poor to be sterilized and might set up sperm banks to pass on the genes of geniuses (he contributed to a privately organized sperm bank; there is no record of the results). But Shockley is dismissed as excessively eccentric. Whether his proposal to pay the poor to be sterilized is more eccentric than Murray's proposal to abolish welfare payments and face the short-term consequences for the hapless children on the receiving end of the change, readers will judge for themselves.

Affirmative action greatly preoccupies Herrnstein and Murray. Oddly enough in discussing it, they back away from an insistence on the genetic determination of IQ. All that matters is that IQ predicts performance at work and in the academy, and cannot be increased by short-term educational and environmental enrichment. In academic matters, they are much bothered by the probability that the SAT scores of black students at the best universities are anything up to 200 points lower than those of their white peers, with obvious consequences for the clustering of black students among the least successful and therefore least happy members of the college community. Herrnstein and Murray argue that we do such students no favor by putting them in a situation where they are anxious in school and possess an undervalued credential when they leave.

Nor are Herrnstein and Murray any happier about affirmative action in employment. They launch a two-pronged attack. The first is to demonstrate that although the raw income data suggest that black Americans earn less than white Americans, the picture changes when we add in the distribution of intelligence. At this point, we find that black Americans earn relatively more than white Americans—that is, relative to their IQs. What you might call "dollars per IQ point" comes out in favor of African Americans. If your notion of justice is that people should be paid according to their IQs, then this is unjust. On the other hand, you might think that what matters is overall efficiency; and Herrnstein's other argument is that affirmative action damages efficiency. Given even halfway plausible assumptions, of course, it must do so; if IQ predicts competence, anything that makes us appoint people on some basis other than IQ produces some degree of incompetence. Old-fashioned class biases were denounced by British socialists precisely because they helped the incompetent to keep out the competent. Herrnstein advertises himself as an enthusiast for that view.

There is a lot to be said on both sides. In a highly competitive society like ours, it may be true that affirmative action causes anxiety in, say, the student who gets into a place like Princeton or Harvard with SATs well below those of his or her white peers. But this anxiety doesn't seem to affect athletes or "legacies," i.e., the children of alumni—groups whose presence at such places Herrnstein is surprisingly happy about—which suggests that even if this generation of black students does less well in strictly academic terms than their white peers, there are better ways of reducing their anxieties than refusing to admit them in the first place. The same thought applies in employment. It may be that there are many black Americans struggling with jobs they cannot deal with and many white colleagues muttering about them under their breath. It may also be that these are the labor pains of a different sort of society from the one we have had for the past three centuries.

4

This, however, throws one back on the fundamental question raised by *The Bell Curve*—how seriously we should take its science? Is there an intelligence gap between black and white Americans that no passage of time and no social policy can close? If there were, would anything follow about the social policies a humane society should adopt? The answer seems to be that there is a good reason to believe that there is a gap, but no conclusive reason to believe that it is unshrinkable; if there were, it would have a good many implications about the need to balance the search for efficiency against the desire for a more humane social order—but it would not dictate how we strike the balance and it would introduce no moral novelties into the calculation. In particular, a belief in the importance of inherited differences in IQ need not encourage apocalyptic conservatism.[3]

It is an under-remarked feature of arguments over the inheritability of intelligence that an obsession with the presumed incapacities of the poor, the children of the slums, the bastard offspring of dim servant girls, and all the rest was once characteristic of reformers and sexual radicals as much as of anxious conservatives. The unwillingness of the contemporary liberals and the left to think eugenically has everything to do with racism being disgusting and not much to do with logic. In 1916 Bertrand Russell condemned the inner city as a site of "race suicide," but meant only that the slums produced large numbers of undernourished, unfit, and ineducable children. It was a common hope of birth control pioneers that wanted children would be fitter and brighter children.

The label "eugenics" itself was coined by Darwin's cousin, Sir Francis Galton, to describe a program for improving the British stock. Nor was the idea foreign to the Fabians. It is not an ignoble hope that as the welfare state improves the physical health of the citizenry it will also make them brighter, more alert, more interested in their surroundings and themselves. One could fear that the most likely end result would be *Brave New World*, with its Alphas, Betas, and Gammas, but that would not be because eugenic science was disgusting, but because the science would be used by the wrong people for the wrong reasons. It is surely true that an interest in the connections between heredity and intelligence need not be malign. After all, our interest in hereditary disease usually stems from the wish to help the sufferers. One can readily imagine a benign educational program that addresses the different strengths and weaknesses of students more intelligently than contemporary schooling does. But if a concern for inherited intelligence or the reverse need not be driven by panic and superstition, it usually has been.

In the United States, fear of new immigrants rather than optimism about the chances of raising the level of the whole population always seems to have driven the discussion; and fears of the "dilution" of the "pure-bred" white stock by Jewish or Negro blood were the common coin of academic discussion throughout the first forty years of this century. Herrnstein misrepresents this past and the complaint against it. He says that Stephen Jay Gould's famous attack on psychometrics in *The Mismeasure of Man* was unfair to the military psychologists of World War I and to the psychologists on Ellis Island, whom Gould accused of announcing that on first testing 80 percent of the Jews, Hungarians, Italians, and Russians were feebleminded, and that even on re-analysis 50 percent were so. "The intelligence of the average 'third class' immigrant is low," said H. H. Goddard, "perhaps of moron grade." Gould, in essence, claimed that research into the supposed racial differences in intelligence was driven by panic and prejudice, and resulted in absurd findings. Herrnstein responds that the psychologists were looking only for mental defectives, not naturally reported cases of mental deficiency. This, as Herrnstein knows, won't wash in the case of Carl Brigham, the Canadian military psychologist who came to the United States in World War I and stayed to become professor of psychology at Princeton and a leading figure in the work of the Educational Testing Service and the development of the SAT. Herrnstein diverts the argument from the point at issue by claiming that Brigham's book, *A Study of American Intelligence*, had less influence on the Immigration Restriction Act of 1924 than Gould supposed. But that is not the point. Brigham was a leading figure in World War I intelligence testing for the American Army, and Brigham held, and popularized, exactly the views that Gould complained of. Brigham knew that many people thought Jews were clever; having examined large numbers of Russian-born Americans in the war, he thought he knew better. His army sample was "at least one-half Jewish," he thought, and they "had an average intelligence below those from all other countries except Poland and Italy." Taking Negro draftees as his reference, he discovered that 39 percent of the Russian-born were below the Negro average, 42.3 percent of the Italian-born, and 46 percent of the Polish-born. This was not an eccentric's vision of the world but the respectable psychometrics of the day.[4]

Brigham's estimates of the cognitive inferiority of black Americans were, as this would suggest, much greater than Herrnstein's—in which case, the unclosable gap has been closing. Even Brigham acknowledged that putting black Americans in a different environment made a difference to their tested intelligence; and other interwar studies confirmed Brigham's finding that northern blacks did better on his tests than southern blacks. Some even found that northern blacks scored higher on many tests than southern whites. None of this proves that there is no inbuilt difference in cognitive abilities between different human groups, though it is hard to believe that anything of the sort would follow the haphazard lines of self-reported ethnicity. What it does suggest is that either relative cognitive abilities change more rapidly than Herrnstein believed or that our estimates of them are less reliable than he thought.

One other thing it suggests is that we should worry less than Herrnstein did about the danger that American intelligence is declining. Herrnstein was an old-fashioned "deteriorationist," squarely in the Brigham tradition.

When people die, they are not replaced one for one with babies who will develop identical IQs. If the new babies grow up to have systematically higher or lower IQs than the people who die, the national distribution of intelligence changes. Mounting evidence indicates that demographic trends are exerting downward pressure on the distribution of cognitive ability in the United States and that the pressures are strong enough to have social consequences.

Other evidence, also quoted by Herrnstein, suggests that intelligence levels are generally rising. As usual where the evidence points in both directions, Herrnstein and Murray urge us to accept the more frightening scenario.

Herrnstein's fears were partly those that recently alarmed Sir Keith Joseph, Mrs. Thatcher's former education minister. In Britain as elsewhere, the cleverer members of the population have fewer children than the less clever. If g is handed down in the genes, there will be less to go round in each generation. Even if each clever woman had as many children as each less clever woman, there would still be deterioration; the less clever have their children earlier, producing three generations of less bright children, while their intellectual superiors produce two. But Herrnstein also shared Brigham's more American anxieties: the wrong sort of immigrants have been flooding into the country. Small numbers of bright East Asians were no match for large numbers of less bright Latino and Caribbean migrants. Herrnstein knew that his critics would retort that all this was said about the Poles, the Russians, and the Italians a century ago; all he could say in reply that this time the anxiety was justified.

The latest contradictions of *The Bell Curve*'s politics emerges when one contrasts Herrnstein's enthusiastic defense of meritocracy with Murray's final fantasy of a world in which we live in "clans" that are high on self-regard and cheerfully ignore the existence of cleverer and less clever people in the world. Herrnstein essentially wants the world in which clever Jewish kids or their equivalent make their way out of humble backgrounds and end up running Goldman Sachs or the Harvard physics department, while Murray wants the Midwest in which he grew up—a world in which the local mechanic didn't care two cents whether he was or wasn't brighter than the local math teacher. The trouble is that the first world subverts the second, while the second feels claustrophobic to the beneficiaries of the first. The authors are united only in their dislike of the mostly unnamed liberals who have been hostile to Herrnstein's obsessions with race and to Murray's obsessions with the welfare system. *The Bell Curve* is not only sleazy; it is, intellectually, a mess.[5]

NOTES

1. Mickey Klaus, *The End of Equality* (BasicBooks, 1992), cited in *The Bell Curve*, p. 524; Robert Reich, *The Work of Nations* (Knopf, 1991), cited p. 529. I ought to note that Klaus himself describes Murray's views in general as "alien and repellent." The *New Republic*, October 31, 1994, p. 4.

2. It is already becoming clear that the air of dispassionate scientific curiosity that they are at such pains to maintain is at odds with the eccentricity of some of their sources. J. Philippe Rushton's bizarre *Race, Evolution and Behavior* is treated as the work of a serious scholar; but Rushton's view is essentially that sexuality and intelligence are inversely related, or, as Adam Miller reported him as saying, "it's a trade-off; more brain or more penis. You can't have everything" (*Rolling Stone*, October 20, 1994). For what it's worth, the recent report on American sexual behavior suggests that he's wrong: Ashkenazi Jews have higher IQs and more active sex lives than anybody else. Richard Lynn is described as a "leading scholar of racial and ethnic differences," and no mention is made of his fondness for the theories of Nordic superiority that were the common coin of early, twentieth-century scientific racists. See, for instance, Jeffrey Rosen and Charles Lane in *The New Republic*, October 31, 1994.

3. Readers of Christopher Jencks's *Rethinking Social Policy* (Harvard University Press, 1991) will recall his skepticism about affirmative action, and readers of *Who Gets Ahead?* (BasicBooks, 1979) will recall his patient demonstration of the role of IQ differences in explaining income differentials. They will also recall that Jencks remains a cautious liberal, a class of person whose existence Hernstein and Murray simply cannot comprehend.

4. Gould gives a perfectly clear account of H. H. Goddard's search for mental defectives on pp. 158–174 of *The Mismeasure of Man* that does nothing to exculpate him. Perhaps more to the point, Goddard himself came to think his work had been scientifically worthless and politically dangerous, as did Carl Brigham half a dozen years after *A Study of American Intelligence* (Princeton University Press, 1923).

5. I am indebted to Nicholas Lemann for a long and helpful conversation while I was preparing this review.

19

BEHIND THE CURVE

by Leon J. Kamin

The Bell Curve, with 400,000 copies in print just two months after its publication, has created an enormous stir. The authors unabashedly assert that scientific evidence demonstrates the existence of genetically based differences in intelligence among social classes and races. They maintain further that data from some 1,000 publications in the social and biological sciences show that attributes such as employment, income, welfare dependence, divorce and quality of parental behavior are determined by an individual's intelligence. These claims—another eruption of the crude biological determinism that permeates the history of IQ testing—lead Herrnstein and Murray to a number of social policy recommendations. The policies would not be necessary, or humane, even if the cited evidence were valid. But the caliber of the data in The Bell Curve is, at many critical points, pathetic. Further, the authors repeatedly fail to distinguish between correlation and causation and thus draw many inappropriate conclusions.

I will deal first with an especially troubling example of the quality of the data on which Herrnstein and Murray rely. They ask, "How do African-Americans compare with blacks in Africa on cognitive tests?" They reason that low African-American IQ scores might be

The Bell Curve: Intelligence and Class Structure in American Life, by Richard J. Herrnstein and Charles Murray. Free Press, 1994 ($30).

the result either of a history of slavery and discrimination or of genetic factors. Herrnstein and Murray evidently assume that blacks reared in colonial Africa have not been subjected to discrimination. In their view, if low IQ scores of African-Americans are a product of discrimination, rather than genes, black Africans should have higher IQs than African-Americans.

To answer the question they have posed, Herrnstein and Murray call on the authority of Richard Lynn of the University of Ulster in Ireland, described as "a leading scholar of racial and ethnic differences," from whose advice they have "benefitted especially." They state that Lynn, who in 1991 reviewed 11 African IQ studies, "estimated the median black African IQ to be 75 . . . about 10 points lower than the current figure for American blacks." Herrnstein and Murray conclude that the "special circumstances" of African-Americans cannot explain their low average IQ relative to whites. That leaves genetics free to explain the black-white difference.

But why do black Americans have higher scores than black Africans? Herrnstein and Murray, citing "Owen 1992," write that "the IQ of 'coloured' students in South Africa—of mixed racial background—has been found to be similar to that of American blacks." The implication is clear: the admixture of Caucasian and African genes, both in South Africa and in the U.S., boosts "coloured" IQ 10 points above that of native Africans. But the claims made regarding African and coloured IQs cannot withstand critical scrutiny.

Lynn's 1991 paper describes a 1989 publication by Ken Owen as "the best single study of the Negroid intelligence." The study compared white, Indian, and black pupils on the Junior Aptitude Tests; no coloured pupils were included. The mean "Negroid" IQ in that study, according to Lynn, was 69. But Owen did not in fact assign IQs to any of the groups he tested; he merely reported test-score differences between groups, expressed in terms of standard deviation units. The IQ figure was concocted by Lynn out of those data. There is, as Owen made clear, no reason to suppose that low scores of blacks had much to do with genetics: "the knowledge of English

of the majority of black testees was so poor that certain [of the] tests
... proved to be virtually unusable." Further, the tests assumed that
Zulu pupils were familiar with electrical appliances, microscopes and
"Western type of ladies' accessories."

In 1992 Owen reported on a sample of coloured students that had
been added to the groups he had tested earlier. The footnote in *The
Bell Curve* seems to credit this report as proving that South African
coloured students have an IQ "similar to that of American blacks,"
that is, about 85 (the actual reference does not appear in the book's
bibliography). That statement does not correctly characterize
Owen's work. The test used by Owen in 1992 was the "nonverbal"
Raven's Progressive Matrices, which is thought to be less culturally
biased than other IQ tests. He was able to compare the performance
of coloured students with that of the whites, blacks and Indians in
his 1989 study because the earlier set of pupils had taken the Progressive Matrices in addition to the Junior Aptitude Tests. The
black pupils, recall, had poor knowledge of English, but Owen felt
that the instructions for the Matrices "are so easy that they can be
explained with gestures."

Owen's 1992 paper again does not assign IQs to the pupils.
Rather he gives the mean number of correct responses on the Progressive Matrices (out of a possible 60) for each group: 45 for whites,
42 for Indians, 37 for coloureds and 28 for blacks. The test's de-
veloper, John Raven, repeatedly insisted that results on the Progressive Matrices tests cannot be converted into IQs. Matrices
scores, unlike IQs, are not symmetrical around their mean (no "bell
curve" here). There is thus no meaningful way to convert an average
of raw Matrices scores into an IQ, and no comparison with American black IQs is possible.

The remaining studies cited by Lynn, and accepted as valid by
Herrnstein and Murray, tell us little about African intelligence but
do tell us something about Lynn's scholarship. One of the 11 entries
in Lynn's table of the intelligence of "pure Negroids" indicates that
1,011 Zambians who were given the Progressive Matrices had a

lamentably low average IQ of 75. The source for this quantitative claim is given as "Pons 1974; Crawford-Nutt 1976."

A. L. Pons did test 1,011 Zambian copper miners, whose average number of correct responses was 34. Pons reported on this work orally; his data were summarized in tabular form in a paper by D. H. Crawford-Nutt. Lynn took the pons data from Crawford-Nutt's paper and converted the number of correct responses into a bogus average "IQ" of 75. Lynn chose to ignore the substance of Crawford-Nutt's paper, which reported that 228 black high school students in Soweto scored an average of 45 correct responses on the Matrices—*higher* than the mean of 44 achieved by the same-age white sample on whom the test's norms had been established and well above the mean of Owen's coloured pupils.

Seven of the 11 studies selected by Lynn for inclusion in his "Negroid" table reported only average Matrices scores, not IQs; the other studies used tests clearly dependent on cultural content. Lynn had earlier, in a 1978 paper, summarized six studies of African pupils, most during the Matrices. The arbitrary IQs concocted by Lynn for those studies ranged between 75 and 88, with a median of 84. Five of those six studies were omitted from Lynn's 1991 summary, by which time African IQ had, in his judgment, plummeted to 69.

Lynn's distortions and misrepresentations of the data constitute a truly venomous racism, combined with scandalous disregard for scientific objectivity. Lynn is widely known among academics to be an associate editor of the racist journal *Mankind Quarterly* and a major recipient of financial support from the nativist, eugenically-oriented Pioneer Fund. It is a matter of shame and disgrace that two eminent social scientists, fully aware of the sensitivity of the issues they address, take Lynn as their scientific tutor and uncritically accept his surveys of research.

I turn now to a revealing example of Herrnstein and Murray's tendency to ignore the difference between mere statistical associations (correlations) and cause-and-effect relationships. The authors lament that "private complaints about the incompetent affirmative action hiree are much more common than scholarly examination of the issue." They then proceed to a scholarly and public discussion of "teacher competency examinations." They report that such exams have had "generally beneficial effects," presumably by weeding out incompetent affirmative-action hirees. That view of tests for teachers is not shared by those who argue that because blacks tend to get lower scores, the tests are a way of eliminating competent black teachers. But Herrnstein and Murray assure us that "teachers who score higher on the tests have greater success with their students."

To support that statement, they cite a single study by two economists who analyzed data from a large number of North Carolina school districts. The researchers obtained average teacher test scores (a measure of "teacher quality") and pupil failure rates for each district. They reported that a "1% increase in teacher quality . . . is accompanied by a 5% decline in the . . . rate of failure of students"—that is, there were fewer student failures in districts where teachers had higher test scores. It does not follow from such a correlation, however, that hiring teachers with higher test scores will reduce the rate of student failure. The same researchers found, to their surprise, that "larger class size tends to lead to improved average [pupil] performance." Does it follow that increasing the pupil-to-teacher ratio would further improve student performance? That policy might please many taxpayers, just as firing teachers with lower test scores would please some. But neither policy derives logically from the observed correlations.

To understand why, consider the following. The average proportion of black students across the North Carolina school districts was 31 percent. Suppose—it does not stretch credulity—that black teachers (who have lower test scores) tend to work in districts with large proportions of black pupils (who have higher failure rates). Such nonrandom assignment of teachers would produce a correlation between teacher test scores and pupil failure rates, but one cannot then conclude that the teachers' test scores have any causal relation to student failure. To argue that, one would have to show that for a group of black teachers and for a separate group of white teachers, teachers' test scores predicted the failure rates of their students. No such information was available to the original researchers or to Herrnstein and Murray.

What about the finding that high pupil-to-teacher ratios are associated with good pupil performance? There is no way to be certain, but suppose deprived black children tended to be in small, de facto segregated rural schools, whereas more privileged whites were in larger classrooms. Would cramming more pupils into the rural schools promote academic excellence?

There is an important and general lesson buried in this example: the arithmetical complexity of the multitude of correlations and logistic regressions stuffed into *The Bell Curve* does not elevate their status from mere associations to causes and effects.

The confusion between correlation and causation permeates the book's largest section, which consists of an interminable series of analyses of data taken from the National Longitudinal Survey of Labor Market Experience of Youth (NLSY). Those data, not surprisingly, indicate that there is an association within each race between IQ and socioeconomic status. Herrnstein and Murray labor mightily to show that low IQ is the cause of low socioeconomic status, and not vice versa. The argument is decked out in all the trappings of science—a veritable barrage of charts, graphs, tables, appendices and appeals to statistical techniques that are unknown to many readers. But on close examination, this scientific emperor is wearing no clothes.

The NLSY survey included more than 12,000 youngsters, who were aged 14 to 22 when the continuing study began in 1979. At that time the respondents or their parents gave information about their educations, occupations, and incomes and answered questions about themselves. Those reports are the basis for classifying the childhood socioeconomic status of the respondents. The teenagers also took the Armed Forces Qualification Test, regarded by psychometricians as essentially an IQ test. As they have grown older, the respondents have provided more information about their own schooling, unemployment, poverty, marital status, childbearing, welfare dependency, criminality, parenting behavior, and so on.

Herrnstein and Murray pick over these data, trying to show that it is overwhelmingly IQ—not childhood or adult socioeconomic status—that determines worldly success and the moral praiseworthiness of one's social behaviors. But their dismissal of socioeconomic status rests ultimately on the self-reports of youngsters, which do not form an entirely firm basis.

I do not suggest that such self-reports are entirely unrelated to reality. We know from many sources that children from differing social class backgrounds do indeed differ in measured IQ. And in the NLSY study, after all, the respondents' self-reports are correlated with the objective facts of their IQ scores. But comparing the predictive value of those self-reports with that of test scores is playing with loaded dice.

Further, the fact that self-reports are correlated with IQ scores is, like all correlations, ambiguous. For Herrnstein and Murray, the relation of their index of parental socioeconomic status to the child's IQ means that parents of high status—the "cream floating on the surface of American society"—have transmitted high-quality genes to their offspring. But other interpretations are possible. Perhaps the kinds of people who get high test scores are precisely those who are vain enough to claim exaggerated social status for themselves. That tendency could artificially inflate correlations of IQ both with parental socioeconomic status and with self-reports of success, distorting all tests of the relative predictive power of socioeconomic status and IQ. Such an explanation may seem far-fetched to some readers, but it is clearly a logical possibility. The choice between such alternative interpretations of statistical associations cannot be based on logic alone. There is plenty of elbow room for ideological bias in social science.

The core of the Herrnstein-Murray message is phrased with a

beguiling simplicity: "Putting it all together, success and failure in the American economy, and all that goes with it, are increasingly a matter of the genes that people inherit." Income is a "family trait" because IQ, "a major predictor of income, passes on sufficiently from one generation to the next to constrain economic mobility." Those at the bottom of the economic heap were unlucky when the genes were passed out, and they will remain there.

The correlations with which Herrnstein and Murray are obsessed are of course real: the children of day laborers are less likely than the children of stockbrokers to acquire fortunes or to go to college. They are more likely to be delinquent, to receive welfare, to have children outside of marriage, to be unemployed and to have low-birth-weight babies. The children of laborers have lower average IQs than do the children of brokers, and so IQ is also related to all these phenomena. Herrnstein and Murray's intent is to convince us that low IQ causes poverty and its attendant evils—not, as others hold, vice versa.

For eight dense chapters, the authors of *The Bell Curve* wrestle with data from the NLSY survey, attempting to disentangle the roles of IQ and of socioeconomic status. They employ a number of quantitative tools, most prominently logistic regression, a technique that purports to specify what would happen if one variable were "held constant" while another variable were left free to vary. When socioeconomic status is statistically held constant by Herrnstein and Murray, IQ remains related to all the phenomena described. When IQ is held constant, the effect of socioeconomic status is invariably reduced, usually substantially, and sometimes eliminated.

There are a number of criticisms to be made regarding the ways in which Herrnstein and Murray analyze these data. But for argument's sake, let us suppose that their analyses are appropriate and accurate. We can also grant that, rightly or wrongly, disproportionate salaries and wealth accrue to those with high IQ scores. What then do the Herrnstein-Murray analyses tell us?

The socioeconomic status of one's parents cannot in any immediate sense "cause" one's IQ to be high or low. Family income obviously cannot directly determine a child's performance on an IQ test. But income and the other components of an index of socioeconomic status can serve as rough indicators of the rearing environment to which a child has been exposed. With exceptions, a child of a well-to-do broker is more likely to be exposed to book learning earlier and more intensively than is a child of a laborer. And extensive practice at reading and calculating does affect, very directly, one's IQ score. That is one plausible way of interpreting the statistical link between parental socioeconomic stats and a child's IQ.

The significant question is not whether socioeconomic status, as defined by Herrnstein and Murray, is more or less statistically associated with success than is their measure of IQ. Different measures of socioeconomic status, or different IQ tests, might substantially affect the results they obtained; other scholars, using other indices and tests, have in fact achieved quite different results. The significant question is, why don't the children of laborers acquire the skills that are tapped by IQ tests?

Herrnstein and Murray answer that the children of the poor, like their laborer parents before them, have been born with poor genes. Armed with that conviction, the authors hail as "a great American success story" that after "controlling for IQ," ethnic and racial discrepancies in education, wages and so forth are "strikingly diminished." They reach this happy conclusion on the questionable basis of their regression analyses. But the data, even if true, allow another reading. We can view it as a tragic failure of American society that so few black and low-socioeconomic status children are lucky enough to be reared in environments that nurture the skills needed to obtain high IQ scores. For Herrnstein and Murray, it is only fair that the race should go to the swift, who are blessed with good genes and high IQs. The conception that our society hobbles most of the contestants at the starting line does not occur to them.

In the world of *The Bell Curve*, the explanatory power of IQ is ubiquitous. The authors note that among blue-collar workers who tell researchers that they have cropped out of the labor force because of physical disability or injury, low IQ is common. Why? "An answer leaps to mind: The smarter you are, the less likely that you will have accidents." That answer leapt to mind before the thought that low-IQ workers, in minimum wage jobs, have little incentive to remain in the labor force. Dull young women lack the "foresight and intelligence" to understand that the welfare system offers them a bad deal. Welfare might be a bad deal for Herrnstein and Murray, but I am not so sure that single mothers on welfare have not figured out *their* odds pretty accurately.

People who have low IQs, according to *The Bell Curve*, commit crimes because they lack foresight, and so the threat of prison does not deter them. Further, they cannot "understand why robbing someone is wrong." Then what is to be made of the fact that although "very dull" young males are stopped by the police, booked for an offense and convicted less often than "normal" males, they are nevertheless jailed more than twice as often? "It may be . . . that they are less competent in getting favorable treatment from the criminal justice system. The data give us no way to tell." Perhaps not, but some hints are available. There is no doubt that O.J. Simpson is "competent," but his ability to hire high-price lawyers is not irrelevant to the treatment he will receive from the criminal justice system.

The Bell Curve, near its closing tail, contains two chapters concerned with affirmative action, both in higher education and in the workplace. To read those chapters is to hear the second shoe drop. The rest of the book, I believe, was written merely as a prelude to its assault on affirmative action. The vigor of the attack is astonishing.

Affirmative action "cannot survive public scrutiny." It is based on "the explicit assumption that ethnic groups do not differ in . . . abilities." Hiring and promotion procedures "that are truly fair . . . will produce . . . racial disparities," and "employers are using dual standards for black and white job applicants because someone or something . . . is making them do so." That behavior has resulted in the "degradation of intellectual requirements" in recruiting police, which has affected "police performance on the street." We learn that a veteran of the Washington, D.C., police force has heard "about people in the academy who could not read or write." And a former instructor saw "people diagnosed as borderline retarded graduate from the police academy." These anecdotes take their place among the politically potent folktales about welfare queens driving Cadillacs.

At long last, Herrnstein and Murray let it all hang out: "Affirmative action, in education and the workplace alike, is leaking a poison into the American soul." Having examined the American condition at the close of the 20th century, these two philosopher-kings conclude, "It is time for America once again to try living with inequality, as life is lived. . . ." This kind of sentiment, I imagine, is what led *New York Times* columnist Bob Herbert to the conclusion that *The Bell Curve* "is just a genteel way of calling somebody a nigger." Herbert is right. The book has nothing to do with science.

20

THE TAINTED SOURCES OF *THE BELL CURVE*

Charles Lane

I

For all the shock value of its assertion that blacks are intractably, and probably biologically, inferior in intelligence to whites and Asians, *The Bell Curve* is not quite an original piece of research. It is, in spite of all the controversy that is attending its publication, only a review of the literature—an elaborate interpretation of data culled from the work of other social scientists. For this reason, the credibility of its authors, Charles Murray and Richard J. Herrnstein, rests significantly on the credibility of their sources.

The press and television have for the most part taken *The Bell Curve*'s extensive bibliography and footnotes at face value. And, to be sure, many of the book's data are drawn from relatively reputable academic sources, or from neutral ones such as the Census Bureau. Certain of the book's major factual contentions are not in dispute—such as the claim that blacks consistently have scored lower than whites on IQ tests, or that affirmative action generally promotes minorities who scored lower on aptitude tests than whites. And obviously intelligence is both to some degree definable and to some degree heritable.

The interpretation of those data, however, is very much in dispute. So, too, are the authors' conclusions that little or nothing can or should be done to raise the ability of the IQ-impaired since so much of their lower intelligence is due to heredity. Murray and Herrnstein instead write sympathetically about eugenic approaches to public policy (though they do not endorse them outright). It is therefore interesting that Charles Murray recently expressed his own sense of queasiness about the book's sources to a reporter from *The New York Times*: "Here was a case of stumbling onto a subject that had all the allure of the forbidden," he said. "Some of the things we read to do this work, we literally hide when we're on planes and trains. We're furtively peering at this stuff."[1]

What sort of "stuff" could Murray mean? Surely the most curious of the sources he and Herrnstein consulted is *Mankind Quarterly*—a journal of "anthropology" founded in Edinburgh in 1960. Five articles from the journal are actually cited in *The Bell Curve*'s bibliography (pp. 775, 807, and 828).[2] But the influence on the book of scholars linked to *Mankind Quarterly* is more significant. No fewer than seventeen researchers cited in the bibliography of *The Bell Curve* have contributed to *Mankind Quarterly*. Ten are present or former editors, or members of its editorial advisory board. This is interesting because *Mankind Quarterly* is a notorious journal of "racial history" founded, and funded, by men who believe in the genetic superiority of the white race.[3]

Mankind Quarterly was established during decolonization and the U.S. civil rights movement. Defenders of the old order were eager to brush a patina of science on their efforts. Thus *Mankind Quarterly*'s avowed purpose was to counter the "Communist" and "egalitarian" influences that were allegedly causing anthropology to neglect the fact of racial differences. "The crimes of the Nazis," wrote Robert Gayre, *Mankind Quarterly*'s founder and editor-in-chief until 1978, "did not, however, justify the enthronement of a doctrine of *a-racialism* as fact, nor of egalitarianism as ethnically and ethically demonstrable."[4]

Gayre was a champion of apartheid in South Africa, and belonged to the ultra-right Candour League of white-ruled Rhodesia.[5] In

1968, he testified for the defense at the hate speech trial of five members of the British Racial Preservation Society, offering his expert opinion that blacks are "worthless."⁶ The founders of *Mankind Quarterly* also included Henry E. Garrett of Columbia University, a one-time pamphleteer for the White Citizens' Councils who provided expert testimony for the defense in *Brown v. Board of Education*;⁷ and Corrado Gini, leader of fascist Italy's eugenics movement and author of a 1927 Mussolini apologia called "The Scientific Basis of Fascism."⁸

Mainstream anthropologies denounced *Mankind Quarterly*. "It is earnestly hoped that *The Mankind Quarterly* will succumb before it can further discredit anthropology and lead to even more harm to mankind," G. Ainsworth Harrison wrote in a 1961 article in *Man*, the journal of Britain's Royal Institute of Anthropology.⁹ Bozo Skerlj, a Slovene anthropologist who had survived Dachau, resigned in protest from his post on the editorial advisory board of *Mankind Quarterly*, saying that he had joined unaware of the journal's "racial prejudice."¹⁰ Undaunted, *Mankind Quarterly* published work by some of those who had taken part in research under Hitler's regime in Germany. Ottmar von Vorschuer, a leading race scientist in Nazi Germany and an academic mentor of Josef Mengele, even served on the *Mankind Quarterly* editorial board.¹¹

Since 1978, the journal has been in the hands of Roger Pearson, a British anthropologist best known for establishing the Northern League in 1958. The group was dedicated to "the interests, friendship, and solidarity of all Teutonic nations." In 1980, Pearson resigned from the ultra-right World Anti-Communist League in a struggle with members who said he was too far to the right.¹² But *Mankind Quarterly* didn't change. Pearson published eugenically-minded attacks on school integration by two American academics, Ralph Scott and Donald Swan, who were alleged to have pro-Nazi affiliations; reports on a sperm bank in which geniuses have deposited their superior genetic material; elaborate accounts of the inherited mental inferiority of blacks; and the fact that Jews first came to South Africa because its gold and diamonds were "attractive" to them.

Pearson's Institute for the Study of Man, which publishes *Mankind Quarterly*, is bankrolled by the Pioneer Fund, a New York foundation established in 1937 with the money of Wickliffe Draper. Draper, a textile magnate who was fascinated by eugenics, expressed early sympathy for Nazi Germany, and later advocated the "repatriation" of blacks to Africa. The fund's first president, Harry Laughlin, was a leader in the eugenicist movement to ban genetically inferior immigrants, and also an early admirer of the Nazi regime's eugenic policies.[13]

The Pioneer Fund's current president, Harry Weyher, has denied any Nazi or white supremacist connections. But the fund's current agenda remains true to the purpose set forth in its charter of 1937: "race betterment, with special reference to the people of the United States." In a letter in 1989, the fund proposed that America abandon integration, on the grounds that "raising the intelligence of blacks or others still remains beyond our capabilities."[14] The fund not only underwrites *Mankind Quarterly* and many other Pearson publications, but has also provided millions of dollars in research grants to sustain the "scholars" who write for it and serve on its editorial board.[15]

Which brings us back to Murray and Herrnstein. They cite in their book no fewer than thirteen scholars who have benefitted from Pioneer Fund grants in the last two decades—the grants total more than $4 million. Many of *The Bell Curve*'s sources who worked for *Mankind Quarterly* were also granted Pioneer money.[16]

Most of *The Bell Curve* does not explicitly address the relationship between race, genes, and IQ—as Murray has taken great pains to point out. Rather, the book couches its arguments about the impact of IQ on social behavior in terms of class, mostly using examples drawn from data on whites. But in view of the characteristic overlaps between race and class in American society, the insinuation is that all the connections between social pathology and low IQ which the authors find for whites must go double for blacks. It is only after one factors in their argument that IQ itself is mostly inherited (however hedged that argument may be), that the racial connotations of their policy prescriptions become evident.

And many of *The Bell Curve*'s most important assertions which establish causal links between IQ and social behavior, and IQ and race, are derived partially or totally from the *Mankind Quarterly*–Pioneer Fund scholarly circle. The University of California's Arthur Jensen, cited twenty-three times in *The Bell Curve*'s bibliography, is the book's principal authority on the intellectual inferiority of blacks. He has received $1.1 million from the Pioneer Fund.[17] To buttress Jensen's argument, Murray and Herrnstein draw on a book edited by University of Georgia psychologist R. Travis Osborne (the book, co-edited by former *Mankind Quarterly* editorial advisory board member Frank McGurk, is also cited by Murray and Herrnstein as an authority on the link between low IQ and criminality: pp. 277, 339). Osborne, the recipient of $387,000 from Pioneer, once testified as an expert witness for plaintiffs in a federal suit to overturn the *Brown v. Board of Education* decision.[18]

Other scholars who have received substantial amounts of money from Pioneer include Robert A. Gordon, a Johns Hopkins sociologist cited by Murray and Herrnstein on the causal link between low IQ and black criminality (pp. 321, 327, and 338); Linda Gottfredson of the University of Delaware, cited on the disproportionate representation of lower-IQ blacks in the profession; and University of Pennsylvania demographer Daniel Vining, Jr., a former *Mankind Quarterly* editorial advisory board member, cited on incipient "dysgenesis," or biological decline, in America, owing to the falling birthrate among the most intelligent members of society.[19]

2

The tainted funding of some of the scholars Murray and Herrnstein cite does not by itself invalidate those scholars' findings. After all, history is full of examples of scientists who were pilloried as crackpots in their own times but are hailed as geniuses today. However shocking it may be that some of Murray and Herrnstein's sources have chosen to affiliate themselves with such organizations, their work—and those parts of *The Bell Curve* that draw upon it—must be judged on the scholarly merits.

Take the case of Richard Lynn. A professor of psychology at the University of Ulster in Coleraine, Northern Ireland, Lynn was particularly influential in guiding the two authors of *The Bell Curve* through their review of the literature. In the book's acknowledgements, they say they "benefitted especially" from the "advice" of Lynn, whom they identify only as "a leading scholar of racial and ethnic differences" (pp. xxv, 272).

Lynn is an associate editor of *Mankind Quarterly*, and has received $325,000 from the Pioneer Fund.[20] One of his articles expressed support for the view that "the poor and the ill" are "weak specimens whose proliferation needs to be discouraged in the interests of the improvement of the genetic quality of the group, and ultimately of group survival."[21] He has also written that the genetic mental superiority of the Jews may be a happy Darwinian byproduct of "intermittent persecutions which the more intelligent may have been able to foresee and escape."[22]

Lynn's work is cited twenty-four times in *The Bell Curve*'s bibliography.[23] It is used to support three important claims: that East Asians have a higher average IQ than whites; that most immigrants come from groups with subpar IQs; and that the IQ score of blacks in Africa is "substantially below" the American black average. Each of these seemingly discrete claims has a key role in the formulation of *The Bell Curve*'s broader suggestions about the relationship among race, heredity, IQ, and social structure.

The assertion about inferior black African intelligence has particularly far-reaching implications. If it can be shown that low IQ predicts social ills such as crime, poverty, and unstable families, current views of Africa and of the sources of its tragic problems would have to be significantly revised. The finding would also support the claim that the IQ superiority of whites is genetic, because the African-American edge over blacks in Africa could be attributed to their admixture of white genes. (Murray and Herrnstein note pointedly that South African "coloureds" have about the same IQ as American blacks.) And lagging African IQ could also be taken to refute the claim that black Americans' lower IQ is a legacy of racism—assuming, as Murray and Herrnstein put it, that "the African black population has not been subjected to the historical legacy of American black slavery and discrimination and might therefore have higher scores" (p. 288).

Setting up their discussion of Lynn's data, Murray and Herrnstein contend that the comparison between black Americans and black Africans is a valid exercise because IQ scores have been found to predict job and school performance of black Africans as well as those of black Americans (p. 288). They also attribute the paucity of published estimates of an overall average IQ score for blacks in Africa to the fact that these scores have been extremely low—the implication being that researchers are reluctant to publish such politically incorrect findings (p. 289).

These assertions are based on a highly selective reading of the article Murray and Herrnstein cite to support them: a comprehensive 1988 review titled "Test Performance of Blacks in Southern Africa," by the South African psychologists I. M. Kendall, M. A. Verster, and J. W. V. Mollendorf (p. 289). The main point of these three researchers' argument is to question sweeping comparisons such as the one Lynn attempts, and Murray and Herrnstein repeat. The three South African psychologists write:

It would be rash to suppose that psychometric tests constitute valid measures of intelligence among non-westerners. The inability of most psychologists to look beyond the confines of their own culture has led to the kind of arrogance whereby judgments are made concerning the "simplicity" of African mental structure and "retarded" cognitive growth.[24]

Given the host of environmental and cultural factors that hamper black Africans' test performance, they also say, "one wonders whether there is any point in even considered genetic factors as an additional source of variance between the average performance levels of westerners and Africans.[25]

Nevertheless, Murray and Herrnstein venture an estimate of African IQ, drawn mainly from an article by Lynn that appeared in *Mankind Quarterly* in 1991. It should be noted, for a start, that the authors of *The Bell Curve* misreport Lynn's data. They say he found a median IQ of 75 in Africa (p. 289). But in his article, "Race Differences in Intelligence: The Global Perspective," Lynn said that the mean African IQ—not the median—was 70.[26]

In any event, how did Lynn arrive at his number? First, he assembled eleven studies of the intelligence of "pure African Negroids," drawn from different tests of several different peoples and widely varying sample sizes in the years from 1929 to 1991. Then, he decided which was the "best": a 1989 study from South Africa. In this test, he says, 1,093 sixteen-year-old black students (who had been in school for eight years and were therefore familiar with pencil-and-paper tests) scored a mean of 69 on the South African Junior Aptitude Test. Finally, Lynn rounded this result up to 70, and declared it a valid approximation of black IQ in the continent of Africa as a whole.[27]

This methodology alone invites skepticism. But Lynn also seems to have misconstrued the study. Its author, Dr. Ken Owen, told me his test was "not at all" an indication that intelligence is inherited. He blamed the low performance of blacks on environmental factors such as poorer schooling for blacks under apartheid and their difficulty with English. Owen said his results "certainly cannot" be taken as an indication of intelligence among blacks in Africa as a whole.[28]

Lynn further defends his choice of 70 as a "reasonable" mean for Africa on the grounds that 70 was the median of the average IQ scores reported in the eleven studies he had found. This statistical artifact aside, his list of studies is dubious. It includes what he calls "the first good study of the intelligence of pure African Negroids": an experiment in 1929 in which 293 blacks in South Africa were given the U.S. Army Beta Test, and got a mean score of 65.[29]

The test was administered by M. L. Fick, whom Kendall, Verster, and Mollendorf call an "extreme protagonist" of the view that blacks are inherently inferior to whites.[30] The Beta test, which was developed for illiterate recruits in the U.S. military, shows blatant cultural bias. One question presents a picture of people playing tennis without a net; respondents are supposed to sketch in the net to get full credit. In 1930, just a year after the Beta test was given in South Africa, C. C. Brigham, who had been its leading proponent in the U.S., finally admitted that the test was invalid for non-Americans. Lynn does not mention this fact.[31]

Far from refuting the thesis that the legacy of racism is to blame for black Americans' lower IQ scores vis-à-vis whites, as Murray and Herrnstein contend, Lynn's data actually support it (to the extent that they have any meaning at all). Of Lynn's eleven studies, five were conducted in South Africa under apartheid (and one in the Belgian Congo in 1952).[32] If any country oppressed black people more than the United States, it was South Africa. Indeed, as the modern South African psychologists now acknowledge, one of the main uses of IQ tests under apartheid was to provide "scientific" justification for that system.

The assertion of an East Asian IQ advantage over whites, though essentially a success story, also plays a subtle, but crucial, supporting role in *The Bell Curve*'s overall argument about the connections among IQ, social achievement, and race. Coming before the discussion of black-white differences, it helps prepare the reader to accept racial categories as units of social analysis. It also conforms to readers' preconceptions, shaped both by the media and by everyday experience, about the amazing brilliance of Asian immigrants and their offspring.

The authors would seem to be on firmer ground invoking Lynn here, since his specialty is the inherited mental superiority of East Asians, or "Mongoloids," as he refers to them. In *Mankind Quarterly*, he has contended that the Japanese "have the highest intelligence in the world."[33] In an article in *Nature* in 1982, Lynn claimed the Japanese enjoy a ten-point IQ advantage over European whites, and that this difference is growing. He suggested that this helps to explain the postwar economic miracle in Japan.[34]

But two American psychologists, Harold W. Stevenson and Hiroshi Azuma, pointed out in a rebuttal in *Nature* that the Japanese sample Lynn used was made up of children of relatively well-off urban parents—a fact Lynn failed to disclose in his article. Lynn's result was thus fatally flawed: he had tried to compare this socially skewed sample with a much broader and more representative American one.[35] Murray and Herrnstein's sole mention of this is a footnote: "For a critique of Lynn's early work, see Stevenson and Azuma 1983" (p. 716).

At the opening of their section headed "Do Asians Have Higher IQs Than Whites?" Murray and Herrnstein seem to be struggling to salvage some meaning from Lynn's data. The basic problem is the enormous difficulty of drawing conclusions about the relative intelligence of people who come from vastly different civilizations. They cite a string of Lynn's comparisons that suggest East Asians are superior, but eventually back off, conceding that the various test results he has assembled are not really comparable. Finally, the authors note: "Given the complexities of crossnational comparisons, the issue [of relative East Asian-white-black intelligence] must eventually be settled by a sufficient body of data obtained from identical tests that are comparable except for race" (pp. 272–274).

Murray and Herrnstein write that they "have been able to identify three such efforts." In the first, they say, "samples of American, British, and Japanese students ages thirteen to fifteen were administered a test of abstract reasoning and spatial relations"—the British and American students did far worse than the Japanese, naturally. In the second "set of studies," they write, nine-year-olds in Japan, Hong Kong, and Britain, drawn from comparable socioeconomic populations, were administered the Ravens Standard Progressive Matrices. Once again, the British children lost out by "well over half a standard deviation" (p. 274).

Only by checking the footnotes (at the back of the 845-page book) can readers discover that the author of both these studies is Richard Lynn. With regard to the first case, *The Bell Curve*'s test leaves the impression that the tests were conducted with similar samples in the three countries at more or less the same time. This is not quite what happened, as one learns from reading the 1987 *Mankind Quarterly* article from which these data are drawn. Lynn and his assistants gave the test in 1985 to 178 Japanese children. The tiny sample was not checked to reflect the social makeup of Japan as a whole (some 57 percent of the test-takers were boys). The test-givers merely showed up at two schools, one rural and one urban, and gave the tests to whoever was present. Lynn then compared this result to results from an American test that had been given thirteen years earlier to 64,000 subjects screened for their representativity, and to the results of a test given in 1978 to a similarly representative sample of 10,000 students in Britain. His conclusion that Japanese children do better was arrived at by distributing extra points among the three groups to "adjust" for the time lag among the three tests.[36]

The second "set of studies" is in the same 1991 *Mankind Quarterly* article in which Lynn presented his claims about "pure African Negroids." He says that a group of 118 Hong Kong nine-year-olds scored a 113 IQ, a sample of 444 children got a 110 IQ, and a sample of 239 British children got a 100 IQ. He asserts that all three samples were "representative" and drawn from "typical public primary schools," as Murray and Herrnstein report. But in the article Lynn does not explain how he assured the "representativity" of the samples, or the "typicality" of the schools.[37]

Murray and Herrnstein then go on to describe a third set of studies done by Harold Stevenson of Minnesota. In contrast to their seeming circumspection about Lynn's identity, they mention Stevenson's name in the main text of the book. As they note, he "carefully matched the children on socioeconomic and demographic variables"—and found no difference at all between the IQs of Japanese, Taiwanese, and American children (pp. 274–275).

"Where does this leave us?" Murray and Herrnstein then ask. On the one hand, we have two methodologically dubious studies by Lynn, a professor who believes, as he wrote in the *Mankind Quarterly* article, that "the Caucasoids and the Mongoloids are the only two races that have made any significant contribution to civilization."[38] On the other hand is a rigorous study by a social scientists with no known axe to grind, who finds no IQ disparity between whites and Asians. But Murray and Herrnstein portray this as a debate among a large number of contentious and equally reputable experts. "We will continue to hedge," they write; and simply split the difference. They venture that East Asians IQ exceeds that of whites by three points, a figure which "most resembles a consensus, tentative though it still is" (p. 276).

By the time Murray and Herrnstein get around to talking about immigrants, their "tentative consensus" on the East Asian-white IQ gap has grown by two points, and hardened into a datum firm enough to be factored into immigration policy. Drawing, once again, on Lynn's 1991 article in *Mankind Quarterly*, they assign East Asians a mean IQ of 105, whites 100, "Pacific" populations a score of 91, and blacks 84. Without reference to Lynn or any other source, Murray and Herrnstein give "Latinos"—a designation empty of meaningful "racial" content—a mean IQ of 91. They give no data on IQs of South Asians and Middle Eastern people, who supplied 11 percent of the immigrants in the 1980s. They're just "omitted from the analysis," as the authors put it. From this hodge-podge of assumptions Murray and Herrnstein produce the "basic statement" that 57 percent of legal immigrants in the 1980s came from ethnic groups with average IQs less than that of American whites, and therefore the mean for all immigrants is probably below that of all native-born Americans (pp. 359–360).

Even if their "basic statement" is true, it says nothing at all about the scores of the individuals who actually did immigrate to the U.S. Thus Murray and Herrnstein must deal with the common-sense notion that immigrants generally represent the brightest and most energetic members of their former societies, by virtue of their willingness to get up and go to the U.S. This the authors try to do by citing numbers from the National Longitudinal Survey, or NLSY. They find that foreign-born NLSY members had a mean IQ ".4 standard deviation" lower than the rest of the NLSY sample (p. 360).

But the NLSY began in 1979, as a survey of people who were fourteen to twenty-two years old at the time, and have then been re-examined and re-interviewed each succeeding year. Thus it has no bearing at all on people who arrived in the United States after 1979, when immigration from the third world reached its height—as Murray and Herrnstein themselves report. (Probably for this reason, the sample did not include a statistically significant percentage of East Asians.) The authors also acknowledge that the slightly poorer IQ performance of those Latino immigrants who were interviewed in the NLSY probably reflects their weak command of English. That normally improves in a few years, and IQ rises along with it. Finally, Murray and Herrnstein find that foreign-born blacks in the NLSY score five points higher than native-born blacks

(p. 360)—a fact they are utterly at a loss to explain, perhaps because some of the immigrants must have come from Africa, and they have just finished alleging that black Africans are even stupider than American blacks.

"Nonetheless," Murray and Herrnstein assert, "keeping all of these qualifications in mind, the kernel of evidence that must also be acknowledged is that Latino and black immigrants are, at least in the short run, putting some downward pressure on the distribution of intelligence" (pp. 360–361). One hundred eighty-nine pages later, this strained contention is used to justify their inclination toward a more eugenically minded—and, hence, restrictive—U.S. immigration policy. Yet other than Lynn's flawed survey, and their own bald assertion that Latinos have a mean IQ of 91, there is no "kernel of evidence" of the kind they refer to (p. 360).

3

Murray and Herrnstein aren't answerable for every belief of every ember of the racialist crowd they rely on for so much of their data. (And they didn't get any money from Pioneer.) Still, there are two matters on which their book and the intellectual mission of the men who founded *Mankind Quarterly* overlap: both sought to restore the scientific status of race, and to reintroduce eugenic thinking into the public policy debate.

The more pertinent issue here is full disclosure, or what used to be called intellectual honesty. Just as Murray blushingly covered some of his materials on the Delta shuttle, so *The Bell Curve* tiptoes around facts that might have an inconvenient influence on its readers' evaluation of the book's sources and data—not to mention the judgment of its authors in choosing those sources. Geoffrey Cowley of *Newsweek*, in a sympathetic review of the book, pronounced its scholarship "overwhelmingly mainstream."[39] Would he have done so if Murray and Herrnstein had provided a full account of the provenance of their data? Indeed, would this heavily-marketed book have achieved the same sales success and as much respectful press attention if it had leveled with readers about all of its sources? There is no way to isolate the scholarship of Richard Lynn, and that of the other *Mankind Quarterly* contributors, from their racial and political views. Social science is not so easily insulated from ideology, as Murray and Herrnstein are quick to emphasize when railing against their critics. The scholarly subcultures on which the authors of *The Bell Curve* depend for information are hardly less biased than those they are summoned to rebut. The bias of the *Mankind Quarterly* contributors, however, is much nastier. And as we have seen, some of the scholars Murray and Herrnstein rely on distort the evidence, which in key cases does not support *The Bell Curve*'s contentions.

NOTES

1. Jason DeParle, "Daring Research or Social Science Pornography?" *The New York Times Magazine*, October 9, 1994, p. 51.
2. Richard J. Herrnstein and Charles Murray, *The Bell Curve* (Free Press, 1994).
3. According to the bibliography of *The Bell Curve*, and to back issues of the *Mankind Quarterly*, the seventeen are W. J. Andrews, Cyril Burt, Raymond B. Cattell (eight citations), Hans J. Eysenck, Seymour Itzkoff, Arthur Jensen (twenty-three citations), Richard Lynn (twenty-four citations), Robert E. Kuttner, Frank C.J. McGurk (six citations), C. E. Noble, R. Travis Osborne (three citations), Roger Pearson, J. Philippe Rushton (eleven citations), William Shockley, Audrey Shuey, Daniel Vining (three citations), and Nathanial Weyl.
    The ten who are or were either editors or members of the editorial board are: Cattell, Eysenck, Itzkoff, Kuttner, Lynn, McGurk, Noble, Pearson, Shuey and Vining.
4. Robert Gayre, "The Mankind Quarterly Under Attack," *The Mankind Quarterly*, Vol. 2, No. 2 (October-December 1961), p. 79. Emphasis in original.
5. Michael Billig, *Die Rassistische Internationale* (Frankfurt: Neue Kritik, 1981), p. 101. This is the German edition of Billig's 1979 book *Psychology, Racism, and Fascism* (Birmingham, England: A. F. and R. Publications/Searchlight, 1979).
6. Billig, *Die Rassistische Internationale*, p. 97.
7. Billig, *Die Rassistische Internationale*, pp. 103–104, and Adam Miller, "Professors of Hate," *Rolling Stone*, October 20, 1994, p. 113. Garrett also wrote in 1961 that "Hitler's persecution of the Jews has greatly oversensitized the American Jew toward anything which smacks of racial distinction. The preoccupation of the Jews with racial matters today is evident in the activities of various Jewish organizations. Most of these belligerently support the equalitarian dogma which

they accept as having been 'scientifically' proven." *Mankind Quarterly*, Vol. 1, No. 4 (1961), p. 256.

8. Billig, *Die Rassistische Internationale*, p. 104.

9. G. Ainsworth Harrison, "The Mankind Quarterly," *Man*, September 1961, p. 164.

10. Bozo Skerlj, "Correspondence," *Man*, November 1960, pp. 172–173.

11. Billig, *Die Rassistische Internationale*, p. 106; Stefan Kühl, *The Nazi Connection: Eugenics, American Racism, and German National Socialism* (Oxford University Press, 1994), pp. 102–103.

12. Kühl, *The Nazi Connection*, p. 4; Miller, "Professors of Hate," p. 113; and Tim Kelsey and Trevor Rowe, "Academics 'were funded by racist American trust,'" *The Independent*, March 4, 1990, p. 4.

13. Kühl, *The Nazi Connection*, p. xv passim.

14. Kühl, *The Nazi Connection*, p. 6; Miller, "Professors of Hate," p. 114; and Kelsey and Rowe, "Academics 'were funded by racist American trust.'"

15. Miller, "Professors of Hate," Kühl, *The Nazi Connection*, pp. 9, 10; and Kelsey and Rowe, "Academics 'were funded by racist American trust.'" See also copies of federal form 990-PF tax returns filed by the Pioneer Fund, which are available on microfiche at The Foundation Center, Washington, D.C.

16. The numbers were derived by cross-checking the Murray-Herrnstein bibliography with Kühl, Billig, Miller, and Kelsey, back issues of *Mankind Quarterly*, and copies of federal form 990-PF filed by the Pioneer Fund.

17. Miller, "Professors of Hate," p. 114.

18. Miller, "Professors of Hate," p. 113.

19. Miller, "Professors of Hate," p. 114, and the federal 990-PF forms filed by the Pioneer Fund at The Foundation Center. Vining is also thanked in the book's acknowledgements. The amounts of the Pioneer Grants are often in the hundreds of thousands of dollars over several years. Another major recipient, J. Philippe Rushton of Canada's University of Western Ontario, is cited eleven times in *The Bell Curve* bibliography, and receives a two-page mention in the book's appendix (pp. 642–643) defending his highly controversial work. Rushton believes that blacks have been selected by evolution to have low intelligence. They have small heads, large genitalia, and other supposed racial features, because they developed in the warm savannah and jungle climates of Africa, where natural selection favored a reproductive strategy of high birth rate and low parental investment. In other words, Rushton believes that black people are genetically programmed to be irresponsible parents; he has also written that this genetic predisposition to sexual excess explains why so many blacks have AIDS.

20. Miller, "Professors of Hate," p. 114.

21. Richard Lynn, "Civilization and the Quality of Population," *Journal of Social, Political and Economic Studies*, Vol. 16, No. 1 (Spring 1991), p. 123. This is another Roger Pearson publication.

22. Richard Lynn, "Orientals: The Emerging American Elite?" *Mankind Quarterly*, Vol. 31, Nos. 1 and 2 (Fall/Winter 1990), p. 189.

23. Six of the Lynn articles cited by Murray and Herrnstein appeared in *Personality and Individual Differences*, a British journal edited by Hans J. Eysenck. Eysenck is the recipient of $250,000 in Pioneer grants and a frequent contributor to *Mankind Quarterly*. In 1990, two years after the University of London barred Eysenck from taking any more funds from Pioneer, Lynn channeled $30,000

from one of his Pioneer grants to Eysenck. All told, eighteen of *The Bell Curve's* bibliographical citations are from Eysenck's journal. See Pioneer Fund's 990-PF forms at The Foundation Center, and Kelsey and Rowe, "Academics 'were funded by racist American trust.' "

24. I. M. Kendall, Mary Ann Verster, and J. W. Von Mollendorf, "Test Performance of Blacks in Southern Africa," in S. H. Irvine and J. W. Berry, editors, *Human Abilities in Cultural Context* (Cambridge University Press, 1988), p. 328.

25. Kendall, Verster, and Mollendorf, "Test Performance of Blacks in Southern Africa," p. 326.

26. Richard Lynn, "Race Differences in Intelligence: A Global Perspective," *The Mankind Quarterly*, Vol. 31, No. 3 (Spring 1991), p. 255 passim.

27. Lynn, "Race Differences in Intelligence: A Global Perspective," p. 272.

28. Interview with the author.

29. Lynn, "Race Differences in Intelligence: A Global Perspective," p. 272.

30. Lynn, "Race Differences in Intelligence: A Global Perspective," p. 267; Kendall, Verster, and Mollendorf, "Test Performance of Blacks in Southern Africa," p. 300.

31. Steven Jay Gould, *The Mismeasure of Man* (Norton, 1981), p. 233.

32. Lynn, "Race Differences in Intelligence: A Global Perspective," p. 269.

33. Richard Lynn, Susan L. Hampson, and Sabura Iwakawi, "Abstract Reasoning and Spatial Abilities Among American, British and Japanese Adolescents," *The Mankind Quarterly*, Vol. 27, No. 4 (Summer 1987), p. 379.

34. Lynn, "IQ in Japan and the United States shows a growing disparity," *Nature*, Vol. 297 (May 20, 1982), pp. 222–223.

35. Harold Stevenson and Hiroshi Azuma, "IQ in Japan and the United States," *Nature*, Vol. 306 (November 17, 1983), pp. 291–292.

36. Lynn, "Abstract Reasoning and Spatial Abilities Among American, British, and Japanese Adolescents," pp. 400 and 401.

37. Lynn, "Race Differences in Intelligence: A Global Perspective," pp. 275, 278.

38. Lynn, "Race Differences in Intelligence: A Global Perspective," p. 284.

39. Geoffrey Cowley, "Testing the Science of Intelligence," *Newsweek*, October 24, 1994, p. 56.

21

"SCIENCE" IN THE SERVICE OF RACISM

C. Loring Brace

Thirty years ago, Charles Silberman made the somewhat belated observation that "the United States . . . is a racist society in a sense and to a degree that we have refused so far to admit, much less face" (1964, 9–10). This was written a decade after the United States Supreme Court in *Brown v Board of Education* declared that, since racially segregated schools were inherently unequal, the "separate-but-equal" educational policy widely followed since the *Plessy v Ferguson* decision of 1896 was unconstitutional. If there is one thing demonstrated by Herrnstein and Murray's new book, *The Bell Curve*, it is that Silberman's statement remains true a generation later. Despite all the denials, disclaimers, and dodges, and the straw men erected to test "other" views, this book is a manifestation of conclusions that are based, in a word, on racism.

It is a compendious tome, filled with graphs and charts. More than twenty chapters are apportioned into four parts, and each is provided with a copious section of notes at the end of the volume. (Incidentally, there is an error in the rendering of the formula for the standard deviation—presumably a proofreader's slip—in the notes on chapter 3). The notes are preceded by seven appendices for the presentation of material of a more technical or detailed nature than was deemed appropriate for the main text. Right at the beginning, the authors lay out their half dozen basic assumptions:

1) human cognitive ability is a single general entity—Spearman's "g"—in which there are individual and group differences;
2) IQ tests measure this accurately;
3) IQ tests measure how "smart" or "intelligent" people are;
4) IQ scores are fixed for much of a life span;
5) IQ tests are *not* biased in regard to "race," ethnic group, or social or economic status;
6) Cognitive ability has a heritability of between forty and eighty percent.

These six assumptions are presented at the beginning as "conclusions" that are "beyond significant technical dispute" (22). Actually, these points are taken as axiomatic to the extent that they are treated more as givens than as hypotheses open to test or falsification.

The only real concern in regard to the status of these assumptions in the whole volume is an occasional *ad hoc* effort to counter some of those who have demonstrated that one or another of them cannot be sustained. In truth, defense of the *status quo* (and particularly ante 1960) is obviously one of the main motivations. Since their first assumption concerning the reality and importance of "g" has no scientific basis (Flynn 1987*b*:20), assumptions two, three, and four become irrelevant. Assumptions five and six are both demonstrably false—points I shall return to later—which means that there is in fact no scientific justification for the book as a whole. The evident underlying thrust is a backward-looking nostalgia for an idealized rural past that is more myth than reality. In their efforts towards the resurrection of this unreal entity, they exemplify a traditional form of "political correctness" that enjoys wide credence at the present time, but it should never be confused with anything that could be called "science."

Part I presents the view that, in contrast to the hereditary stratification that used to characterize European countries, the United States of America is generating a "cognitive elite" with all of the desirable and high-paying positions going to the best and the brightest, and that these will in effect become an endogamous caste genetically distinct from the rest of the population. Part II develops the view that a consideration of "intelligence" is essential in order to make sense out of America's "social problems." Those "problems" are to be found where inherent intellectual incompetence inevitably generates poverty, low social status, and crime. These also are regarded as genetically destined to be self-perpetuating and, according to the authors' alarmist cant, they are disproportionately outbreeding everyone else—illustrating amongst other things the complete failure of the authors to comprehend the pattern of inheritance in a trait under complex polygenic control. Part III considers a national context of different ethnic constituents where each is assumed to differ in cognitive ability. The final section—Part IV—is entitled "Living Together," and it suggests that all would be well if the congenitally inferior could be brought to accept their lot and be happy hewing the wood and drawing the water for their cognitive betters. This again is far from anything that could be called "science," based as it is on an idealized myth of the America of some generations ago prior to the development of agribusiness, the postindustrial ghetto-isation of the cities, and the export of labor-intensive jobs to emerging Third-World work forces. The authors are realists enough to view the chances of "turning back the clock" as being highly unlikely. Their prognosis, then, is one of gloom and pessimism, but their conservative political convictions are such that they opt for the question that Cain chose as an answer to the Lord's query concerning the status of his brother rather than the one that Christ asked concerning who was a neighbor to whom in his parable of the Good Samaritan.

For such a ponderous work, it is eminently readable. The tone, however, alternates between patronizing condescension for the limited powers of comprehension granted to the greater bulk of humankind and a flattering inclusion of the reader into the lofty reaches of the "Very Bright." The "bell curve" of the title, of course, is the standard "normal distribution" that statisticians plot from the accumulated individual values for any measured aspect of the natural world. In this instance, it refers to the graphed results of human-intelligence measurements as they are derived from IQ scores. The authors divide the curve into five "Cognitive Classes": I, Very bright; II, Bright; III, Normal (fifty percent of the population); IV, Dull; and V, Very dull (which "sounds to us less damning than the standard 'retarded' ") (122). And you, dear reader—"meaning the self-selected person who has read this far into this book—and, in all likelihood, almost all of your friends and professional associates belong among the top 5% in that Class I slice" (121)

The book is a working example of how to mobilize statistics to support claims that are in direct contradiction to the data used. More than one reviewer has already noted that Herrnstein and Murray have started with a preconceived political position—and assumption that current social organization in the United States, the status quo, is the way things ought to be—and that this is just the inevitable result of the biologically innate capabilities of the various constituent human groups involved (Gould 1994; Lane 1994; Beardsley 1995; Kamin 1995). If there is a hierarchy of social stratification with a causative "racial" element, this is only to be expected, and it warrants documentation by quantitative methods. Differences in rank in that hierarchy are assumed to be the result of differences in general intelligence, and the authors start with the assumption that the latter is a single entity that corresponds to Spearman's "g." It is the same approach as that taken some years back by the Berkeley educational psychologist Arthur R. Jensen. Principal-components analysis will always generate a summary-first factor simply as a consequence of the method (Thurstone 1940: 208; Mercer 1988:202), but to invest this with identifiable meaning entails a substantial leap of faith based more on prior commitment than on anything inherently present in what is being analyzed. As has been previously noted, this is tantamount to "statistical theology," where "divinity" is denoted by a lower-case but italicized "g" (Brace 1980, 334).

In one of the most trenchant reviews of *The Bell Curve*, Stephen Jay Gould noted that not only is it biologically highly unlikely that human behavioral capacities should all be subsumed under a single entity called "g" or anything else, but also that the factor analysis studies of L. L. Thurstone have conclusively shown that human behavioral capability involves a series of unrelated and uncorrelated dimensions (Gould 1994, 144). Gould had made this point effectively in his book *The Mismeasure of Man* (1981, 310), and had gone on to quote John Stuart Mill on the human tendency to believe in the independent existence of whatever has received a name. He has used the occasion of his review to repeat his quote of Mill's observation, and the point should be well taken (1994, 149). Herrnstein and Murray, of course, are perfectly aware of the body of critical literature, but they have simply chosen to ignore it. This and the repeated instances of citing important studies and omitting their considered conclusions stimulated an angry Gould to comment on the "pervasive disingenuousness" of their course of argument (1994, 140), and Gould is absolutely right.

A manifestation of that disingenuousness can be seen in the fact that, although they recognize that heritability is not a property of traits but calculated from populations under given circumstances, nevertheless they go on to adopt a fixed figure of 0.6 for the heritability of intelligence which, they suggest with misplaced magnanimity, may err on the low side (105). What they never tell the reader is that heritability is not a fixed measure of the contribution made by heredity: it is actually a measure of the *proportion* of the relative variance of the environmental and genetic contributions (Feldman and Lewontin 1975). In fact, the magnitude of "heritability" actually serves as an indicator of favorable environmental circumstances. Under optimum developmental conditions where all individuals have the best possible chance for the realization of genetic potential, the only measurable differences will be those contributed by the genes. Where conditions are least favorable for the realization of genetic potential, "heritability" will be at a minimum.

Heritability can vary between 0.0 and 1.0 for the same subjects, and the differences in its value, rather than saying anything about variation in the genetic contribution, actually serve as an inverse measure of *environmental* influence on the development of the trait in question—a point that is the complete antithesis of what is assumed by the authors of this book. An illustration of this can be seen in the fact that the measured heritability of intelligence varies from 0.8 in the affluent white suburbs that Arthur Jensen uses as his standard (Jensen 1969*b*) to 0.4 for the indigent inner cities (Scarr-Salapatek 1971).

Gould also noted that the chosen multiple regression technique favored by Herrnstein and Murray yields only very low levels of association. Building on that, one could add that the authors have also ignored a fundamental caveat of scientific research: correlation does not necessarily have anything to do with cause (Kamin 1986, 1995). In a number of instances, they have evidently chosen to regard their observed correlations as documentation for cause-and-effect conclusions when in fact the studies they have cited have demonstrated that this is not the case. The correlations are real enough, but it is just possible that the reasons may be precisely the opposite of those favored by the authors; that is, high socioeconomic status may actually be part of the circumstances that create high IQ scores in the offspring raised by those who have been born to privilege. Herrnstein and Murray never consider the possibility that status may be as important in creating IQ as IQ is in creating status, and they do not consider how one would test that question although they cite the literature that actually deals with such problems (Skodak and Skeels 1949; Scarr and Weinberg 1976, 1978, 1983; Horn 1983; Stevenson and Azuma 1983; Weinberg et al. 1992). And then they simply ignore the conclusions.

This brings up the question of the possibility of test bias, an issue that was treated at exhaustive if irrelevant length by Jensen in his *Bias In Mental Testing* (1980). Herrnstein and Murray follow Jensen in denying that bias in the tests can account for the mean "racial" differences in the scores achieved, but like Jensen, they make no effort to assure that the background conditions of those being tested are certified as being equal. They continue the tradition of noting that, since IQ tests predict school performance quite well, by definition they are not biased. In effect, the IQ test is regarded as a yardstick, and there can be nothing inherently biased about such a measuring instrument. The problem lies in the meaning of what is being measured. The unbiased results of the use of a yardstick to measure stature of Americans of African ancestry prior to the turn of the century would have indicated that African-Americans could never anticipate success as basketball players. The same yardstick applied to African-Americans born after World War II, however, leads to very different conclusions. In like fashion, the rise in IQ scores in the European-American population over the span of a single generation starting in the early 1930s is almost exactly equal to the present African-American/European-American difference, although there is no faint hint that a genetic change of any sort has been involved (Flynn 1984). Evidently, then, IQ tests are no better at automatically getting at the underlying inherited intellectual essence of the human mind than yardsticks are at getting at the inherited linear essence of the human body. The bias comes on the part of those who assume that tests, administered without any attempt to control for other contributing factors, can reveal a single inherited essence. Like Jensen, Herrnstein and Murray are quick to draw conclusions that express their preconceived bias.

Since the authors take it as axiomatic that human variation is best understood in terms of group differences and that there must by definition be cognitive differences between those groups, they charge that it is just an elitist liberal hypocrisy to refuse to talk about "it" (297). Although they assume as a given that the "cognitive elite" deserves its dominant status because of its genetic superiority, yet when members of that same group, presumably as a result of their inherited intelligence, articulate the warning that *The Bell Curve* is a product of the politics of self-interest by an *economic* elite and not the result of science, they denigrate this as merely representing "the elite wisdom" (315). "Elite" is used as a word of praise when linked with "cognitive," but denigration when its exemplars disagree with the authors' politically based stance.

Gould has complained that Herrnstein and Murray have in fact created an unwarranted cognitive entity by the expedient of lumping all aspects of the cognitive domain under a single simplistic name—"g." In like fashion, a similar complaint should be raised concerning their assumption of another unwarranted entity that exists solely by virtue of the assignation of another simplistic name—this being "race." They have at least recognized one minor critique of that concept in noting the problem of discerning biological boundaries between human populations, but, while they grant the existence of "blurred lines," they never doubt the essential reality of "the races" in the first place (296). They never once consider the possibility that human biological variation can only be understood when the concept of "race" is abandoned, and that the biologically adaptive dimensions in which people differ are best understood when each is handled separately in terms of its own clinal distribution (Livingstone 1962, 1964; Brace 1964, 1995*a*, n.d.; Brace and Hunt 1990). Instead, they state that "Races are by definition groups of people who differ in characteristic ways" (272)—whatever that may mean—and then, ignoring the actual nature of human variation, they "classify people according to the way they classify themselves" (271). Their classification, then, is at best a kind of folk taxonomy without any validity from the perspective of evolutionary biology.

On top of all this, the authors never consider the likelihood that, for very good evolutionary reasons, cognitive ability, of all the significant adaptive aspects of human variation, may very well be the only one that does *not* vary in clinal fashion—being uniformly distributed throughout the human world (Brace 1995*b*, 177). Even to consider this is something that they put down to an almost hysterical "denial" on the part of "the elite" (315) or "conventional wisdom" (23, 70). They do not pursue the issue very far, but their evident role model in the use of "g," Arthur R. Jensen, has attempted to justify the assumption that there are significant "racial" differences in cognitive ability by suggesting that the various living "races" are adapted to the "civilizations" with which they are associated (1969*a*, 14).

Here is where a bit of anthropological perspective is sorely needed. In fact *no* present human population is living under the circumstances that served to shape the human condition in the past. Even the often-maligned Australian aborigines were pursuing an extraordinarily sophisticated post-Pleistocene form of Mesolithic subsistence strategy with all kinds of complicated resource extraction techniques that allowed them to take advantage of a spectrum and quantity of plant foods not available for human use throughout the span of the Pleistocene when human cognitive capabilities were being evolved (Brace 1995*b*, 130). From two million to ten thousand years ago, whether people lived in the tropics or the temperate zone, the problems that had to be overcome by human ingenuity were essentially the same from one end of the inhabited world to the other (Brace 1995*b*, 177). This is overwhelmingly documented by the essential functional identity of human tool categories at any one time throughout the entire span of human existence. This picture only began to change with the development of farming within the last 10,000 years. The consequent measurable changes during this period are best shown in the single most well-preserved and easily measured aspect of human form—the teeth. During this time span, these have undergone a reduction of ten percent at most, and even this is barely distinguishable from measurement error (Brace et al. 1987, 1991). There is no justifiable reason for expecting that cognitive capacities, with their vastly more complex genetic background, should have changed as much, or even that they should have changed at all (Brace 1980).

While Herrnstein and Murray deride those who they claim deny the role of heredity in contributing to cognitive ability—and they grossly overstate their case—on their own part, they simply dismiss the evidence that supports any important environmental contribution to the kind of record of intellectual achievement that is actually shown on IQ tests. In the most careful long-term study of the effects of transracial adoption, it has been shown that infants of African-American parentage raised in upper-middle-class European-American homes have IQ scores a full standard deviation above the scores of their biological parents, being slightly higher than the European-American mean value (Scarr and Weinberg 1976, 1978, 1983; Weinberg et al. 1992). This difference is fully the equivalent of the mean-measured differences between African-American and European-American scores for the population at large. The authors of these studies, after all due caveats and considerations, have concluded that this is clearly the result of the nongenetic contributions made by the environment in the adoptive homes.

The authors of *The Bell Curve*, however, simply ignore those considered conclusions and restrict their focus to the mean fifteen-point IQ deficit displayed by Americans of African ancestry when their scores are compared with those of European origin. Without taking into account the legacy of slavery, segregation, social barriers, and substandard educational opportunities, the authors remain true to their *a priori* assumptions that the difference is solely of genetic origin. Given their faith in that conviction and the fact that the genetic make-up of African-Americans, on the average, is between one-quarter and one-third European, with its presumably "superior" cognitive contribution, the authors conclude that the obvious reason for those lower scores is the genetic input from an original African source of still lower cognitive capability. This then impelled them to look for evidence indicating intellectual inferiority in native Africans. For this, they turned to the Ulster racialist Richard Lynn, who has defended the view that indigenous African IQ is approximately yet another standard deviation below that reported for African-Americans (Lynn 1991). At that, Lynn simply left out mention of the Soweto-township high-school sample where the black Matrices score is higher than the British norm (Owen 1992:150; Kamin 1995:100).

What *The Bell Curve* authors do not say, however, is that those figures he assembled come principally from simple diagram tests administered in the segregated, substandard school systems in KwaZulu and the Transvaal in South Africa, and that there is no defensible way of converting those scores into IQ figures (Owen 1992, 149; Kamin 1995, 100). These were used by the advocates of *apartheid* for the purpose of defending their own cherished racist ideology. The majority of the testees had such a rudimentary comprehension of English that the instructions had to be given by gestures. In spite of the fact that the administrator of the tests felt that no confidence could be extended to the scores generated (Lane 1994:16), our authors have seen nothing amiss in the conversion of those results into IQ scores and using this instance to generalize about all the inhabitants of the continent of Africa past and present (289). This, then, is the source of their conviction that the non-European ancestors of African-Americans were congenitally ranked in the lowest of the categories in their IQ spectrum.

When the generally high performance of those of East Asian ancestry is recognized, Herrnstein and Murray declare that this as the result of an inherited "racial" element. Although they cite the work of Harold Stevenson and his colleagues, they omit mention of the fact that this has concluded, after extensive and elegant analysis, that the basic reasons are to be found in the value of intellectual performance stressed by the families and the societies in which the subjects were raised (Stevenson and Azuma 1983; Stevenson et al. 1993). The high IQ scores achieved by East Asians and Jews are much more likely to be because those two groups represent the bearers of the two oldest traditions of unbroken literate continuity in the world than because there is anything inherently biological in the literary achievements of their representatives. In each of those traditions, the stress on intellectual achievement is valued both for the family honor and for the individual satisfaction to be gained. Both of those examples illustrate what has been called "behavioral Lamarckism" (Angier 1995, B9), where maternal investment in the shaping of behavioral styles and the transmission of social learning can continue for generations in the absence of selecting control by any genetic aspect of variation (Avital et al. 1994). And of course the converse is equally true for those descendants of a formerly enslaved group where any recognized connection between lifetime success and intellectual performance was either completely absent or actively discouraged.

In addition to the various adoption studies that fundamentally belie the whole Herrnstein-Murray hypothesis, there are two other sets of data that are at least as damaging. On the one hand, there is an accumulation of evidence which shows that IQ has risen dramatically over the span of a single generation in a whole series of countries. In a good half dozen of these, the rise has been by fifteen points or even more, which is greater than the maximum difference between the "races" tested (Flynn 1987*a*). In these instances, however, there is no hint of genetic change or population replacement. Nor is there any evidence for differential reproduction or drastic selection at work. As in comparable changes in stature that have taken place in various parts of the world over the last century-and-a-half, these are obviously "secular" rather than genetic changes and simply reflect alterations in environmental conditions.

Finally, Herrnstein and Murray have taken the evidence for higher visuospatial and lesser verbal scores on the parts of Chinese, Japanese, Inuit, and Amerindian samples as evidence for a "common genetic history of racial East Asians" (301). The score differences involved are not very large, but they are persistent. Presumably the tests performed in Asia are not "biased" because they were administered in the languages of the students involved. What the reader is not told, however, is the fact that the very business of learning to read Chinese characters (*zi* in Chinese and *kanji* in Japanese) requires a visuospatial kind of learning completely absent in what is needed to master the Western alphabet (Chan and Vernon 1988, 346). In addition, the tests were administered via the written language. However, mastering a reading vocabulary in a language that is based on ideographs entails a process of rote memory to an extent not true in the Western world where, with the use of prefixes, suffixes and roots, one can readily identify the meaning of words never before encountered. There is no such comparable possibility in Chinese or Japanese, and the number of words in the reading vocabulary of a literate East Asian is always less for a given educational level than is true in the West.

As for the Inuit and Amerindians, they were not tested in their native languages, which could well account for lower verbal scores. Furthermore, since most of those groups were still engaged in hunting and foraging, they had been raised in circumstances where the use of spatial memory had been honed since infancy. Consequently, visuospatial recognition was developed to a high degree (McShane and Berry 1988). When one takes all of this into account, Herrnstein and Murray's confident pronouncement that "Any simple socioeconomic, cultural, or linguistic explanation is out of the question" (301) constitutes an assertion that is transparently without foundation.

One of the themes that reverberates throughout the book is the sense of alarm expressed by the claim that the people who represent the lower tail of the IQ curve are reproducing at a much greater rate than the people who represent the Bright and Very Bright end. Although they repeatedly state that "it matters little whether the genes are involved at all" (312), this is simply a continuing manifestation of their pervasive disingenuousness. The whole message of the book is that genetically determined capabilities are of vital significance for the future of society, and the authors regularly and erroneously denounce other scholars for denying a genetic component in the realization of intelligence. If the reader has fallen for their grossly and simplistically unacceptable assumptions concerning the inheritance of intelligence, then one can hardly avoid their

implied but coyly unstated conclusion that the population of the
United States of America is sliding into a sink of genetically determined stupidity. It is the same view as the one expressed by that
inflammatory bigot Lothrop Stoddard in his tract *The Revolt Against
Civilization*, subtitled *The Menace of the Under-Man* (1922), a work
which followed his influential book *The Rising Tide of Color: Against
White World-Supremacy* (1920). The "under-man"—"the underclass" in the current version (518)—is said to be alive and well and
reproducing himself with alarming speed in the scenario presented
by Herrnstein and Murray.

   This gambit had been previously expressed by Stoddard's friend,
Madison Grant, in *The Passing of the Great Race: Or the Racial Basis
of European History* (1916). These works conditioned the American
public to support the passage of the Immigration Restriction Act of
1924 and to give favorable consideration to Harry Laughlin's Model
Sterilization Law, which was adopted with such enthusiasm by Nazi
Germany in 1933. Madison Grant, on his part, contributed money
for the establishment of the Pioneer Fund in 1936, a source of support for the eugenics movement and for the promotion of Nazi
racial propaganda in America (Allen 1986, 246). As Stefan Kühl has
recently observed, the list of recent recipients of Pioneer Fund
grants "reads like a 'Who's Who' of scientific and political racism
in the United States, Canada, Great Britain, and Ireland" (1994, 9).
It is interesting to note that the surviving author of *The Bell Curve*,
Charles Murray, has refused a request to be interviewed on his relationship with the Pioneer Fund (ABC World News Tonight, Nov.
22, 1994).

   I began this review with the claim that, in essence, *The Bell Curve*
is a manifestation of "racism." In saying this, I have used the word
in Todorov's sense as an "ubiquitous form of behavior" directed
towards representatives of a perceived "race." This is in contradis-
tinction to his use of the word "racialism" as merely indicating the
assumption that particular physical and behavioral characteristics are
associated with each supposed "race" (Todorov 1985, 372; and note

that this, in effect, is the opposite of the meanings assigned by Banton 1967, 8). Gates has complained that the racist's "error" is also one of "thought" as well as of behavior (1985, 404), and it is a legitimate issue. Not to make too fine a point of it, however, the real manifestation of damage comes with action, and it is useful to have a definition of "racism" that can be specifically measured in terms of its tangible consequences.

Elsewhere Murray has declared that "there is no such thing as an undeserving five-year-old" (1984, 223). However, one of the main points of *The Bell Curve* is that such programs as welfare and Head Start should be abolished. Evidently the five-year-olds who will be affected deserve the consequences of the poverty of their parents who in turn are poor because they are considered to be stupid and, in large numbers, presumed to be stupid because of their African heritage. At bottom, then, those five-year-olds presumably deserve the consequences of their position because of their perceived "race." By the definitions I have adopted above, it is clear that those who would devise and implement such policies are "racists," which is why *The Bell Curve* is "a manifestation" of "racism."

The final chapter of the book is entitled "A Place for Everyone," and it advocates a return to the fabled "individualism" of yesteryear and the situation where social control was vested in the "neighborhood" or "municipality." This is nothing less than the argument for "states' rights" that the Southern states had promoted from before the Civil War in their effort to defend their "peculiar institution," and it was the same argument that led to the disenfranchisement of African-Americans as Reconstruction collapsed during the 1870s and slavery was re-established in everything but the name. The adage from which the chapter title was borrowed tacitly suggests its completion. And if indeed "A Place for Everyone" implies, in addition, "Everyone in His Place," presumably there will always be a representative of the "cognitive elite" to emulate the youthful Charles Murray and burn a cross on a nearby hill (De Parle 1994, 51) just in case the genetically determined mental defectives need to be reminded to stay in their appropriate place and not get too uppity.

Not one of the often-reviled students of sociobiology has suggested such a grim picture of rigid biological predestination. Perhaps those almost Calvinistic echoes may account for its popularity with the American public. As an antidote, the reader would do well to peruse the arguments amassed two years earlier in *The Learning Gap* (Stevenson and Stigler 1992), a work ignored by Herrnstein and Murray. This amounts to a definitive rebuttal of *The Bell Curve* written in advance. After comparing the patterns of expectation and achievement in Asian and American traditions of education, the authors in essence predict Herrnstein and Murray's forthcoming assertions of prejudice, and comment: "We suggest that the American emphasis on innate abilities is harmful and is undermining the pursuit of public education—indeed, of democracy itself" (Stevenson and Stigler 1992, 95).

As a whole, *The Bell Curve* is a massive manifestation of genteel bigotry. Herrnstein and Murray have used their status and authority to cram several categories of Americans into a single Procrustean bed imposed despite the fact that their backgrounds are not comparable. The different degrees of fit are assigned different values in the same manner that the hierarchy of worth was assumed by the Europeans who initially conquered the Western hemisphere. That evaluation of differential worth is at bottom a reflection of long-standing political power. *The Bell Curve*, then, is a creation of Political Correctness, and, when it is used to justify social inequalities in the world to which it is applied, it can only have suffocating consequences of the same kind that Sylvia Plath perceived as she contemplated the descent of an imagined *Bell Jar* over her own unhappy self (1966, 196). Both instances are manifestations of an evident departure from sanity.

REFERENCES

Angier, N. 1995. Heredity's more than genes, new theory proposes. *New York Times.* Jan. 3:B5, B9.

Allen, G. E. 1986. The eugenics record office at Cold Spring Harbor, 1910–1940: An essay in institutional history. *Osiris* 2:225–264.

Avital, E., and E. Jablonka. 1994. Social learning and the evolution of behaviour. *Animal Behaviour* 48:1195–1199.

Banton, M. 1967. *Race relations.* London: Tavistock Publications.

Beardsley, T. 1995. For whom the bell curve really tolls. *Scientific American* 272:14, 16–17.

Brace, C. L. 1964. "A non-racial approach toward the understanding of human diversity." In *The Concept of Race,* ed. M. F. A. Montagu, 103–152. New York: The Free Press.

———. 1980. Social bias in mental testing. Review of *Bias in Mental Testing* by Arthur R. Jensen. *The Behavioral and Brain Sciences* 3:333–334.

———. 1995a. Region does not mean race: Reality vs. convention in forensic identification. *Journal of Forensic Sciences* 40:29–33.

———. 1995b. 5th edition. *The stages of human evolution.* Englewood Cliffs. N.J.: Prentice-Hall.

———. 1995. "A four-letter word called 'race.' " In *Race and Other Miscalculations, and Mismeasures: Papers in Honor of Ashley Montagu,* ed. L. J. Reynolds and L. Lieberman. Dix Hills, N.Y.: General Hall Publishers.

Brace, C. L., and K. D. Hunt. 1990. A non-racial craniofacial perspective on human variation: A(ustralia) to Z(uni). *American Journal of Physical Anthropology* 88:341–360.

Brace, C. L., K. R. Rosenberg, and K. D. Hunt. 1987. Gradual change in human tooth size in the late Pleistocene and post-Pleistocene. *Evolution* 41:705–720.

Brace, C. L., S. L. Smith, and K. D. Hunt. 1991. "What big teeth you had Grandma! Human tooth size past and present," in *Advances in Dental Anthropology,* ed. M. A. Kelley and C. S. Larsen, 33–57. N.Y.: Wiley-Liss.

Chan, J. W. C., and P. E. Vernon. 1988. "Individual differences among the peoples of China." In *Human Abilities in Cultural Context,* ed. J. W. Berry, 340–357. Cambridge: Cambridge University Press.

De Parle, J. 1994. Daring research or 'social science pornography'? Charles Murray. *New York Times Magazine,* Oct. 9:48–53, 62, 70–71, 74, 78, 80.

Feldman, M. W., and R. C. Lewontin. 1975. The heritability hang-up. *Science* 190: 1163–1168.

Flynn, J. R. 1984. The mean IQ of Americans: Massive gains 1932 to 1978. *Psychological Bulletin* 95:29–51.

———. 1987a. Massive IQ gains in 14 nations: What IQ tests really measure. *Psychological Bulletin* 101:171–191.

———. 1987b. "The ontology of intelligence." In *Measurement, Realism and Objectivity: Essays on Measurement in the Social and Physical Sciences,* ed. J. Forge, 1–40. Dordrecht: D. Reidel Publishing Company.

Gates, H. L., Jr. 1985. "Talkin' that talk," in *"Race," Writing, and Difference,* ed. H. L. Gates, Jr., 402–409. Chicago: University of Chicago Press.

Gould, S. J. 1981. *The Mismeasure of Man.* N.Y.: W. W. Norton.

———. 1994. Curveball. Review of *The Bell Curve*, by R. J. Herrnstein and C. Murray. *New Yorker* 70:139–149.

Grant, M. 1916. *The Passing of the Great Race: Or the racial basis of European history.* N.Y.: C. Scribner's Sons.

Horn, J. M. 1983. The Texas adoption project: Adopted children and their intellectual resemblance to biological and adoptive parents. *Child development* 54:268–275.

Jensen, A. R. 1969a. Edited reply to letter by D. N. Robinson. *New York Times Magazine.* Sept. 21, 14.

———. 1969b. How much can we boost IQ and scholastic achievement? *Harvard Educational Review* 39:1–123.

———. 1980. *Bias in mental testing.* N.Y.: The Free Press.

Kamin, L. J. 1986. Is crime in the genes? The answer may depend on who chooses what evidence. Review of *Crime and Human Welfare*, by J. Q. Wilson and R. J. Herrnstein. *Scientific American* 254:22–27.

———. 1995. Behind the curve. Review of *The Bell Curve*, by R. J. Herrnstein and C. Murray. *Scientific American* 272:99–103.

Kühl, S. 1994. *The Nazi Connection: Eugenics, American racism and German national socialism.* N.Y.: Oxford University Press.

Lane, C. 1994. The tainted sources of *The Bell Curve. The New York Review of Books* 41:14–19.

Livingstone, F. B. 1962. On the non-existence of human races. *Current Anthropology* 3:279–281.

———. 1964. "On the nonexistence of human races." In *The Concept of Race*, ed. M. F. A. Montagu, 46–60. N. Y.: The Free Press.

Lynn, R. 1991. Race differences in intelligence: A global perspective. *Mankind Quarterly* 31:254–296.

McShane, D., and J. W. Berry. 1988. "Native North Americans: Indians and Inuit abilities," in *Human Abilities in Cultural Context*, ed. S. H. Irvine and J. W. Berry, 385–426. Cambridge: Cambridge University Press.

Mercer, J. R. 1988. Ethnic difference in IQ scores: What do they mean? (A response to Lloyd Dunn). *Hispanic Journal of Behavioral Science* 10:199–218.

Murray, C. A. 1984. *Losing Ground: American social policy 1950–1980.* N.Y.: Basic Books.

Owen, K. 1992. The suitability of Raven's Standard Progressive Matrices for various groups in South Africa. *Personality and Individual Differences* 13:149–159.

Plath, S. 1966. *The Bell Jar.* London: Faber Paperbacks.

Scarr, S., and R. A. Weinberg. 1976. IQ test performance of black children adopted by white families. *American Psychologist* 31:726–739.

———. 1978. The influence of "family background" on intellectual attainment. *American Sociological Review* 43:674–692.

———. 1983. The Minnesota adoption studies: Genetic differences and malleability. *Child Development* 54:260–267.

Scarr-Salapatek, S. 1971. Race, social class, and IQ. *Science* 174:1285–1295.

Silberman, C. E. 1964. *Crisis in black and white.* N.Y.: Random House.

Skodak, M., and H. M. Skeels. 1949. A final follow-up study of one hundred adopted children. *The Journal of Genetic Psychology* 75:85–125.

Stevenson, H. W., and H. Azuma. 1983. IQ in Japan and the United States: Methodological problems in Lynn's analysis. *Nature* 306:291–292.

Stevenson, H. W., C. Chen and S-Y. Lee. 1993. Mathematics achievement of Chinese, Japanese, and American children: Ten years later. *Science* 259:53–58.

Stevenson, H. W., and J. W. Stigler. 1992. *The Learning Gap: Why our schools are failing and what we can learn from Japanese and Chinese education.* N.Y.: Summit Books.

Stoddard, L. 1920. *The Rising Tide of Color: Against white world-supremacy.* N.Y.: Blue Ribbon Books.

———. 1922. *The Revolt Against Civilization: The menace of the under-man.* N.Y.: Charles Scribner's Sons.

Thurstone, L. L. 1940. Current issues in factor analysis. *Psychological Bulletin* 37:189–236.

Todorov, T. 1985. " 'Race,' writing, and culture, in *"Race," Writing, and Difference,* ed. H. L. Gates, Jr., 370–380. Chicago: University of Chicago Press.

Weinberg, R. A., S. Scarr and I. D. Waldman. 1992. The Minnesota transracial adoption study: A follow-up of IQ test performance at adolescence. *Intelligence* 16: 117–135.

22

HOW HERITABILITY MISLEADS ABOUT RACE[1]

Ned Block

The Bell Curve's main argument for black genetic inferiority in IQ
depends for its persuasive force on conceptual confusions that have
been tacitly accepted to some degree even by many of the book's
sharpest critics. The book contains two lines of thought. One, which
I will accept for present purposes, is: that IQ tests substantially measure "general intelligence," that IQ is socially important, and that
IQ is sixty percent heritable within whites. (I'll explain heritability
below.) The second main line of thought—which I will be contesting—is the argument for genetic inferiority of American blacks. Before I get to their argument for this conclusion, I want to be clear
about the conclusion itself. Murray has recently complained about
misinterpretation in an article entitled "The Real Bell Curve" (Murray 1994). He grumbles about critics, such as Stephen Jay Gould,
who read the book as saying that racial differences in IQ are mostly
genetic. He quotes from the book:

> If the reader is now convinced that either the genetic or environmental
> explanations have won out to the exclusion of the other, we have not
> done a sufficiently good job of presenting one side or the other. It
> seems highly likely to us that both genes and environment have some-
> thing to do with racial differences. What might the mix be? We are

Reprinted with permission from *The Journal of Cognition*, published by Elsevier Science B.V. Copyright ©1995 by Elsevier Science B.V.

resolutely agnostic on that issue; as far as we can determine, the evidence does not yet justify an estimate." (*Bell*, 311)

But the *resolute agnosticism* we see here is on the issue of which is *more* responsible for the low IQs of blacks, bad environment or genetic inferiority. What they are very much *not* agnostic about is that *part* of the IQ difference between blacks and whites is genetic, and (given their way of thinking about the matter) to the extent that *any* of this difference is genetic, blacks are genetically inferior.[2]

What is their argument? It proceeds from two facts: the first is the 60 percent heritability of IQ within whites and the second is the average fifteen point IQ difference between whites and blacks.[3] A crude version of the argument goes like this. If IQ were completely genetic in whites and completely genetic in blacks, the IQ difference between whites and blacks would have to be completely genetic; but given that IQ is *largely* genetic (at least in whites), surely it is very probable that the IQ difference between blacks and whites is at least *partly* genetic in origin. The argument is more subtle than that; they raise issues about the pattern and the magnitude of the differences that I will get to later.

Herrnstein and Murray's argument depends on thinking of the fifteen-point IQ difference as divisible into a genetic chunk and an environmental chunk. This way of thinking dictates the following three alternatives:

Extreme Environmentalism	Blacks are genetically on a par with whites, so all of the IQ gap is environmental
Extreme Geneticism	Blacks are environmentally on a par with whites, so all of the IQ gap is genetic.
The Reasonable View	Blacks are worse off *both* genetically and environmentally: some of the gap is genetic, some environmental.

Option 1, Extreme Environmentalism, is thought to be excluded by the 60 percent heritability of IQ. Option 2, an equally Extreme Geneticism, is excluded by well-known environmental effects on IQ together with differences between black and white environments that are acknowledged by Herrnstein and Murray. So we are left with option 3, which on this way of putting the matter is The Reasonable View—and it postulates *some black genetic inferiority*. But their way of putting the alternatives blots out a *crucial possibility*, namely that blacks are *much* worse off than whites environmentally and actually *better* off genetically. Allowing this option, we get a different set of alternatives: *genetically, blacks are worse off—or better off—or equal to whites.*

The idea of the missing alternative arises from the possibility that genetic IQ differences and actual measured IQ differences go in *opposite directions*. Even if you think that races are likely to differ genetically in IQ, the question remains of the *direction* of the genetic difference. In this scenario, black environments for the development of IQ are on the average sufficiently worse than white environments as to lower average black IQ *more* than fifteen points. I don't say that this is *likely*, but I do say it is *possible*, and its possibility is important. What you consider as *possible* affects what you think is an *extremist* position. The critics of Herrnstein and Murray have tended to trip over this possibility.

For example, in a *New York Times* op-ed critique that describes *The Bell Curve* as "bogus" and "nothing but a racial epithet" (Herbert 1994), Bob Herbert insists that "the overwhelming consensus of experts in the field is that environmental conditions account for most of the disparity when the test results of large groups are compared." In effect, he uses known environmental effects on IQ to argue for a *low degree of genetic inferiority* in blacks. Even Stephen Jay Gould (in an otherwise excellent article in *The New Yorker* [Gould 1994]) missteps here. Apparently accepting *The Bell Curve's* way of conceiving of the issue, he complains that Herrnstein and Murray wrongly minimize the large environmental malleability of

IQ. He says that they turn "every straw on their side into an oak, while mentioning but downplaying the strong circumstantial case for substantial malleability and little average genetic difference." Gould does little to guard against the natural interpretation of "little average genetic difference" in the context of discussion of *The Bell Curve* as *little average genetic inferiority of blacks*. Jim Holt's critique in the *New York Times* (Holt 1994) asks "How then do we account for the sizable gap in measured IQ?" and then goes on to emphasize prenatal explanations of most of "the racial gap." (Low birth weight is almost three times as common in black babies as in white babies; see Lieberman 1995.) But if one accepts the Herrnstein and Murray framework, it is a *stretch* to appeal to prenatal differences to reduce the size of the genetic inferiority all the way to zero. A somewhat different version of the same fallacy is a misplaced agnosticism. *U.S. News & World Report* (Leo 1994), attempting to be neutral and unbiased, says of the IQ gap that "we don't know . . . how much is genetic, or how much environmental factors are responsible." That is, we don't know *how genetically inferior* blacks are. The *expectation*, that is, is that blacks are genetically inferior to *some* extent, but lacking information, we don't know *how much*. A number of the critics in *The New Republic* (Oct. 31, 1994), in turn, wonder about the size of the "genetic component of the black-white difference" (10), thereby buying into the same way of thinking. Again, we can see that what you take as possible affects what you take as actual. As with the passage from Herrnstein and Murray that I quoted earlier, agnosticism ends up as agnosticism about just how genetically inferior blacks are.

If you accept *The Bell Curve's* way of putting the options, evidence for environmental effects at best shows that the amount of genetic inferiority is little or nothing, and so the critics find themselves up against the wall of zero genetic difference. Given the set of alternatives provided by Herrnstein and Murray, the idea that the environmental difference between blacks and whites is big enough to account for fifteen IQ points looks like an *extremist* hypothesis. But given the *actual* alternatives, that blacks are genetically on a par with whites, or worse off, or better off, zero genetic difference doesn't seem extremist at all.

But isn't the idea of black genetic superiority in IQ a desperate and pathetic attempt to exploit a mere logical possibility? Roses are red, violets are blue. Color is genetic, so the color difference is genetic. Is there any real possibility that the genetic color difference is the opposite of the observed one? Toe number is genetic in sloths and in humans, and humans are observed to have five toes whereas sloths (that is, the diurnal sloths) are observed to have three toes. Is there any real possibility that the genetic toe difference between humans and sloths goes in the *opposite direction* from the observed toe-number gap? Well, there is a very remote possibility that the three-toed sloth evolved six toes, but the three toes we observe are a result of a thalidomide-like chemical which has polluted their food during the years in which we have observed them.[4] But this possibility is only worth mentioning as an example of something *extremely unlikely*. And that leads to a principle that underlies all of Herrnstein and Murray's thinking on race even though it is never articulated. Recall that the crude form of their argument is that if IQ were completely genetic in blacks and whites, then the black-white difference would have to be completely genetic as well; so given that IQ is sixty percent heritable within whites, very likely the black-white difference is partly genetic. The underlying principle is: *if a characteristic is largely genetic and there is an observed difference between two groups, then there is "highly likely"* (I allude to their term from the passage quoted in the first paragraph of this article) *to be a genetic difference between the two groups that goes in the same direction as the observed difference.* So given the substantial heritability of IQ, if East Asians are superior in measured IQ, then they are highly likely to be *genetically* superior; and if blacks are inferior in measured IQ, then they are highly likely to be *genetically* inferior in IQ.

Here is a roadmap to the rest of this article. The principle just mentioned is right on one sense of "genetic" and wrong on another.

However, the sense in which it is *wrong* is the one that employs the figure of sixty percent heritability. In the sense in which the principle is right, IQ is not genetic. In the next section, I will explain the ambiguity in "genetic." Then I will explain why the principle just mentioned is wrong on the sense of "genetic" that really counts for their argument, *heritability*.

HERITABILITY VS. GENETIC DETERMINATION

The key to part of the fallacy of *The Bell Curve* is the distinction between two concepts: *genetic determination* and *heritability*. The concept of inheritance which allows us to speak of number of toes as genetic is the ordinary commonsensical idea of *genetic determination*. But the *scientific concept*, on which all Herrnstein's and Murray's data rely, is *heritability* and not *genetic determination*. Heritability has to do with what causes *differences* in a characteristic, whereas genetic determination is a matter of what causes the characteristic *itself*. Heritability of number of toes is a matter of genetic differences causing *variation* in number of toes, whereas it is the number of toes itself—not variation in it—that is genetically determined. Heritability is *defined* as a fraction: the ratio of *genetically caused* variation to *total* variation (environmental and genetic). *Genetic determination*, by contrast, is an informal and intuitive notion that has no quantitative definition (for reasons that I will explain later). It depends on the idea of a normal environment. A characteristic could be said to be genetically determined if it is coded in and caused by the genes and bound to develop in a normal environment. Genetic determination in a single person makes sense: my brown hair color is genetically determined. By contrast, heritability makes sense only relative to a population in which individuals differ from one another. You can't ask "What's the heritability of *my* IQ?"

We can get a handle on the difference by noticing that the number of fingers on a human hand or toes on a human foot is genetically determined: the genes code for five fingers and toes in almost everyone, and five fingers and toes develop in any normal environment. However, interestingly, the *heritability* of numbers of fingers and toes in humans is almost certainly very *low*. What's going on? If you look at cases of unusual numbers of fingers and toes, you find that most of the variation is environmentally caused, often by problems in fetal development. For example, when pregnant women took thalidomide some years ago, many babies had fewer than five fingers and toes. And if we look at numbers of fingers and toes in adults, we find many missing digits as a result of accidents. Genetic coding for six toes is rare in humans (though apparently not in cats). Heritability, you will recall, is a fraction, the ratio of genetically produced variation to total variation (total variation = variation due to all causes, genetic and environmental). If the genetically caused variation is small compared to the environmentally caused variation, then the heritability is low, even when the characteristic in question is genetically determined. So toe number is genetically determined but nonetheless low in heritability.[5]

Conversely, a characteristic can be *highly heritable* even if it is *not genetically determined*. Some years ago when only women wore earrings, the heritability of having an earring was high because differences in whether a person had an earring were "due" to a genetic (chromosomal) difference, XX vs XY. Now that earrings are less gender-specific, the heritability of having an earring has no doubt decreased. But neither then nor now was having earrings genetically determined in anything like the manner of having five fingers. The heritability literature is full of high measured heritabilities for characteristics whose genetic determination is doubtful. For example, the same methodology that yields 60 percent heritability for IQ also yields 50 percent heritability of academic performance and 40 percent heritability of occupational status (Plomin, DeFries and McClearn, 1990, 393). Obviously, occupational status is not genetically determined. The genes do not code for working in a printed-circuit factory. More significantly, a child's *environment* is often a heritable characteristic, strange as this may seem. If degree of musical talent is highly heritable and if variation in the number of music lessons a child gets depends on variation in musical talent, then the number of music lessons that a child gets may be heritable too, despite not being genetically determined. This is not an idle speculation. Recent studies of heritabilities of various features of children's environments show substantial heritabilities for many environmental features, for example, the "warmth" of the parents' behavior toward the child. Even number of hours of TV watched and number and variety of a child's toys shows some heritability (Plomin and Bergeman, 1991; see also Scarr and McCartney, 1983). If this seems unintelligible, think of it this way: variation in these environmental properties is in part due to variation in heritable characteristics of the child, and so the environmental characteristics themselves are heritable. People who read *The Bell Curve* often suppose that a heritable characteristic is one that is passed down in the genes, but this identification is importantly flawed. The number and variety of a child's toys is not passed down in the genes. Heritability is a matter of the causation of differences, not what is "passed down."

By contrast, a characteristic is genetically determined if the characteristic itself—not differences in it—is caused by the genes. A characteristic can be genetically determined even if there is no genetically caused variation. Number of heads in humans is genetically determined even if there is no genetic variation in number of heads at all. I've mentioned physical characteristics, but there are many mental features that are genetically determined too. For example, if you put a pacifier of one of a number of shapes (e.g., spherical or cubical or knobbly) in a newborn baby's mouth, the baby will look preferentially at a picture of the same shape. So something about the coordination between vision and feel is very likely genetically determined. But there may be little or no genetic variation in such mental characteristics, so they are genetically determined without, perhaps, being heritable.[6]

What "genetic determination" comes to depends heavily on what we count as a "normal" environment, as Kitcher (1996) notes. For example, we could think of a normal environment as one that is usual, or rather differently, as one that allows people to thrive, even if it is uncommon. On the former notion, PKU was once a genetically determined form of mental retardation. But on the latter, given that retardation can be avoided by a diet that is low in phenylalanine, it is not genetically determined. This example illustrates something that we will return to in the last section of the paper, namely that (as Kitcher notes), increasing knowledge often leads us to move from thinking of the genes determining X to the genes determining the tendency to develop X in certain environments. We now tend to think of what is genetically determined in the case of PKU not as retardation but rather as an inability to metabolize phenylalanine that can cause retardation if there is phenylalanine in the diet. (I am making use of a somewhat idealized description of PKU; I am told that a more complex picture is emerging.)

So what is genetically determined depends on what we count as a normal environment. But not so for heritability. It depends *not at all* on what environments are normal, but only on the balance of genetic and environmental differences in the causation of differences in the characteristic. We will return to this point later.

I have given examples of traits that are genetically determined but not heritable and, conversely, of traits that are heritable but not genetically determined. But the reader may be suspicious: what relevance do these weird examples have to the case of IQ? Maybe there is a range of normal cases, of which IQ is an example, for which the oddities that I've pointed to are just irrelevant?

Not so! In fact IQ is a great example of a trait that is highly heritable but not genetically determined. Recall that what makes toe number genetically determined is that having five toes is coded in and caused by the genes so as to develop in any normal environment. By contrast, IQ is enormously affected by *normal environmental variation* (and in ways that are not well understood). As Herrnstein and Murray concede, children from very low socioeco-

nomic status backgrounds who are adopted into high SES backgrounds have IQs that are dramatically higher than their parents.
The point is underscored by what Herrnstein and Murray call the
Flynn Effect: IQ has been rising about three points every ten years
worldwide. Since World War II, IQ in many countries has gone up
fifteen points, about the same as the gap separating blacks and
whites in this country. As Herrnstein and Murray note, no one
knows why IQ has been rising. In some countries, the rise has been
especially dramatic. For example, average IQ in Holland rose
twenty-one points between 1952 and 1982 (Flynn, 1987a). In a species in which toe number reacted in this way with environment (e.g.,
a centipede-like creature which grows legs depending on how much
it eats) I doubt that we would think of number of toes as genetically
determined. The dramatic rises in IQ in Holland (and other countries) is a very significant fact to which I will return.

I said that these dramatic increases in IQ show that IQ is enormously affected by normal environmental variation. But this claim
may appear to be in conflict with the following fact: that the correlations among adopted children in the same family are very small,
near zero, by late adolescence. (See Plomin and Daniels, 1987 and
Plomin and Bergeman, 1991.) Doesn't that show that normal environmental variation has no effect? This is the opposite of the correct conclusion from these data. The low correlations among
adopted children show that normal variation of the sort that exists
even *within* families has a large effect. It should also be noted that
the bottom of the socioeconomic distribution is scanted in these
data because this segment of the population is not favored by adoption agencies. Unfortunately, this segment of the population is all
too normal. So what does not appear to have much of an effect on
IQ (after adolescence) is variation in socioeconomic status within
the middle range, and in addition, number of books in the home,
cultural activities of the parents and the like—in short, the sort of
thing that psychologists measure about shared family environment.

One very important conclusion from both the Flynn data and the low-correlation data just mentioned is that no one understands very much about how environmental variation differentially affects IQ. The cause of the large increases in Holland is simply unknown. Even Herrnstein and Murray concede that of the environmental variation in IQ, "relatively little can be traced to the shared environments created by families. It is, rather, a set of environmental influences *mostly unknown at present*, that are experienced by individuals as individuals" (*Bell*, 108; emphasis added.)

The crucial factor that has enabled the research that Herrnstein and Murray report to exist at all is the fact that one can measure the heritability of a characteristic without even having much of an idea of what the characteristic *is*. We needn't know what IQ tests measure in order to calculate the heritability of IQ—we need only be able to measure IQ—whatever it is—in various circumstances. Suppose you could place two pairs of genetically identical (one-egg) twin human fetuses in randomly chosen wombs, and then give them IQ tests after they had grown up in different environments (including different prenatal environments). Suppose twins Sally and Sarah were reared in very different environments, one impoverished, the other rich in intellectual stimulation, yet both ended up with the same high IQ; and twins Fred and Ted, also reared in very different environments, both had the same low IQ. That would indicate that the genetic differences in the population were contributing more to IQ variation than the environmental differences. So heritability of IQ would be high. The opposite procedure would be rearing genetically unrelated individuals in the same environment (note— same environment, not similar family, since that appears not to provide the same environment). To the extent that heritability is high, unrelated children reared in the same environment should not resemble one another any more than people chosen at random from the population. To the extent that heritability is low, their IQs should be highly correlated.

A common method for measuring heritability relies on comparisons of the correlations of IQ among one-egg twins raised by their biological parents compared with two-egg twins raised by their biological parents. Suppose you give IQ tests to two children and they get the same score. One has a one-egg (identical) twin, the other has a two-egg (fraternal) twin. Suppose that you can predict the score of the one-egg twin reliably, but that your prediction of the score of the two-egg twin is much less reliable. This would be an indication of high heritability of IQ because one-egg twins share all their genes whereas two-egg twins normally share half their genes.

Heritability studies of IQ *within white* populations in the US and northern Europe have tended to yield moderately high heritabilities. Herrnstein and Murray's sixty percent is a reasonable figure. But it is important to note that no one would do one of these heritability studies in a mixed black/white population. Why not? If you place a pair of black one-egg twins in different environments "at random," you automatically fail to randomize environments, because the black twins will bring part of their environment with them; they are both black and will be treated as black.

I mentioned that heritability—unlike genetic determination—can be very different in different populations. For example, the heritability of IQ could be decreased if half the population were chosen at random to receive IQ-lowering brain damage. The quantity a/b gets smaller if b *gets larger*. By damaging the brains of some people, you make the environmentally caused variation larger. Another example that illustrates the same point: suppose we could make a million clones of Newt Gingrich, raising them in very different environments so there would be some variation in IQ, all environmentally caused. The quantity a/b is zero if a is zero. So heritability in that population would be zero because the ratio of genetic variation to total variation is zero if the genetic variation is zero. To take a real example, the heritability of IQ increases throughout childhood into adulthood. Plomin (1990a) gives heritability figures of under twenty percent in infancy, about thirty percent in childhood, fifty percent in adolescence, and a bit higher in adult life. (Plomin notes that the results are not a consequence of increasing reliability of IQ tests.) Studies of older twins in Sweden (Pedersen, et al. 1992) report an eighty percent heritability figure for adults by age fifty as compared to a fifty percent heritability for children. One possible reason for the rise in heritability is that although the genetic variation remains the same, environmental variation decreases with age. Children have very different environments; some parents don't speak to their children, others are ever verbally probing and jousting. Adults in industrialized countries, by contrast, are to a greater degree immersed in the same culture (e.g., the same TV programs). With more uniform environments, the heritability goes up.[7] Heritability can even be different in men and women. Suppose, for example, that variation in hair length in women depends on heritable variation in the hair itself, whereas hair length in men depends on nonheritable variation in conventions in peer groups. Then hair length would have higher heritability in women than in men. (I'll give an example later on which there are actual data.) I hope these points remove the temptation (exhibited in *The Bell Curve*) to think of the heritability of IQ as a constant (like the speed of light). Heritability is a population statistic just like birth rate or number of TVs and can be expected to change with changing circumstances. There is no reason to expect the heritability of IQ in India to be close to the heritability of IQ in Korea.

These issues are pathetically misunderstood by Murray, as shown by a recent CNN interview reported in *The New Republic* (Wright 1995). Murray declared "When I—when we—say 60 percent heritability, it's not 60 percent of the variation. It is 60 percent of the IQ in any given person." Later, he repeated that for the average person, "60 percent of the intelligence comes from heredity" and added that this was true of the "human species," missing the points made above that heritability makes no sense for an individual and that heritability statistics are population-relative. In a letter to the editor that complains about being quoted out of context (Murray 1995), Murray quotes more of what he had said, viz. ". . . your IQ may have been determined overwhelmingly by genes or it may have been—yours personally—or overwhelmingly by environment. That can vary a lot from individual to individual. In the human species as a whole, you have a large genetic component." Though Murray embarrasses himself, *The Bell Curve* itself does not make these crude mistakes. Herrnstein, the late co-author, was a professional on these topics. But the upshot of part of this essay is that the book's main argument depends for some of its persuasive force on a more subtle conflation of heritability and genetic determination. And Murray's confusion serves to underscore just how difficult these concepts can be, even for someone so numerate as Murray.

Again, the critics of the book are often confused on this topic. A recent op-ed critique of Herrnstein and Murray in *The New York Times* (Hofer 1994) describes the basic thesis of the book as the claim that "genes, rather than experience, primarily determine the development of the complex sets of behaviors that underlie general intelligence." The article goes on to describe the book as linking "inherited intelligence" with race, and as drawing unwarranted conclusions about "genetic influences on general intelligence." Throughout the article, the language of genetic determination is substituted for the language of heritability. No wonder the article ends up conceding "the small differences in IQ between races and other genetically distinct groups that Mr. Murray and Professor Herrnstein set forth in endless detail."

What's the upshot of the distinction between genetic determination and heritability[8] for the argument of *The Bell Curve?* Let's go back to the sloth example: Toe number is genetic in sloths and in humans; there is a difference in toe number (three vs. five); so the toe number difference is genetic. This is a good argument: it strains the imagination to suppose that the genetic toe difference between sloths and humans goes in the opposite direction from the actual observed toe difference. The idea that our genes code for two toes despite the five toes we see at the beach is ludicrous. So in this sense the Herrnstein and Murray argument works for the concept of *genetic determination*. But the data on genes and IQ *do not* concern genetic determination, but rather *heritability*.

Is IQ genetically determined as well as heritable? No! As I already pointed out, IQ is very reactive to changes in environments in the *normal* range. Recall the example of the large rise in Holland. Surely both 1952 and 1982 count as *normal!* (Of course it is one thing for IQ to be plastic to environmental changes and quite another thing for the changes to be ones that we know how to *manipulate;* in fact, as Herrnstein and Murray note, no known environmental intervention short of adoption changes IQ very much.) Further, the claim that IQ is genetically determined is not the kind of quantitative claim on which Herrnstein and Murray would want to base their claims about genes and race.

Where are we? Here is an outline of the argument so far:

1. The basic Herrnstein and Murray argument says: IQ is largely genetic in whites; there is a fifteen point black/white difference; so part of the difference is probably genetic.
2. "Genetic" is ambiguous.
3. In the sense of *genetic determination*, IQ is not genetic in whites or anyone else, and in any case the issue is not quantitative.
4. In the sense of *heritable*, IQ is largely genetic (among whites in the US at least). But, I will argue below, in this sense of "genetic," the argument does not work.

I said at the outset that the confusion between genetic determination and heritability is partially responsible for the persuasive force of Herrnstein and Murray's argument. But even when this confusion is cleared up, their argument can appear very persuasive. In what follows, I will be leaving behind the issues just discussed about the distinction between genetic determination and heritability. I will be focusing on the logic of the argument from heritability to racial genetic differences. The upshot will be that the logic of the argument is flawed and that heritability is an uninteresting and misleading statistic.

HERITABILITY AND RACE DIFFERENCES

Arthur Jensen's 1969 article in the *Harvard Educational Review* started off the current controversy by arguing from heritability within whites to genetic differences between whites and blacks. In 1970, Richard Lewontin gave a graphic example that illustrates why this is a mistake. Suppose you buy a bag of ordinary seed corn from a hardware store. This is ordinary genetically variegated (not cloned) corn. You grow one handful of it in a carefully controlled environment in which the seeds get uniform illumination and uniform nutrient solution. The corn plants will vary in height and since the environment is uniform, the heritability of height will be 100 percent. Now take another handful of corn from the same bag which you grow in a similarly uniform environment but with a uniformly poor nutrient solution. The plants will vary in height again but all will be stunted. The heritability of height in both groups is 100 percent, but the difference in height between the groups is entirely environmentally caused. So heritability can be *total* within groups even if there is no genetic difference between groups.

The application to race is obvious: heritability is high within whites. But high heritability within groups licenses no conclusion about differences between groups.[9]

So we see that high heritability within groups does not dictate any genetic difference between groups. Nor does high heritability within groups dictate the *direction* of any genetic difference between groups. The stunted corn could have been genetically taller, with the genetic advantage outweighed by the environmental deprivation.

In reply to Lewontin's critique, Jensen focused on a principle very much like the one that underlies Herrnstein and Murray's reasoning. He said:

The real question is not whether a heritability estimate, by its mathematical logic, can prove the existence of a genetic difference between the two groups, but whether there is any probabilistic connection between the magnitude of the heritability and the magnitude of group differences. Given two populations (A and B) whose means on a particular characteristic differ by x amount, and given the heritability (h_A^2 and h_B^2) of the characteristic in each of the two populations, the probability that the two populations differ from one another genotypically as well as phenotypically is some monotonically increasing function of the magnitudes of h_A^2 and h_B^2 (Jensen, 1970, 104).

This argument has been repeated many times, by Jensen and others.[10]

Now if we knew nothing at all about two groups *except* that they differed by fifteen points in IQ and that IQ has some heritability in both, and we had to *guess* the causes, for all I've said so far, it would make sense to guess that the lower scoring group was disadvantaged *both* genetically and environmentally. (In the last section of the paper I'll show that even this weak principle is wrong.) However, the principle has no application to the *actual* racial question because we know *more* than nothing: we know that the environment can have huge effects on IQ (e.g., the Flynn effect of three points per decade and the twenty-one point increase in Holland and that blacks are environmentally disadvantaged in a way that has been shown to count. But without being able to *measure* the effect of being treated as subnormal and the effect of a legacy of slavery and discrimination from the past, how do we know whether its average effect is sufficient to lower black IQ fifteen points, or less than that—or *more* than that? Given the social importance of this issue, *guessing* is not appropriate.

I said that if we knew nothing except that there is a difference between two groups in a characteristic and that the characteristic has some heritability in both groups, we could guess that the lower group was disadvantaged both genetically and environmentally. Of course the reasoning is equally good for what Plomin, DeFries, and

McClearn call "environmentality," the "converse" of heritability (i.e., the proportion of variation due to environmental differences in the population). The danger of such guesswork in the absence of an evaluation of the relative environments is illustrated by gender and height. Women are shorter than men and height has some heritability and some "environmentality" in both groups. But the guess that women are deprived in environmental variables that affect height would be wrong. And an evaluation of these environmental variables would save us from a wrong guess here.

It is worth emphasizing the solidity of the data about the large increases in IQ in Holland. The twenty-one point increase reported by Flynn is based on comprehensive testing of all Dutch eighteen-year-olds who pass a medical exam (and there has been no change in the pass rate). The test used is Raven's Progressive Matrices, a widely respected "nonverbal test that is an especially good measure of *g*." (*Bell*, 273). Even Richard Lynn, the arch-Jensenist who is the source of much of *The Bell Curve*'s data on race concedes this point. He says, "The magnitude of the increase has generally been found to be about three IQ points per decade, making fifteen points over a fifty year period. There have, however, been some larger gains among 18 year-old conscripts in The Netherlands and Belgium amounting to seven IQ points per decade." Lynn also mentions that similar results have been found in France. (Lynn 1992, 382.) Herrnstein and Murray concede that "In some countries, the upward drift since World War II has been as much as a point a year for some spans of years." (308) In an area where the facts are often contested, it is notable that this set of facts seems to be accepted by both sides.

Another fact that is widely accepted by all sides is that when it comes to specific identified genes and their products (e.g., genes for blood types) only about seven percent of all human genetic variation lies between the major races of Africa, Asia, Europe, and Oceana. (Lewontin, 1982). About eighty-five percent of this genetic variation is within ethnic groups, and about eight percent is between ethnic groups within a single race (e.g., between Spaniards and Italians).

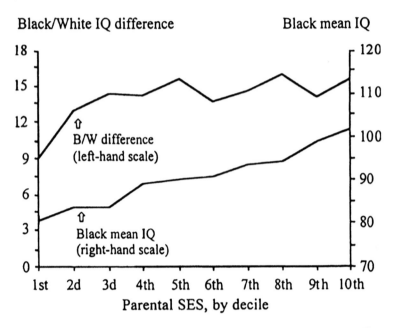

Figure 20.1 The difference between average black and white IQ is smallest for the lowest thirty percent of socioeconomic status (Adapted from Bell, 288).

Herrnstein and Murray have heard appeals to the legacy of slavery and discrimination. They have a response, and their response forms part of their argument that I have not yet mentioned. They appeal to the pattern and the magnitude of racial differences. First, the pattern. They remind us that the black/white IQ difference is smallest at the lowest socioeconomic levels. (See Figure 20.1.) And this leads them to ask:

> Why, if the B/W difference is entirely environmental, should the advantage of the "white" environment compared to the "black" be greater among the better-off and better-educated blacks and whites? We have not been able to think of a plausible reason. An appeal to the effects of racism to explain ethnic differences also requires explain-

ing why environments poisoned by discrimination and racism for some other groups—against the Chinese or the Jews in some regions of America, for example—have left them with higher scores than the national average. (*Bell,* 299)

But these facts are actually not hard to understand. Blacks and whites are to some extent separate cultural groups, and there is no reason to think that a measure like socioeconomic status means the same thing for every culture. Herrnstein and Murray mention the work of John Ogbu, an anthropologist who has distinguished a number of types of oppressed minorities (Ogbu 1986). A key category is that of "caste-like" minorities who are regarded by themselves and others as inferior, and who, if they are immigrants, are not voluntary immigrants. This category includes the Harijans in India, the Buraku and Koreans in Japan, and the Maori in New Zealand. He distinguishes them from groups like Chinese and Jews who are voluntary immigrants and have a culture of self-respect. If higher-socioeconomic-status blacks still are to some extent part of a caste-like minority, then they will be at an environmental disadvantage relative to higher-socioeconomic-status whites. But low-status blacks and whites are more likely to share a caste background. Note in Figure 20.1 that for the bottom thirty percent in socioeconomic status, blacks and whites are more similar in IQ than the for the top seventy percent. As Henry Louis Gates points out (Gates 1994), affirmative action has had the effect of quadrupling the size of the black middle class since 1967. Most middle-class blacks have arrived in the middle classes relatively recently, many of them under less than ideal conditions for the development of self-respect. It would be surprising if children of these newly middle-class blacks were to have fully escaped their caste background in so short a time.

Ogbu notes that where IQ tests have been given, "the children of these castelike minorities score about 10–15 points . . . lower than dominant group children." He notes further that differences remain "when minority and dominant group members are of similar socioeconomic background." But when "members of a castelike minority group emigrate to another society, the twin problem of low IQ test scores and low academic achievement appears to disappear" (Ogbu 1986, 32–33). Data suggests that the Buraku who have emigrated to this country do "at least as well at school and the work place" as other Japanese.[11]

That was the pattern; now let's move to the magnitude issue. Herrnstein and Murray calculate that "the *average* environment of blacks would have to be at the 6th percentile of the distribution of environments among whites . . . for the racial differences to be entirely environmental . . . differences of this magnitude and pattern are implausible" (299). That is, ninety-four percent of whites would have to have an environment that is better for the development of IQ than the environment of the average black—if the fifteen-point difference is to be explained environmentally. Herrnstein and Murray think this is implausible because when you look at measures of the environment such as income of parents, quality of schools and the like, you do not find that ninety-four percent of whites have a better environment than the average black. But this calculation ignores the effect of being in Ogbu's category of a caste-like minority, and it also ignores the fact mentioned earlier that variables such as income of parents, quality of schools, etc., have no differential impact within middle-class families. Compare the Dutch eighteen-year-olds of 1982 with their fathers' cohort, the eighteen-year-olds of 1952. The difference is entirely environmental despite the probable substantial heritability within each group. Using the same procedures as Herrnstein and Murray, Flynn calculates that ninety-nine percent of the 1982 group had to have a better environment for the development of IQ than the average member of the 1952 group (Flynn 1987b). Given differences of this magnitude among people of a uniform culture who are separated by only a single generation, is it really so implausible that ninety-four percent of whites have an environment better than a black at the fiftieth percentile?[12]

Let me sum up the argument of this section.

1. If we knew nothing at all about two groups *except* that they differed by fifteen points in IQ and that IQ is moderately heritable in both, then, for all I've said so far, we could guess that the lower scoring group was disadvantaged both genetically and environmentally.
2. We know that IQ has risen three points per decade in very many industrialized countries since World War II (the Flynn Effect) and that in some countries IQ has risen seven points per decade for three decades or more. These large changes in IQ (equal to or larger than the black/white IQ gap) cannot be due to any genetic change.
3. We know that only seven percent of identified human genetic variation is within races.
4. It appears that when members of caste-like minorities emigrate, the IQ gap narrows or disappears.

Conclusion: Environmental differences, including the sort that affect blacks in this country, are known to have large effects on IQ. We have no way at present of quantifying this effect. So we should draw no conclusion about the probability of any black genetic IQ advantage or disadvantage.

INDIRECT HERITABILITY

Earlier I said that genetic determination is not quantitative. Now I will explain why. Genetic determination is a species of causation. And causation is context-relative, as John Stuart Mill taught us.

To see this, imagine that a man is shot in the chest and dies. What caused his death? Of course he was shot, but, in addition, many other parts of the causal net—both conditions and events— were part of the mechanism by which the death was produced, such as bullet-permeable clothes, the intentions of the assassin, or going further back in time, the invention of gunpowder. We do not usually think of such factors as causes, but in some contexts we do. You can

cause someone's death by replacing some of the kevlar in his bul-
letproof vest with cotton when you know he will be targeted by a
sharpshooter who aims for the heart.

The *entire* causal net—the totality of factors that influence an
event—is an objective matter, but which *parts* of the net count as
"the cause" or even "a cause" is dependent on context. Notice that
this context-relativity of what counts as a cause is no mere verbal
matter. It really counts in ethics, law, and politics. If you kill someone by replacing the kevlar in his vest with cotton, you can be convicted of murder. The bullet-permeability of his vest caused his
death. To quantify causation—to ascribe X percent of the causation
to the bullet and Y percent to the bullet-permeability of his vest—
would require some way of standardizing contexts and interests, and
then the notion would not be very useful for other contexts and
interests.

But wait! Heritability is a causal notion too! It is the ratio of
variation *caused by* genetic differences to total variation. So doesn't
the same point apply to heritability? Why is heritability quantifia-
ble? The answer is that the actual methods for measuring heritability involve the *tacit acceptance* of a uniform policy as to what will
count as a cause and what will not that has nothing to do with our
ordinary socially important ideas of causation and is often violently
in conflict with them.

An example (cf. Jencks, et al. 1972) will help to make this point.
Consider a culture in which red-haired children are beaten over the
head regularly, but all other children are treated well. This effect
will increase the measured heritability of IQ because red-haired
identical twins will tend to resemble one another in IQ (because
they will both have low IQs) no matter what the social class of the
family in which they are raised. The effect of a red-hair gene on red
hair is a "direct" genetic effect because the gene affects the color via
an internal biochemical process. By contrast, a gene affects a characteristic *indirectly* by producing a direct effect which interacts with
the environment so as to affect the characteristic. See Figure 20.2.

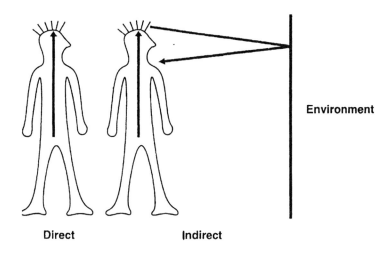

Direct Indirect Environment

Figure 20.2 A gene affects IQ directly via an internal biochemical process. A gene affects IQ indirectly by having a direct effect on something else (hair) which interacts with the environment so as to affect IQ.

In the hypothetical example, the red hair genes affect IQ indirectly. In the case of IQ, no one has any idea how to separate out direct from indirect genetic effects because no one has much of an idea how genes and environment affect IQ. For that reason, we don't know whether or to what extent the roughly sixty percent heritability of IQ found in white populations is *indirect heritability* as opposed to direct heritability. (I coined the term "indirect heritability" many years ago [Block and Dworkin 1974], but it is now sometimes called reactive heritability [Tooby and Cosmides 1990].)

As I mentioned, we typically think of some but not other events or conditions in a causal chain as causes. The methodology used to measure heritability counts differences in characteristics as caused by genetic differences if there is a genetic difference, even if there is *also an environmental difference*, thus distorting the ways in which we normally think about causation. For instance, the heritability methodology focuses on the difference between the red-hair genes and genes for other hair colors, not on the fact that red-haired children—unlike blond children—are beaten.

Recall that earlier I said that wearing earrings used to be highly heritable because differences were "due" to the XY/XX difference. I put "scare quotes" around "due" because it is a by-product of the methodology for measuring heritability to adopt a tacit convention that *genes are taken to dominate environment*. Variation in earrings was as much a social matter as a genetic matter, but it still counted as highly heritable. If there is a genetic difference in the causal chains that lead to different characteristics, the difference counts as genetically caused even if the environmental differences are just as important. If we adopted the opposite convention, the convention that any environmental difference in two causal chains shows that the difference counts as environmentally caused, then we could not use current methodology for measuring heritability, because we have no general method of detecting indirect genetic effects using current techniques. Heritabilities using the two different conventions would be radically different if there are substantial indirect genetic effects.

Recall the examples mentioned earlier about the *measured heritabilities* of such quantities as number of hours of watching TV. No one should suppose that there is variation in genes for watching TV; this is a matter of indirect effects. Here is a good example of the never-never land of indirect heritability. A recent questionnaire study showed large heritabilities for many surprising "environmental" variables. (The method used was comparisons of one-egg and two-egg twins in nonadoptive environments. The more similar one-egg twins are to one another compared to two-egg twins, the higher the heritability.) The twins were asked to indicate "things you have done during the past year." For "baby-sat" the heritabilities were thirty-five percent for males and forty-seven percent for females. For "had your back rubbed," heritabilities were ninety-two percent for males and twenty-one percent for females (Schönemann and Schönemann 1991, 1994). How could heritability be different for males and females? Suppose (just for illustration) that male babysitters are chosen on the basis of weight and female babysitters are chosen on the basis of height. Height is more highly heritable than weight, so the indirect pathway would explain the difference. The result is *intelligible*, but it does show that heritability is a *strange* statistic.

Consider the fact that no one would do a heritability study on a mixed black/white population. I mentioned earlier that if you place a pair of black one-egg twins in different homes, you automatically fail to randomize environments, because the black twins will bring part of their environment with them; they are both black and will be treated as black. This is an indirect genetic effect *par excellence*. Implicitly, everyone in this field recognizes that, yet more subtle possibilities of indirect effects are typically ignored.

Recall that heritability is defined as a fraction: variation due to genetic differences divided by total variation. The measure of variation that is always used (though alternatives are available) is a statistical quantity known as variance. One factor that raises variance is a positive correlation between genetic and environmental variables. Suppose that children whose genes give them an advantage in musical talent tend to have parents who provide them with an environment conducive to developing that talent—music lessons, concerts, a great CD collection, musical discussions over dinner, etc. Suppose further that other children who have a genetic disadvantage also have an environment that stultifies their musical talents. Hence there will be a correlation between genes and environment that will move children towards the extremes of the distribution, increasing the variance in musical skills. Variance due to gene/environment correlation (gene/environment "covariance") should not be counted in the genetic component of the variance, and there are a variety of methods of separating out such variance. It is common in behavior genetics to distinguish among a number of different types of covariance (Loehlin and DeFries 1987; Plomin, DeFries, and Loehlin 1977; Plomin 1990a). The kind just mentioned in which parents provide genes for musical talent and an environment that develops it is called "passive" covariance because it doesn't depend on what the child does. Reactive covariance is a matter of the environment reacting to the child's qualities, as when a school gives extra music classes to children who exhibit musical talent. Active covariance is a matter of the child creating a gene environment correlation, as when a musically talented child practices musical themes in the imagination or pays attention to the musical environment. Passive covariance can be controlled in heritability calculations by attention to adoption studies in which the double-advantage/double-disadvantage does not exist. But reactive and active covariance cannot be measured without specific hypotheses about how the environment affects IQ. And it is just *a fact about IQ that little is known* about how the environment affects it. So reactive and active covariance is on the whole beyond the reach of the empirical methods of our era's "behavior genetics," for those methods do not include an understanding of what IQ *is* (e.g., whether it is information processing capacity, or whether it has more to do with how information processing capacity is deployed, that is, whether it is mainly attention) or how the environment affects it.

Perhaps you think that my claim that no one understands very much about how the environment affects IQ would be hotly contested by behavior geneticists who agree with Herrnstein and Murray. *I doubt it!* Recall that earlier I mentioned that most of the environmental variation that affects IQ variation (in whites) is *within* families rather than *between* families. I mentioned the low correlations of adopted children raised in the same families. And I quoted Herrnstein and Murray agreeing that of the environmental variation in IQ, "relatively little can be traced to the shared environments created by families. It is, rather, a set of environmental influences, *mostly unknown at present,* that are experienced by individuals as individuals" (*Bell,* 108; italics mine). Recall also that Herrnstein and Murray concede that no one has explained the Flynn effect.

The points about covariance just made assume that there are genes *for IQ* and that these genes may affect the environment so as to produce effects on IQ that are correlated with the ones that the genes themselves produce. But to think of the issue this way is to very seriously underestimate its significance. For as the red-hair example illustrates, indirect genetic effects needn't work through anything that should be thought of as "IQ genes."

Since we don't know much about how variation in environment differentially affects IQ, we can only guess about how variation in genes differentially affects IQ indirectly, via the environment. Suppose, for example, that a child's perceived attractiveness and self-confidence strongly affects how adults interact with children in a way that largely accounts for the variation in IQ. Scarr and Mc-Cartney (1983), for example, say "It is quite likely that smiley, active babies receive more social stimulation than sober, passive infants. In the intellectual area, cooperative, attentive preschoolers receive more pleasant instructional interactions from the adults around them than uncooperative distractible children. [427] . . . The social psychology literature on attractiveness . . . would seem to support our view that some personal characteristics evoke differential responses . . ." (433). Of course, adults could give some children more attention than others without making a difference to the children's IQs. That is, differential response on the part of adults does not show differential effect on IQ. But it could be so.

Suppose further that personal attractiveness and self-confidence are highly heritable. Then we would have an indirect effect par excellence, and such an effect could, for all we know, largely account for the heritability of IQ. Without an understanding of how the environment affects IQ, we simply have no way of determining how much of the variance in IQ is indirect genetic variance of this sort. Of course, if we knew that some specific adult behavior that is triggered by some specific heritable property of children was responsible for a large component of IQ variation, then we could measure that behavior. But there is no theory of intelligence or IQ that would allow us to have any synoptic grip on such factors. The point is underscored by the possibility that the differences in environment might be partly *internal* to the child's interaction with stimuli rather than a matter of differences in the stimuli themselves. As Scarr and McCartney note, "The toddler who has "caught on" to the idea that things have names and who demands the names for everything is experiencing a fundamentally different verbal environment from what she experienced before, even though her parents talked to her extensively in infancy." (425).

This point is often (at least partially) acknowledged by behavior geneticists. For example, Plomin, DeFries, and Loehlin (1977, 321) say: "Because it is not possible to measure all aspects of the environment (including everybody and everything) that might correlate with children's genotypes, it will probably never be possible to assess completely the effects of active and reactive genotype-environment correlations."

The upshot is that there may be a large component of heritability due to indirect genetic effects, including (but not limited to) gene-environment correlation, that is outside the boundaries of what can be measured given the mainly atheoretical approach that is available today. Where does the "gene-environment covariance" show up in heritability calculations? Answer: active and reactive effects that we don't know how to measure inevitably are included in the genetic component. This is often regarded by behavior geneticists as perfectly OK. In an often-quoted passage, Roberts (1967) says:

The genotype may influence the phenotype either by means of biochemical or other processes, labelled for convenience as "development," or by means of influencing the animal's choice of environment. But this second pathway, just as much as the first, is a genetic one; formally it matters not one whit whether the effects of the genes are mediated through the external environment or directly though, say, the ribosomes. (218)

Jensen (1973) notes "Generally, CovGE [that is, gene-environment covariance] is included in h^2 [heritability] . . . either on the assumption that the covariance is due to the genotype and/or because the particular method of estimating h^2 does not permit separation of V_G [genetic variance] and CovGE" (369). Indeed, Jensen argues that "much if not most, of this effect should be included in the genetic variance, because, in part, r_{GE} [the correlation of genes and environment] is a result of the genotype's selective utilization of the environment" (54). In practice, if researchers were to actually identify an "unmeritocratic" effect such as the red-hair indirect effect mentioned earlier, they would no doubt ignore Roberts's advice, counting the variance produced by the effect as covariance rather than genetic variance. The problem is that we have *no idea* how much of the sixty percent of the variance in IQ that is said to be genetic is of this sort. So in actual practice, covariance due to indirect effects that people actually know how to measure—at least if it is flagrantly nonmeritocratic—is not counted in the heritability; but other indirect effects are counted as genetic. So what counts as genetic variance, inflating heritability, has two very peculiar properties:

1. It is flagrantly a matter of *value judgements* (e.g., whether red hair is meritorious). Effects that everyone would agree are unmeritocratic are removed from the genetic variance.
2. Variance due to indirect effects whose nature is *not known* (namely, practically all of it) is counted as genetic variance.

In effect, the field has adopted as an axiom that *heritability of IQ can be measured by current methods*. Without this assumption, the right conclusion would be that since we cannot separate indirect genetic effects, (including certain kinds of gene/environment covariance) from pure genetic variance, no heritability estimate can be made. Behavior geneticists have chosen to count indirect genetic effects as genetic even if they are also environmental. Why does the field adopt this axiom? I cannot help thinking that part of the explanation is that behavior genetics is a young field (see Plomin 1990a) struggling for acceptance and funding, and heritability is a flag that attracts attention to it. Surely the right conclusion is that heritability as it is construed by the field is a second-class concept that does not belong in anything that can be counted as a science.

Let us return to the speculation mentioned above that the sixty percent heritability of IQ (within whites) is entirely indirect and due to differential treatment of children on the basis of heritable characteristics. Then the direct heritability of IQ would be zero and we would have no reason to think that anything that could be called genes *for* IQ (e.g., genes for information-processing capacity) vary in the white population, and no reason to look for such differences to explain the fifteen-point difference between blacks and whites. Indeed, we would have reason to look for differences in the ways adults interact with children to explain the black-white IQ difference. So indirect heritability suggests an environmental hypothesis about the measured black-white IQ difference, maybe one that could be the object of social policy. Are there reasons to expect indirect genetic effects in the black-white difference? I mentioned the obvious example of genes for skin color above. But there may be less obvious indirect effects as well. I mentioned earlier that there are many more low-birth-weight black babies than white babies. Nothing known appears to rule out a genetic explanation (Lieberman 1995). If blacks are more likely to have genes for low-birth-weight babies, perhaps the effect could be neutralized by diet or by drug intervention in pregnancy. Certainly, no one should think of genes for low birth weight as "IQ genes."[13]

Let us return to the topic of the last section, the issue of whether heritability within groups yields any probability judgement about the genetic differences between groups. I commented that (for all I'd said so far) if we knew nothing at all about two groups *except* that they differed by fifteen points in IQ and that IQ is heritable in both, and we had to *guess* the causes, it would make sense to guess that the lower scoring group was disadvantaged *both* genetically and environmentally. But the points I've just made about indirect heritability show that any such guess would be misguided. The reasoning behind the guess assumed that the heritability of IQ within whites reflected differences in IQ caused by differences in *IQ genes*. But what the points about indirect heritability show is that we don't know whether *any* of the variation within whites is due to variation in IQ genes. If we have no real grip on what kinds of causal mechanisms result in the sixty percent heritability within whites, we can have no confidence in any extrapolation to blacks. Here is a very closely related point: the Jensen-Herrnstein-Murray reasoning assumed that there was a well-defined space of alternative genotypes for IQ that vary within whites and that can be used to apportion probabilities. Any reasoning about probability in the absence of data requires some way of dividing the possibilities into equi-probable alternatives. But what the direct/indirect distinction reveals is that the well-behaved space of IQ genotypes that would be required for such reasoning cannot be assumed to exist.

Let's call a person's genome (his total set of genes) genetically inferior with respect to IQ if that genome yields low IQ in any normal environment. But what is to count as a normal environment? In the example discussed earlier, genes for red hair yield low IQ within environments that are normal in the environment of the hypothetical society, but in environments that *we* would consider normal, the red-hair genes are irrelevant to IQ. What if the heritabilities observed for IQ are a result of indirect effects that can be changed by changing social practice? Then phrases like "genetically inferior in IQ" and "genetic disadvantage in IQ" will *only* apply to genomes such as that of Down's Syndrome that yield low IQ no matter what the social practices.

Another consequence of the point about indirect heritability is to cast doubt on Herrnstein and Murray's ideas about genetic social stratification within whites based on IQ. If the sixty percent heritability does not reflect IQ genes, then there is no reason to suppose that social classes differ at all in IQ genes. Herrnstein and Murray worry about pollution of the gene pool by immigrants and by large numbers of children of low-IQ parents. But if the heritability of IQ is mainly indirect, their emphasis on genes is misdirected. If we lived in a culture that damaged the brains of red-haired children, should we complain about genetic pollution when large numbers of red-haired immigrants arrived? No, we should try to change the social practices that deprive those with certain genes of an equal chance.[14]

GENETIC BUCKET THEORY

Though IQ is not genetically determined, something close to it might be said to be genetically determined: namely *potential IQ*. The genes, it might be said, determine the size of the mental bucket and then the environment fills the bucket to one level or another. (Herrnstein and Murray are far from alone in talking this way. Vernon, in 1969, for example, introduced the term "intelligence A" for the size of the bucket.)

To see what is wrong with this idea, and also to see why heritability is much less relevant to social policy than many have supposed, we need the concept of a *norm of reaction*. Suppose that of the many plants growing on a mountain, some do well at high altitudes but poorly at low altitudes, and others are exactly the opposite. We could graph the situation as in Figure 20.3. One type of plant—gen-

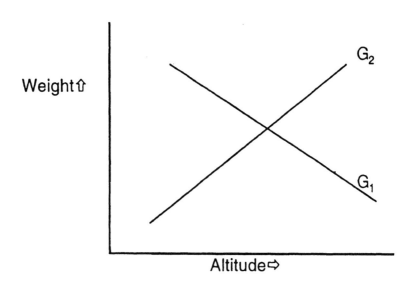

Figure 20.3 One genetic type of plant does better at high altitudes, another does better at low altitudes.

otype G_1—thrives at low altitudes (as measured by the weight of the plant), and the other thrives at high altitudes. The norm of reaction is simply the function from environment to phenotype for a specific genotype. Two norms of reaction, one for each type of plant are illustrated in the diagram.

What is most truly genetically determined is the norm of reaction for a trait rather than any specific trait, as every population geneticist knows. The concept of the norm of reaction allows us to see that heritability data can tell us nothing about the genetic bucket

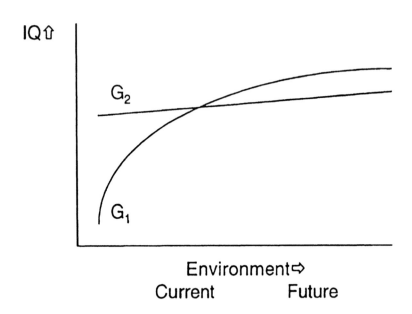

Figure 20.4 Two hypothetical genotypes show a large difference in IQ in current environments, but the difference decreases and the order changes in another environment.

theory. Consider some *hypothetical* norms of reaction for IQ as in Figure 20.4. (Note: G_1 and G_2 are not intended as a guess about any actual races.)

One point illustrated is that current environments may have nothing to do with anything that could be thought of as *maximum* capacity, the potential size of the genetic bucket. That might be a ceiling we bump up against only in environments very different from ones available to us now (or perhaps there is no ceiling at all). If this seems unlikely to you, remember the Flynn effect. The IQ gap between us now and ourselves and our relatives of 1950 is about the same as between blacks and whites now. Another point that doesn't depend on IQ: when Gödel's Theorem and General Relativity were young, it was said that there were only a handful of people smart enough to understand them. Now any reasonably industrious and with-it college undergraduate has a good grasp of both within his reach. The change is improved understanding on the part of the intellectual community which allows difficult ideas to be made digestible. A similar point could be made with respect to athletic skills. The techniques (diet, shoes, training regime) required to run a four-minute mile put within the reach of many runners an achievement that was not available even to the very top runners of a hundred years ago.

A second point illustrated by the graph is a much more significant one. Consider a population clustered on the left-hand side in the Current Environments section. If the population is equally split between G_1 and G_2, we can expect substantial heritability. But as the environment improves and moves into Future Environments, we get the following results: heritability decreases, IQ increases and G_1 and G_2 reverse. The point of course is not that anyone knows that this is what norms of reaction for IQ look like. The point is just the opposite—that no one does know how any human genotypes may react to environments that involve new intellectual machinery, new software for the brain. As Lewontin (1974; see also Feldman and Lewontin 1975) has emphasized, heritability gives a local analysis that depends on the environmental conditions and the distribution of genotypes that happens to exist at a given time. It tells us nothing about the effect of introducing environments that are either new or not now common. If we want to know the effects of a new or uncommon environment, we should *ignore heritability* and just try changing the environments. This is yet another reason why heritability is a bad statistic.

A third point (closely connected to the previous two) is that the talk of genetic advantage and disadvantage that I allowed at the

outset of this paper is problematic. Even if some genotypes determine lower IQs than others in some environments, that tells us
nothing about what will happen in other environments. Perhaps in
ideally favorable environments most genotypes yield more or less
the same phenotype. Talk of part of the black/white difference being
genetic is even more problematic. We could try to make sense of
the notion of part of an IQ difference being genetic as follows.
Suppose there is a ten point IQ difference between you and me. If
we were both raised in an average environment, the difference
would have been only two points. Then we might be tempted to
say that the environmental part is eighty percent of the difference
and the genetic part is twenty percent. But as we can see from the
curves of the last figure, if our actual environment is far from the
average, what happens at the average environment may have little
or nothing to do with the actual causes of our IQ difference. Indeed,
you may have a "genetic advantage" in our actual environments, but
I may have a "genetic advantage" in the average environment. Further, any statistic that depends on the average environment has the
problem of the heritability statistic—that it provides a local analysis
that may have nothing to do with environments outside the current
range.

Genetic determinists often react to data like those that I mentioned earlier on the large IQ changes in Holland by saying that
though IQ scores are very environmentally malleable, the relative
positions of individuals and groups are not. In effect, what they are
supposing is that the norms of reaction are always parallel. There
is some evidence for this within a very narrow range of environments of the current correlational studies. (See Plomin 1990b for
the standard behavior genetics point of view on this, but see also
Wahlsten 1990 for a discussion of problems with this point of view.)
But there is no evidence at all outside that range. I think the right
thing to say is that we don't know what the shape of the norms of
reaction are, and if we are curious, we should ignore heritability
statistics and simply *try out improved environments*.

Further, it is not difficult to think of possibilities in which norms of reaction for IQ might not be parallel. Suppose, for example, that the brain is in a certain respect like a muscle: the activity of abstract thinking makes dendrites sprout whereas not thinking makes them shrivel. Then the more one *does* think, the better one *can* think. (Perhaps this would help to explain why college graduates appear to be at lower risk for Alzheimer's disease.) Then over the long run, differences in confidence and motivation will make for differences in ability. If there are environments that encourage some genotypes but discourage others, then we could expect to see norms of reaction for cognitive abilities that are far from parallel (and to the extent that IQ tests tap cognitive abilities, we could expect to see the same for IQ norms).

I mentioned earlier Kitcher's observation that though it was once said that PKU was a form of genetic retardation, we now feel that what is genetic in the case of PKU is the inability to properly metabolize phenylalanine. More generally, the more we know about the mechanisms of causation, the more we tend to see that what is genetic is not any specific phenotypic characteristic, but rather a tendency to develop certain phenotypic characteristics in certain environments. The notion of a norm of reaction allows us to see why that is the right way to think. Generally, what is genetic is simply a mapping from environment to actual (phenotypic) characteristics.

I would like to end with a brief comment on affirmative action. Herrnstein and Murray suppose that affirmative-action policies depend on an assumption of genetic equality. But the main justifications for affirmative action do not so depend. Affirmative action is justified as a remedy for current discrimination, to make up for past discrimination and for the provision of role models. Issues about a genetic involvement in race differences have no relevance to these justifications.[15]

NOTES

1. This article is reprinted from *Cognition* 56, 2 (1995) with the permission of the publisher, Elsevier Science B.V.
2. I am going along with a dangerous way of thinking here. As I will point out in the last section of this paper, this talk of *part* of an IQ difference is deeply problematic.
3. This is a widely accepted figure, but Nisbett (1995) gives some plausible arguments that the gap has narrowed. As he says, no study in the last two decades indicates a narrowing of the gap by less than 4.2 points. I am using Herrnstein and Murray's figure, putting aside disagreements about the data so as to concentrate on the conceptual issue.
4. Roses are red, violets are blue, color is genetic, so the color difference is genetic. This sounds like a tautology, but it isn't. Perhaps the easiest way to see that is to think of what it is for color to be genetic to implicitly involve appeal to the idea of a normal environment. If the environment is not normal (as in the thalidomide example) the conclusion may be false even when the premises are true.
5. I am using a very liberal notion of genetic determination. On a finer grained notion, one might want to distinguish between "the genes code for x" and "the genes code for y, but the result, given normal development, is x."
6. What psychologists usually have in mind when they say that aspects of syntax are genetically determined (Chomsky [1975], Fodor, Bever and Garrett [1974]) or that aspects of the concept of an object are genetically determined is that the source of the *information* that people end up with is the genes. This model does not apply to IQ.
7. Another possibility mentioned by Scarr and McCartney (1983) is that older children and adults make their own environments to a larger extent than younger children do.
8. The distinction between genetic determination and heritability might be challenged as follows: whenever a characteristic is genetically determined but not highly heritable, we can always increase its heritability by expanding the relevant population. Thus, number of digits has low heritability in people, but high heritability in the population that includes both people and animals that have different numbers of digits. (This line of thought appears in Sober, 1993, 190.) Briefly, there are two problems with this reasoning. First, there is no guarantee that there will be other species that differ in the required way. To appeal to merely *possible* species would be a mistake, since *everything* is heritable relative to *some* range of possible species. Second, this reply does nothing to counter the cases of characteristics that are heritable but not genetically determined.
9. Herrnstein and Murray mention Lewontin's point, but they do so in a way that distorts its crucial features. They leave out the 100 percent heritability within groups. In their version of the example, two handfuls of "genetically identical seed corn" are planted, one in Iowa and the other in the Mojave Desert (*Bell*, 298). So the heritabilities within the groups are zero (or undefined if all the corn in the Mojave dies). Also, their statement of the point conflates genetic determination with heritability. They say "That a trait is *genetically transmitted in individuals* [emphasis added] does not mean that group differences in that trait are also genetic in origin" (298). However, the effect of Herrnstein and Murray's

having *mentioned* Lewontin's point, even in a distorted way, is that the critics have ignored it. And the effect of that is that the audience doesn't know about it.

10. The latest incarnation is an article in *The Wall Street Journal* (Arvey, et. al. 1994) by fifty-two behavior geneticists and psychometricians which is intended to correct misinformation in the debate about *The Bell Curve*. They mention the high heritability of IQ within whites and they add "The reasons that blacks differ among themselves in intelligence appear to be basically the same as those for why whites (or Asians or Hispanics) differ among themselves. Both environment and genetic heredity are involved." And they hint at a conclusion much like that of Jensen and of Herrnstein and Murray about a probable black genetic deficiency. Herrnstein and Murray, however, are more cautious in not making claims about heritability within blacks.

11. In personal communication, Ogbu tells me that it is difficult to get data on Buraku immigrants to this country partly because there are not very many of them and partly because no one wants to be identified as a Buraku. One of the studies he cites in Ogbu, 1986 was actually published under a pseudonym.

12. Herrnstein and Murray have a number of other independent arguments for black genetic inferiority, some of which are directly relevant to the point about caste-like minorities. In particular, they claim that the IQ of blacks in African countries in which they are not an oppressed caste is lower than that of American blacks. I am not impressed with the data that they provide. See Kamin (1995) on this topic.

13. This is an oddball case but I still count it as an indirect genetic effect. The mother's genes produce a direct effect on her reproductive system that has an additional effect on the environment of the baby. It should be noted that the direct/indirect distinction, as with any distinction involving causation, is itself context-relative. All direct genetic effects involve the environment in some way (if the environment had been different in the appropriate way the effect would have been different) so in some contexts such environmental dependencies can make the effect indirect.

14. The ideas in this section were developed from my contribution to Block and Dworkin, 1974 (section 1) in lectures that I gave in the 1970s, and in part stimulated by Jencks, et. al., 1972. While this paper was in press I read Jencks, 1980, which makes a number of overlapping points.

15. I am grateful to the following people for their comments on earlier drafts: Eliza Block, Alex Byrne, Susan Carey, Noam Chomsky, Josh Cohen, Delia Graff, Ned Hall, Michael Hardimon, Paul Horwich, Emily Jenkins, Johanna Jenkins, Philip Kitcher, Leonard Katz, Peter Klein, Amy Lang, Richard Lewontin, Karen Neander, Charles Nesson, Wayne O'Neil, Steven Pinker, Georges Rey, Sahotra Sarkar, Sandra Scarr, Elliott Sober, Judith Thomson, and an anonymous referee for *cognition*.

REFERENCES

Arvey, R., et al. 1994. Mainstream Science on Intelligence. *Wall Street Journal*, Dec. 13.

Block, N. And Dworkin, G. 1974. IQ, Heritability and Inequality, Part II, *Philosophy and Public Affairs* 4, 1:40–99. Reprinted in Block and Dworkin, 1976.

Block, N. and Dworkin, G. 1976. *The IQ Controversy*. N.Y.: Pantheon.

Chomsky, N. 1975. On Cognitive Capacity, Chapter 1 of *Reflections on Language*. N.Y.: Pantheon. This chapter is reprinted in N. Block, *Readings in Philosophy of Psychology* Vol. 2, Cambridge: Harvard University Press, 1981, 305–323.

Feldman, M. and Lewontin, R. 1975. The Heritability Hangup. *Science* 190, 4220: 1163–1168.

Flynn, J. R. 1987a. Massive IQ Gains in 14 Nations: What IQ Tests Really Measure. *Psychological Bulletin* 101, 2, 171–191.

Flynn, J. R. 1987b. Race and IQ: Jensen's Case Refuted. In S. Modgil and C. Modgil, eds. *Arthur Jensen: Consensus and Controversy*. London: Falmer Press, 221–232.

Fodor, J., Bever, T. and Garrett, M. 1974. The Specificity of Language Skills. In *The Psychology of Language*. N.Y.: McGraw-Hill. 436–441 and 449–462, by the same authors. These passages are reprinted in N. Block, *Readings in Philosophy of Psychology* Vol. 2, (Cambridge: Harvard University Press. 1981), 324–338.

Gates, H. L. Jr. 1994. Why Now? *The New Republic* 211, no. 18, issue 4163, Oct. 31: 10

Gould, S. J., 1994. Curveball. *The New Yorker* LXX, 139–149. Reprinted in *The Bell Curve Wars*, Steven Fraser, ed. (N.Y.: Basic Books, 1995), 11–22; and in *The Bell Curve Debate*, Russell Jacoby and Naomi Glauberman, eds. (N.Y.: Random House, 1995), 3–13.

Herrnstein, R. J., and Murray, C. 1994. *The Bell Curve*, N.Y.: The Free Press.

Herbert, Bob. 1994. Throwing a Curve. *The New York Times* Oct. 26: Op-Ed page.

Hofer, M. 1994. Behind the Curve. *The New York Times* Dec. 26: Op-Ed page.

Holt, J. 1994. Anti-Social Science. *The New York Times* Oct. 19: Op-Ed page.

Jencks, C., Smith, M., Acland, H., Bane, M. Cohen, D., Gintis, H., Heyns, B., and Michelson, S. 1972. *Inequality: A Reassessment of the Effect of Family and Schooling in America*. N.Y.: Basic Books.

Jencks, C. 1980. Heredity, Environment and Public Policy Reconsidered. *American Sociological Review* 45:723–736.

Jensen, A. R., 1969. How much can we boost IQ and scholastic achievement? *Harvard Educational Review*, 39:1–123

Jensen, A. R. 1970. Race and the genetics of intelligence: a reply to Lewontin, *Bulletin of the Atomic Scientists*. Reprinted in Block and Dworkin, 1976, 93–107.

Jensen, A. R. 1973. *Educability and Group Differences*. N.Y.: Harper and Row.

Kamin, L. 1995. Lie, Damned Lies, and Statistics. In *The Bell Curve Debate*, R. Jacoby and N. Glauberman, eds., NY: Random House, 81–105.

Kitcher, P. 1996. Fascinating Genetalk. Chapter 11 of *An Unequal Inheritance*. NY: Simon and Schuster.

Leo, J. 1994. Why IQ isn't destiny/The Return of the IQ Wars, *U.S. News and World Report*, Oct 24:73–80/24.

Lewontin, R. 1970. Race and Intelligence. *Bulletin of the Atomic Scientists* 26, 3:2–8. Reprinted in Block and Dworkin, 1976.

Lewontin, R. 1974. The Analysis of Variance and the Analysis of Causes. *American Journal of Human Genetics* 26:400–411. Reprinted in Block and Dworkin, 1976.

Lewontin, R. 1982 *Human Diversity*. N.Y.: Scientific American Library.

Loehlin, J. and J. DeFries. 1987. Genotype-Environment Correlation and IQ. *Behavior Genetics* 17, 3:263–277.

Lynn, R. 1992. Lynn Replies to Flynn. In J. Lynch, C. Modgil and S. Modgil, *Cultural Diversity and the Schools.* Falmer.

Lieberman, E. 1995. Low Birth Weight—Not a Black-and-White Issue. *New England Journal of Medicine* 332, 2:117–118.

Murray, C. 1994. The Real Bell Curve. *The Wall Street Journal* Dec. 2.

Murray, C. 1995. Letter to the Editors. *The New Republic* Jan. 30:5.

Nisbett, R. Race, IQ and Scientism. In *The Bell Curve Wars*, S. Fraser, ed. N.Y.: Basic Books.

Ogbu, J. 1986. The Consequences of the American Caste System. In U. Neisser, ed. *The School Achievement Of Minority Children: New Perspectives.* Hillsdale, N.J.: Lawrence Erlbaum, 19–56.

Pedersen, N. L., Plomin, R., Nesselroade, J. and McClearn, G. 1992. A quantitative genetic analysis of the cognitive abilities during the second half of the life span. *Psychological Science* 3, 6:346–353.

Plomin, R. 1989. Environment and Genes. *American Psychologist* 44, 2:105–111.

Plomin, R. 1990a. *Nature and Nurture.* Pacific Grove: Brooks-Cole.

Plomin, R. 1990b. Trying to shoot the messenger for his message. *The Behavioral and Brain Sciences* 13, 1:144.

Plomin, R. and C. Bergeman. 1991. The nature of nurture: genetic influence on "environmental" measures. *The Behavioral and Brain Sciences* 14:3:373–386.

Plomin, R. and D. Daniels. 1987. Why are children in the same family so different from one another? *The Behavioral and Brain Sciences* 10, 1:1–60.

Plomin, R., DeFries, J. and J. Loehlin. 1977. Genotype-environment interaction and correlation in the analysis of human behavior. *Psychological Bulletin* 84, 2:309–322.

Plomin, R., J. DeFries, J. and G. McClearn. 1990. *Behavioral Genetics: A Primer.* N.Y.: Freeman.

Plomin, R., J. Loehlin, J. DeFries. 1985. Genetic and environmental components of environmental influences. *Developmental Psychology* 21, 3:391–402

Roberts, R. C. 1967. Some concepts and methods in quantitative genetics. In *Behavior-Genetic Analysis*, ed. J. Hirsch. N.Y.: McGraw-Hill, 214–257.

Scarr, S. 1995. Human differences and political equality: the dilemma of group differences. In *Issues in Science and Technology*, ???

Scarr, S. and K. McCartney. 1983. How people make their own environments: A theory of genotype →environment effects. *Child Development* 54:424–435

Schönemann, P. and S. Schönemann. 1991. We wondered where the errors went. *The Behavioral and Brain Sciences* 14:3:404–405.

Schönemann, P. and S. Schönemann. 1994. Environmental versus genetic models for Osborne's personality data on identical and fraternal twins. *Cahiers de Psychologie Cognitivite/European Bulletin of Cognitive Psychology* 13, 2:141–167.

Sober, E. 1988. Apportioning Causal Responsibility. *Journal of Philosophy* LXXXV, 6:303–318.

Sober, E. 1993. *Philosophy of Biology.* Boulder: Westview.

Tooby, J. and L. Cosmides. 1990. On the universality of human nature and the uniqueness of the individual: the role of genetics and adaptation. *Journal of Personality* 58, 1:17–67.

Vernon, P. 1969. *Intelligence and cultural environment.* London: Methuen.
Wahlsten, D. 1990. Insensitivity of the analysis of variance to heredity-environment interaction. *The Behavioral and Brain Sciences* 13, 1:109–120.
Wright, R. 1995. Has Charles Murray read his own book? *The New Republic,* Jan. 2:6.

Printed in the United Kingdom by
Lightning Source UK Ltd., Milton Keynes
136892UK00001B/154/A

9 780195 102215